THE PLAYS OF EURIPIDES

ORESTES

D1526708

General editor

Professor Christopher Collard

CONCORDIA COLLEGE LIBRARY
BRONXVILLE, N.Y. 10708

PA
3973
.07
1987

EURIPIDES

Orestes

edited with translation and commentary by

M. L. West

ARIS & PHILLIPS LTD

C16II

CONCORDIA COLLEGE LIBRARY
BRONXVILLE, N.Y. 10708

© M.L. West 1987. All rights reserved. No part of this publication may be reproduced, stored in a retrieval system, or transmitted in any form by any means without the prior written permission of the publishers.

 British Library Cataloguing in Publication Data

Euripides
  [Orestes. *English*] Orestes. --(Classical
  texts)
  I. [Orestes. *English*] II. Title
  III. West, M.L. IV. Series
  882'.01   PA 3975.07

ISBN 0 85668 310 8 *cloth*
ISBN 0 85668 311 6 *limp*

Printed and published in England by ARIS & PHILLIPS Ltd, Teddington House, Warminster, Wiltshire. BA12 8PQ, England.

CONTENTS

GENERAL EDITOR'S FOREWORD

Euripides' remarkable variety of subject, ideas and methods challenges each generation of readers – and audiences – to fresh appraisal and closer definition. This Series of his plays is in the general style of Aris and Phillips' Classical Texts: it offers university students and, we hope, sixth-formers, as well as teachers of Classics and Classical Civilisation at all levels, new editions which emphasise analytical and literary appreciation. In each volume there is an editor's Introduction which sets the play in its original context, discusses its dramatic and poetic resources, and assesses its meaning. The Greek text is faced on the opposite page by a new English prose translation which attempts to be both accurate and idiomatic. The Commentary, which is keyed wherever possible to the translation rather than to the Greek, pursues the aims of the Introduction in analysing structure and development, in annotating and appreciating poetic style, and in explaining the ideas; since the translation itself reveals the editor's detailed understanding of the Greek, philological comment is confined to special phenomena or problems which affect interpretation. Those are the guidelines within which individual contributors to the Series have been asked to work, but they are free to handle or emphasise whatever they judge important in their particular play, and to choose their own manner of doing so. It is natural that commentaries and commentators on Euripides should reflect his variety as a poet.

This volume is the second in the Series. The first, *Trojan Women* by Shirley A. Barlow (1986), included a General Introduction to the Series written by Dr. Barlow; it is reprinted in this volume, pp.1-25. I have updated the General Bibliography (p.47-52). For *Orestes*, Professor Martin West has prepared a new edition of the Greek text, with a selective critical *apparatus*; I record my own and the publisher's gratitude to him and Dr. James Diggle, who has again helped the series by giving Professor West access to collations of manuscripts made for his forthcoming edition in the Oxford Classical Texts.

University College of Swansea   Christopher Collard

PREFACE

This edition has the modest aim of providing a readable text (i.e. one in which the plausible emendation is generally preferred to the cautious crux); a not wholly unreadable translation, in which, however, absolute naturalness of expression has sometimes been sacrificed in the interests of accurate reflection of the meaning and the varying stylistic levels of the Greek; and a concise commentary, usable both by those reading the play in translation and by those reading it in Greek, with the main emphasis placed on dramatic and poetic technique rather than linguistic or textual matters.

I have two major debts to acknowledge with great gratitude. The first is to Sir Charles Willink, who most generously placed drafts of his excellent large-scale commentary at my disposal in advance of its publication. This was an enormous help, which I hope I have not abused by excessive borrowing. I have been able to pass over many problems of detail in the knowledge that those interested will have his thorough discussions to turn to. The second debt is to Dr. James Diggle for his unfailing helpfulness in commenting on ideas and in answering queries, and more especially for providing me with a complete fair copy of his extensive manuscript collations. This enabled me to put my critical apparatus, highly selective as it is, in a crisper and more accurate form. Any errors that may be discovered in it should in the first instance be assumed to be mine. I must further thank Christopher Collard, the editor of this Euripides series, for all his assistance, encouragement, and constructive criticism.

Royal Holloway & Bedford New College, London   M.L. West
August 1986

Note to the second printing (1988):
I have now discussed a number of the play's problems in more detail in *Classical Quarterly* 37 (1987) 281-93 – mainly textual points, but also the question of author's afterthoughts, and the staging of the Phrygian's entry.

GENERAL INTRODUCTION TO THE SERIES

I. The Ancient Theatre

The contemporary theatre consists of many different types of performance, and these are on offer most of the time at numerous small theatres in many places, particularly in centres like London and New York where the cultural choice is vast. Audiences go to only one play at a time – unless, that is, they are attending something special like Wagner's *Ring Cycle* – and they go primarily for entertainment, not to be overtly instructed or to discharge a religious obligation. The choice includes musicals, ballets, operas, variety shows, classical plays, contemporary plays, thrillers, serious prose plays, verse dramas, domestic comedies and fringe theatre. Audiences range from the highly intellectual, who might be devotees of serious opera, or of Becket or Eliot or Stoppard, to the self-acknowledged low-brow, who go to the theatre to escape from real life and have a night out away from the harassments of home and work. In spite, however, of this range in type of audience, the English speaking theatre-going public has long been, and probably still is, predominantly middle class. It is not representative of all strata of the population.

I mention all these obvious things merely to draw a contrast with the ancient theatre. For the classical Greek theatre did not have this fragmentation of genre, location or audience. The genres were few, all in verse, consisting of only four types – tragedy, satyric drama, comedy and dithyramb. There were neither scattered small theatres, nor performances on offer all the time. Theatres were outdoor, few and far between, and performances were concentrated into one or two dramatic festivals held at select times of the year. One could not go to the theatre all the time in ancient Greece. Audiences were vast mass ones (probably 14,000, for instance, at the theatre of Dionysus in Athens) and were drawn from a wide section of the population. Moreover their reasons for going were as much religious, or to glean instruction, as for pure entertainment. They would not have expected their tragedies to allow them to escape into a fantasy world which

1

bore little relation to reality – or to escape into another *private* domestic world which had no public relevance.

Greek Tragedy was in no way portrayed on a small canvas, nor was it personal in character. It was grand and large, and it dealt with elevated social, political, religious, and moral issues in elevated poetic language. It conveyed these themes through traditional myth, and was thus communal in another sense than just having a mass audience – it had a mass audience with a shared heritage about to be presented on stage. This heritage had both religious and secular associations.

First, religious. Tragedy, like the other dramatic genres, was an offering to the God Dionysus whose statue stood in the theatre throughout dramatic performances. The main festival at Athens, the Great Dionysia, happened once a year for a few days in the Spring when tragedies, comedies, satyr plays and dithyrambs were performed in open competition in Dionysus' honour. The occasion was for the whole community and a kind of carnival air reigned. The law courts were closed. Distraints for debt were forbidden. Even prisoners were released, according to Demosthenes, and any outrage committed during the performance was treated as a sacrilegious act.

Although such *religious* ceremonial was essential to the presentation of drama at Athens, it was the state which managed the production side. A selected official, an archon, in charge of the festival, initially chose the poets and plays, and was responsible for the hiring and distribution of actors. Thus the theatre was also a state function.

Peisistratus had been the one to institute tragic contests recognised by the state, and the first competition was held in 534 B.C. when Thespis won first prize. At each festival from then on, three poets were appointed as competitors, and each exhibited four plays (three tragedies and a satyr play). The general name for the group of plays was *didaskalia* or teaching, because the author taught (*edidaxe*) the plays to the actors.

A herald proclaimed the victorious poet and his choregus (trainer of the Chorus), and these were crowned with ivy garlands. The poet and choregus who won a prize were listed on public monuments, and in later times actors' names were also recorded on official lists. The monuments of stone erected near the Theatre of Dionysus at Athens, as well as private monuments set up by the choregus, or the dedication of masks, marble tablets or sculptural reliefs and the *didaskaliai*, show how high a place the tragic poet held in society. The place of the poet in ancient fifth century society is thus different from the way poets or dramatists are regarded by most people today. His place was in a context of the whole community and so was the subject matter of his plays.

Note
The most scholarly and detailed discussions and evidence for the festivals, staging and performances of the ancient Greek theatre may be found in A.W. Pickard-Cambridge, *The Dramatic Festivals of Athens* and *The Theatre of Dionysus in Athens*. Shorter and more easily digestible treatments, also suitable for the Greekless reader, may be found in P.D. Arnott, *Introduction to the Greek Theatre*, H.C. Baldry, *The Greek Tragic Theatre*, E. Simon, *The Ancient Theatre*, and T.B.L. Webster, *Greek Theatre Production*. (See General Bibliography, Section VIII). A.E. Haigh's *The Attic Theatre* (Oxford, 1907[3]), though very old now, and in many ways superceded, has some very useful details on ancient sources.

II. Greek Tragedy

Greek Tragedy treats passions and emotions of an extreme kind (fear, anger, hate, madness, jealousy, love, affection) in extreme circumstances (murder, suicide, incest, rape, mutilation). Its potency is felt all the more because such circumstances and such emotions occur within the close confines of a family.[1] Were the protagonists unrelated, such intensity would be lacking. Yet offsetting all this violence is the concentrated and controlled form of the plays which serves as a frame for the action. Of all art forms Greek Tragedy is one of the most formalised and austere. The combination of such formality with the explosive material it expresses, is what gives this drama its impact.

In life, extremes of emotion do not often have shape and ordered neatness. They are incoherent and chaotic. The newspapers show everyday the havoc wrought by acts like murder, incest, rape and suicide – the very stuff of Greek Tragedy. Amid such havoc the perpetrators or victims of violent deeds seldom have either the temperament or the opportunity to express in a shaped form how they feel or felt

3

at the time. Lawyers may later impose an order for them, but it cannot be *their own* response as it was at the actual moment of disaster. What Greek Tragedy does is to create an imagined action, through myth, where the characters *are* able to articulate the thoughts and emotions which drive them, and where the audience is given also the thoughts and emotions of those involved with the main actors, i.e., relatives, friends, outsiders. It does this moreover in such a way that the lasting effect is not one of repugnance, but of acceptance and understanding.

The material of Greek Tragedy is shaped and transformed into art in two main ways. One is through the creative harnessing of ancient myth and more modern insights. The other is through the formal conventions of language and structure.

First the combination of myth with more contemporary elements. By this I mean the blending of traditional stories, the shared heritage, with the perspectives which come from the city state, particularly fifth century Athens. This means an explosive mixture of past and present. Consider first the mythical element:–

1) Myth means *the past* to a Greek tragedian, a past which he has inherited over centuries, ever since the earliest stories were recited to his ancestors.

2) This past myth is usually concerned with the *heroic* – the great heroes as they are presented in epic and lyric poetry.

3) In this telling of the heroic, the *individual* is important. It is the single figure and his greatness which stands out, whether Achilles or Agamemnon or Odysseus or Ajax or Philoctetes or Heracles.

4) This single figure is so glorified that he may often have become, in epic and particularly in lyric poetry, a *model*, an archetype of heroic qualities.

Against this let us set the other side – the contemporary world of the poet which must confront this mythical material.

1) It is the present with present values and attitudes.

2) It is not a heroic world – it is the *city state* with its keen interest in contemporary politics and social issues.

3) It is interested in *collective values* much more than in the lone outstanding individual. The community matters.

4

4) It is interested in asking *questions*, not in eulogising the great heroes – at least not exclusively. As Vernant says, when past heroes become incorporated into contemporary tragedy, they turn into problems and cease to be models.

In the creation of tragedy, therefore, we have the meeting of the mythical past, with its stress on the greatness of the hero, with the contemporary present, with its stress on collective values and the asking of fundamental questions. Vernant puts it very elegantly. "Tragedy is a debate with a past that is still alive" and "Tragedy confronts heroic values and ancient religious representations with new modes of thought that characterise the advent of law within the city state".[2]

So too Nestlé, "Tragedy is born when myth starts to be considered from the point of view of an (ordinary) citizen".[3]

The heritage of myth is well represented by epic poetry in the shape of Homer, and lyric poetry in the shape of Pindar.

Tragedy borrows heavily from the stories told by Homer. In fact Aeschylus was said to have called his plays "rich slices from the banquet of Homer".[4] From the *Iliad* we meet again in tragedy the heroes Agamemnon, Ajax, Menelaus, and Odysseus, as well as Hecuba, Andromache, Helen and Clytemnestra. Other figures from the other epic cycles such as Philoctetes, Heracles, Theseus and Oedipus form the main subject of tragedies.

Agamemnon for instance plays a leading role in Homer's *Iliad* and Aeschylus' *Oresteia*, yet in the transformation from one author to another, setting, concept and climate have changed. Agamemnon is no longer seen as prestigious leader against the backdrop of a glorious war. The new domestic situation in which he is depicted strips him both of prestige and of a glorious cause. The righteousness of the Trojan war is questioned, Agamemnon's motives are questioned, his weaknesses dwelt upon rather than merely lightly indicated. In this new setting our concept of the hero is found to undergo a change, but it is not only that the setting alone brings about that change, it is that the tragic poet explores a complexity of motive, both human and divine, which would have been inconceivable in Homer's day. It is not simply the *greatness* of the heroic figure which interests Aeschylus, but the weakness and complex negative traits which underlie the *reputation* of

5

that heroic greatness. He uses the familiar epic frame in which to paint a new picture in a dramatic form.

In Homer, whatever the heroes' faults, they are unquestionably great and glorious. Eulogy is implicit in the very epithets used to describe them. Pindar also eulogises several of the great hero figures who become later the subject of tragedies. Among them are Ajax, Heracles, Jason and Philoctetes.

Homer and Pindar both celebrate Ajax's greatness, particularly his physical strength. Homer calls him "great", "huge", "strong", "tower of defence", "rampart of the Achaeans", "like a blazing lion".[5] He defended the ships against the onslaughts of Hector. He was pre-eminent in the battle for the body of Patroclus. He held a special place of honour at one end of the Greek encampment.[6] Even in the *Odyssey*, in the Underworld, where he turns his back on Odysseus, his silence is majestic and impressive.[7] Pindar glorifies Ajax in the fourth *Isthmian* and pays tribute also to Homer's celebration of the hero's greatness. Neither Homer nor Pindar, however, ask fundamental questions about the nature of the man – they are content merely to celebrate him as a hero. But Sophocles begins from where Homer and Pindar left off. He too acknowledges this hero's greatness, but he asks stringent questions at the same time. His play *Ajax* is the vehicle for such questions: How can the world comfortably contain such an individual? How can society function properly with one such as him in its midst? How can Ajax himself survive when he confuses so tragically the rôles of comrade-in-arms and arch enemy? What does it mean to him mentally to take the decision to kill himself?

In this play we see Ajax not only as a glorious single heroic figure, but also as a tragic character who is so because he is isolated from others, and is unable to communicate with them successfully. He is seen in the perspective of those around him – Odysseus, Tecmessa, Teucer, Agamemnon and Menelaus. Undoubtedly he has that epic *star quality* which the others do not possess and the continuity with the heroic past is important and a fundamental part of the whole conception – but that is not the whole of it. He is a problem both for himself and for others, and because he is a problem we see the tragedy unfold. The heroic individual is balanced against the collective values of a more modern society, represented particularly by Odysseus, and to some extent by

6

Agamemnon and Menelaus – odious though they are.[8] What makes the drama of the play is precisely this tension between the old heroic individual concerns (the core of the myth), and the newer collective values of society which had more relevance to Sophocles' own time. Of course this is an over-simplification – there are problems *implicit* in epic too, as in Achilles' case, but they are not articulated as problems, they are just told and the audience must draw its own conclusions.

One of the most eulogised heroes in Pindar is Heracles. He is celebrated as the glorious hero *par excellence* – monster-slayer and civiliser of the known world. In the first *Nemean* Pindar introduces him, and then goes on to describe his miraculous exploits as a baby when Hera sent snakes to destroy him in his cradle.[9] In the ninth *Pythian* are the words:

> Stupid is the man, whoever he be, whose lips defend not
> Herakles,
> who remembers not the waters of Dirke that gave him life,
> and Iphicles.
> I, who have had some grace of them, shall accomplish my
> vow to bring them glory; let only the shining
> light of the singing Graces fail me not.[10]

In the fourth *Isthmian* he speaks of Heracles' ascension to Olympus after civilising the known world, and in the second *Olympian* he greets Heracles as the founder of the Olympic games.[11]

Euripides takes the spirit of the Pindaric celebration and incorporates it early in his play, *The Mad Heracles*, in an ode somewhat reminiscent of Pindar.[12] In it the chorus eulogises the great labours of Heracles, stressing his superhuman strength and effortless valour. But this dramatist too is concerned ultimately not with mere celebration but with problems. The end of the play shows a transformation: not the glorious invincible hero, but a vulnerable human being struck down by madness. This is a disgraced and humiliated Heracles who is broken and dependent. It is society who rescues him in the shape of Theseus his friend and Amphitryon his father. As the hero is brought down to the level of others, the superhuman isolation goes and human social values are seen to count. Once again the tension between the lone heroic figure and socially co-operative values are worked through in the course of the drama.

7

Perhaps nowhere is this blend of archaic myth and more recent thought, of the clash between the heroic individual and collective co-operation, seen more clearly than in Aeschylus' *Oresteia*. There, an archaic story of the heroic Mycenaean age ends up in Athens – not famous in Mycenaean times at all, and an Athens, at that, with contemporary resonances. The old story of a family's blood feud is played out in the *Agamemnon* and *Libation Bearers* where the tribal law of vendetta rules, and blood is shed for blood in seemingly endless succession. In the last play of the trilogy – the *Eumenides* – a modern legal solution is imposed, and by means of a new jury system at the court of the Areopagus at Athens, a public not a private judgement is made on the crime of murder. The setting up of this court in the play reflects a historical event, the confirmed attribution to the Areopagus of homicide cases in 462 B.C. by Ephialtes, and the patronage which Athene, the patron goddess of Athens, extended to this institution and to Athens as a whole. Thus the present community of the whole city is inextricably blended with what is ostensibly an archaic drama recounting an ancient myth.

Thirty two tragedies survive, and of these, nineteen have as their setting a city or *polis*, a *polis* with a ruler, a community and political implication which have a bearing on contemporary issues. Of these nineteen, the *Eumenides* is set in Athens itself, Sophocles' *Oedipus at Colonus* is set at Colonus, very near Athens, Euripides' *Suppliants* is set at Eleusis very near Athens, and his *Heracleidae* is set in Athens itself. The rest are in Greek cities like Corinth, Thebes, Mycenae, or Troizen. All these cities have a *turannos* or sole ruler. The setting and the form of rule are ostensibly archaic to fit the traditional myth, but again and again the dramatist imports contemporary resonances which will be of particular interest to his audience.

Two of Sophocles' plays – the *Antigone* and *Oedipus the King* – are set in a *polis*, though that of Thebes not Athens, and both, particularly the *Antigone*, are to some extent concerned with the question of rule in relation to the ruler and his citizens.

Sophocles was not on the whole aiming to make *specific* references to the contemporary political scene[13] although the plague at Thebes in *Oedipus the King* will have awoken familiar echoes in the audiences' minds of their own privations from

8

plague at Athens in the opening years of the Peloponnesian War.[14] But this aside, Sophocles was concerned in these plays much more with general questions of what makes a good ruler in a city, what stresses affect him and what should be his relations with the citizens. Such questions would be of perennial interest to the inhabitants of a city like Athens, even though the mechanisms of rule were no longer the same as they had been under the tyrants, and even though the dramatic location was Thebes not Athens.

Such examples show that in Greek tragedy the archaic myths are transmitted not only to preserve their traditional features – though this transmission of the past is a vital ingredient of the dramatic conceptions and indeed forms an assumption from which to view the whole dramatic development[15] – but they are also permeated by a sense of what the present and the city state mean. The old hero is put in a new context where new judgements are made on him. There is a sense of the community, sometimes represented by the comments of the chorus as ordinary citizens, e.g. in the *Antigone, Oedipus the King, Medea* and *Hippolytus* and sometimes by the comments of other characters who represent the common good like Odysseus in the *Ajax*, Theseus in the *Heracles*, the messengers in the *Bacchae*. The hero may have greatness, as he often has in Sophocles, but the greatness does not go unchallenged. It is not flawless. In Euripides the greatness may disappear altogether, as in the case of Jason, once the great hero of the Argonauts, and now a paltry mean-minded person caught in a shabby domestic situation, or Menelaus as he appears in the *Helen* or Agamemnon in the *Iphigenia in Aulis*.

This questioning spirit so characteristic of Greek Tragedy is also important when one considers it as a religious event. It has often been said that tragedy's origins lie in ritual.[16] This may be true. But that implies repetition, dogma and unquestioning belief, and classical tragedy was never like this, although its performance was sacred to a god, and its content still reflected to some extent the relations between gods and men. For gods as well as heroes were inherited from earlier myth and the innovations the dramatists bring to religious consciousness are just as important as the developing complexity in their grasp of human behaviour. In fact the two are inextricably linked. It is not too much to say that the gods dominate the world of tragedy and those gods are no

9

longer the sunny Olympians of Homer. In the interval between the eighth century and the fifth, moral consciousness has been born and the gods become associated with the implacable punishment of men's wrongdoing. Whether Aeschylus' all-seeing Zeus who is associated with Justice, or Sophocles' relentless oracles which always come true in the fulness of time, or Euripides' pitiless Aphrodite or Dionysus, the gods hover above the heroes' actions watching men trip themselves up. And whether it is the passionate belief of Aeschylus, or the inscrutable acceptance of Sophocles, or the protesting criticism of Euripides, the gods are always there at the heart of tragedy and the new problematic lives of the heroes must be seen against this divine background. But tragedies are not sacred texts. By classical times the art form was emancipated, and the authors free to change traditional treatments, criticise even the divine figures and sometimes, as Euripides did, show radical scepticism about the gods, their morals and even their very existence. This is all the result of a creative meeting between two worlds – the archaic, traditional, aristocratic, heroic world of myth, and the newer contemporary values of the democratic, highly social city state where the ordinary citizen's views counted in the general reckoning of human conduct and achievement, and where contemporary thinkers were questioning moral and theological issues.

The tragedians had available to them all the resources of inherited myth which they incorporated into their own experience as beings within the *polis*. They also had to work through the contrived shapes of language and structure which conventionally belonged to the dramatic genre of tragedy. As we see them, these contrived shapes are overt and analysable, and their variety of style and development is largely responsible for the rich and complex experience which comes from watching this drama. Through them the dramatic action is assimilable: through them the reactions of those watching and listening are orchestrated. In other words they filter through their disciplined structures the inherent turbulence of the basic material, thus controlling by form and pace the responses of the audience.

First the verse form. Greek Tragedy was written in verse in an elevated and traditional poetic language. Most translations, even the verse ones, are misleading in that they do not record the variety of verse forms employed in the different sections of the plays. Spoken dialogue was in iambic

10

trimeter. The sung portions, choral odes and solo arias, and some exchanges between actor and chorus, were in lyric metres of which there was a wide range and variety to express different moods. Rhyme was not used. Music would accompany the lyric portions, often on the pipe but the music accompanying the drama has unfortunately not survived except for tiny almost unintelligible fragments.

The long spoken episodes, rather like acts, stand between shorter sung choral odes, or *stasima* as they are sometimes called, of which there are usually three or four in the course of the play. A processional song called the *parodos* marks the first entrance of the chorus into the orchestra and the name is clearly associated with that of the *parodoi* or side-entrances.

The choral odes were danced as well as sung, and had elaborate choreography which again has not survived. Modern productions have to use imagination in providing steps and music in which to express the lyric parts of tragedy, but they can on the whole successfully reproduce the basic metrical rhythms and recurring patterns of the words themselves. The language in which iambic speech and choral lyric are written, differs. The former is in the Attic dialect, the latter includes elements from a Doric form of Greek, perhaps reflecting the Peloponnesian origins of choral songs. There is the utmost contrast in Greek Tragedy between the spoken portion and the lyric. The former, though in verse, resembles more nearly ordinary conversation and, with occasional colloquialisms, particularly in Euripides, its language also owes much to rhetoric, particularly in the set debate and the longer speeches. Euripides' language here is outstanding for its fluency and clarity of diction whether employed in argument, appeal, statement of feeling or philosophical reflection.[17]

The lyrics on the contrary are in more elaborate metres and highly poetic language containing more ornament, more images, more condensed syntactical structures and more compressed thought patterns.[18] They are composed in the tradition of the great lyric poets, particularly Pindar whose somewhat obscure but highly colourful and elaborate style was famous in antiquity and would have been familiar to the dramatists' audience.

It is hard to communicate in a few words just what the lyric metres achieve in Greek Drama. And indeed we do not always know. But one can say that they characterise and control pace, mood, and tone. They act as a kind of register

11

of emotion. Certain metres, like the dochmiac, for instance, are associated with high points of excitement, others like the ionic rhythms have cult associations, others, like the dactylic, convey a strong sense of insistent and forward movement, or may recall the hexameter beat of epic. Frequently it is the subtle blend and changing of rhythms which create special effects as for instance when the opening ionics of the *Bacchae parodos*, evoking religious and cult associations, turn eventually through choriambs and glyconics to excited dactyls as the pace gathers momentum and the women sing of rushing off to the mountains,[19] or when the primarily iambic first *stasimon* of the *Trojan Women* is given an epic flavour at the beginning by its opening dactyls

The lyric metres, more emotional than iambic trimeters, are often used in contrast with the trimeter in mixed dialogues where one actor sings in lyrics and another replies in spoken utterance or where an actor will speak his lines and the chorus reply in sung lyrics. In this way the different emotional levels are offset as for instance at *Alc.* 244, where Alcestis, in a semi-delirious trance, as she has a vision of approaching death, is given lyrics, and the uncomprehending Admetus speaks in iambics.

The chorus are always at the heart of the play. Singing and dancing to music, they have a function which is both a part of, and yet slightly separated from, the main action. Placed in the orchestra, the circular dancing space, the chorus are physically distanced from the actors and like the messenger they are usually, though not always, outsiders who look at the happenings from a slightly different point of view from the protagonists. They are ordinary citizens,[20] the protagonists are not. The chorus' task is to change the gear of the action, interrupting its forward flow and examining it in new perspectives. Their look at events allows time for reflection and judgement, leisure to consider motivation and causal explanations. They may as so often in Aeschylus – e.g. in the *parodos* of the *Agamemnon* (40 ff.) – bring to light a whole realm of background material which sets into relief the immediate events, or they may as in the ode on Man in the *Antigone* (332 ff.), cast specific actions in a more universal context. Their rôle is that of an interested commentator who is able not only to reflect, but to look *around* as well as directly *at* an action, providing a sort of philosophical pause in highly poetic form. But sometimes, as in the *Bacchae*, for instance, they are strongly involved in the action as participants, and here their songs actually enact the religious rituals which are at the heart of the play's experience. Here there is no detachment, only devotion to the god. The choral function is complex and multiple, and varies from context to context, particularly in Euripides. The varied lyric metres show a fine register of different emotions and indicate tone and mood. Frequently they change as an ode proceeds.

Lyric is however not restricted to the chorus, and the solo aria is often a *tour de force* in the play and associated with high emotion expressed through the lyric metres in which it is cast. This actor's song in lyric is called a monody. Not all plays have one but some, as for instance the *Ion*, *Trojan Women* and *Phoenician Women* of Euripides, have two or more. The monodies of Greek tragedy formed high points of sympathetic identification with hero or heroine – more usually the latter since only a very few male characters are given one to sing in all of extant Greek tragedy. Here the author sought to move his audience with stirring music and words that excited pity. The monody is often designed to present a subjective and partial point of view which reflects the strong preoccupations of the singer, but which may be at variance with other views presented in the play. Euripides, the most renowned composer of monodies, gives his singers just such passionate commitment and bias.[21] Examples are Ion's adoration of Apollo, Creousa's blasphemy against the same god, Hecuba's aching despair, Cassandra's delirious wedding song, or Electra's passionate grief.[22] The monody has a lyric non-logical structure with images, personal apostrophes, laments and prayers predominating.[23]

Among the spoken parts of the play are certain set pieces, easily recognisable in formal terms, such as the messenger speech, *agon* (debate), *rhesis* (single set speech) and *stichomythia* (line dialogue). In Euripides these are much more obviously marked off than in Sophocles and Aeschylus so that they sometimes seem almost crystallised and isolable in themselves rather than merging into one another or growing naturally. Euripides no doubt had his own reasons for this and indeed often the sharp contrast between modes creates a dramatic excitement of a peculiarly impelling kind.[24]

The messenger speech, much beloved by Euripides, is one such spoken device.[25] It is a set narrative speech in iambics, reporting offstage action to the actors on the stage and to the audience. Perhaps here the rôle of the imagination for the audience is at its height. A whole scene is set for the

13

spectator with exact detail sketched in so that visual and auditory images etch themselves sharply on the mind. Gone are the personal apostrophes, images, laments and prayers of the lyric style. Here, instead, is ordered narrative in strict chronological sequence, full of verbs of action and graphic physical detail. Unlike the monodist, the messenger is an outsider, a third person objective witness who records events in an unbiassed way and in such a manner that the audience can make their own judgements.

It would be a mistake to think of the messenger's report as a poor substitute which fails to make up for what cannot be shown on the stage. On the contrary it is superior to spectacle. The Greeks delighted in narrative ever since the performances of the epic rhapsodes were formally instituted by Peisistratus, and long before that no doubt, and such extended reports will have given special pleasures in themselves. As Aristotle saw, there were disadvantages to mere horror spectacles even had it been feasible to stage them.[26] For they produce confusion and shock – so that their impact would preclude proper assimilation of the events. What the messenger does is to control and stage the experience so that it is assimilable to the spectator bit by bit in an ordered way.

Euripides' messenger speeches with their quiet pictorial beginnings, their slow build-ups, their fragments of recorded conversation, and their graphic descriptions of the climactic acts of horror in visual terms, are masterpieces of the art of narrative. The two in the *Bacchae* for instance not only tell the audience *what* has happened, but make imaginable through pictures the whole Bacchic experience. Here the narrative is indispensable, for it is inconceivable that the audience would ever be able to view directly the mass attack of the women upon the cattle or upon Pentheus. It would be utterly beyond stage resources. But if by any chance they were allowed to view it, it is unlikely that they would emerge with as clear and as objective a picture as the messenger is able to give. Narrative enables greater total understanding than mere spectacle, and can condense more into a short space of time. In that it is one degree removed from direct sight, and is delivered by an impartial witness, it practises a kind of *distancing* which reduces the crude horror of the tragic action and requires balanced judgement as well as an emotional response.

Many tragedies contain a set debate or 'agon' where one

14

character presents a case in formal terms, and another, as adversary, responds point for point in a counter speech. Euripides, particularly, formalised such debates, so that they often resembled law-court speeches, and they are indeed sometimes cast in formal rhetorical terms.[27] Examples are Medea's great debate with Jason, or Hecuba's with Helen in the *Trojan Women*. In these, logical and orderly exposition is more important than naturalism. It is never possible entirely to separate feelings from reasoned thought – nor should it be. But the modes of tragedy assault both, in differing degrees, by different routes. The solo aria is a direct appeal to the feelings through emotive sound and image, through words of personal address and reaction. The messenger speech appeals to the audience's consciousness through an ordered evocation of the senses so that one perceives and hears a chronological sequence of events in the mind's eye and ear. The *agon*, on the other hand, captures the audience's hearts and minds by persuasion through reasoned argument. Although the result may involve the emotions, the method is more intellectual than in either the aria or the messenger speech. Thus the *agon* in the *Trojan Women* with its sharp development of points of debate gives an academic edge to an action which is otherwise predominantly lyric in mood.

The *rhesis* is a set speech of an actor which works by persuasive and ordered logic and which may none the less often make strong appeal to the emotions. It is the commonest of all dramatic forms and one of the most varied, and overlaps with other parts. It may, for example, form part of a debate scene, it may convey extended dialogue or it may stand on its own in monologue. Its tenor may be argumentative, reflective, pathetic, informative or questioning. Many set speeches take the form of a monologue where the speaker examines his or her motives and actions in an intense process of self-examination.[28] Such are Medea's speech to the women of Corinth at *Med*. 214 ff. or her monologue at 1021 ff., Phaedra's speech at *Hipp*. 373 ff. or 616 ff., Hecuba's speech at *Hec*. 585 ff.

Often it is hard to separate the emotional element from the thought element when the poet gets the balance right. For instance Medea's speech at *Med*. 1021 ff., where she debates whether she can bring herself to kill her own children, has a tight logical structure, but through this makes strong appeal also to the emotions.[29] There is a delicate balance between direct apostrophe, a simple expression of raw feeling, and reasoned alternatives which are worked out logically. But the

15

dramatist brilliantly gives the impression that the logic is forced out desperately by a person fighting for control in a situation where the emotions threaten to take over. The result is a powerful speech which assaults both our emotional and our thinking faculties, made no less effective by the violent swings of stance which Medea takes as she is torn between the immediate sight of her children before her, and the more long-term thought of her future life as it must follow from present circumstances.

Stichomythia is a special kind of formal dialogue where the characters speak in single line exchanges. It is not the only kind of dialogue or even the commonest in tragedy but I single it out here because of its regular and easily identifiable form. Such a tight and formal framework permits speed, concentrated and pointed utterance within its compass.[30] It is particularly suited to scenes of interrogation such as we see in the *Bacchae* where it communicates with its economy and rapid pace the extreme tension and changing shifts between the god Dionysus and Pentheus the King.[31]

All these items, monody, choral ode, messenger speech, set debate, *rhesis* and *stichomythia* make up the 'formal' elements of Greek Tragedy. Now 'formal' sometimes conjures up an image of fossilisation and aridity, but this is far from the case. On the contrary, the variety of metre, language, dialect and mode within the compass of one tragedy, and the alternation of song and speech, and of lyric and dialogue, made Greek Tragedy a rich experience offering a range seldom even dreamt of today. Each mode approaches the same dramatic action in a new way, with its own perspective and its own style, so that the audience is constantly exposed to shifts of perception, and the contrasts such shifts imply. Moreover each mode would have had its own associations – lyric arousing echoes of the great lyric tradition in Greece, narrative, reminiscent of epic, catering for the pleasure in story-telling the Greeks always had. And each mode carried with it its own responses which contrasted with others. Thus the great debates provided intellectual stimulus and were set off against the more emotional colouring of choral odes and arias. All were combined within the one dramatic action.

With great range of form went an economy and concentration lacking in much modern drama. The action was usually confined to twenty-four hours in one place, and was so arranged that all the parts could be taken by three actors. Scenery was sparse, subtle gestures and expressions were precluded by masks, heavy costumes and the sheer size of the theatre. But these things in themselves explain why the burden must be on the language (speech and song) and why the words were so important. In them were all the things which today are done by elaborate costume, make-up, close-up photography, lighting, scenery, stage directions, and all the rest. To the Greeks the expressed utterance was all - or almost all.[32]

So it was that the very great range of form in Greek Tragedy evinced in the different modes of speech and sung lyric, was matched by an equal range of expressions of complex human emotion, action, and thought made to fit those forms and channelled into patterns of plot, setting and action of extreme economy. It was this rich content within a controlling structure which involved too a creative harmonising of past and present attitudes through use of myth, as I outlined at the beginning, which gave, and still does give, Greek tragedy its forceful, concentrated impact.

III. Euripides

Euripides was the youngest of the three great Athenian tragedians (c.484-406 B.C.) although Sophocles, his slightly older contemporary, outlived him by a few months. In his lifetime he was not as popular with the Athenian public as the others, winning fewer prizes (four first prizes out of twenty two occasions) and ending his life in voluntary exile away from Athens at the court of Archelaus of Macedon.[33] More of his work has survived than the meagre seven plays each we have of Aeschylus and Sophocles. Nineteen plays entire have come down to us under his name, including the satyr play Cyclops, the Alcestis, a substitute for a satyr play, and the probably spurious Rhesus. Perhaps because of the wider sample known to us, part of which has been preserved by accident and not by deliberate selection, his work seems uneven and diverse in range.[34] There are the great tragedies of a very high order such as the Medea, Hippolytus, Trojan Women and Bacchae. But there are also plays where tragic themes mix with lighter elements and the ending is happy, such as the Alcestis, Ion, Iphigenia in Tauris, Helen. Attempts to categorise Euripides' style and plot by chronological criteria, thematic groupings, or structural elements, have largely failed, since there always seem to be exceptions which prevent such categories being

17

watertight.[35] Euripides is the most elusive of dramatists and the most resistant to fixed labels.

Not that his contemporaries hesitated to fix labels upon him. The comic poet Aristophanes was one such, a sharp critic who parodied him for his choice of subject matter, characters, plots, opinions and style.[36] Aristophanes saw him as ultra-trendy, undermining traditional religious and moral beliefs in a dangerous way and introducing outrageous musical innovations. He saw Euripides' characters, particularly his women characters, as unprincipled and shameless, too clever for their own or anybody else's good. He thought that Euripides elevated the ordinary to an absurd degree, making the trivial seem important, and low characters appear too significant. He therefore saw him as destroying the old heroic values and introducing instead ambiguous moral standards.[37] A rebel in fact of a most subversive kind.

This is quite a catalogue of blemishes. How misleading is it? Aristophanes is concerned of course mainly with raising a laugh – and for this, gross exaggeration is necessary. None the less much of his criticism is apt, if in a superficial way.

Euripides does introduce women characters who are criminal in their actions, like Medea who kills her children and two others, or like Phaedra who falsely incriminates her stepson thus indirectly causing his death. But Aeschylus had portrayed Clytemnestra – surely a woman of towering criminality. Why the fuss now? Perhaps because Euripides led the audience to see the action from these characters' points of view, whereas Aeschylus hardly encourages us to sympathise with Clytemnestra. Euripides was able to show what it *felt* like to have to kill your children or your mother; to be consumed by devouring jealousy or a desire for revenge; to fight an overmastering love and struggle with the consequences of madness.[38] And in so doing, unlike Sophocles, who on the whole portrayed characters who retained their wholeness and integrity throughout their tragedies, he explored weakness not strength, and exposed those elements in character which revealed disintegration and the split *persona*. Electra, Orestes, Pentheus, Phaedra, Admetus and even Medea or the great Heracles all reveal in some degree traits which characterise such disintegration and a nature divided against itself.[39]

To say that in so presenting his characters Euripides was debunking the heroic is only part of the truth. Undeniably in a play like the *Electra* all the old heroic assumptions and

18

settings are undermined or changed. Electra and Orestes are no longer the single-minded champions of justice. Clytemnestra and Aegisthus are no longer the uncompromising villains they were in Aeschylus. The murders are no longer performed in such a way that they can be seen as heroic actions. Even the setting has changed from grand palace to impoverished hovel.

And in other plays too such as *Iphigenia in Aulis*, great leaders of the heroic tradition like Agamemnon and Menelaus appear in particularly despicable lights, shifting their ground, arguing for expediency and promoting personal ambition at the expense of principles.

Yet it would be a mistake to say that Euripides had no concept of what it meant to be heroic if we think of this word not in its narrow archaic sense of military and physical valour, but in more general terms. It is that often he redefines traditional heroic qualities or else transfers them to *women*, placed in different situations from male heroes. Medea for instance, although a woman, shows many of the great heroic qualities of say an Ajax or an Achilles: bravery, desire to preserve her own honour, refusal to be laughed at by her enemies, the decisive nature to act in revenge.[40] What makes her interesting is the combination of these traditional qualities with her rôle as a woman and mother.

In the *Trojan Women*, Hecuba the old queen of Troy is heroic in her endurance of the sufferings inflicted on her by the Greeks, and in her fight to preserve her family. And when Euripides in the first stasimon makes the chorus "Sing, Muse, of Ilium, a lament consisting of *new* songs"[41] he is redefining the old epic notions of glorious war and transferring them to a setting where it is the victims who are seen as the true heroes – a point Cassandra also makes in her speech at *Tro.* 365 ff.

Several women characters voluntarily surrender their lives for a noble cause – such as Iphigeneia in *Iphigenia in Aulis*, the *parthenos* in the *Heracleidae*, or Evadne in the *Suppliants*, not to mention Alcestis who dies to save her husband. These are all examples of heroism, though not in the traditional masculine mould.

In the *Heracles* where the protagonist is male, Euripides contrasts the old traditional and active heroism of Heracles in performing the labours, with the more passive qualities of endurance he must display in facing up to the terrible consequences of his subsequent madness. He rejects the

19

traditional hero's solution to disgrace, namely suicide – the way Ajax had taken – and decides to live on in the company of his humiliation and misery. A new heroism perhaps for a newer age.[42]

Aristophanes, through the mouthpieces of Aeschylus and Dionysus in the *Frogs*, regretted the passing of the old standards and saw nothing but demeaning and undignified negativism in their place. *"Oikeia pragmata"*, "ordinary things", to him were not worthy of tragedy. But Euripides' celebration of the ordinary, if so it may be called, is often a positive and important part of the way he saw events and actions.

It is not only in settings and small actions we see it at work,[43] but also in characters. Again and again relatively humble characters play a significant rôle in a play's events. The former husband of Electra is arguably the only sane person in the *Electra*. The old servant in the *Hippolytus* has the wisdom Hippolytus lacks. The two messengers in the *Bacchae* grasp the truth of the Dionysiac phenomenon with an instinctive sense denied to all the other characters in the play.[44] They in fact carry the message of the play – that it is dangerous to deny such instinctive wisdom and to mock at belief. Aristophanes was therefore right when he said that Euripides introduced the ordinary into tragedy. He did. The ordinary person is listened to and often proved right. And if this is regarded as an overturning of values, it is a positive and significant one, and should not be dismissed as mere rabble rousing.

What Aristophanes saw as frivolity and irresponsibility in Euripides in fact sprang from a deep care for the world and a wish to protest at its wrongs. This is what his characters show. It was not to abandon a portrayal of the heroic but to redefine it. And all the charges of agnosticism or heresy which the comic poet loved to heap upon Euripides' shoulders are likewise superficially true, but in a deeper sense misleading.

Aristophanes was wrong to see Euripides' own views in every character who railed against the gods. Indeed his own views are difficult to recognise since he is usually much too good a dramatist to intrude his own *persona*. His characters display as many different beliefs as their rôle and the occasion demands. It is true however that attack on the gods is a persistent and recurring theme from major characters. Repeatedly his leading characters – Hecuba, Iphigeneia, Amphitryon, Heracles, Ion, Creousa, Electra, Orestes –

20

express their despair at a Universe negligently managed by divine beings.[45] But this despair springs not from a reluctance to believe at all on their part, but from an outrage that gods, as they are commonly understood, can be so amoral and utterly uncaring of human well-being. It is the disillusion of the perfectionist that Euripides so often portrays. As Heracles is made to say,[46]

> but I do not believe the gods commit
> adultery, or bind each other in chains.
> I never did believe it; I never shall;
> nor that one god is tyrant of the rest.
> If god is truly god, he is perfect,
> lacking nothing. These are poets' wretched lies.

Such sentiments come not from the frivolity of his characters, but from their taking the Universe too seriously. If there is a fault it is the latter not the former, that should be laid against Euripides' door. And no one who has heard or read the *Bacchae* could possibly accuse its creator of either agnosticism or superficiality. There are depths in it still being explored today.

The very characteristics in Euripides' work which disturbed Aristophanes and his contemporaries – his moral ambiguity, his scepticism, his anti-heroic stance and his common touch – are what appeal to the modern reader for they seem more in keeping with our own age. In the twentieth century we have been preoccupied with doubt and disintegration, demythologising and rationalising, and this is what Euripides epitomises. We can admire the sheer brilliance with which he manipulates the myths in a way which both uses and exposes their assumptions. While keeping the traditional stories as a frame, he yet undercuts them by rationalising many of the attitudes which have previously underpinned them. Notions of the very gods he uses come under attack: old conceptions about pollution and guilt are questioned; traditional criteria for judging character are scrutinised and found wanting. And in this problematic climate his characters like Electra, Orestes, Medea, Phaedra or Pentheus, pick their way, on the verge of collapse under the strain, as their rational grip loses the battle with the forces of disintegration.

But the drama he created did not always offer purely negative perspectives. Again and again positive human values are seen to triumph over divine neglect or apathy – the friendship of Amphitryon and Theseus, the supporting love of

21

Hecuba for her family and her courage, the integrity of Ion, the compassion of Cadmus and Agave, the selfless sacrifice of Iphigeneia, Alcestis, the *parthenos* in the *Heracleidae*, and the cheerful sanity of ordinary people like messengers, or servants.

In the importance he attached to supporting rôles and to the close interaction between his characters, Euripides prefers not to focus upon one dominating protagonist. The *whole* social context is what matters, and environment and social factors play a much larger part in determining the main character's rôle and the course of the action than they do in Sophocles (with the exception perhaps of the *Philoctetes*).[47]

In short Euripides was adventurous – adventurous above all in his treatment of myth. And adventurousness here meant an entirely new perspective on plot, character, moral and religious values, and social factors. But he was adventurous too in treatment of form and structure. He experimented with music and lyrics, with metrical forms and with the breaking up of dialogue. He increased the rôle of the solo aria and messenger speech and he sometimes changed the traditional function of the chorus. He introduced more colloquialism into the dialogue and more elaboration than Sophocles into the late lyrics, thus increasing contrasts between the modes.

What is clear is that he reshaped tragedy in a radical way so that it could never be quite the same again. He went as far as he could in giving it a new image without abandoning its basic conventions. And there is common agreement that his work is, at its best, of the first rank.

Of course there are faults and unevennesses in the plays: echoes from the soap-box occasionally, irrelevant rhetorical excrescences sometimes, self-indulgence in over-elaborate ornamentation of some of the later lyrics, too blatant melodrama perhaps in certain plays, loose plot construction in others.[48] But informing all is an understanding of a very powerful sort, a mind which for all its critical sharpness, also knew the human heart and dissected it not only with uncanny perception but also with compassion. It was Aristotle who called Euripides *tragikōtatos tōn poētōn*, "the most emotionally moving of the poets",[49] a paradox one might think for one who was also the most intellectual of dramatists, but a paradox that for him somehow makes sense.

Shirley A. Barlow

Notes to General Introduction

1. Aristotle, *Poetics*, ch. XIV, 1453 b, 19-22.
2. Vernant & Vidal-Naquet, 10; 4.
3. Cited *ib.*, 9.
4. Athenaeus, 347e.
5. Homer, *Il.* 23. 708, 842; 3. 229; 7. 211; 17. 174, 360; *Od.* 11. 556; *Il.* 3. 229; 6. 5; 7. 211.
6. *Il.* 11. 5-9.
7. *Od.* 11. 543 ff.
8. See especially Soph. *Aj.* 121 ff. where Odysseus rejects the traditional Greek view of the rightness of hating one's enemies and 1067 ff. where Menelaus complains of the problems an individual such as Ajax poses for the army as a whole and its discipline.
9. Pindar, *Nem.* 1. 33 ff.
10. *Pyth.* 9. 87 ff., transl. by R. Lattimore.
11. *Isth.* 4. 56 ff. *Ol.* 2. 3 ff.
12. *H.F.* 348 ff.
13. Unless the use of *ton stratēgon* 'the commander' *Ant.* 8, and *andrōn prōton* 'first of men' *O.T.* 33 are veiled references to Pericles who was *stratēgos* 'general', and whose influence was very much that of first citizen. See Thuc. II.65.10; V. Ehrenberg, *Sophocles and Pericles* (Oxford 1954) 105 ff.
14. *O.T.* 168 ff.
15. In fact Aristophanes set great store by what he saw as the rôle of tragedy to preserve traditional heroic features and criticised Euripides strongly for debasing such features. See next section.
16. For a recent analysis of ritual elements in Greek Drama see F.R. Adrados, *Festival, Comedy and Tragedy* (Leiden, 1975), chs. II, VII, VIII, XI.
17. Collard (1981) 20-23, 25-27.
18. *ib.* 26-27.
19. *Ba.* 64 ff. and Dodds' analysis, *Bacchae* (1960) 72-74.
20. Not in the technical sense of course since women were not full citizens but in the sense of people concerned at issues in the community.
21. On the function of the monody see Barlow, ch. III, 43 ff.
22. *Ion* 82 ff., 859 ff.; *Tro.* 308 ff., 98 ff.; *El.* 112 ff.
23. e.g. *Hipp.* 817 ff.; *Ion* 82 ff., 859 ff.; *Tro.* 98 ff. See also Barlow, 45 ff.

24. See for instance the contrasts in *Trojan Women* between the prologue and Hecuba's monody, between Cassandra's monody and her iambic *rhesis*, between the great debate and the subsequent choral ode, between the iambic dialogue at 1260 ff. and the lyric *kommos* which ends the play.
25. On the messenger speech see Barlow 61 ff.
26. Aristotle, *Poetics*, ch. XIII, 1453 b, 8–10.
27. On the *agon* see C. Collard, *G & R*, 22 (1975), 58–71; J. Duchemin, *L'Agōn dans la tragédie grecque* (Paris, 1945).
28. Collard (1981) 21–22.
29. I am assuming here that 1056–80 are genuine as it seems to me they must be (*pace* Diggle, Tomus I (1984) of his Oxford Classical Text).
30. Collard (1981) 22.
31. *Ba.* 463–508, 647–655, 802–841. N.B. the change to *two*-line dialogue, i.e. *distychomythia*, at 923–962.
32. But for the rôle of the non-verbal in theatrical performance see Taplin (1978) *passim*.
33. See the chart of chronology and award of prizes in Collard (1981) 2.
34. Collard (1981) 3; Barrett, *Hippolytos* (1964) 50 ff.
35. Collard (1981) 5.
36. Criticisms of Euripides occur extensively in *Frogs, Thesmophoriazusae*, substantially in *Acharnians* and in scattered references throughout Aristophanes' other works. See G.M.A. Grube, *The Greek and Roman Critics* (London, 1965) 22–32; P. Rau, *Paratragodia* (München, 1967); K.J. Dover, *Aristophanic Comedy* (London, 1972) 183–189.
37. Religious beliefs: *Frogs* 888 ff. Immorality: *Frogs* 771 ff., 1079 ff., *Thesm.* 389 ff. Musical innovations: *Frogs* 1298 ff., 1331 ff. Women characters: *Frogs* 1049 ff., *Thesm.* 389 ff. Cleverness: *Frogs* 775 ff., 956 ff., 1069 ff. Stress on the ordinary or sordid, the antiheroic: *Frogs* 959 ff., 1013 ff., 1064, *Ach.* 410 ff.
38. A point made by Vickers 563–4 and 566 (apropos of the *Electra*). See Medea's agonised speech at 1021 ff., Electra's remorse at 1183 ff., Hermione's vindictive jealousy expressed in the scene at *And.* 147 ff., Hecuba's gloating revenge over Polymestor *Hec.* 1049 ff. and her justification before Agamemnon 1233 ff., Phaedra's

struggle with her love at *Hipp*. 373 ff. particularly
380–381 and 393 ff., Heracles' struggle to face the
consequences of his madness from *H.F.* 1089 to the end.

39. Electra and Orestes in the *Electra* both suffer remorse
for their murder of their mother. Orestes in the *Orestes*
is reduced to madness through guilt and tormented by
conscience (*sunesis*). Pentheus is destroyed by the very
thing he professes to despise, ending his life as
voluntary spectator at a Bacchic revel from which he had
previously dissociated himself. Phaedra knows how she
should be but cannot achieve it. Her love overrides her
better judgement as does Medea's hate (*Hipp*. 380–381,
Med. 1078–9). Admetus suffers acute remorse for letting
Alcestis give her life for him (*Alc*. 861 ff. and 935 ff.).
Heracles is on the brink of total disintegration (*H.F.* 1146
ff.).

40. B.M.W. Knox, 'The *Medea* of Euripides', *YCS* 25 (1977),
193–225, esp. 198–9.

41. *Tro*. 511 ff. See my note on this passage.

42. See esp. H.H.O. Chalk, 'Arete and Bia in Euripides'
Herakles', JHS 82 (1962), 7 ff.

43. Settings such as the farmer's cottage in the *Electra* or
the drab tents of the Greek encampment in the *Trojan
Women*. Often ordinary actions are described such as
when the chorus and companions are doing the washing
(*Hipp*. 121 ff., *Hel*. 179 ff.) or Ion is sweeping out the
temple with a broom (*Ion* 112 ff.) or Hypsipyle sweeping
the step (*Hyps*. fr. 1. ii Bond), or the chorus describe
themselves getting ready for bed (*Hec*. 914 ff.).

44. *Ba*. 769 ff., 1150 ff.

45. *Trojan Women* 469 ff., 1240 ff., 1280 ff. *I.T.* 384 ff.
H.F. 339 ff., 1340 ff. *Ion* 435 ff., 1546 ff., 911 ff. *El*.
979, 981, 1190, 1246.

46. 1341–1346 transl. by W. Arrowsmith, cf. *I.T.* 384 ff.

47. See n. 43.

48. These points are covered by Collard (1981) e.g.
rhetorical excrescences 25-26, over-ornamentation of
lyrics 26-27, melodrama to be seen in last minute rescues
or recognitions 6. Many plays have been criticised for
their plot construction in the past; see my article on
H.F. in *G & R* 29(1982), 115–25, although, as I have
pointed out, opinions on this subject are now changing.

49. Aristotle, *Poetics*, ch. XIII, 1453 a, 28–30.

INTRODUCTION TO *ORESTES*

I. *Orestes* in the Development of Tragedy

Orestes was produced in 408 B.C.[1] Within the next year or so Euripides left Athens for Aegae in Macedon, accepting the patronage of Archelaus, the king of that country. By spring 406 he was dead. In a matter of months the nonagenarian Sophocles followed him to the grave, and the great age of Attic tragedy was suddenly over.

It had evolved considerably in the 66 years since the *Persians*, the earliest play now extant. To mention only externals: painted scenery had been introduced, normally representing a house or temple, giving the action a more definite location and an additional entry/exit point; the number of speaking actors had risen from two to three, giving the possibility of more complex interactions among characters; the chorus had grown from twelve to fifteen, but its share in the whole had been reduced; the music had become more varied and elaborate; there had come to be solo arias from actors as well as choral songs and sung dialogue between actor and chorus; the average length of a play had increased by fifty per cent. The greater length was mainly due to greater complexity of plots, the inclusion of a larger quantity of incident. Underlying this is a striving after a greater variety of emotional responses within the ambit of a single story. Early tragedy portrays, imaginatively and artistically but comparatively straightforwardly, the moods of a group of people before and after a decisive event. In time it was found that certain types of scene were particularly effective in the theatre, for example, those that created tension or mixed expectations in the audience, and those in which they saw characters on the stage acting under a misapprehension. To exploit these specifically theatrical effects, the tragedians contrived their plots so as to multiply such situations, depicting not just apprehension before the crisis and grief after it, but such things as mystification by oracles, false hopes, false fears, misplaced anger, premature rejoicing, belated enlightenment, ignorant encounters leading to joyous

26

recognition, deadly stratagems that might or might not succeed.

This prompted a good deal of invention, since the traditional myths as told by the epic and lyric poets and the logographers did not of themselves imply many of those effects. Euripides in particular, at least in his later years, sometimes went so far as to write plays in which, while the characters and some elements of the initial situation were traditional, the plot was entirely a fiction of his own. (Agathon took the extreme step of composing a tragedy in which even the characters were invented.) *Iphigeneia in Tauris, Ion, Helen* and *Orestes* are of this type. They are often called melodramas, a term which has no ancient equivalent but serves to convey the idea of works concerned more with emotional ups and downs (tending to find expression in song) than with profound tragic issues. In each of them there is romance, excitement, danger, suspense – in a word, "drama" – and a happy ending with nobody hurt except sometimes a number of barbarian underlings.

Orestes may claim to be the most brilliant of the set: skilfully constructed, rich in novel theatrical effects, building up to a spectacular dénouement. By objective technical criteria it represents the culmination of Euripides' development. He had been using resolved and anapaestic feet in his iambic trimeters with increasing frequency year after year, at least since the mid 420s. The figures reach a peak in this play, and fall back in the subsequent *Bacchae* and *Iphigeneia in Aulis*. One might attribute this to the steadying influence of being in Macedon, except that Sophocles shows a curiously parallel pattern, reaching very pronounced peaks in regard to the same metrical features in *Philoctetes* (409 B.C.) and retreating from them in *Oedipus at Colonus.*[2] It is as if an instinctive reaction had set in – as if tragedy suddenly seemed to have gone as far as it could go in the direction it was going, and drew back from the dizzy summit to which its exuberance had carried it. *Orestes* almost goes "over the top", with touches of self-commentary and self-parody (cf. nn. on 850, 1426–8, 1503) of a kind that would, if unchecked, have turned tragedy into pantomime in a few more years. One can imagine that the actors who performed this play were bubbling over with it (cf. 279 n.). Then the pendulum started to edge back. *Iphigeneia in Aulis* is another melodrama, but a more restrained one, while *Bacchae* is a reversion to an older type.

27

Not many people, if asked to nominate the greatest Greek tragedy, would choose *Orestes*. For true tragic greatness we expect horrific indignity faced with terrific dignity; we look to the doom-laden atmospherics of *Agamemnon*, the ruthless mechanism of *Oedipus Tyrannus*, the harrowing psychology of *Medea* or *Philoctetes*. We do not admit the "melodramas" as having a serious claim. But there is a sense in which *tragōidia*, considered not as a sublime abstraction but as theatre for the people, did not realise its full potential until Euripides perfected the art of balancing one emotion against another, one expectation against another, one sympathy against another, and of running his audience through a gamut of sensations to a final tonic chord of satiety and satisfaction. If there is one play in which this perfection may be said to have been achieved, it is *Orestes*.

We do not know whether the judges awarded Euripides the first prize in 408; we must remember that *Orestes* was only one of three tragedies that he presented.[3] But certainly after his death *Orestes* was his most popular play, indeed the most popular of all tragedies. It is parodied and alluded to in Old, Middle and New Comedy, and quoted by authors of all periods. Fragments of inscriptions[4] attest a production in 340 B.C. and another sometime in the following century. There must have been many more: an Alexandrian scholar whose commentary partly underlies the scholia refers several times to what "present-day actors" do in performing the play, and Dionysius of Halicarnassus, making a point about the setting of words to music which he could have illustrated from any tragedy he had seen, in fact illustrates it from the first sung words in *Orestes*, no doubt having the sound in his head (see on 140-207). In the late second century A.D. a scene from *Orestes* adorned a house wall in Ephesus.[5] Snobs may dismiss this popularity as evidence of debased taste. Let them. *Orestes* is not an *Agamemnon* or an *Oedipus*, but it is first-rate theatre, a rattling good play that deserves the attention of everyone interested in ancient drama.

II. The Story

The plot is an unorthodox version of the aftermath of Orestes' killing of Clytaemestra. As in earlier accounts (Aeschylus' *Choephoroe* and *Eumenides*, Euripides' own

28

Electra and *Iphigeneia in Tauris*), he is persecuted by his mother's Erinyes, who imperil his mental and physical health. But instead of being driven by them into immediate exile, as usual, he has remained on a sickbed at Argos, tended by his sister. The major novelty is that the city has reacted to the matricide with horror. It has excommunicated Orestes and Electra, and threatens to sentence them to death. In traditional mythology homicide and its punishment are matters between individuals or families. The community may applaud or lament, but it has no judicial role. In the case of Orestes' deed the assumption had always been that Argos rejoiced at its liberation from the tyranny of an evil couple (see especially *Cho.* 935–72, 1044–7); Orestes' immediate departure eliminated the problem of the pollution that according to common belief would be caused by the presence of a man who had shed kindred blood. By the time he came back he was purified. Aeschylus did indeed bring him before a court, but an Athenian, aristocratic one created by Athena to give service in post-mythical times. The idea of the trial comes from her, not from the city, which has no pre-existing machinery for it. Hellanicus (*FGrH* 323a F 22) had Orestes prosecuted by Clytaemestra's kinsmen, but he knew no other venue for the trial than Athens. Euripides is the first to imagine Argos as a *polis* concerning itself with Orestes' guilt and issuing decrees on the subject. He supplies the social dimension that is lacking in the traditional version. This is a notable instance of the tendency, discussed by Shirley Barlow in the General Introduction to this series (above, pp. 4 ff.), for tragedy to interpret heroic myths in the light of contemporary, community-oriented values.

Euripides does not, however, represent the Argives' condemnation as the inevitable and proper response of a city to an act such as Orestes'. Their assembly is not a wise and responsible body like Aeschylus' Areopagus, but a volatile crowd liable to be swayed this way and that by skilful oratory, or for that matter by coarse ranting. It is goaded on by Orestes' enemies (431 ff.), but the death sentence is the outcome of a debate in which contrary opinions are heard (884 ff.). Orestes is condemned, not because Euripides thinks he deserved it, but because he wants to create a desperate situation for the young hero and his friends to extricate themselves from, in other words, to promote dramatic excitement. The measures to which they resort – attempting to

29

CONCORDIA COLLEGE LIBRARY
BRONXVILLE, N.Y. 10708

assassinate Helen, and taking her young daughter hostage - are equally devoid of traditional foundation.

Two other elements in the plot do have a basis in tradition, though not both in the same tradition. Menelaus' belated return from Troy, just after the killing of Aegisthus and Clytaemestra, was given by the epic *Nostoi* (and *Od.* 3.311, 4.547; Eur. *El.* 1276-9). Euripides makes use of it in order to have both Menelaus and Helen on the scene: Menelaus to raise hopes of salvation that are later dashed, and Helen to become the object of the assassination attempt. The other traditional element is Helen's apotheosis, which goes back to Stesichorus. In *Helen* 1666-9 (four years before *Orestes*) Euripides had put the apotheosis at the end of Helen's natural life on earth, but in this play it is neatly combined with the new fiction of Orestes' attempt to kill her. In *Helen* he had used Stesichorus' story of a phantom that went to Troy in lieu of the real Helen, and he has the phantom fly off to heaven after the war when its job is done. In this play the phantom is discarded, but the same idea is exploited: Helen was only the gods' instrument for bringing the war about (1639 f.), and now that it is over she herself is carried up to heaven.

The other "traditional" characters in the play are Hermione, Tyndareos, and Pylades. Euripides has a good use for each of them, but has to invent reasons for their being at Argos at this juncture (see nn. on 63-4, 471, 763). Hermione serves as a hostage to frustrate Menelaus when he tries to avenge the (supposed) murder of Helen, and she ends up being named as Orestes' bride (traditional, 1654 n.). On Tyndareos' role see the nn. on 348-724 and 622. Pylades provides Orestes with moral and material support, as traditionally at the killing of Clytaemestra and Aegisthus. His future marriage to Electra (also traditional, 1078 n.) fits conveniently with his presence in this adventure.

To sum up, the entire action of the play is newly invented. The elements taken from tradition are either incorporated in the starting situation (Orestes' persecution by the Erinyes, Menelaus just returned from Troy) or in what Apollo in the closing scene announces as due to follow (Helen's reception among the gods, Pylades' marriage to Electra, Orestes' to Hermione, and also his exile in Arcadia and trial at Athens). Apollo's speech reinstates tradition: the new story does not replace existing accounts of what became of Orestes, it is interpolated into them as an extra episode.

III. Literary Sources and Models

Although the plot is a new creation, there is much in the play for which we can trace literary antecedents: ideas and motifs used in working out the story, and mythological material assumed as background or mentioned incidentally. As regards mythology, the following come into question:

Homer and the poems of the Epic Cycle (especially *Nostoi*, but also *Cypria, Aethiopis*, and *Little Iliad*; on these works see *OCD*[2] s.v. Epic Cycle).

The pseudo-Hesiodic *Catalogue of Women* (sixth century; all Hesiodic fragments cited are from this work, on which see West [1985]).

Lyric poets, especially Stesichorus' *Oresteia* and Helen-Palinode (sixth century).

Prose mythographers, especially Pherecydes of Athens (c.450-440) and Hellanicus (still active at the time of *Orestes*).

Above all: previous tragedy. For the killing of Clytaemestra and Orestes' subsequent tribulations Euripides was especially conscious of Aeschylus' *Oresteia* (458 B.C., perhaps revived in the 420s), of his own *Electra* (c.420), and of Sophocles' *Electra* (later than Euripides'?). The motif of Helen's apotheosis and the relation to Euripides' *Helen* has been mentioned in the preceding section. Where Euripides refers to earlier episodes in the saga of the Pelopid family, he seems to have in view previous tragedies either of his own (*Oenomaus, Cretan Women*) or of Sophocles' (*Atreus, Thyestes in Sicyon*); see the nn. on 14, 16, 18, 988, 1002. Elsewhere we may observe or suspect that he is remembering Aeschylus' *Glaucus Pontius* (363 n.), Sophocles' *Hermione* (1654-7 nn.), his own *Andromache* (1654-7 nn.) and Trojan trilogy (432-3, 1364-5 nn.).

The detailed dramatic invention often draws on motifs used in earlier plays. The idea of sending Hermione to Clytaemestra's grave-mound with libations and hair-offerings derives from the similar offerings made to Agamemnon in *Choephoroe* (96 n.). The scene where Orestes sleeps while Electra and the chorus sing, anxious not to wake him, has a close precedent in *Heracles* (140-207 n.), and also owes something to Sophocles' *Philoctetes* and *Electra* (174, 202-7 nn.). The following sickbed scene has further echoes of *Philoctetes* (218, 226 nn.), besides a motif that we recognize from *Hippolytus* (232 n.). In depicting Orestes' mad fit

31

Euripides draws on *Choephoroe* and on his own *Iphigeneia in Tauris* (238, 255-7, 259, 260 nn.). The idea of road blocks preventing escape (444) had been used in at least two of Euripides' earlier plays. Orestes' desire to hide in shame from the approaching Tyndareos (459) seems modelled on a passage of *Heracles*. When he wins from the Argives a stay of execution till the end of the day, we recall *Medea* (946 n.). The scene between Orestes, Electra and Pylades following the Argive debate contains more reminiscences of *Iphigeneia in Tauris* (1039, 1070-93, 1177). It ends with a set-piece antiphonal invocation of Agamemnon (1225-45) on the same pattern as one that Euripides had written in *Electra* on the model of one in *Choephoroe*. The following lyric dialogue between Electra and the chorus, during which Helen's cries are heard, has a number of parallels with the corresponding part of Sophocles' *Electra* (1246-1310, 1296, 1297, 1301, 1302 nn.). Later, when Menelaus is locked out of the palace and Orestes addresses him from the roof, there is another strong echo of *Medea* (1567 n.).

The plays that survive are only a fraction of those that existed. If we had the rest, we should no doubt be able to see that in writing *Orestes* Euripides drew even more largely on the stock of established motifs and devices than is now evident. Some of the parallels noted above might be superseded by closer ones. But it is clear that the comparative material at our disposal is more than a random selection. It includes a number of plays that Euripides quite definitely had in mind: Aeschylus' *Choephoroe*, Sophocles' *Electra* and *Philoctetes*, his own *Electra*, *Heracles*, *Iphigeneia in Tauris*, and *Helen*. The influence of *Philoctetes* is particularly noteworthy. This, the most Euripidean among Sophocles' tragedies, was produced the year before *Orestes*, and it evidently made a deep impression on Euripides. We find many verbal echoes in addition to the points of contact already mentioned.[6]

IV. Characters. Ethics. Contemporary Background

"The play is one of those that enjoy success on the stage, but its ethics are dreadful: apart from Pylades everyone is bad." Such is the pithy judgment of an ancient critic in one of the Hypotheses prefixed to the text. Aristotle

32

had earlier pointed to the Menelaus of this play as a character whom Euripides had gratuitously made bad (*Poet*. 1454a29, 1461b21), and both Menelaus and Helen are repeatedly criticized in the scholia. But did Euripides intend his characters to be judged so adversely?

Consider first Orestes and Electra. They are there at the beginning, and we follow their fortunes throughout. There can be no doubt that we are meant to sympathize with them in their desperate plight and rejoice at their salvation. For at least the first two thirds of the play there is nothing in their behaviour with which anyone could find fault. True, Orestes has killed his mother, and Electra helped him; but this is a fixed datum of the tradition, it is the very definition of Orestes and Electra, not something Euripides has used to give them a bad character. They did it on Apollo's instructions, and Orestes is racked with remorse and doubt at having done it (285–93, 396–8, 1668–9). On the positive side, the brother and sister show a self-effacing mutual devotion and loyalty of which the audience must have approved warmly. Their reaction must have been similar in the scene between Orestes and Pylades (729–806), where the two friends exhibit the same qualities towards each other. Towards his grandfather, Tyndareos, Orestes feels a proper shame and diffidence (459 ff., 544 ff.). He summons up the strength and courage to go to the debate and defend himself. Returning under sentence of death, he comports himself as a man should; his sister gives way to womanly tears, but for his sake as much as for her own. Pylades yields to neither of them in nobility of demeanour, determined to share their fate although there is no necessity for him to do so.

In the last third of the play these paragons turn without a qualm to murder, hostage-taking, and arson in the hope of (a) taking revenge on Menelaus for failing to save them and (b) escaping with their lives. They would certainly have used bombs if they had had any. Now it is easy for us to say "Why, they are behaving like a modern terrorist group: this we can only condemn". But the ancient Athenian spectator will have applied different categories. Where we see crimes, he saw resourcefulness, a brilliant plan being carried out boldly and efficiently. It was self-evident to him that one seeks to preserve one's life and one's friends' lives and injure one's enemy. In Greek eyes the application of cunning and ruthlessness to such ends is admirable, whether in a Homeric

33

hero or in a Resistance fighter, to all who sympathize with the cause. Our ancient spectator held no brief for Menelaus or Helen, and after seeing the affair from Orestes' and Electra's point of view all the way through, he was not going to be alienated by their use of an unscrupulous stratagem in order to come out on top. If Euripides had wanted him to be, his chorus would have shown the way. But the chorus remains supportive of Orestes and Electra: despite its horror at the murder of Clytaemestra, it approves of the murder of Helen.

I do not claim that either chorus or audience would cheerfully have accepted the slaughter of the guiltless Hermione. That Orestes threatens to kill her is the greatest stumbling-block for the modern critic, the proof of "how thoroughly Orestes' inner universe has been perverted" (H. Parry). But nothing the conspirators say convicts them of a genuine readiness to kill the girl: it is only a threat, to be maintained as long and as convincingly as necessary to persuade Menelaus (1193-1202; the tense of *sphaze* in 1199 is crucial, see 1195 n.).

I shall come back to Orestes and Electra, but it is time to move on to Menelaus and the others. Menelaus cannot be called an impressive figure. From the moment he comes into view the audience's feelings about him are ambivalent: he has a glamorous appearance, but it is a suspect kind of glamour (1532 n.). His niece and nephew hope that he will take command of the situation, rather as Heracles does when he returns from Hades in *HF* 523. But Menelaus is no Heracles. He takes his time in appraising the situation. He keeps talking about what the "intelligent" or "enlightened" person should do or say (397 n.), as if he had graduated from the Cogitatorium of the *Clouds* (490 n.). He decides that a careful approach to the problem is called for (698-9 n.). Of the heroic temper he shows not a flicker. Orestes is disgusted by his response (717 n.). We might think this unjust – Menelaus' assessment of the practical possibilities seems level-headed and realistic – were it not that when the time comes he fails even to try what he thought he could and said he would try. Evidently he has taken account in his calculations of Tyndareos' threat to exclude him from his Spartan kingdom if he supports Orestes (624-6). He is a man of reason adrift in a drama of emotion: he lacks nerve, and when those about one expect blind unhesitating loyalty, lack of nerve is equated with lack of virtue.

Tyndareos is also a kind of misfit in the world of
Orestes-plays. While Menelaus represents prudent pragmatism,
Tyndareos represents commitment to a civic law-code. He is an
old man and believes in following old-established procedures,
not from sheer conservatism but because it is his considered
judgment that they were wisely conceived. But in the
traditional Orestes legend these procedures never came into
play. So Tyndareos' views about what ought to have been done
with Clytaemestra are academic; his views of what ought to be
done with Orestes carry the day in the political setting
postulated in the play, but it is impossible that they should be
implemented in contradiction of tradition. Tyndareos is not, of
course, merely a mouthpiece of the law. He is a reasoning,
principled man, but he has robust passions too. He grieves for
Clytaemestra his daughter, while recognizing that she deserved
to die, and when roused to anger he becomes a formidable and
implacable opponent. It is anger, not principle, that leads him
to interfere in the Argives' debate and induce them to
sentence his grandchildren to death by stoning. This
immoderate response must be the reason for his inclusion in
the ancient critic's wholesale condemnation of the play's
characters.

Hermione certainly does not deserve her inclusion in it.
She is just an innocent young girl, rather naive (1323 n.),
and that is all there is to be said about her. As for her
mother, Helen, she has of course one great stain on her
record, and this is considered to mark her for life as "a bad
woman". But from Homer onward she is regarded as having
repented of her lapse long before Troy's overthrow; she does
not misbehave further, and is perfectly sweet to everybody.
In this play we see her mainly through the hostile eyes of
Electra and Orestes. For them she is an irredeemable Fallen
Woman, responsible for the loss of countless lives and indeed
for their own plight (130 f.), incurably vain (128, 1110-4),
possessive (1108), pretending concern but really malicious
(1122). In the short scene where she appears on stage,
however, (71-125) she gives us little reason to find fault. We
must accept Electra's point (128) that she has cut off less of
her hair in her dead sister's honour than she might have. But
nothing she says does her discredit. While grieving for
Clytaemestra, she shows every sympathy for Electra and
Orestes. When Electra is tart (99), she answers mildly. It may
seem thoughtless of her to suggest that Electra of all people

should take her offerings to Clytaemestra's grave. But if the poet had meant this point to be taken, he would have made Electra expostulate about it. He can give Helen some trifling feminine weaknesses, but he cannot commit himself to a damning picture of one who is in the end to be deified.

Not a few critics have found in the play significant reflections of the political and moral climate of Athens in the period following the short-lived oligarchical government of 411. With the Assembly restored to power, demagogues and hotheads like Cleophon once again came to the fore. There was a wave of recriminations against all those compromised by the revolution. Hundreds were prosecuted and fined, deprived of civic rights, or put to death. As the witch-hunt continued, the unscrupulous took the opportunity to enrich themselves by blackmail or to settle private scores by malicious denunciation (Lysias 20.7, 25.25 f.). Democracy was not seen at its best in those years.

Now it is certainly no coincidence that *Orestes*, in which Euripides transforms the traditional story by showing the young aristocrats beleaguered and hounded to death by an enraged demos, was written at such a time. His remarks on the unmanageability of public fury (696-703) and his account of the assembly proceedings (884-949) must be based on Athenian experience, and the two speakers described in 902 ff. and 917 ff. represent types, if not actual individuals, that the audience would have recognized. There are other details that may plausibly be related to recent events; see nn. on 903/904, 923, 943. On the other hand, we should be sceptical of the notion that the conduct of Orestes, Pylades and Electra in the latter part of the play is meant to reflect the contemporary corruption of morality and easy acceptance of violence. People like to cite Thucydides' famous chapter (3.82) on the perversion of values in times of revolution:

> Foolish daring was regarded as bravery and loyalty to comrades, and prudent hesitation as cowardice in disguise ... whoever forestalled another in doing something bad was praised, as was whoever proposed it to someone who had not thought of it. Even kinship became less close than comradeship because of the latter's greater readiness for daring without justification ... they confirmed their trust in each other not so much by sacred oaths as by companionship in crime ... it was held more

36

important to take revenge on someone than to avoid being hurt in the first place,
and so on. There is much in this that may be applied to Orestes and his friends by a critic who, aloof as Thucydides, reads the play in his study. But Euripides was not writing for such persons. He was writing for a theatre audience whose emotions he had enlisted on Orestes' side. What does the academic critic think that Orestes and Electra ought to have done? Taken their medicine like sportsmen, or like Socrates, hymning the supremacy of law, leaving Menelaus and Helen in possession of Agamemnon's house and throne? Apollo could still have stepped in at the end and put things right, of course. But what a lame play that would have made, in comparison with the one we have got.

V. Production

In reading a Greek tragedy it is important to keep in mind the layout of the ancient theatre. The main action of *Orestes* took place on a stage 100 feet wide. In front of it, on a slightly lower level, was the *orchestra*, a large circular area in which the chorus danced and remained between dances. At the back of the stage was a painted wooden structure representing the front of the palatial house that had been Agamemnon's. In its centre was a big double door. Behind the façade the house was imagined as having many rooms, outhouses, stables, etc. The actors could reach the stage either through the central door, if they were coming out of the house, or by one of the *eisodoi* if coming from elsewhere. The *eisodoi* ("ways in") were broad ramps leading up to the orchestra at each side of the stage from the lower ground beyond. An actor who exited via one of the *eisodoi* could reappear (in a different role, of course) from the house, and vice versa. Those approaching by the *eisodoi* could be seen while still a little way off.[7]
Four offstage locations are mentioned: the harbour at Nauplia; the town of Argos; the tomb of Clytaemestra; and the tomb of Agamemnon. Menelaus, arriving from Nauplia, has evidently not passed through the town. Tyndareos, coming from Clytaemestra's tomb, is making his way in the direction of Nauplia in the hope of meeting Menelaus (471 ff.); his entry is therefore from the opposite side, the same side as the town of

Argos. Pylades, arriving from Phocis, has come through the town. When Orestes sets out for the town, he intends to visit his father's tomb on the way, but to bypass his mother's (796-8). So one of the *eisodoi* represents the road to Nauplia and is used by Menelaus for his first entrance, while the other represents the road to the tombs and Argos and is used for all later entries and exits apart from those in and out of the house. An Athenian producer might naturally think of the harbour as being to the right, in the direction of Athens' own harbour, the Piraeus.[8]

In the final scene there are people on the roof of the house, behind a parapet (1569).[9] Apollo and Helen appear at a still higher level, in the sky. Either they stand on a platform of which the support is concealed by a screen painted to resemble the sky (the *theologeion* described by Pollux 4.130) or, more likely, they are suspended from the *mechane*, a kind of crane, which was certainly in use by this time for aerial appearances.[10] It is not necessary to suppose that Apollo delivers his long speech from a chest-harness. He and Helen may have occupied a winged chariot.[11]

The speaking parts had to be divided among three actors. By observing which characters appear on stage together, we arrive at the following as the most probable allocation:
1. Orestes.
2. Electra, Menelaus, the Phrygian.
3. Helen, Tyndareos, Pylades, the Old Man, Hermione, Apollo.

Only one actor is required to sing, as Electra and as the Phrygian. The nature of these two roles would seem to call for a voice with a high register, and this is confirmed both by what the scholiast records about the music of 176 ff. (see n. on 140-207) and by the Phrygian's reference to a "chariot melody" (1384 n.). It has the interesting implication that Menelaus too may have been represented as having a rather high, not particularly manly voice.

For what is known in general about tragic masks and costumes, *DFA*[2] 180-209 may be consulted. The text of *Orestes* gives a number of particular clues. Orestes has a wild and wasted aspect, with unkempt, straggly hair (223-6, 385-91). Later he and Pylades are described as wearing voluminous purple-bordered robes (1457 f., cf. 1125), and his feet are in *arbylai*, some kind of boot (1470). (They are inside the house by then, but the descriptions must be in accord with what they have worn on stage. On the other hand, Helen's golden sandals [1468] could be indoor wear, not corresponding to what she wore in 71-125.) Menelaus has blond shoulder-locks (1532); the same mask may have been adapted for Dionysus in *Bacchae* three years later (cf. *Ba.* 235 f., 493). Tyndareos probably has grey or white hair (cf. 550). It is cut short in mourning (458), and his dress is dark-coloured for the same reason (457). The Phrygian slave wears shoes of an oriental type (1370 n.), and no doubt the rest of his costume is barbarian. The chorus-women wear *arbylai* (140), and they have hair that hangs down over their cheeks (1267 n.; cf. 1427-9 of Helen).

The music that accompanied the sung parts of the play, the final anapaests, and perhaps certain other passages (348 n., 729-806 n.) was provided by a single instrumentalist who led the chorus in and out of the orchestra. He played a pair of *auloi*, pipes with a vibrating-reed mouthpiece, for which the best English equivalent is "shawm" (the ancestor of the oboe). The common translation "flute" is badly misleading, as flutes have no reed. The *aulos* produced a buzzing, blaring or droning tone which Aristophanes represents as *mümü, mümü* (*Knights* 10). The player played in unison with the singers, with decorative extra notes here and there. We know a good deal about the rhythms of the music, because they are reflected in the metres of the verse, but almost nothing about its melody. However, *Orestes* is one play for which, in consequence of its popularity, we do have some scraps of information.[12] See the nn. on 140-207 and 316-47.

VI.   From Euripides' Text To Ours

What Euripides wrote down consisted essentially of the words to be spoken or sung. He probably did not add musical notation but taught the melodies orally to his chorus, his singing actor and his aulete, and they were written down later, sporadically, by professional performers. He probably marked changes of speaker, if at all, only by punctuation: the practice of identifying the speakers throughout seems to be no older than the fifth century A.D. (N.G. Wilson, *CQ* 20 [1970] 305). This means that the editor of a tragedy (or comedy) is free to allocate lines to speakers or singers as best fits the sense, whatever the manuscripts may indicate. Again,

39

Euripides probably wrote no stage directions – at any rate, there are none in the manuscripts. The directions inserted in my translation are deduced from indications in the spoken text.

In composing his play, Euripides naturally sometimes had second thoughts, and altered or expanded a passage he had already written. I believe this is occasionally detectable from mild discontinuities or interruptions of logical sequence, and in the notes I postulate "afterthoughts" by the poet to account for them.

More often we have to reckon with insertions by later actors or producers. Classical tragedies, or those that were popular enough to go on being performed, suffered from this especially in the fourth century B.C.[13] Sometime in the 330s or early 320s, Lycurgus got a law passed that an official text of Aeschylus, Sophocles and Euripides should be kept, and actors not allowed to depart from it (Plutarch, *Lives of Orators* 841F). This no doubt had at least some effect in curbing interpolation at Athens, though by this time touring actors were performing frequently in other places (see *DFA*[2] 279 ff.). An Alexandrian commentator whose note survives in the scholium on *Or.* 57 criticizes the actors of his time for showing Helen arriving at the house early in the morning, with the spoils of Troy; in other words a gratuitous procession was prefixed to the play for the sake of spectacle (cf. Taplin [1977] 77). This may have been a dumb show. But the Alexandrian text certainly contained many spurious lines, some of which, critics noted, were not present in all copies (see nn. on 957-9, 1227-30, 1394). By my reckoning the text as we have it contains at least 25 interpolations (not counting mere intrusive glosses), the great majority being probably of pre-Alexandrian date. All but six consist of a single line, or less than a whole line, and only two (906-13 and 1227-30) exceed three lines. Nearly all can be assigned to one of the following categories:

1. alterations to suit a new manner of production (349-51, 957-9; 1366 if not genuine);
2. addition of references to characters or themes of the play in places where they seemed to have been passed over (33, 51, 537, 663, 1564-6);
3. expansion for its own sake (367?, 593, 602-4 [probably borrowed from some other play], 906-13, 933, 1224 with 1227-30, 1394, 1430);

4. a line added to supplement a tersely expressed phrase (361, 677, 856, 916, 1024, 1647);
5. words added to existing words to make up an iambic trimeter (141, 478).

Aristophanes of Byzantium (c.270-190) was the first major Alexandrian scholar to concern himself with tragedy. He was interested in the authenticity of the text, and he probably had access to Lycurgus' official Athenian copy, which Ptolemy III filched for the Alexandrian library. He produced an edition in which the lyric portions were for the first time divided into lines on metrical criteria, and also brief Hypotheses containing factual details about the plays. (See the second Hypothesis to *Orestes* and the notes to it.) He appears not to have published a commentary, but much of his learning was embodied in a commentary by his pupil Callistratus.[14] This was excerpted by the industrious compiler Didymus (first century B.C.), whose work, together with that of one Dionysius (unkown, probably late), apparently supplied the meat of the extant scholia. Some of the material in these scholia is merely Byzantine paraphrase of the text, but some goes right back, via Didymus and Callistratus, to Aristophanes. This may well include the valuable remarks in a few places about what "present-day" actors do when they perform the play (schol. 57, see above; nn. on 268 and 644), since a scholium on *Hipp*. 171 cites Aristophanes as using an argument from stage practice, and the reference to Stesichorus in the comment on *Or*. 268 can be connected with Aristophanes' citation of that poet at line 1287.

Papyri and quotations provide some further evidence of the state of the text in antiquity. Fragments of fourteen ancient manuscripts (thirteen papyrus, one parchment) are so far known, ranging in date from about 200 B.C. to the sixth or seventh century A.D. Only occasionally (at 141, 206, 1340, 1394, 1441) do they have good readings that are not to be found in at least some of the medieval manuscripts, and it looks as if the better medieval copies are giving us a text not greatly inferior to that of the average copy of the later Hellenistic or Roman period. The picture from ancient writers' quotations of the play is much the same. Despite the large number of quotations - lists may be found in the editions of Di Benedetto and Biehl - they preserve better readings than the manuscripts in only two places (141 again, 351).

By the Roman period the number of Euripidean plays that were widely read had been reduced to a fraction of the original total. A set of ten, perhaps the ten most popular, survived at Constantinople into the Middle Ages together with ancient commentaries. They survived probably in a small handful of fifth- or sixth-century copies which, after lying unread for many generations, were rediscovered in the ninth or early tenth century and made the basis for a new edition in minuscule script with marginal variants and scholia. The transliteration from uncial to minuscule involved the writing of accents and other lectional signs regularly instead of merely sporadically, as had been the ancient custom, and it therefore demanded a considerable scholarly effort of interpretation. It is possible that this effort was made independently by more than one person, but the prevalent opinion is that it was made only once, and that the product, laden with variant readings good and bad culled from the old manuscripts, became the sole archetype of the later medieval tradition.[15]

The ten plays in question – often referred to as the "select" plays, or "the selection" – are *Hecuba, Orestes, Phoenissae, Hippolytus, Medea, Andromache, Alcestis, Rhesus, Troades*, and *Bacchae*. *Bacchae* has lost its scholia, but we have scholia for the other nine. In addition to the select plays there survived by a lucky chance a codex containing nine further plays, without scholia. These are known as the "alphabetic" plays, because their titles all come from the same part of the alphabet (E-H-I-K), and they evidently represent a portion (or two not quite contiguous portions) of Aristophanes' complete edition of Euripides' works, arranged alphabetically by initial. This must have been a great rarity even in late antiquity. The alphabetic plays – *Helen, Electra, Heraclidae, Heracles, Suppliants*, the two *Iphigeneias, Ion, Cyclops* – remained almost unread until about 1300, and they are preserved only in one manuscript of that date and another copied from it.

By contrast, most of the select plays exist in a good number of manuscripts, and the first three, *Hecuba, Orestes* and *Phoenissae*, in over two hundred. The reason is that these three plays, the so-called Byzantine triad, were prescribed on the regular school syllabus.[16] Of this mass of manuscripts a large part has still not been collated, five hundred years after the invention of printing; if scholars had devoted as much effort to this basic research as they have put into writing "interpretations" of tragedy, we should be further forward. However, the older manuscripts at least have been investigated, and the likelihood that important variant readings remain to be discovered is low (though not zero).

The manuscripts regularly cited in the critical apparatus are:

H (Hierosolymitanus *taphou* 36), the Jerusalem palimpsest, 10th or 11th century. Only 507 lines of the play (from various parts) are preserved, and these partly obscured by a commentary on the Old Testament prophets which was written across them some three hundred years later.

M (Marcianus graecus 471). 11th century.

B (Parisinus graecus 2713). 11th century.

O (Laurentianus 31.10). Latter part of the 12th century.

V (Vaticanus graecus 909). *c*.1250–80. The pages containing lines 1205–1504 are lost, and for this section V's place is taken by a manuscript copied from it, namely Va (Palatinus graecus 98, 14th century).

A (Parisinus graecus 2712). Late 13th century.

The following are sporadically mentioned:

gnomol. Vatoped. A gnomology found in a manuscript on Mt. Athos (Vatopedianus 36). 12th century.

gnomol. Scorial. Another in a manuscript in the Escorial (Scorial. gr. X.1.13). Early 14th century.

F (Marcianus graecus 468). Late 13th century.

K (Laurentianus conventi soppressi 66). Late 13th century.

Pr (Rheims, Bibl. de la ville 1306). Late 13th century.

Sa (Vaticanus graecus 1345). Late 13th century.

G (Ambrosianus L 39 sup.). Early 14th century.

L (Laurentianus 32.2). Early 14th century. This is the manuscript that also preserves the alphabetic plays.

ξ Collective symbol for a group of three manuscripts of the earlier 14th century (Bodleianus Auct. F.3.25; Bodleianus Barocci 120; Laurentianus conventi soppressi 71).

Other 14th- or 15th-century manuscripts are cited unspecifically as "rec." or "recc." (recentior(es)).

The manuscripts do not, for the most part, group themselves in recognizable families. The readings they offer have to be judged on their merits, and not according to the number or age of the manuscripts in which they occur; sometimes the superior variant appears only in one of the later ones. The main thing to bear in mind is that after about 1280 there were scholars who studied Euripides and other poets in a critical spirit, and who were much more liable than earlier

43

copyists to correct errors (or what they too: to be errors) on their own initiative: in particular Maximus Planudes, Manuel Moschopulus, Thomas Magister, and Demetrius Triclinius.[17] In the case of L we know that it was produced in the school of Planudes, and much corrected by Triclinius. Other corrections in Triclinius' hand are found in a manuscript in Rome, Angelicus graecus 14. The ξ manuscripts carry the scholia of Moschopulus and therefore perhaps some corrections by him. Another group of manuscripts carries Thomas' scholia. In general, with the manuscripts of this period and later, we have to consider carefully whether their more plausible readings represent genuine tradition or only scholarly emendation. Decision is sometimes difficult, depending as it does on one's assessment of what the Byzantine scholars were likely to find fault with and what sorts of correction were likely to occur to them. Triclinius (c.1280 to after 1332) was certainly the most important among them. He made a particular contribution by realizing that the lyric strophes and antistrophes were supposed to agree with each other metrically: he made efforts to analyse the metres, and to correct the text where the responsion broke down. It is not certain whether he was the first to do anything of the sort, but whatever had been achieved in this field before him was negligible.

From the Renaissance to the present day scholars have continued striving, according to their lights, to purify the text. Progress has been greater since the late 18th century, when the dramatists' linguistic and metrical habits began to be studied in a more systematic way. Advances are still being made. But as often as old problems are solved, new ones are identified; and solutions are seldom accepted by everybody. There can never be a definitive text of a Greek play, only improved ones. By no means every edition is an improvement on its predecessors. But the overall trend, these last five centuries, has been upward – that is, closer to Euripides.

Notes to Introduction to *Orestes*

1. The date is given by the scholiast on line 371, in the form "when Diocles was archon". Callimachus had published a great chronological table of dramatic productions, drawing on an earlier work of Aristotle; Aristotle's information came from the official Athenian archives. So where we have such dates, they seem to be reliable.
2. For the details see West (1982) 82, 85.
3. The identity of the others is unknown. The satyr-play produced on this occasion may have been the *Cyclops*, cf. R. Seaford, *JHS* 102 (1982) 163 ff.
4. Most conveniently found in *TrGF* i. 26 and 41.
5. V.M. Strocka, *Gymnasium* 80 (1973) 366 ff. and pl. 18.
6. The more striking are mentioned in the notes (on 34-5, 640, 656, 903, 1598, 1670/1679-80). Cf. also T.M. Falkner, *CJ* 78 (1982/3), 290-3.
7. The theatre underwent alterations and improvements from time to time. The above sketch refers to its probable state in the late fifth century. For detailed information see the works listed in section VIII of the General Bibliography.
8. The statement of Pollux 4.126 that "the right-hand *parodos* [later equivalent of *eisodos*] leads from the country or the harbour or the town, while those arriving on foot from elsewhere enter by the other" probably reflects only a convention of the Hellenistic theatre, and as it puts harbour and town on the same side, it is not much use to us.
9. For another use of the roof see 1366-8 n.
10. Cf. Barrett on *Hipp.* 1283; Hourmouziades 30, 146-69; Stevens on *Andr.* 1229; Taplin (1977) 443-7.
11. Cf. *PV* 135, 279, *Med.* 1321, *HF* 880 f. In several plays characters rode on a flying animal (*PV*, Euripides' *Stheneboea* and *Bellerophon*, Aristophanes' *Peace*).
12. The only other one is *Iphigeneia in Aulis*, for which a few musical notes are preserved on papyrus; see T.J. Mathiesen, *Acta Musicologica* 53 (1981), 15-32. For an introduction to ancient Greek music see R.P. Winnington-Ingram in *OCD*^{2} 705-13 or in *The New Grove Dictionary of Music and Musicians* (1980) vii. 659-72.
13. Cf. D.L. Page, *Actors' Interpolations in Greek Tragedy* (Oxford, 1934), especially pp. 1-19 and (on our play) 41-55.

14. See Page, op. cit. 5 f.; Barrett, *Hippolytos*, 47 f., 56 f.; Zuntz (1965) 251 f.; R. Pfeiffer, *History of Classical Scholarship* i (1968) 190.

15. See on this, and on the matter of this whole paragraph, Barrett, op. cit. 50–61; Zuntz, op. cit. 254–75.

16. Among the plays of Aeschylus this status was enjoyed by the triad *Prometheus, Seven against Thebes*, and *Persians*; among those of Sophocles, by the triad *Ajax, Electra*, and *Oedipus Tyrannus*.

17. See N.G. Wilson, *Scholars of Byzantium* (1983) 229–56.

GENERAL BIBLIOGRAPHY

(This Bibliography has been compiled by the General Editor, and concentrates on works in English; a supplementary Bibliography for *Orestes* follows, compiled by the editor of this volume).

I : complete critical editions
The standard edition is by J. Diggle in the Oxford Classical Texts: Tomus I (1984) *Cyclops, Alcestis, Medea, Heraclidae, Hippolytus, Andromacha, Hecuba;* Tomus II (1981) *Supplices, Electra, Hercules, Troades, Iphigenia in Tauris, Ion;* until Tomus III is published, its predecessor, by G. Murray (1913[2]), will remain standard for *Helena, Phoenissae, Orestes, Bacchae, Iphigenia Aulidensis, Rhesus.*

The edition of R. Prinz and N. Wecklein (Leipzig, 1878–1902) is still useful for its *apparatus* and *appendices.* The 'Collection Budé' edition, by L. Méridier and others (Paris, 1923 onwards), still lacks *Rhesus;* it has French translation, introductory essays and some notes. The 'Bibliotheca Teubneriana' issues plays singly, each with bibliography and some with brief critical notes, by different editors (Leipzig, 1964 onwards).

Fragments: when it is published, Volume V of *Tragicorum Graecorum Fragmenta, Euripides,* ed. R. Kannicht, will at last unite in one book the many long-known and frequently re-edited fragments with modern finds. For the present, see *Hypsipyle,* ed. G.W. Bond (Oxford, 1963); *Phaethon,* ed. J. Diggle (Cambridge, 1970); A. Nauck, *Tragicorum Graecorum Fragmenta* (Leipzig, 1889[2], reprinted Hildesheim, 1964 with *Supplementum* by B. Snell); D.L. Page, *Greek Literary Papyri* ('Loeb', London, 1942); C. Austin, *Nova Fragmenta Euripidea in Papyris Reperta* (Berlin, 1967).

History of the text: W.S. Barrett, *Euripides: Hippolytos* (Oxford, 1964) 45–90; G. Zuntz, *An Inquiry into the Transmission of the Plays of Euripides* (Cambridge, 1965) esp. 249–88; J. Diggle, *Praefatio* to his *OCT* Tomus I, v–xiv.

II : complete commentaries
F.A. Paley (London, 1857[1]–1889[2]) (commonsensical and still useful).

E. Schwartz, *Scholia in Euripidem* (Berlin, 1887–91) (nine plays only; a more widely based edition of the ancient and medieval scholia is needed).

47

'Reference' commentaries on single plays are: W.S. Barrett, *Hippolytos* (Oxford, 1964); G.W. Bond, *Heracles* (Oxford, 1981); C. Collard, *Supplices* (Groningen, 1975); J.D. Denniston, *Electra* (Oxford, 1939); J. Diggle, *Studies on the Text of Euripides* (Oxford, 1981); E.R. Dodds, *Bacchae* (Oxford, 1960); R. Kannicht, *Helena* (Heidelberg, 1969); R. Seaford, *Cyclops* (Oxford, 1984); U. von Wilamowitz-Moellendorff, *Herakles* (Berlin, 1895[2]; reprinted Bad Homburg 1959); C.W. Willink, *Orestes* (Oxford, 1986).

Commentaries on the other tragedians important for reference are: E. Fraenkel, *Aeschylus: Agamemnon* (Oxford, 1950); R.C. Jebb, *Sophocles* (7 vols., Cambridge, 1883[1]-1903[3]); A.C. Pearson, *The Fragments of Sophocles* (3 vols., Cambridge, 1917).

III : complete English translations
D. Grene, R. Lattimore (eds.), *The Complete Greek Tragedies: Euripides* (2 vols., Chicago, 1958-9)
P. Vellacott, *Euripides* (4 vols., Harmondsworth, 1953-72) ('Penguin Classics')

IV : lexicography
J.T. Allen, G. Italie, *A Concordance to Euripides*, Berkeley/London 1954, reprinted Groningen 1970; *Supplement* by C. Collard, Groningen 1971.

V : bibliographical aids
L'Année Philologique has recorded publications since 1924.
Anzeiger für die Altertumswissenschaft has published occasional evaluative surveys since 1948.
From Section VI below, see Burian, *Cambridge History of Greek Literature, I*, Collard (evaluative), Lesky (1983; bibliography only till 1971) and Webster (esp. lost plays).

VI : general studies and handbooks (Greek Tragedy; Euripides)
A. Brown, *A New Companion to Greek Tragedy* (London, 1983) (a 'dictionary').
P. Burian (ed.), *New Directions in Euripidean Criticism* (Durham, U.S.A., 1985).
A.P. Burnett, *Catastrophe Survived: Euripides' plays of mixed reversal* (Oxford, 1971).
Cambridge History of Classical Literature, Volume I: Greek Literature ed. P.E. Easterling, B.M.W. Knox, (Cambridge, 1985), 258-345, 758-73 (chapters by leading scholars).

C. Collard, *Euripides*, 'Greece and Rome' New Surveys in the
   Classics No. 14 (Oxford, 1981) (brief survey with biblio-
   graphical emphasis).
D.J. Conacher, *Euripidean Drama: Myth, Theme and Structure*
   (Toronto, 1967) (best general introduction of its kind).
A.M. Dale, *Collected Papers* (Cambridge, 1969) (on many
   aspects of drama).
K.J. Dover (ed.), *Ancient Greek Literature* (Oxford, 1980),
   53-73 (Ch. 4, 'Tragedy', by K.J. Dover).
G.F. Else, *Aristotle's Poetics: the Argument* (Harvard, 1957).
Entretiens sur l'Antiquité Classique, VI: Euripide (Vandoeuvres-
   Genève, 1960) (seven papers, and transcribed discussion, by
   leading scholars).
L.H.G. Greenwood, *Aspects of Euripidean Drama* (Cambridge,
   1953).
G.M. Grube, *The Drama of Euripides* (London, 1961^2) (handbook).
J. Jones, *On Aristotle and Greek Tragedy* (London, 1962).
H.D.F. Kitto, *Greek Tragedy: a Literary Study* (London,
   1961^3).
B.M.W. Knox, *Word and Action* (Baltimore, 1979) (collected papers
   on drama).
W. Kranz, *Stasimon* (Berlin, 1933) (fundamental work on the
   Chorus).
R. Lattimore, *The Poetry of Greek Tragedy* (Oxford, 1958).
- *Story Patterns in Greek Tragedy* (London, 1964).
A. Lesky, *Greek Tragedy*, trans. H. Frankfort (London,
   1967) (basic text-book).
- *Greek Tragic Poetry*, trans. M. Dillon (New Haven, 1983)
   (scholar's handbook).
D.W. Lucas, *Aristotle:Poetics* (Oxford, 1968) (commentary).
G. Murray, *Euripides and his Age* (London, 1946^2) (an
   'evergreen').
A.W. Pickard-Cambridge, *Dithyramb, Tragedy and Comedy*,
   2. ed. by T.B.L. Webster (Oxford, 1962).
A. Rivier, *Essai sur le tragique d'Euripide* (Paris, 1975^2).
L. Séchan, *Etudes sur la tragédie grecque dans ses rapports
   avec la céramique* (Paris, 1926).
E. Segal (ed.), *Oxford Readings in Greek Tragedy* (Oxford,
   1984) (important essays by leading scholars reprinted).
W.B. Stanford, *Greek Tragedy and the Emotions* (London, 1983).
O. Taplin, *The Stagecraft of Aeschylus* (Oxford, 1977)
   (important for all Tragedy).
- *Greek Tragedy in Action* (London, 1978) (vigorous introduction).

A.D. Trendall, T.B.L. Webster, *Illustrations of Greek Drama* (London, 1971) (vase-paintings and the plays).
P. Vellacott, *Ironic Drama: a Study of Euripides' Method and Meaning* (Cambridge, 1976) (the plays as veiled social criticism).
J.P. Vernant, P. Vidal-Naquet, *Tragedy and Myth in Ancient Greece*, English trans. (Brighton, 1981).
B. Vickers, *Towards Greek Tragedy: Drama, Myth, Society* (London, 1973).
P. Walcot, *Greek Drama in its Theatrical and Social Context* (Cardiff, 1976).
T.B.L. Webster, *The Tragedies of Euripides* (London, 1967) (a profile of the dramatic and poetic career as it developed).
Yale Classical Studies 25 (1977): *Greek Tragedy* (papers invited from prominent scholars).

VII : Euripides and contemporary events and ideas
R.G. Buxton, *Persuasion in Greek Tragedy: a Study of 'Peitho'* (Cambridge, 1982).
K. Reinhardt, *Tradition und Geist* (Göttingen, 1960) 223-56 ('Die Sinneskrise bei Euripides': classic discussion of Euripide intellectualism and its reflection in his dramaturgy).
P.T. Stevens, 'Euripides and the Athenians', *JHS* 76 (1976), 76-84 (contemporary reception).
R.P. Winnington-Ingram, 'Euripides: Poiētēs Sophos', *Arethusa* 2 (1969), 127-42 (need for balanced interpretation of Euripides cleverness).
G. Zuntz, *The Political Plays of Euripides* (Manchester, 1963[2]).
Cf. esp. Lesky (1983), Murray, Vellacott, Vernant, Vickers and Walcot from Section VI above.

VIII : theatre and production
P.D. Arnott, *Introduction to the Greek Theatre* (London, 1959).
- *Greek Scenic Conventions in the Fifth Century B.C.* (Oxford, 1962).
H.C. Baldry, *The Greek Tragic Theatre* (London, 1971).
M. Bieber, *The History of the Greek and Roman Theatre* (Princeton, 1961[2]) (copious illustrations).
R.C. Flickinger, *The Greek Theater and its Drama* (Chicago. 1936[4]).
A.W. Pickard-Cambridge, *The Theatre of Dionysus in Athens* (Oxford, 1946).
- *The Dramatic Festivals of Athens*, 2. ed. by J. Gould, D.M. Lewis (Oxford, 1968).

E. Simon, *The Ancient Theatre*, trans. C.E. Vafopoulo-Richardson (London, 1982).
T.B.L. Webster, *Greek Theatre Production* (London, 1970²)
Cf. esp. Dale, Taplin (1978), Trendall and Walcot in Section VI above; Bain, Halleran, Hourmouziades, Jens and Mastronarde in Section IX below.

IX : dramatic form and theatrical technique
D. Bain, *Actors and Audience: a study of asides and related conventions in Greek drama* (Oxford, 1977).
M.R. Halleran, *Stagecraft in Euripides* (London, 1985).
N.C. Hourmouziades, *Production and Imagination in Euripides* (Athens, 1965).
W. Jens (ed.), *Die Bauformen der griechischen Tragödie* (München, 1971).
D.J. Mastronarde, *Contact and Discontinuity: Some Conventions of Speech and Action on the Greek Tragic Stage* (Berkeley, 1979).
W. Schadewaldt, *Monolog und Selbstgespräch* (Berlin, 1926).
W. Steidle, *Studien zum antiken Drama unter besonderer Berücksichtigung des Bühnenspiels* (München, 1968).
H. Strohm, *Euripides: Interpretationen zur dramatischen Form* (München, 1957).
Cf. esp. Burnett, Kranz, Lesky (1983) and Taplin (1977) from Section VI above.

X : language and style
S.A. Barlow, *The Imagery of Euripides* (London, 1971) (widest appreciative study).
W. Breitenbach, *Untersuchungen zur Sprache der euripideischen Lyrik* (Stuttgart, 1934) (*Index Locorum* by K.H. Lee, Amsterdam, 1979).
P.T. Stevens, *Colloquial Expressions in Euripides* (Wiesbaden, 1977).
Cf. Section IV above; Lattimore (1958), Lesky (1983) and Stanford from Section VI above; Buxton from Section VII above.

XI : verse and metre
A.M. Dale, *The Lyric Metres of Greek Drama* (Cambridge, 1968²).
- *Metrical Analyses of Tragic Choruses*, BICS Supplement 21.1 (1971); 21.2 (1981); 21.3 (1983) (index of Choruses in 21.3)
D.S. Raven, *Greek Metre* (London, 1962) (analyses many complete odes).

51

M.L. West, *Greek Metre* (Oxford, 1982) (standard handbook).
- *Introduction to Greek Metre* (Oxford, 1987) (abridged and slightly simplified version of *Greek Metre*).
U. von Wilamowitz-Moellendorff, *Griechische Verskunst* (Berlin, 1921) (analyses and interprets many complete odes).

BIBLIOGRAPHY TO *ORESTES*

Texts and Commentaries
(See also General Bibliography I and II)
N. Wedd, *The Orestes of Euripides edited with Introduction, Notes and Metrical Appendix* (Cambridge, 1895)
V. Di Benedetto, *Euripidis Orestes. Introduzione, testo critico, commento e appendice metrica* (Florence, 1965)
W. Biehl, *Euripides' Orestes erklärt* (Berlin 1965: commentary only)
– , *Euripides, Orestes* (Leipzig, 1975: Teubner text)
C.W. Willink, *Euripides, Orestes* (Oxford, 1986: large-scale scholarly edition and commentary)

Interpretation
(See also General Bibliography VI, in particular Burnett, Conacher, Grube, Lesky 1983, Vickers, Webster)
Burkert, W., "Die Absurdität der Gewalt und das Ende der Tragödie: Euripides' Orestes", *Antike und Abendland* 20 (1974), 97–109
Falkner, T.M., "Coming of Age in Argos. Physis and Paideia in Euripides' Orestes", *Classical Journal* 78 (1983), 289–300
Fuqua, C., "Studies in the use of myth in Sophocles' Philoctetes and Euripides' Orestes", *Traditio* 32 (1976), 29–95
– , "The world of myth in Euripides' Orestes", *Traditio* 34 (1978), 1–28
Greenberg, N.A., "Euripides' Orestes: an interpretation", *HSCP* 66 (1962), 157–92
Mullens, H.G., "The meaning of Euripides' Orestes", *CQ* 34 (1940), 153–8
Parry, H., "Euripides' Orestes, The quest for salvation", *TAPA* 100 (1969), 337–53
Rawson, E., "Aspects of Euripides' Orestes", *Arethusa* 5 (1972), 155–67
Schein, S.L., "Mythical illusion and historical reality in Euripides' Orestes", *Wiener Studien* 9 (1975), 49–66
Smith, W.D., "Disease in Euripides' Orestes", *Hermes* 95 (1967), 291–307
Will, F., "Tyndareus in the Orestes", *Symbolae Osloenses* 37 (1961), 96–9
Wolff, C., "Orestes", in E. Segal (ed.), *Oxford Readings in Greek Tragedy* (Oxford, 1983), 340–56

53

ABBREVIATIONS

AJP	*American Journal of Philology*
ARV²	J.D. Beazley, *Attic Red-Figure Vase Painters*, 2nd edition (Oxford 1963)
BICS	*Bulletin of the Institute of Classical Studies*
Burkert (1983)	W. Burkert, *Homo Necans*, English edition (California, 1983)
Burkert (1985)	W. Burkert, *Greek Religion* (Harvard, 1985)
CEG	P.A. Hansen, *Carmina Epigraphica Graeca saeculorum VIII-V a. Chr. n.* (Berlin & New York, 1983)
Collard (1975)	see General Bibliography II
Collard (1981)	see General Bibliography VI
CQ	*Classical Quarterly*
CR	*Classical Review*
Denniston	J.D. Denniston, *The Greek Particles*, 2nd edition (Oxford, 1954)
DFA²	A.W. Pickard-Cambridge, *The Dramatic Festivals of Athens*, see General Bibliography VIII
DK	H. Diels & W. Kranz, *Die Fragmente der Vorsokratiker*, 6th edition (Berlin, 1951-2)
Dodds	E.R. Dodds, *The Greeks and the Irrational* (Berkeley, 1951)
Dover	K.J. Dover, *Greek Popular Morality in the Time of Plato and Aristotle* (Oxford, 1974)
FGrH	F. Jacoby, *Die Fragmente der griechischen Historiker* (Berlin, Leiden, 1923-58)
Fraenkel	E. Fraenkel, see General Bibliography II
GRBS	*Greek, Roman & Byzantine Studies*
Halleran	see General Bibliography IX
Hourmouziades	see General Bibliography IX
HSCP	*Harvard Studies in Classical Philology*
JHS	*Journal of Hellenic Studies*
LSJ	H.G. Liddell & R. Scott, *A Greek-English Lexicon*, 9th edition (Oxford, 1925-40)
MacDowell	D.M. MacDowell, *Athenian Homicide Law in the Age of the Orators* (Manchester, 1963)
Moorhouse	A.C. Moorhouse, *The Syntax of Sophocles* (Leiden, 1982)
OCD²	*The Oxford Classical Dictionary*, 2nd edition (Oxford, 1970)

Parker	R.C.T. Parker, *Miasma. Pollution and Purification in Early Greek Religion* (Oxford, 1983)
PMG	D.L. Page, *Poetae Melici Graeci* (Oxford, 1962)
RÉA	*Revue des Études anciennes*
Shisler	F.L. Shisler, "The Use of Stage Business to Portray Emotion in Greek Tragedy", *AJP* 66 (1945) 377-97
SLG	D.L. Page, *Supplementum Lyricis Graecis* (Oxford, 1974)
Stevens	see General Bibliography X
TAPA	*Transactions of the American Philological Association*
Taplin (1977), (1978)	see General Bibliography VI
TrGF	B. Snell & Others, *Tragicorum Graecorum Fragmenta* (Gottingen, 1971-)
West (1966)	M.L. West, *Hesiod, Theogony* (Oxford, 1966)
West (1982)	see General Bibliography XI
West (1985)	M.L. West, *The Hesiodic Catalogue of Women* (Oxford, 1985)
ZPE	*Zeitschrift für Papyrologie und Epigraphik*

SIGLA

Papyrus fragments		Century
Π3	Oxyrhynchus 1616	5th
Π4	Columbia inv. 517A	1st B.C.
Π6	Vienna G 2315 (Rainer inv. 8029)	3rd-2nd B.C.
Π7	Oxyrhynchus 1370	5th
Π11	Geneva inv. 91	2nd-3rd
Π13	Oxyrhynchus 1178	2nd-1st B.C.
Π14	Herculaneum 1012 vi (quotation of *Or.*)	1st B.C.
Π15	Berlin 17051 + 17014	6th-7th
Π16	Cologne 131	2nd-1st B.C.
Π17	Florence PL III/908	2nd B.C.
Π18	Oxyrhynchus 3716	2nd-1st B.C.
Π19	Oxyrhynchus 3717	2nd
Π20	Oxyrhynchus 3718	5th

Medieval manuscripts
See above, p. 43

Other sigla

Σ_λ	scholium
Σ^λ	lemma (heading) of scholium
M^1, M^2	M as corrected by first/second hand
M^{ac}, M^c	M before/after correction
M^s	suprascript reading in M
$M^{\gamma\rho}$	reading recorded in M as alternative
[Π16]	reading of Π16 inferred from width of gap in papyrus
+	plus unlisted manuscripts

ORESTES

ΥΠΟΘΕΣΙΣ ΟΡΕΣΤΟΥ

Ὀρέστης τὸν φόνον τοῦ πατρὸς μεταπορευόμενος ἀνεῖλεν Αἴγισθον καὶ Κλυταιμήστραν· μητροκτονῆσαι δὲ τολμήσας παραχρῆμα τὴν δίκην ἔδωκεν ἐμμανὴς γενόμενος. Τυνδάρεω δὲ τοῦ πατρὸς τῆς ἀνῃρημένης κατηγορήσαντος κατ᾽ αὐτοῦ, ἔμελλον Ἀργεῖοι κοινὴν ψῆφον ἐκφέρεσθαι περὶ τοῦ τί δεῖ παθεῖν τὸν ἀσεβήσαντα· κατὰ τύχην δὲ Μενέλαος ἐκ τῆς πλάνης ὑποστρέψας νυκτὸς μὲν Ἑλένην εἰσαπέστειλε, καθ᾽ ἡμέραν δὲ αὐτὸς ἦλθεν. καὶ παρακαλούμενος ὑπ᾽ Ὀρέστου βοηθῆσαι αὐτῷ, ἀντιλέγοντα Τυνδάρεων μᾶλλον ηὐλαβήθη. λεχθέντων δὲ λόγων ἐν τοῖς ὄχλοις, ἐπηνέχθη τὸ πλῆθος ἀποκτείνειν Ὀρέστην. <παρῃτήσατο δὲ πρὸς μίαν ἡμέραν βιοῦν Ὀρέστης> ἐπαγγειλάμενος ἑαυτὸν ἐκ τοῦ βίου προΐεσθαι. συνὼν δὲ τούτοις ὁ Πυλάδης, φίλος αὐτοῦ, συνεβούλευσε πρῶτον Μενελάου τιμωρίαν λαβεῖν Ἑλένην ἀποκτείναντας. αὐτοὶ μὲν οὖν ἐπὶ τούτοις ἐλθόντες διεψεύσθησαν τῆς ἐλπίδος, θεῶν τὴν Ἑλένην ἁρπασάντων· Ἠλέκτρα δὲ Ἑρμιόνην ἐπιφανεῖσαν ἔδωκεν εἰς χεῖρας αὐτοῖς. οἳ δὲ ταύτην φονεύειν ἔμελλον· ἐπιφανεὶς δὲ Μενέλαος καὶ βλέπων ἑαυτὸν ἅμα γυναικὸς καὶ τέκνου στερούμενον ὑπ᾽ αὐτῶν, ἐπεβάλλετο τὰ βασίλεια πορθεῖν· οἳ δὲ φθάσαντες ὑφάψειν ἠπείλησαν. ἐπιφανεὶς δὲ Ἀπόλλων Ἑλένην μὲν αὐτὸς ἔφησεν εἰς θεοὺς διακομίζειν, Ὀρέστῃ δὲ ἐπέταξεν αὐτὸν μὲν Ἑρμιόνην λαβεῖν, Πυλάδῃ δὲ Ἠλέκτραν συνοικίσαι, καθαρθέντι δὲ τὸν φόνον Ἄργους δυναστεύειν.

ΑΡΙΣΤΟΦΑΝΟΥΣ ΓΡΑΜΜΑΤΙΚΟΥ ΥΠΟΘΕΣΙΣ

Ὀρέστης διὰ τὴν τῆς μητρὸς σφαγὴν ἅμα καὶ ὑπὸ τῶν Ἐρινύων δειματούμενος καὶ ὑπὸ τῶν Ἀργείων κατακριθεὶς θανάτῳ, μέλλων φονεύειν Ἑλένην καὶ Ἑρμιόνην ἀνθ᾽ ὧν Μενέλαος παρὼν οὐκ ἐβοήθησε, διεκωλύθη ὑπὸ Ἀπόλλωνος. παρ᾽ οὐδενὶ κεῖται ἡ μυθοποιία.

HYPOTHESIS OF *ORESTES*

Orestes, seeking retribution for his father's murder, killed Aegisthus and Clytaemestra; but having ventured this act of matricide, he straightway paid the penalty by going mad. Tyndareos, the father of the murdered woman, prosecuted him, and the Argives were preparing to have a public vote on what should be done to the sinner. As it happened, Menelaus then arrived home from his travels: he sent Helen in during the night, and came himself by day. Being implored by Orestes to help him, he preferred to play safe with regard to Tyndareos who argued against it; and when the debate took place before the mob, the majority was led to vote for putting Orestes to death. <Orestes, however, secured a day's grace> by promising to dispatch himself out of this life. His friend Pylades, who was present, proposed to him that they should first take vengeance on Menelaus by killing Helen. So they went off with this intention, but were cheated of their hopes when the gods snatched Helen away. But Electra delivered Hermione (who appeared just then) into their hands. They were preparing to murder her, when Menelaus appeared, and seeing himself about to lose both his wife and his child, he set himself to storm the palace; but they forestalled him by threatening to set it on fire. Then Apollo appeared and said that he was transporting Helen to the gods, and instructed Orestes to take Hermione for himself and give Electra to Pylades as wife, and, after undergoing purification for the killing, to rule over Argos.

ARISTOPHANES THE GRAMMARIAN'S HYPOTHESIS

Orestes, suffering from the terrors both because of his slaughter of his mother and by agency of the Erinyes, and condemned to death by the Argives, intended to murder Helen and Hermione (in retaliation for Menelaus' failing to help him, although he was at hand); but he was stopped by Apollo. The story does not occur in any author.

59

ἡ μὲν σκηνὴ τοῦ δράματος ὑπόκειται ἐν Ἄργει· ὁ
δὲ χορὸς συνέστηκεν ἐκ γυναικῶν Ἀργείων, ἡλικιω-
τίδων Ἠλέκτρας, αἳ καὶ παραγίνονται ὑπὲρ τῆς τοῦ
Ὀρέστου πυνθανόμεναι συμφορᾶς. προλογίζει δὲ
Ἠλέκτρα. τὸ δρᾶμα κωμικωτέραν ἔχει τὴν καταστρο-
φήν.
    ἡ δὲ διασκευὴ τοῦ δράματός ἐστι τοιαύτη· πρὸς τὰ
τοῦ Ἀγαμέμνονος βασίλεια ὑπόκειται Ὀρέστης κάμνων
ὑπὸ μανίας καὶ κείμενος ἐπὶ κλινιδίου, ᾧ προσκαθέ-
ζεται πρὸς τοῖς ποσὶν Ἠλέκτρα. διαπορεῖται δὲ τί
δήποτε οὐ πρὸς τῇ κεφαλῇ καθέζεται· οὕτως γὰρ <ἂν>
μᾶλλον ἐδόκει τὸν ἀδελφὸν τημελεῖν, πλησιαίτερον
προσκαθεζομένη. ἔοικεν οὖν διὰ τὸν χορὸν ὁ ποιητὴς
οὕτω διασκευάσαι· διηγέρθη γὰρ ἂν Ὀρέστης, ἄρτι
καὶ μόγις καταδραθείς, πλησιαίτερον αὐτῷ τῶν κατὰ
τὸν χορὸν γυναικῶν παρισταμένων. ἔστι δὲ ὑπονοῆσαι
τοῦτο ἐξ ὧν φησιν Ἠλέκτρα τῷ χορῷ· "σῖγα, σῖγα,
λεπτὸν ἴχνος ἀρβύλης". πιθανὸν οὖν ταύτην εἶναι
τὴν πρόφασιν τῆς τοιαύτης διαθέσεως.
    τὸ δρᾶμα τῶν ἐπὶ σκηνῆς εὐδοκιμούντων, χείριστον
δὲ τοῖς ἤθεσι· πλὴν γὰρ Πυλάδου πάντες φαῦλοι ἦσαν.

ΤΑ ΤΟΥ ΔΡΑΜΑΤΟΣ ΠΡΟΣΩΠΑ

Ἠλέκτρα	Πυλάδης
Ἑλένη	ἄγγελος
χορός	Ἑρμιόνη
Ὀρέστης	Φρύξ
Μενέλαος	Ἀπόλλων
Τυνδάρεως	

The scene of the play is set in Argos. The chorus consists of women of Argos, companions of Electra, and they come to enquire about Orestes' calamity. The opening speech is spoken by Electra. The play has a dénouement more of the comic type.

———

The arrangement of the play is as follows. At Agamemnon's palace Orestes is represented laid low by madness and lying on a couch, while Electra sits by him at his feet. It is a problem why she does not sit at his head: in that way she would give more of an impression of caring for her brother, by sitting closer. Well, it seems to be because of the chorus that the poet arranged it so. Orestes would have been woken up – and he had only recently and with difficulty fallen asleep – with the chorus women standing any closer to him. This can be inferred from what Electra says to the chorus, "Quietly, quietly, light set down your shoe-tread" (140). So it is plausible that this is the ground for arranging it like that.
The play is one of those that enjoy success on the stage, but its ethics are dreadful: apart from Pylades everyone is bad.

DRAMATIS PERSONAE

Electra	Pylades
Helen	Newsbringer*
Chorus	Hermione
Orestes	Phrygian
Menelaus	Apollo
Tyndareos	

*This is how the manuscripts name this character. In the translation I have substituted "Old Man".

ΗΛΕΚΤΡΑ

Οὐκ ἔστιν οὐδὲν δεινὸν ὧδ' εἰπεῖν ἔπος
οὐδὲ πάθος οὐδὲ ξυμφορὰ θεήλατος,
ἧς οὐκ ἂν ἄραιτ' ἄχθος ἀνθρώπου φύσις.
ὁ γὰρ μακάριος – κοὐκ ὀνειδίζω τύχας –
Διὸς πεφυκώς, ὡς λέγουσι, Τάνταλος   5
κορυφῆς ὑπερτέλλοντα δειμαίνων πέτρον
ἀέρι ποτᾶται· καὶ τίνει ταύτην δίκην,
ὡς μὲν λέγουσιν, ὅτι θεοῖς ἄνθρωπος ὢν
κοινῆς τραπέζης ἀξίωμ' ἔχων ἴσον
ἀκόλαστον ἔσχε γλῶσσαν, αἰσχίστην νόσον.   10
    οὗτος φυτεύει Πέλοπα, τοῦ δ' Ἀτρεὺς ἔφυ,
ᾧ στέμματα ξήνασ' ἐπέκλωσεν θεά
ἔριν, Θυέστῃ πόλεμον ὄντι συγγόνῳ
θέσθαι. τί τἄρρητ' ἀναμετρήσασθαί με δεῖ;
ἔδαισε δ' οὖν νιν τέκν' ἀποκτείνας Ἀτρεύς. 15
    Ἀτρέως δέ – τὰς γὰρ ἐν μέσῳ σιγῶ τύχας –
ὁ κλεινός, εἰ δὴ κλεινός, Ἀγαμέμνων ἔφυ
Μενέλεώς τε Κρήσσης μητρὸς Ἀερόπης ἄπο.
γαμεῖ δ' ὃ μὲν δὴ τὴν θεοῖς στυγουμένην
Μενέλαος Ἑλένην, ὃ δὲ Κλυταιμήστρας λέχος 20
ἐπίσημον εἰς Ἕλληνας Ἀγαμέμνων ἄναξ·
ᾧ παρθένοι μὲν τρεῖς ἔφυμεν ἐκ μιᾶς,
Χρυσόθεμις Ἰφιγένειά τ' Ἠλέκτρα τ' ἐγώ,
ἄρσην δ' Ὀρέστης, μητρὸς ἀνοσιωτάτης,
ἣ πόσιν ἀπείρῳ περιβαλοῦσ' ὑφάσματι   25
ἔκτεινεν· ὧν δ' ἕκατι, παρθένῳ λέγειν
οὐ καλόν· ἐῶ τοῦτ' ἀσαφὲς ἐν κοινῷ σκοπεῖν.
    Φοίβου δ' ἀδικίαν μὲν τί δεῖ κατηγορεῖν;
πείθει δ' Ὀρέστην μητέρ' ἥ σφ' ἐγείνατο
κτεῖναι, πρὸς οὐχ ἅπαντας εὔκλειαν φέρον· 30
ὅμως δ' ἀπέκτειν' οὐκ ἀπειθήσας θεῷ·
κἀγὼ μετέσχον, οἷα δὴ γυνή, φόνου.
[Πυλάδης θ', ὃς ἡμῖν συγκατείργασται τάδε.]

_____

2   συμφορὰν θεήλατον MB^{ac}O²ΥᵖV Dio Chrys., Stob. v.l.
13   Ἔρις ΣΥᵖVˢ
24   δ' Elmsley: τ' codd.
33   del. Herwerden

*[Orestes lies on a bed, under wraps and asleep. Electra
is sitting beside him.]*

ELECTRA. There is no thing so fearful to
relate or to suffer, nor any contingency god may
impose, of which humankind is not liable to have
to take up the burden. That fortunate man (and
I am not being sarcastic about his fate), Zeus'
offspring, as they say – Tantalus – hovers in mid   5
air in dread of a rock that looms above his
head; he pays this penalty – so they say – because,
a mortal enjoying equal status with gods at the
shared table, he caught that most horrid disease,
an unchecked tongue.   10
He fathered Pelops, and from him Atreus was
born, upon whom the goddess, raking out her wool-
coils, spun strife – to make fight with Thyestes
his own brother. Why need I recount those
obscenities? Anyway, Atreus feasted him on his   15
slaughtered children.
From Atreus – I say nothing of intervening
events – the glorious Agamemnon sprang, if
glorious he be, and Menelaus, from a Cretan
mother, Aërope. And he, Menelaus, married her
whom the gods abhor, Helen; while the lord   20
Agamemnon took Clytaemestra, a notable marriage
in Greek eyes. To him three of us girls were
born from the one mother – Chrysothemis,
Iphigeneia, and myself, Electra – and a male
child, Orestes: from a mother most unholy, who
wrapped her husband in an endless cloth and   25
killed him. For what reasons, it is not seemly
for an unwed woman to say; I leave this vague,
for public consideration.
Then Phoebus – how should Phoebus be accused
of wrong? But he urged Orestes to kill the
mother who bore him – not in everyone's eyes a   30
thing bringing good repute, but still he killed
her and did not reject the god's bidding. I too
took part in the murder, such part as a woman
might. [And so did Pylades, who has done this
deed with us.]

63

ἐντεῦθεν ἀγρίᾳ συντακεὶς νόσῳ νοσεῖ
τλήμων Ὀρέστης ὅδε πεσών <τ´> ἐν δεμνίοις   35
κεῖται· τὸ μητρὸς δ᾽ αἷμά νιν τροχηλατεῖ
μανίαισιν· ὀνομάζειν γὰρ αἰδοῦμαι θεὰς
Εὐμενίδας, αἳ τόνδ᾽ ἐξαμιλλῶνται φόβῳ.
ἕκτον δὲ δὴ τόδ᾽ ἦμαρ ἐξ ὅτου σφαγαῖς
θανοῦσα μήτηρ πυρὶ καθήγνισται δέμας,   40
ὧν οὔτε σῖτα διὰ δέρης ἐδέξατο,
οὐ λούτρ᾽ ἔδωκε χρωτί· χλανιδίων δ᾽ ἔσω
κρυφθείς, ὅταν μὲν σῶμα κουφισθῇ νόσου,
ἔμφρων δακρύει, ποτὲ δὲ δεμνίων ἄπο
πηδᾷ δρομαῖος, πῶλος ὡς ὑπὸ ζυγοῦ.   45
ἔδοξε δ᾽ Ἄργει τῷδε μήθ᾽ ἡμᾶς στέγαις,
μὴ πυρὶ δέχεσθαι, μηδὲ προσφωνεῖν τινα
μητροκτονοῦντας· κυρία δ᾽ ἥδ᾽ ἡμέρα,
ἐν ᾗ διοίσει ψῆφον Ἀργείων πόλις,
εἰ χρὴ θανεῖν νὼ λευσίμῳ πετρώματι.   50
[ἢ φάσγανον θήξαντ᾽ ἐπ᾽ αὐχένος βαλεῖν.]
ἐλπίδα δὲ δή τιν᾽ ἔχομεν ὥστε μὴ θανεῖν·
ἥκει γὰρ εἰς γῆν Μενέλεως Τροίας ἄπο,
λιμένα δὲ Ναυπλίειον ἐκπληρῶν πλάτῃ
ἀκταῖσιν ὁρμεῖ, δαρὸν ἐκ Τροίας χρόνον   55
ἅλαισι πλαγχθείς· τὴν δὲ δὴ πολύστονον
Ἑλένην, φυλάξας νύκτα, μή τις εἰσιδὼν
μεθ᾽ ἡμέραν στείχουσαν, ὧν ὑπ᾽ Ἰλίῳ
παῖδες τεθνᾶσιν, εἰς πέτρων ἔλθῃ βολάς,
προύπεμψεν εἰς δῶμ᾽ ἡμέτερον· ἔστιν δ᾽ ἔσω   60
κλαίουσ᾽ ἀδελφὴν συμφοράς τε δωμάτων.
ἔχει δὲ δή τιν᾽ ἀλγέων παραψυχήν·
ἣν γὰρ κατ᾽ οἴκους ἔλιφ᾽ ὅτ᾽ εἰς Τροίαν ἔπλει
παρθένον ἐμῇ τε μητρὶ παρέδωκεν τρέφειν
Μενέλαος ἀγαγὼν Ἑρμιόνην Σπάρτης ἄπο,   65
ταύτῃ γέγηθε κἀπιλήθεται κακῶν.
βλέπω δὲ πᾶσαν εἰς ὁδόν, πότ᾽ ὄψομαι
Μενέλαον ἥκονθ᾽· ὡς τά γ᾽ ἄλλ᾽ ἐπ᾽ ἀσθενοῦς

35 τ᾽ add. Reiske
38 del. Nauck
45 ὑπὸ Herwerden: ἀπὸ codd.
51 del. Herwerden
61 συμφοράς Π3 KGΞ: συμφοράν MBOVA

64

Hence it is that poor Orestes here is sick,
wasted with a savage sickness, and has taken   35
to his bed: his mother's blood bowls him along
in frenzy-fits - I am shy of naming the
goddesses, the Benign Ones, who are putting him
through ordeals of terror. This is now the
sixth day since our mother, after dying in
carnage, became cleansed in the fire; and during   40
these days he has swallowed no food, not given
his skin a wash. Hidden inside his wraps, when
his body gets relief from the illness he is sane
and he cries, but at other times he jumps from
the bed, running wild like a colt from under   45
the yoke.
    This city of Argos has decreed that no one
is to give us hospitality of roof or fire, or
speak to us, matricides that we are. And this
is the appointed day when the community of
Argives will divide its vote on whether the pair
of us must die by stoning [or sharpen a sword   50
and strike at our necks].
    But we do have some hope of avoiding death,
because Menelaus has arrived in the land from
Troy. Filling the harbour of Nauplia with his
oarage he is moored at the headlands, who for   55
long after Troy went wandering astray. As for
that source of so much grief, Helen, he took
care to wait for night-time, in case any of
those whose sons lie dead below Ilion, seeing
her walking abroad by day, should take to
throwing stones, and he sent her ahead to our   60
house. She is indoors, weeping for her sister
and the house's calamities.
    But she does have some comfort for her
sufferings: the daughter Menelaus left at home
when he was sailing for Troy and brought from
Sparta and gave to my mother to bring up -   65
Hermione - in her she rejoices, and puts her
troubles out of mind.
    I am watching every road for when I shall
see that Menelaus has arrived; we have but

65

ῥώμης ὀχούμεθ᾽, ἤν τι μὴ κείνου πάρα
σωθῶμεν. ἄπορον χρῆμα δυστυχῶν δόμος.   70

ΕΛΕΝΗ

ὦ παῖ Κλυταιμήστρας τε κἀγαμέμνονος,
παρθένε μακρὸν δὴ μῆκος Ἠλέκτρα χρόνου,
πῶς, ὦ τάλαινα, σύ τε κασίγνητός τε σός
τλήμων Ὀρέστης, μητρὸς ὃς φονεὺς ἔφυ;
προσφθέγμασιν γὰρ οὐ μιαίνομαι σέθεν,   75
εἰς Φοῖβον ἀναφέρουσα τὴν ἁμαρτίαν.
καίτοι στένω γε τὸν Κλυταιμήστρας μόρον,
ἐμῆς ἀδελφῆς, ἥν, ἐπεὶ πρὸς Ἴλιον
ἔπλευσ᾽ ὅπως ἔπλευσα θεομανεῖ πότμῳ,
οὐκ εἶδον, ἀπολειφθεῖσα δ᾽ αἰάζω τύχας.   80
ΗΛ.   Ἑλένη, τί σοι λέγοιμ᾽ ἂν ἅ γε παροῦσ᾽ ὁρᾷς,
ἐν συμφοραῖσι τὸν Ἀγαμέμνονος γόνον;
ἐγὼ μὲν ἄϋπνος πάρεδρος ἀθλίῳ νεκρῷ
(νεκρὸς γὰρ οὗτος οὕνεκα σμικρᾶς πνοῆς)
θάσσω· τὰ τούτου δ᾽ οὐκ ὀνειδίζω κακά·   85
σὺ δ᾽ ἡ μακαρία μακάριός θ᾽ ὁ σὸς πόσις
ἥκετον ἐφ᾽ ἡμᾶς ἀθλίως πεπραγότας.
ΕΛ.   πόσον χρόνον δὲ δεμνίοις πέπτωχ᾽ ὅδε;
ΗΛ.   ἐξ οὗπερ αἷμα γενέθλιον κατήνυσεν.
ΕΛ.   ὦ μέλεος· ἡ τεκοῦσά θ᾽, ὡς διώλετο.   90
ΗΛ.   οὕτως ἔχει τάδ᾽· ὥστ᾽ ἀπείρηκεν κακοῖς.
ΕΛ.   πρὸς θεῶν, πίθοι᾽ ἂν δῆτά μοί τι, παρθένε;
ΗΛ.   ὡς ἄσχολός γε συγγόνου προσεδρίᾳ.
ΕΛ.   βούλῃ τάφον μοι πρὸς κασιγνήτης μολεῖν –
ΗΛ.   μητρὸς κελεύεις τῆς ἐμῆς; τίνος χάριν;   95
ΕΛ.   κόμης ἀπαρχὰς καὶ χοὰς φέρουσ᾽ ἐμάς;
ΗΛ.   σοὶ δ᾽ οὐχὶ θεμιτὸν πρὸς φίλων στείχειν τάφον;

---

71   susp. Haslam
74   ὃς Porson: ὅδε MBVA, ὧδε O
79   ὅπως B^cΣ: ὅπως δ᾽ MB^{ac}OVA: ὅπως δὴ ᾽πλευσα Reiske
82   susp. Kirchhoff
86-7 del. Klinkenberg
86   ἡ V+: εἰ MBOAΣ

feeble strength to buoy us up otherwise, if we
do not find some salvation from him. It is a
helpless thing, a house in ill fortune.   70
[*Helen comes out of the house without attendants. She
carries a tray on which are jugs and a lock of hair.*]
   HELEN. Child of Clytaemestra and Agamemnon,
so long unwed - Electra - how are you, poor
creature, and your brother, unhappy Orestes, who
became his mother's murderer? Speaking to you
does not affect me with pollution, you see,   75
because it is to Phoebus that I attribute the
misdeed. Yet I do bewail the fate of my sister
Clytaemestra, whom I never saw after I sailed
to Ilion as I did from the heaven-sent madness
that was my lot. I am bereaved, and lament   80
what has befallen.
   EL. Helen, why would I tell you what you
see with your own eyes, Agamemnon's children in
calamity? I sit sleepless attending a miserable
corpse (for a corpse is what he is, by the
feebleness of his breath; I am not being
sarcastic about his troubles); and you the   85
fortunate one, and your fortunate husband, find
us in miserable plight.
   HEL. How long has he been sunk on his bed?
   EL. Ever since he did the deed of parental
carnage.
   HEL. O pitiable - and his mother too, the   90
way she perished.
   EL. That is how it is; and so he has broken
down.
   HEL. Niece, I beg you, would you do something
for me?
   EL. Well, I am rather occupied in sitting
by my brother.
   HEL. Do you mind going to my sister's tomb -
   EL. My mother's you want me to go to? What   95
for?
   HEL. To take an offering of hair and some
libations from me.
   EL. Is it improper for you to visit a
family tomb?

ΕΛ. δεῖξαι γὰρ 'Αργείοισι σῶμ' αἰσχύνομαι.
ΗΛ. ὀψέ γε φρονεῖς εὖ, τότε λιποῦσ' αἰσχρῶς δόμους.
ΕΛ. ὀρθῶς ἔλεξας, οὐ φίλως δέ μοι λέγεις.   100
ΗΛ. αἰδὼς δὲ δὴ τίς σ' εἰς Μυκηναίους ἔχει;
ΕΛ. δέδοικα πατέρας τῶν ὑπ' 'Ιλίῳ νεκρῶν.
ΗΛ. δεινὸν γάρ, "Αργει τ' ἀναβοᾷ διὰ στόμα.
ΕΛ. σύ νυν χάριν μοι τὸν φόβον λύσασα δός.
ΗΛ. οὐκ ἂν δυναίμην μητρὸς εἰσβλέψαι τάφον.   105
ΕΛ. αἰσχρόν γε μέντοι προσπόλους φέρειν τάδε.
ΗΛ. τί δ' οὐχὶ θυγατρὸς 'Ερμιόνης πέμπεις δέμας;
ΕΛ. εἰς ὄχλον ἔρπειν παρθένοισιν οὐ καλόν.
ΗΛ. καὶ μὴν τίνοι γ' ἂν τῇ τεθνηκυίᾳ τροφάς.
ΕΛ. ὀρθῶς ἔλεξας, πείθομαί τέ σοι, κόρη,   110
     καὶ πέμψομέν γε θυγατέρ'· εὖ γάρ τοι λέγεις.
     ὦ τέκνον, ἔξελθ', 'Ερμιόνη, δόμων πάρος
     καὶ λαβὲ χοὰς τάσδ' ἐν χεροῖν κόμας τ' ἐμάς·
     ἐλθοῦσα δ' ἀμφὶ τὸν Κλυταιμήστρας τάφον
     μελίκρᾶτ' ἄφες γάλακτος οἰνωπόν τ' ἄχνην, 115
     καὶ στᾶσ' ἐπ' ἄκρου χώματος λέξον τάδε·
     "'Ελένη σ' ἀδελφὴ ταῖσδε δωρεῖται χοαῖς,
     φόβῳ προσελθεῖν μνῆμα σόν, ταρβοῦσά τε
     'Αργεῖον ὄχλον." πρευμενῆ δ' ἄνωγέ νιν
     ἐμοί τε καὶ σοὶ καὶ πόσει γνώμην ἔχειν   120
     τοῖν τ' ἀθλίοιν τοῖνδ', οὓς ἀπώλεσεν θεός·
     ἃ δ' εἰς ἀδελφὴν καιρὸς ἐκπονεῖν ἐμέ,
     ἅπανθ' ὑπισχνοῦ νερτέρων δωρήματα.
     ἴθ' ὦ τέκνον μοι, σπεῦδε, καὶ χοὰς τάφῳ
     δοῦσ' ὡς τάχιστα τῆς πάλιν μέμνησ' ὁδοῦ.   125

111 πέμψομαί HB³ᵛᶜA
118 γε recc.
119 πρευμενῆ Mʸᵖ V²ʸᵖ : εὐμενῆ HMBOVA
122 ἐμέ OL+ : ἐμήν HMBVA

68

HEL. Well, you see, I am ashamed to show my
person to the Argives.
    EL. Belated wisdom: you left the house
brazenly enough that other time.
    HEL. You speak truly, though not amiably.   100
    EL. And what inhibition is it you feel
towards the Mycenaeans?
    HEL. I am afraid of the fathers of those
lying dead below Ilion.
    EL. A case for fear indeed, and you are
loud on Argos' lips.
    HEL. So will *you* do me this kindness, and
relieve my fear?
    EL. I would not be able to face my mother's
tomb.   105
    HEL. But it does not look good that servants
should be the bearers.
    EL. Why do you not send your daughter
Hermione?
    HEL. It is not seemly for girls to go out in
public.
    EL. But then, she would be repaying
Clytaemestra for bringing her up.
    HEL. That's true; I accept what you say,   110
niece. Yes, I'll send my daughter. A good
suggestion. - My child! Hermione! Come out to
the front - [*Hermione appears*] and take these
libations and this hair of mine. Go to the
edge of Clytaemestra's tomb and pour out the
milk honey-mix and the sprinkle of wine. Then 115
stand on top of the mound and say, "Helen your
sister presents you with these libations, afraid
to approach your memorial and fearing the Argive
populace". Ask her to keep a kindly attitude
toward me, and you, and my husband - and this   120
unhappy pair whom a god has ruined - and
promise all the mortuary offerings that it is
appropriate for me to make for my sister.
[*Hermione takes the tray and starts to leave.*] Go, my
child, be brisk, and when you have given the
libations to the tomb, mind you come back as   125
quickly as you can. [*Exit Hermione. Helen returns*

ΗΛ. ὦ φύσις, ἐν ἀνθρώποισιν ὡς μέγ' εἶ κακόν –
σωτήριόν τε τοῖς καλῶς κεκτημένοις.
εἴδετε, παρ' ἄκρας ὡς ἀπέθρισεν τρίχας,
σῴζουσα κάλλος; ἔστι δ' ἡ πάλαι γυνή.
θεοί σε μισήσειαν, ὥς μ' ἀπώλεσας   130
καὶ τόνδε πᾶσάν θ''Ελλάδ'. ὦ τάλαιν' ἐγώ·
αἵδ' αὖ πάρεισι τοῖς ἐμοῖς θρηνήμασιν
φίλαι ξυνῳδοί· τάχα μεταστήσουσ' ὕπνου
τόνδ' ἡσυχάζοντ', ὄμμα δ' ἐκτήξουσ' ἐμὸν
δακρύοις, ἀδελφὸν ὅταν ὁρῶ μεμηνότα.   135
ὦ φίλταται γυναῖκες, ἡσύχῳ ποδί
χωρεῖτε, μὴ ψοφεῖτε, μηδ' ἔστω κτύπος.
φιλία γὰρ ἡ σὴ πρευμενὴς μέν, ἀλλ' ἐμοί
τόνδ' ἐξεγεῖραι συμφορὰ γενήσεται.

ΧΟ. σῖγα σῖγα, λεπτὸν ἴχνος ἀρβύλας   str.1
τίθετε, μὴ κτυπεῖτ'.   141
ΗΛ. ἀποπρὸ βᾶτ' ἐκεῖσ', ἀποπρό μοι κοίτας.
ΧΟ. ἰδού, πείθομαι.
ΗΛ. ἆ ἆ, σύριγγος ὅπως πνοὰ   145
λεπτοῦ δόνακος, ὦ φίλα, φώνει μοι.
ΧΟ. ἴδ', ἀτρεμαῖον ὡς ὑπόροφον φέρω
βοάν.   ΗΛ. ναί, οὕτως.
κάταγε κάταγε, πρόσιθ' ἀτρέμας, ἀτρέμας ἴθι·
λόγον ἀπόδος ἐφ'ὅτι χρέος ἐμόλετέ ποτε·   150
χρόνια γὰρ πεσὼν ὅδ' εὐνάζεται.

ΧΟ. πῶς ἔχει; λόγου μετάδος, ὦ φίλα·   ant.1
τίνα τύχαν εἴπω; [τίνα δὲ συμφοράν;]
ΗΛ. ἔτι μὲν ἐμπνέει, βραχὺ δ' ἀναστένει.   155
ΧΟ. τί φής; ὦ τάλας.
ΗΛ. ὀλεῖς, εἰ βλέφαρα κινήσεις

---

128 ἴδετε FKᶜL Tricl. ad Aesch. Ag. 536
136-9 del. Wilamowitz
137 κτύπος codd., sch. Nic. Th. 423: ψοφος Π16
138 ἐμοὶ HMBOVA: ομω[ς Π16, ὅμως rec.
140 λεπτὸν HᶜMB²Oᵞᵖ V²ᵞᵖ A sch. Nic.: λευκὸν Hᵃᶜ BOVΣᵞᵖ Dion.
     Hal. sch. Eur. Ph. 202: utrumque Diog. Laert. codd.
141 κτυπεῖτ' [Π16] Dion. Hal.: κτυπεῖτε μηδ'ἔστω κτύπος codd.
154 τίνα δὲ συμφοράν; del. Schenkl

70

indoors.]

EL. O Nature, what a curse you are to
mankind - and what a preservative for the lucky
ones! Did you notice how she had shorn her
hair along the edge, to save her beauty? She is
the woman she used to be. May the gods' hate
fall upon you, for being the ruin of me, of   130
him here, and of all Greece! [*The Chorus, led
by the shawm-player, comes into view on one of the side
ramps.*] Oh dear, here they are again, my
friends who sing with me in my laments. They
will soon shift him from the sleep he rests in,
and dissolve my eye in tears when I see my
brother in his frenzy.   135

Dearest women, come with quiet step, make
no noise, let there be no clatter. Your
devotion is kindly, but to me his rousing will
be a calamity.

CHORUS [*piano*]
    Quietly, quietly, light set down   140
    your shoe-tread, do not stamp.
EL. Keep well clear, that way, please well
    clear of the bed.
CH. There, I do as you say!
EL. No, no - like breath of a panpipe's   145
    slight reed, as I love you, make your voice.
CH. [*pianissimo*] There, gentle as if indoors
    I bring my song.
EL. Yes, like that! Draw in, draw in,
    come up gently, gently come: give account
    of whatever business it is you have come for:
    It is a long time since he fell asleep   151
    like this.

CH. How is it with him? Share what you can tell,
    as I love you. What shall I say is his
    case? [What his plight?]
EL. He still breathes, but with shallow groan. 155
CH. What? O, poor man!
EL. You'll finish me if you disturb his closed

71

```
        ὕπνου γλυκυτάταν φερομένῳ χάριν.
ΧΟ.   μέλεος ἐχθίστων θεόθεν ἐργμάτων,              160
      τάλας.    ΗΛ. φεῦ μόχθων.
      ἄδικος ἄδικα τότ᾽ἄρ᾽ ἔλακεν ἔλακεν, ἀπό-
        φονον ὅτ᾽ ἐπὶ τρίποδι Θέμιδος ἄρ᾽ ἐδίκασε
        φόνον ὁ Λοξίας ἐμᾶς ματέρος.                165

ΧΟ.   ὁρᾷς; ἐν πέπλοισι κινεῖ δέμας.              str.2
ΗΛ.   σὺ γάρ νιν, ὦ τάλαινα,
      θωΰξασ᾽ ἔβαλες ἐξ ὕπνου.
ΧΟ.   εὕδειν μὲν οὖν ἔδοξα.
ΗΛ.   οὐκ ἀφ᾽ ἡμῶν, οὐκ ἀπ᾽ οἴκων              170
      πάλιν ἀνὰ πόδα σὸν εἱλίξεις μεθεμένα κτύπου;
ΧΟ.   ὑπνώσσει.    ΗΛ. λέγεις εὖ.
        πότνια πότνια Νύξ,
      ὑπνοδότειρα τῶν πολυπόνων βροτῶν,          175
      ᾽Ερεβόθεν ἴθι, μόλε μόλε κατάπτερος
      τὸν ᾽Αγαμεμνόνιον ἐπὶ δόμον.
      ὑπὸ γὰρ ἀλγέων ὑπό τε συμφορᾶς             180
      διοιχόμεθ᾽ οἰχόμεθ᾽ - ἆ, κτύπον ἠγάγετ᾽·
        οὐχὶ σῖγα σῖγα φυλασσομένα
      †στόματος ἀνὰ κέλαδον† ἀπὸ λέχεος ἤ-       185
      συχον ὕπνου χάριν παρέξεις, φίλα;

ΧΟ.   θρόει τίς κακῶν τελευτὰ μένει.             ant.2
ΗΛ.   θανεῖν, τί δ᾽ ἄλλο γ᾽ εἴπω;
      οὐδὲ γὰρ πόθον ἔχει βορᾶς.
ΧΟ.   πρόδηλος ἄρ᾽ ὁ πότμος.                     190
ΗΛ.   ἐξέθυσ᾽ ὁ Φοῖβος ἡμᾶς
      μέλεον ἀπόφονον αἷμα δοὺς πατροφόνου ματρός.
ΧΟ.   δίκα μέν.    ΗΛ. καλῶς δ᾽ οὔ.
        ἔκανες ἔθανες, ὦ                         195
      τεκομένα με μᾶτερ, ἀπὸ δ᾽ ὤλεσας
      πατέρα τέκνα τε τάδε σέθεν ἀφ᾽ αἵματος·
```

---

159 χάριν A^{1s}: χαράν codd.
167 γὰρ et ὦ del. Porson. cf. ad 187
181 οἰχόμεθ᾽· ἆ Biehl, Willink: οἰχόμε(σ)θα codd.
186 χάριν Σ: χαράν codd.
188 θανεῖν <θανεῖν> Lachmann: θανεῖν <νιν> Willink
     γ᾽ εἴπω K^{c}G: γ᾽ εἴπας HSa+: γ᾽ OB^{2}γ^p: om. MBVA

	eyes while he enjoys the sweet boon	
	of sleep.	
CH.	Pitiable for his horrible god-sent acts!	160
	Poor man!	
EL.	Oh, these toils: wrongful the god that	
	day, wrongful his oracle, oracle,	
	when on Themis' tripod Loxias passed	
	sentence that murder be followed by murder	
	of my mother!	165

CH. Do you see - he stirs in his wraps.
EL. Yes, because you with your wretched halloos
have jolted him awake.
CH. But no, I think he sleeps.
EL. Won't you leave us, leave the house,   170
retrace your steps and let your stamping be?
CH. He slumbers.   EL. That's well then.
   O mistress, mistress Night,
thou giver of sleep to mortals and all
   their toils,   175
come forth from the cosmic dark, come,
   come on thy wings
to the house that was Agamemnon's,
for by suffering and by calamity   180
we are lost, are lost - Oh! You made
   a clatter!
Won't you quietly, quietly, careful to
avoid clamorous voice, away from the bed,   185
allow him the peaceful boon of sleep,
   as I love you?

CH. Cry it aloud, what ending of his ills awaits.
EL. Death: what else can I say?
He has not even appetite for food.
CH. Plain to foresee then is his fate.   190
EL. Sacrificial victims Phoebus made of us,
by assigning that piteous sequential
murder of father's murderer, mother!
CH. It *was* just -   EL. But *not good*.
   You slew and were slain, o   195
mother who bore me; you put an end to
father and to us children of your blood.

ὀλόμεθ' ἰσονέκυες, ὀλόμεθα·   200
σύ τε γὰρ ἐν νεκροῖς, τό τ'ἐμὸν οἴχεται
βίου τὸ πλέον μέρος ἐν στοναχαῖσί τε
   καὶ γόοισι δάκρυσί τ' ἐννυχίοις,   205
ἄγαμος †ἐπὶ δ'ἄτεκνος ὅτε† βίοτον ἀ
μέλεος εἰς τὸν αἰὲν ἕλκω χρόνον.

ΧΟ.   ὅρα παροῦσα, παρθέν' 'Ηλέκτρα, πέλας,
      μὴ κατθανών σε σύγγονος λέληθ' ὅδε·
      οὐ γάρ μ' ἀρέσκει τῷ λίαν παρειμένῳ.   210
ΟΡΕΣΤΗΣ
      ὦ φίλον ὕπνου θέλγητρον, ἐπίκουρον νόσου,
      ὡς ἡδύ μοι προσῆλθες, ἐν δέοντί γε.
      ὦ πότνια Λήθη τῶν κακῶν, ὡς εἶ σοφή
      καὶ τοῖσι δυστυχοῦσιν εὐκταία θεός.
      πόθεν ποτ' ἦλθον δεῦρο; πῶς δ' ἀφικόμην;   215
      ἀμνημονῶ γάρ, τῶν πρὶν ἀπολειφθεὶς φρενῶν.
ΗΛ.   ὦ φίλταθ', ὥς μ' ηὔφρανας εἰς ὕπνον πεσών.
      βούλῃ θίγω σου κἀνακουφίσω δέμας;
ΟΡ.   λαβοῦ λαβοῦ δῆτ', ἐκ δ' ὅμορξον ἀθλίου
      στόματος ἀφρώδη πελανὸν ὀμμάτων τ' ἐμῶν.   220
ΗΛ.   ἰδού· τὸ δούλευμ' ἡδύ, κοὐκ ἀναίνομαι
      ἀδέλφ' ἀδελφῇ χειρὶ θεραπεύειν μέλη.
ΟΡ.   ὑπόβαλε πλευροῖς πλευρά, καὐχμώδη κόμην
      ἄφελε προσώπου· λεπτὰ γὰρ λεύσσω κόραις.
ΗΛ.   ὦ βόστρυχ', ὦ πινῶδες ἄθλιον κάρα,   225
      ὡς ἠγρίωσαι διὰ μακρᾶς ἀλουσίας.
ΟΡ.   κλῖνόν μ' ἐς εὐνὴν αὖθις· ὅταν [μ']ἀνῇ νόσος
      μανιάς, ἄναρθρός εἰμι κἀσθενῶ μέλη.
ΗΛ.   ἰδού. φίλον τοι τῷ νοσοῦντι δέμνιον,
      ἀνιαρὸν ὂν τὸ κτῆμ', ἀναγκαῖον δ' ὅμως.   230

_____

201   σύ τε [Π17] codd.: ὅδε Weil: fort. ὃ τε
206   οτε Π17: ἄτε codd.
212   γε: τε Π17 ξ Stob., Plut. v.l.
216   φρενῶν codd.: κακων Π4
224   κόραις codd.: νόσῳ Σ^γρ,]ωι Π4
225   βόστρυχ', ὦ Paley: βοστρύχων codd. Σ
227   μ' (et Π4?) del. Heath
228   μανιάς et μανίας Σ, μανίας codd.

We are destroyed, as good as dead,   200
   destroyed,
for you are among the dead, and my life
is gone, the greater part of it,
in groaning, lamenting, weeping in the night,
as marriageless, childless too - unhappy me -
I drag out my years for evermore.

   CHORUS-LEADER. Look, Electra - you are
there beside him - see your brother hasn't died
without your noticing. I don't like the look
of him, he's too limp. [*Anxious pause.*]   210
   ORESTES [*waking*]. O friendly enchantment of sleep,
help against sickness, how sweet was your
coming, just when I needed it. O mistress
Oblivion of Ills, how clever you are, and for
those in misfortune a goddess worth praying to.
   Wherever did I get here from? How did I   215
get here? I've no recollection, my former
mind has deserted me.
   EL. Dearest, how glad you made me by
falling asleep. Would you like me to deal with
you and make you comfortable?
   OR. Take hold, take hold, yes, and wipe the
sticky foam from my suffering mouth and eyes.   220
   EL. There. The menial task is a pleasure;
I don't decline to tend brother's body with
sister's hand.
   OR. Support my side with yours, and take
this drab hair out of my face. I can't see
very well.
   EL. O lock of hair, o dirty, suffering   225
head; how unkempt you are through long lack
of washing.
   OR. Lay me down again. When the madness
abates, I am limbless, I have no strength in
my body.
   EL. There. The sick man loves his couch -
a nuisance of a thing to have, but necessary   230
nonetheless.

OP. αὖθίς μ᾽ ἐς ὀρθὸν στῆσον, ἀνακύκλει δέμας·
     δυσάρεστον οἱ νοσοῦντες ἀπορίας ὕπο.
ΗΛ. ἦ κἀπὶ γαίας ἁρμόσαι πόδας θέλεις,
     χρόνιον ἴχνος θείς; μεταβολὴ πάντων γλυκύ.
OP. μάλιστα· δόξαν γὰρ τόδ᾽ ὑγιείας ἔχει.   235
     κρεῖσσον δὲ τὸ δοκεῖν, κἂν ἀληθείας ἀπῇ.
ΗΛ. ἄκουε δή νυν, ὦ κασίγνητον κάρα,
     ἕως ἐῶσί σ᾽ εὖ φρονεῖν Ἐρινύες.
OP. λέξεις τι καινόν· κεἰ μὲν εὖ, χάριν φέρεις·
     εἰ δ᾽εἰς βλάβην τιν᾽, ἅλις ἔχω τοῦ δυστυχεῖν.
ΗΛ. Μενέλαος ἥκει, σοῦ κασίγνητος πατρός,   241
     ἐν Ναυπλίᾳ δὲ σέλμαθ᾽ ὥρμισται νεώς.
OP. πῶς εἶπας; ἥκει φῶς ἐμοῖς καὶ σοῖς κακοῖς
     ἀνὴρ ὁμογενὴς καὶ χάριτας ἔχων πατρός;
ΗΛ. ἥκει – τὸ πιστὸν τόδε λόγων ἐμῶν δέχου –   245
     Ἑλένην ἀγόμενος Τρωϊκῶν ἐκ τειχέων.
OP. εἰ μόνος ἐσώθη, μᾶλλον ἂν ζηλωτὸς ἦν·
     εἰ δ᾽ ἄλοχον ἄγεται, κακὸν ἔχων ἥκει μέγα.
ΗΛ. ἐπίσημον ἔτεκε Τυνδάρεως εἰς τὸν ψόγον
     γένος θυγατέρων δυσκλεές τ᾽ ἀν᾽ Ἑλλάδα.   250
OP. σύ νυν διάφερε τῶν κακῶν· ἔξεστι γάρ·
     καὶ μὴ μόνον λέγ᾽ ἀλλὰ καὶ φρόνει τάδε.
ΗΛ. οἴμοι, κασίγνητ᾽, ὄμμα σὸν ταράσσεται,
     ταχὺς δὲ μετέθου λύσσαν, ἄρτι σωφρονῶν.
OP. ὦ μῆτερ, ἱκετεύω σε, μὴ ᾽πίσειέ μοι   255
     τὰς αἱματωποὺς καὶ δρακοντώδεις κόρας.
     αὗται γὰρ αὗται πλησίον θρῴσκουσί μου.

---

240 εἰς om. Π4
    τοῦ B²OV¹A: τὸ MBV²: τῶ Vᵃᶜ
242 νεώς O: νεῶν MBVA

OR. Set me up straight again ... swivel me
round. There's no pleasing the sick in their
helplessness.
    EL. Do you want me to set your feet down
on the ground? It's a long time since you
did. A change is always nice.
    OR. Yes, by all means. This has the   235
semblance of health, and it's better to have
the semblance, even if it falls short of
reality.
    EL. Now, listen, dear brother, while the
Erinyes are letting you think straight.
    OR. You're going to tell me some news. Well,
if it's good, I'm pleased, but if it points to
harm of some sort, I have enough misfortune.   240
    EL. Menelaus is come, your father's brother;
his galley is moored at Nauplia.
    OR. What's that? He's come, light of
deliverance for my troubles and yours, our
kinsman who owes gratitude to our father?
    EL. He's come – this certainty you may take   245
from what I say – bringing Helen home from the
walls of Troy.
    OR. If he had survived alone, he would be
more to be envied. If he comes with wife, he
comes with a load of trouble.
    EL. It was a notable brood of daughters
that Tyndareos fathered, with regard to such
censure, and of ill fame in Greece.   250
    OR. You be different from those bad women,
then, you have the option; and don't just say
you will, but mean it. [He suddenly shows signs
of distress.]
    EL. Oh, my dear brother, your eye is
becoming disturbed; you have soon switched to
madness, when just now you were sane.
    OR. Mother, I beg you, don't threaten me   255
with those blood-eyed, snaky maidens! For
here they come, here they come, bounding up
to me! [He begins to jerk up and down convulsively.
Electra tries to calm him.]

ΗΛ. μέν᾿, ὦ ταλαίπωρ᾿, ἀτρέμα σοῖς ἐν δεμνίοις·
     ὁρᾷς γὰρ οὐδὲν ὧν δοκεῖς σάφ᾿ εἰδέναι.
ΟΡ. ὦ Φοῖβ᾿· ἀποκτενοῦσί μ᾿ αἱ κυνώπιδες,   260
     γοργῶπες ἐνέρων ἱέρεαι, δειναὶ θεαί.
ΗΛ. οὔτοι μεθήσω· χεῖρα δ᾿ ἐμπλέξασ᾿ ἐμήν
     σχήσω σε πηδᾶν δυστυχῆ πηδήματα.
ΟΡ. μέθες· μί᾿ οὖσα τῶν ἐμῶν Ἐρινύων
     μέσον μ᾿ ὀχμάζεις ὡς βάλῃς εἰς Τάρταρον.   265
ΗΛ. οἲ ᾿γὼ τάλαινα, τίν᾿ ἐπικουρίαν λάβω,
     ἐπεὶ τὸ θεῖον δυσμενὲς κεκτήμεθα;
ΟΡ. δός τόξα μοι κερουλκά, δῶρα Λοξίου,
     οἷς μ᾿ εἶπ᾿ Ἀπόλλων ἐξαμύνασθαι θεάς
     εἴ μ᾿ ἐκφοβοῖεν μανιάσιν λυσσήμασιν.   270
     βεβλήσεταί τις θεῶν βροτησίᾳ χερί,
     εἰ μὴ ᾿ξαμείψει χωρὶς ὀμμάτων ἐμῶν.
     οὐκ εἰσακούετ᾿; οὐχ ὁρᾶθ᾿ ἑκηβόλων
     τόξων πτερωτὰς γλυφίδας ἐξορμωμένας;
     ἆ ἆ·
     τί δῆτα μέλλετ᾿; ἐξακρίζετ᾿ αἰθέρα   275
     πτεροῖς· τὰ Φοίβου δ᾿ αἰτιᾶσθε θέσφατα.
     ἔα·
     τί χρῆμ᾿ ἀλύω, πνεῦμ᾿ ἀνεὶς ἐκ πλευμόνων;
     ποῖ ποῖ ποθ᾿ ἡλάμεσθα δεμνίων ἄπο;
     ἐκ κυμάτων γὰρ αὖθις αὖ γαλήν᾿ ὁρῶ.
     σύγγονε, τί κλαίεις κρᾶτα θεῖσ᾿ εἴσω πέπλων;
     αἰσχύνομαί σε, μεταδιδοὺς πόνων ἐμῶν   281
     ὄχλον τε παρέχων παρθένῳ νόσοις ἐμαῖς.
     μὴ τῶν ἐμῶν ἔκατι συντήκου κακῶν·
     σὺ μὲν γὰρ ἐπένευσας τάδ᾿, εἴργασται δ᾿ ἐμοί
     μητρῷον αἷμα· Λοξίᾳ δὲ μέμφομαι,   285
     ὅστις μ᾿ ἐπάρας ἔργον ἀνοσιώτατον
     τοῖς μὲν λόγοις ηὔφρανε, τοῖς δ᾿ ἔργοισιν οὔ.
     οἶμαι δὲ πατέρα τὸν ἐμόν, εἰ κατ᾿ ὄμματα
     ἐξιστόρουν νιν, μητέρ᾿ εἰ κτεῖναί με χρή,
     πολλὰς γενείου τοῦδ᾿ ἂν ἐκτεῖναι λιτάς   290

260-1 et 264-5 inter se commut. F.W.Schmidt
269 [οἷς εἶπ᾿] Ἀπόλλων μ᾿ anon. P.Oxy.2506 fr.26 ii 20
     ἐξαμύνασθαι OV: -εσθαι Μ(ἐπ-),ΒΑ
273 εἰσακούετ᾿ Μ^{c}Β^{s}Ο^{c}V^1: εἰσακούσετ᾿ Μ^{ac}Β^{ac}γα^{c}α^{c}α$_A$
289 κτεῖναι χρεών L

78

EL. Stay quietly, poor sufferer, on your
bed. You're not seeing any of the things you
think you're sure of.
OR. O Phoebus! They'll kill me, the bitch- 260
faced, fierce-eyed priestesses of the nether
ones, dread goddesses!
EL. I'll not let go: I'll thread my arm in
and restrain your unhappy jumping about.
OR. Let go! You're one of my Erinyes,
you're getting a grip on my waist for a throw   265
- into Tartarus! [He springs free.]
EL. O misery, where am I to get help, when
we've got the powers that be against us? [She
covers her head and begins to weep.]
OR. Give me my horn-drawn bow, Loxias' gift
with which he said to defend myself against the
goddesses if they terrified me with raving fits. 270
There's going to be a deity shot by mortal
hand if she doesn't move away out of my sight!
Aren't you listening? Can't you see the
feathered shafts speeding out from the far-
shooting bow? Ach - why are you waiting, then? 275
Skim the air with your wings! It's Phoebus'
oracles you must hold responsible!
But stay ... What am I doing, raving and out
of breath? Where, oh where have I got to,
springing out of bed? Out of the surge once
more I see calm water. My sister, why are you
crying with your head inside your dress? You   280
make me ashamed for involving you in my troubles
and being a bother to an unmarried woman with
my ailments. Don't pine on account of my ills.
I mean, you agreed to this business, but it's
my doing, mother's murder; and it's Loxias I   285
blame, who put me up to a most unholy deed and
encouraged me with words but not with actions.
I think my father, if I were questioning him
face to face about whether I should kill my
mother, would have reached for my chin with   290

μήποτε τεκούσης εἰς σφαγὰς ὦσαι ξίφος,
εἰ μήτ' ἐκεῖνος ἀναλαβεῖν ἔμελλε φῶς
ἐγὼ δ' ὁ τλήμων τοιάδ' ἐκπλήσειν κακά.
  καὶ νῦν ἀνακάλυπτ', ὦ κασίγνητον κάρα,
ἐκ δακρύων τ' ἄπελθε, κεἰ μάλ' ἀθλίως   295
ἔχομεν. ὅταν δὲ τἄμ' ἀθυμήσαντ' ἴδῃς,
σύ μου τὸ δεινὸν καὶ διαφθαρὲν φρενῶν
ἴσχναινε παραμυθοῦ θ'· ὅταν δὲ σὺ στένῃς,
ἡμᾶς παρόντας χρή σε νουθετεῖν φίλα·
ἐπικουρίαι γὰρ αἵδε τοῖς φίλοις καλαί.   300
ἀλλ' ὦ τάλαινα, βᾶσα δωμάτων ἔσω
ὕπνῳ τ' ἄϋπνον βλέφαρον ἐκταθεῖσα δός
σίτων τ' ὄρεξαι λουτρά τ' ἐπιβαλοῦ χροΐ.
εἰ γὰρ προλείψεις μ' ἢ προσεδρείᾳ νόσον
κτήσῃ τιν', οἰχόμεσθα· σὲ γὰρ ἔχω μόνην   305
ἐπίκουρον, ἄλλων, ὡς ὁρᾷς, ἔρημος ὤν.
ΗΛ. οὔκ ἔστι· σὺν σοὶ καὶ θανεῖν αἱρήσομαι
καὶ ζῆν· ἔχει γὰρ ταὐτόν· ἢν σὺ κατθάνῃς,
γυνὴ τί δράσω; πῶς μόνη σωθήσομαι,
ἀνάδελφος ἀπάτωρ ἄφιλος; εἰ δὲ σοὶ δοκεῖ,   310
δρᾶν χρὴ τάδ'. ἀλλὰ κλῖνον εἰς εὐνὴν δέμας,
καὶ μὴ τὸ ταρβοῦν κἀκφοβοῦν σ'ἐκ δεμνίων
ἄγαν ἀποδέχου, μένε δ' ἐπὶ στρωτοῦ λέχους.
κἂν μὴ νοσῇ γάρ, ἀλλὰ δοξάζῃ νοσεῖν,
κάματος βροτοῖσιν ἀπορία τε γίγνεται.   315

ΧΟ. αἰαῖ·   str.
δρομάδες ὦ πτεροφόροι
ποτνιάδες θεαί,
ἀβάκχευτον αἳ θίασον ἐλάχετ' ἐν
    δάκρυσι καὶ γόοις,   320
μελάγχρωτες Εὐμενίδες, αἵτε τὸν
    ταναὸν αἰθέρ' ἀμπάλλεσθ', αἵματος
τεινύμεναι δίκαν, τεινύμεναι φόνον,

---

291 μήποτε [Π15]BFKLΞΣ: μήπω MOVA
294 κασίγνητον codd. Σ: κασιγνήτη Brunck
303 ἐπὶ χροΐ βάλε fere codd.(βαλοῦ G, βάλευ O, βάλλευ M):
     corr. Hermann
314 ita Callistratus ap. Σ: νοσῇς ... δοξάζῃς fere codd.

many an appeal never to drive my sword into
the neck of her who bore me, if he was not to
get his daylight back and my suffering self
was to endure ills like these.

And now unveil, dear sister head, and leave
your tears, even if we are in very sorry   295
plight. When you see depression on my part,
you must shrink the grim diseased part of my
mind and comfort me; and when it is you that
groans, it is for me to be at hand with
affectionate advice. These are fitting services 300
for people who are close. Now go into the
house, poor sufferer, stretch out and yield
your sleepless lids to sleep, take food, and
wash yourself. For if you are going to give
out on me or catch some illness through
sitting with me, I am lost: you're the only   305
helper I have, for as you see, I am without
any others.

EL.   Impossible. I shall opt even to die
with you, no less than to live. It comes to
the same; for if you die, what can I do, as a
woman? How shall I survive by myself,
brotherless, fatherless, friendless?   310

Yet if you think it best, I must obey. But
lie down on your bed, and be none too receptive
to that panic that startles you from the couch,
but stay on the comfortable bed. For even if
one is not ill but fancies one is, the effect
is fatigue and despair.   315

[*Electra goes indoors. Orestes resumes his place
on the couch. Music.*]

CH.   Ah woe.
      Ye wild-running wingèd
      frenzying goddesses
      who have been assigned an unbacchanal coven
      among tears and wailings: 320
      dark-hued Benign Ones, who dart the length
        of the sky,
      seeking justice for blood,
      seeking payment for murder:

καθικετεύομαι καθικετεύομαι,
τὸν ᾿Αγαμέμνονος   325
    γόνον ἐάσατ᾿ ἐκλαθέσθαι λύσσας
μανιάδος φοιταλέου. φεῦ μόχθων,
οἵων, ὦ τάλας, ὀρέχθεὶς ἔρρεις,
τρίποδος ἄπο φάτιν, ἂν
    ὁ Φοῖβος ἔλακεν ἔλακε, δε-
    ξάμενος ἀνὰ δάπεδον,   330
    ἵνα μεσόμφαλοι λέγονται μυχοί [γᾶς].

ὦ Ζεῦ·   ant.
τίς ἔλεος, τίς ὅδ᾿ ἀγὼν
φόνιος ἔρχεται,
θοάζων σε τὸν μέλεον, ᾧ δάκρυα   335
    δάκρυσι συμβάλλει
πορεύων τις εἰς δόμον ἀλαστόρων
    ματέρος αἷμα σᾶς, ὅ σ᾿ ἀναβακχεύει;
κατολοφύρομαι κατολοφύρομαι.
ὁ μέγας ὄλβος οὐ μόνιμος ἐν βροτοῖς·   340
ἀνὰ δὲ λαῖφος ὥς
    τις ἀκάτου θοᾶς τινάξας δαίμων
κατέκλυσεν δεινῶν πόνων ὡς πόντου
λάβροις ὀλεθρίοισιν ἐν κύμασιν.
τίνα γὰρ ἔτι πάρος οἶ-
    κον ἄλλον ἕτερον ἢ τὸν ἀπὸ   345
    θεογόνων γάμων,
    τὸν ἀπὸ Ταντάλου, σέβεσθαί με χρή;

καὶ μὴν βασιλεὺς ὅδε δὴ στείχει,
    Μενέλαος ἄναξ. [πολὺ δ᾿ ἀβροσύνῃ
    δῆλος ὁρᾶσθαι   350
    τοῦ Τανταλιδᾶν ἐξ αἵματος ὤν.]

---

329 ἔλακε(ν) bis Π15 HMBV: semel OA. cf. ad 345
331 γᾶς del. Triclinius
337 δόμους Π15 codd. Σ: corr. Triclinius
339 ante 338 habuit Π6
345 ἄλλον ἕτερον BV: ἕτερον HMO: ἄλλον A
349-51 πολὺ δ᾿ - ὤν seclusi
    πολὺ HMBO Dio Chrys.(interpol.): πολλῇ B²O¹V¹A, πολῇ
    Vᵃᶜ: πάνυ L.Dindorf | τοῦ Τανταλιδᾶν Dio:
    τοῦ Τανταλιδᾶν sch. Hom.: τῶν Τανταλιδᾶν codd.

I beseech you, beseech you,
let Agamemnon's son   325
free his mind of the fury
of raving and roving. Oh, what toils
you reached your hand at, poor man -
  - and therefore perish -
when from the tripod Phoebus' oracle, oracle,
you received in the precinct   330
where, they say, the central Navel lurks.

O Zeus.
What tragedy, what trial
is this that comes with carnage,
spurring you, hapless one, for whom   335
    some demon
joins tears in stream with tears,
channelling into the house
your mother's blood that drives you wild?
I grieve for you, grieve for you.
Great prosperity among mortals is not   340
lasting:
upsetting it like the sail of a swift sloop
some higher power swamps it in the rough
    doom-waves
of fearful toils, as of the sea.
For what other house yet, but the one   345
sprung from marriage of holy stock -
from Tantalus - am I sooner to revere?

[*Menelaus and attendants come into view, marching up one
of the side ramps.*]

But see now, here the king approaches, lord
Menelaus. [And by his elegance he may be
plainly seen to be of the Tantalids' blood.]   350

ὦ χιλιόναυν στρατὸν ὁρμήσας
εἰς γῆν 'Ασίαν,
χαῖρ'· εὐτυχίᾳ δ' αὐτὸς ὁμιλεῖς,
θεόθεν πράξας ἅπερ ηὔχου.   355

ΜΕΝΕΛΑΟΣ
ὦ δῶμα, τῇ μέν σ' ἡδέως προσδέρκομαι
Τροίαθεν ἐλθών, τῇ δ' ἰδὼν καταστένω·
κύκλῳ γὰρ εἰλιχθεῖσαν ἀθλίοις κακοῖς
οὔπώποτ' ἄλλην μᾶλλον εἶδον ἑστίαν.
'Αγαμέμνονος μὲν γὰρ τύχας ἠπιστάμην   360
[καὶ θάνατον, οἵῳ πρὸς δάμαρτος ὤλετο,]
Μαλέᾳ προσίσχων πρῷραν· ἐκ δὲ κυμάτων
ὁ ναυτίλοισι μάντις ἐξήγγειλέ μοι
Νηρέως προφήτης Γλαῦκος, ἀψευδὴς θεός,
ὅς μοι τόδ' εἶπεν ἐμφανῶς κατασταθείς·   365
"Μενέλαε, κεῖται σὸς κασίγνητος θανών,
λουτροῖσιν ἀλόχου περιπεσὼν πανυστάτοις"·
δακρύων δ' ἔπλησεν ἐμέ τε καὶ ναύτας ἐμούς
πολλῶν. ἐπεὶ δὲ Ναυπλίας ψαύω χθονός,
ἤδη δάμαρτος ἐνθάδ' ἐξορμωμένης,   370
δοκῶν 'Ορέστην παῖδα τὸν 'Αγαμέμνονος
φίλαισι χερσὶ περιβαλεῖν καὶ μητέρα,
ὡς εὐτυχοῦντας, ἔκλυον ἀλιτύπων τινός
τῆς Τυνδαρείας παιδὸς ἀνόσιον μόρον.
   καὶ νῦν ὅπου 'στὶν εἶπατ', ὦ νεάνιδες,   375
'Αγαμέμνονος παῖς, ὃς τὰ δείν' ἔτλη κακά·
βρέφος γὰρ ἦν τότ' ἐν Κλυταιμήστρας χεροῖν,
ὅτ' ἐξέλειπον μέλαθρον εἰς Τροίαν ἰών,
ὥστ' οὐκ ἂν αὐτὸν γνωρίσαιμ' ἂν εἰσιδών.
ΟΡ. ὅδ' εἴμ' 'Ορέστης, Μενέλεως, ὃν ἱστορεῖς.   380
ἑκὼν ἐγώ σοι τἀμὰ μηνύσω κακά·
τῶν σῶν δὲ γονάτων πρωτόλεια θιγγάνω
ἱκέτης, ἀφύλλου στόματος ἐξάπτων λιτάς·
σῶσόν μ'· ἀφῖξαι δ' αὐτὸς εἰς καιρὸν κακῶν.
ΜΕ. ὦ θεοί, τί λεύσσω; τίνα δέδορκα νερτέρων;   385

---

361 del. Dindorf
367 fort. delendum
381 μηνύσω HMB: σημανῶ OVA
384 αὐτὸν Schaefer

84

O thou who launched a thousand-vessel horde
at Asian soil, joy on you; with Success you
consort for your own part, having won from the
gods just what you were praying for.   355

MENELAUS. O palace: in one way I am
delighted to behold you, coming from Troy as I
do, but at the same time I lament, for never
in my life have I seen a hearth more circled
about with grievous ills. Agamemnon's fate I   360
knew [and by what a death he perished at his
wife's hand] as I brought my prow to Malea;
the soothsayer for sailors had announced it to
me out of the waves, the prophet of Nereus,
Glaucus, a god without deceit, who told me,
stationed there before my eyes: "Menelaus,   365
your brother lies dead; he has met his last
ablutions from his wife", and so he filled me
and my sailors with tears in plenty. But after
I touched Nauplian soil, when my wife was
already on her way here and I was thinking to   370
embrace Orestes, Agamemnon's boy, with loving
arms, and his mother, assuming them to be well,
I heard from one of the harbour salts of the
unholy murder of Tyndareos' daughter.
And now tell me where he is, young ladies,   375
Agamemnon's son, who steeled himself to this
horror. He was a babe in Clytaemestra's arms
when I left the house to go to Troy, so I
would not recognize him at sight.
OR. [*running forward from his bed and crouching
before Menelaus*] Here I am, Menelaus, that   380
Orestes you are asking after. Of my own accord
I will lay my plight before you. As a first
offering I touch your knees in supplication,
making contact in prayer uttered without
foliage: save me! You have come, the very man,
at the moment of crisis.
MEN. Ye gods, what am I seeing? Which of   385
the dead do I behold?

85

ΟΡ.	εὖ γ᾽ εἶπας· οὐ γὰρ ζῶ κακοῖς, φάος δ᾽ ὁρῶ.
ΜΕ.	ὡς ἠγρίωσαι πλόκαμον αὐχμηρόν, τάλας.
ΟΡ.	οὐχ ἡ πρόσοψίς μ᾽ ἀλλὰ τἄργ᾽ αἰκίζεται.
ΜΕ.	δεινὸν δὲ λεύσσεις ὀμμάτων ξηραῖς κόραις.
ΟΡ.	τὸ σῶμα φροῦδον· τὸ δ᾽ ὄνομ᾽ οὐ λέλοιπέ με. 390
ΜΕ.	ὦ παρὰ λόγον μοι σὴ φανεῖσ᾽ ἀμορφία.
ΟΡ.	ὅδ᾽ εἰμί, μητρὸς τῆς ταλαιπώρου φονεύς.
ΜΕ.	ἤκουσα· φείδου δ᾽ ὀλιγάκις λέγειν κακά.
ΟΡ.	φειδόμεθ᾽· ὁ δαίμων δ᾽ ἐς ἐμὲ πλούσιος κακῶν.
ΜΕ.	τί χρῆμα πάσχεις; τίς σ᾽ ἀπόλλυσιν νόσος; 395
ΟΡ.	ἡ ξύνεσις, ὅτι σύνοιδα δείν᾽ εἰργασμένος.
ΜΕ.	πῶς φής; σοφόν τοι τὸ σαφές, οὐ τὸ μὴ σαφές.
ΟΡ.	λύπη μάλιστά γ᾽ ἡ διαφθείρουσά με –
ΜΕ.	δεινὴ γὰρ ἡ θεός, ἀλλ᾽ ὅμως ἰάσιμος.
ΟΡ.	μανίαι τε, μητρὸς αἵματος τιμωρίαι. 400
ΜΕ.	ἤρξω δὲ λύσσης πότε; τίς ἡμέρα τότ᾽ ἦν;
ΟΡ.	ἐν ᾗ τάλαιναν μητέρ᾽ ἐξώγκουν τάφῳ.
ΜΕ.	πότερα κατ᾽ οἴκους ἢ προσεδρεύων πυρᾷ;
ΟΡ.	νυκτὸς φυλάσσων ὀστέων ἀναίρεσιν.
ΜΕ.	παρῆν τις ἄλλος ὃς σὸν ὤρθευεν δέμας; 405
ΟΡ.	Πυλάδης, ὁ συνδρῶν αἷμα καὶ μητρὸς φόνον.

---

390 με HBO^{S}A: μοι MOV gnomol. Vatoped.
392 σφαγεύς H
400 μητρὸς ΣL+: μητρός θ᾽ HMBOVA
402 ταλαίνης μητρὸς … τάφον Σ^{γρ}

OR. Well said, for in my plight I am not
alive, though I see the daylight.
MEN. How unkempt you are with your drab hair,
unhappy creature!
OR. It is not my aspect but my actions that
disfigure me.
MEN. And how grimly you gaze with your
wasted eyes!
OR. My body is passed away – but my name   390
has not deserted me.
MEN. O unexpected apparition of unsightliness!
OR. Here I am, my wretched mother's
murderer.
MEN. So I have heard. Be sparing in
mentioning evils.
OR. I am; but Fortune is prodigal of them
towards me.
MEN. What's wrong with you? What sickness   395
is killing you?
OR. My intellect – I am conscious of having
done awful things.
MEN. How do you mean? It's intelligent to
be clear, not obscure.
OR. It is anguish in particular that is
destroying me –
MEN. Yes, she is formidable, that one, but
still curable.
OR. And frenzy-fits, retributions for my   400
mother's blood.
MEN. And when did you start being mad? Which
day was it?
OR. The day I was building up my poor
mother's grave-mound.
MEN. Was it at home, or as you sat by the
pyre?
OR. As I waited in the night for the taking
up of bones.
MEN. Was anyone else there, keeping you   405
upright?
OR. Pylades, my accomplice in blood and
matricide.

ΜΕ. ἐκ φασμάτων δὲ τάδε νοσεῖς ποίων ὕπο;
ΟΡ. ἔδοξ' ἰδεῖν τρεῖς νυκτὶ προσφερεῖς κόρας.
ΜΕ. οἶδ' ἃς ἔλεξας· ὀνομάσαι δ' οὐ βούλομαι.
ΟΡ. σεμναὶ γάρ. εὐπαίδευτα δ' ἀποτρέπου λέγειν.410
ΜΕ. αὗταί σε βακχεύουσι συγγενῆ φόνον.
ΟΡ. οἴμοι διωγμῶν οἷς ἐλαύνομαι τάλας.
ΜΕ. οὐ δεινὰ πάσχειν δεινὰ τοὺς εἰργασμένους.
ΟΡ. ἀλλ' ἔστιν ἡμῖν ἀναφορὰ τῆς ξυμφορᾶς -
ΜΕ. μὴ θάνατον εἴπῃς· τοῦτο μὲν γὰρ οὐ σοφόν.   415
ΟΡ. Φοῖβος, κελεύσας μητρὸς ἐκπρᾶξαι φόνον.
ΜΕ. ἀμαθέστερός γ' ὢν τοῦ καλοῦ καὶ τῆς δίκης.
ΟΡ. δουλεύομεν θεοῖς, ὅτι ποτ' εἰσὶν οἱ θεοί.
ΜΕ. κᾆτ' οὐκ ἀμύνει Λοξίας τοῖς σοῖς κακοῖς;
ΟΡ. μέλλει· τὸ θεῖον δ' ἐστὶ τοιοῦτον φύσει.   420
ΜΕ. πόσον χρόνον δὲ μητρὸς οἴχονται πνοαί;
ΟΡ. ἕκτον τόδ' ἧμαρ· ἔτι πυρὰ θερμὴ τάφου.
ΜΕ. ὡς ταχὺ μετῆλθόν σ' αἷμα μητέρος θεαί.
ΟΡ. οὐ σοφός, ἀληθὴς δ' εἰς φίλους ἔφυ θεός.
ΜΕ. πατρὸς δὲ δή τι σ' ὠφελεῖ τιμωρία;   425
ΟΡ. οὔπω· τὸ μέλλον δ' ἴσον ἀπραξία λέγω.
ΜΕ. τὰ πρὸς πόλιν δὲ πῶς ἔχεις δράσας τάδε;
ΟΡ. μισούμεθ' οὕτως ὥστε μὴ προσεννέπειν.

---

407 ἐκ φασμάτων: φαντασμάτων ξ
411 συγγενῆ φόνον Σ: συγγενεῖ φόνῳ codd.
416 μητρὸς: πατρὸς Hemsterhuys
424 ἔφυ θεός West: ἔφυς κακός codd. Σ: ἔφυν φίλος Brunck

88

MEN. And from what kind of visions are you
being disordered by?
    OR. I thought I saw three maidens that
looked like Night.
    MEN. I know the ones you mean. I don't
care to name them.
    OR. No, they are awesome. Turn to politer   410
matters.
    MEN. It is these that drive you wild on
kindred murder.
    OR. Oh, the chases by which I am hounded!
    MEN. It's not monstrous that monstrous things
be suffered by those who have done them.
    OR. Yet I have a recourse in my calamity –
    MEN. Don't say death: *that* isn't intelligent.415
    OR. In Phoebus who told me to carry out
my mother's murder.
    MEN. Which makes him rather backward in
what is right and proper.
    OR. We are slaves to the gods – whatever
"the gods" are.
    MEN. Then does Loxias provide no relief for
your troubles?
    OR. He is biding his time. Divinity is   420
like that.
    MEN. And how long has your mother's breath
been departed?
    OR. This is the sixth day; the funeral
pyre is still warm.
    MEN. How soon the goddesses have come after
you on account of her blood.
    OR. God may not be intelligent, but he is
true to his own.
    MEN. Does the fact that you have avenged   425
your father help you at all?
    OR. Not so far; and "going to" I reckon
the same as doing nothing.
    MEN. And how do you stand with the town
since doing this deed?
    OR. I am so abhorred that they do not
speak to me.

ΜΕ. οὐδ᾿ ἥγνισαι σὸν αἷμα κατὰ νόμον χεροῖν;
ΟΡ. ἐκκλήομαι γὰρ δωμάτων ὅπῃ μόλω.   430
ΜΕ. τίνες πολιτῶν δ᾿ ἐξαμιλλῶνταί σε γῆς;
ΟΡ. Οἴαξ, τὸ Τροίᾳ μῖσος ἀναφέρων πατρί.
ΜΕ. συνῆκα· Παλαμήδους σε τιμωρεῖ φόνου.
ΟΡ. οὗ γ᾿ οὐ μετῆν μοι· διὰ τριῶν δ᾿ἀπόλλυμαι.
ΜΕ. τίς δ᾿ἄλλος; ἦ που τῶν ἀπ᾿Αἰγίσθου φίλων;   435
ΟΡ. οὗτοί μ᾿ ὑβρίζουσ᾿· ὧν πόλις τὰ νῦν κλύει.
ΜΕ. ᾿Αγαμέμνονος δ᾿ οὐ σκῆπτρ᾿ ἐᾷ σ᾿ἔχειν πόλις;
ΟΡ. πῶς, οἵτινες ζῆν οὐκ ἐῶσ᾿ ἡμᾶς ἔτι;
ΜΕ. τί δρῶντες, ὅτι καὶ σαφὲς ἔχεις εἰπεῖν ἐμοί;
ΟΡ. ψῆφος καθ᾿ ἡμῶν οἴσεται τῇδ᾿ ἡμέρᾳ.   440
ΜΕ. φεύγειν πόλιν τήνδ᾿; ἢ θανεῖν ἢ μὴ θανεῖν;
ΟΡ. θανεῖν ὑπ᾿ ἀστῶν λευσίμῳ πετρώματι.
ΜΕ. κᾆτ᾿ οὐχὶ φεύγεις γῆς ὑπερβάλλων ὅρους;
ΟΡ. κύκλῳ γὰρ εἱλισσόμεθα παγχάλκοις ὅπλοις.
ΜΕ. ἰδίᾳ πρὸς ἐχθρῶν ἢ πρὸς ᾿Αργείας χερός;   445
ΟΡ. πάντων πρὸς ἀστῶν, ὡς θάνω· βραχὺς λόγος.
ΜΕ. ὦ μέλεος, ἥκεις συμφορᾶς εἰς τοὔσχατον.
ΟΡ. εἰς σ᾿ ἐλπὶς ἡμὴ καταφυγὰς ἔχει κακῶν.
      ἀλλ᾿ ἀθλίως πράσσουσιν εὐτυχὴς μολών
      μετάδος φίλοισι σοῖσι σῆς εὐπραξίας,   450
      καὶ μὴ μόνος τὸ χρηστὸν ἀπολαβὼν ἔχε,
      ἀλλ᾿ ἀντιλάζου καὶ πόνων ἐν τῷ μέρει,

---

429 νόμον Μ+: νόμους BOVA
432 Τροίᾳ Musgrave: Τροίας codd.
437 δ᾿οὐ Schirlitz: δὲ codd.

MEN. And have you not purged the blood on
your hands in the prescribed way?

OR. No, I am excluded from homes wherever   430
I go.

MEN. And which of them is it that want to
run you out?

OR. There is Oeax, who blames my father
for the outrage at Troy.

MEN. I know what you mean: he is punishing
you for the killing of Palamedes.

OR. In which I had no part; I am ruined
by it at two removes.

MEN. Who else? Some of Aegisthus' party,   435
perhaps?

OR. Yes, they abuse me; and the town is
led by them nowadays.

MEN. But does the people not let you hold
Agamemnon's sceptre?

OR. How should they, since they will no
longer let me live?

MEN. Why, what are they doing that you can
tell me definitely?

OR. A vote will be taken against me today.   440

MEN. That you should suffer exile? Or is
it life or death?

OR. Death at the citizens' hands by stoning.

MEN. Then aren't you fleeing across the
border?

OR. No, I am encircled all round with full
bronze weaponry.

MEN. By your enemies on their own, or by   445
an Argive force?

OR. By all the citizens - to kill me. It's
as simple as that.

MEN. Oh, unhappy man, you have reached the
ultimate in disaster.

OR. My hope runs to you for refuge from my
troubles. You have come full of success: give
your near ones, who are suffering grievously,   450
a share of your good fortune, don't take all
the benefit and keep it to yourself, but accept

91

χάριτας πατρῴους ἐκτίνων εἰς οὖς σε δεῖ.
ὄνομα γάρ, ἔργον δ' οὐκ ἔχουσιν οἱ φίλοι
οἱ μὴ 'πὶ ταῖσι συμφοραῖς ὄντες φίλοι.   455

ΧΟ. καὶ μὴν γέροντι δεῦρ' ἁμιλλᾶται ποδί
     ὁ Σπαρτιάτης Τυνδάρεως, μελάμπεπλος
     κουρᾷ τε θυγατρὸς πενθίμῳ κεκαρμένος.
ΟΡ. ἀπωλόμην, Μενέλαε· Τυνδάρεως ὅδε
     στείχει πρὸς ἡμᾶς, οὗ μάλιστ' αἰδώς μ'ἔχει 460
     εἰς ὄμματ' ἐλθεῖν τοῖσιν ἐξειργασμένοις.
     καὶ γάρ μ' ἔθρεψε σμικρὸν ὄντα, πολλὰ δέ
     φιλήματ' ἐξέπλησε, τὸν 'Αγαμέμνονος
     παῖδ' ἀγκάλαισι περιφέρων, Λήδα θ' ἅμα,
     τιμῶντέ μ' οὐδὲν ἧσσον ἢ Διοσκόρω·   465
     οἷς, ὦ τάλαινα καρδία ψυχή τ' ἐμή,
     ἀπέδωκ' ἀμοιβὰς οὐ καλάς. τίνα σκότον
     λάβω προσώπῳ; ποῖον ἐπίπροσθεν νέφος
     θῶμαι, γέροντος ὀμμάτων φεύγων κόρας;

ΤΥΝΔΑΡΕΩΣ
     ποῦ ποῦ θυγατρὸς τῆς ἐμῆς ἴδω πόσιν   470
     Μενέλαον; ἐπὶ γὰρ τῷ Κλυταιμήστρας τάφῳ
     χοὰς χεόμενος ἔκλυον ὡς εἰς Ναυπλίαν
     ἥκοι σὺν ἀλόχῳ πολυετὴς σεσωμένος.
     ἄγετέ με· πρὸς γὰρ δεξιάν, αὐτοῦ θέλω
     στὰς ἀσπάσασθαι, χρόνιος εἰσιδὼν φίλον.   475
ΜΕ. ὦ πρέσβυ, χαῖρε, Ζηνὸς ὁμόλεκτρον κάρα.
ΤΥ. ὦ χαῖρε καὶ σύ, Μενέλεως, κήδευμ' ἐμόν.
     ἔα· [τὸ μέλλον ὡς κακὸν τὸ μὴ εἰδέναι·]
     ὁ μητροφόντης ὅδε πρὸ δωμάτων δράκων
     στίλβει νοσώδεις ἀστραπάς, στύγημ' ἐμόν.   480
     Μενέλαε, προσφθέγγῃ νιν, ἀνόσιον κάρα;
ΜΕ. τί γάρ; φίλου μοι πατρός ἐστιν ἔκγονος.
ΤΥ. κείνου γὰρ ὅδε πέφυκε, τοιοῦτος γεγώς;

---

478 τὸ μέλλον - εἰδέναι del. Wecklein
481 ἀνόσιον: ἀκάθαρτον Σ^{γρ}

some toil too in your turn, repaying your debts
of gratitude to my father in the proper quarter.
The name but not the reality is what those
friends have who are not friends in misfortune. 455
    [*Tyndareos is seen approaching with attendants from
the direction of Clytaemestra's tomb.*]
    CHORUS-LEADER. See now, on aged legs the
Spartiate struggles this way, Tyndareos, dark-
robed and shorn in mourning fashion for his
daughter.
    OR. I am lost, Menelaus! Here is Tyndareos
approaching us, the man into whose sight I am   460
most hesitant to come because of what I have
done. He even took care of me when I was small,
with constant expressions of affection, carrying
"Agamemnon's boy" around in his arms, and so did
Leda. They treasured me no less than the Zeus- 465
twins. And o my wretched heart and soul, I have
not repaid them well. What darkness can I find
for my face? What sort of cloud can I put in
front of myself to avoid the old man's eyes?
[*He shrinks back behind Menelaus.*]
    TYNDAREOS. Where, oh where can I catch sight
of my daughter's husband, of Menelaus? I was   471
at Clytaemestra's tomb pouring libations when
I heard he had arrived at Nauplia with his wife,
safe home after all these years. Take me to
him, I want to stand to his right hand and
greet him when I see him again at last.   475
    MEN. Joy to you, old sir, whose pillow was
also Zeus'.
    TY. Ha, joy yourself, Menelaus, my son-in-
law!
    But stay. [What a plague it is not to know
what is coming.] Here's the matricide-serpent
in front of the house, glinting his unhealthy   480
flashes, my bête noire. Menelaus, are you
talking to him, the unholy creature?
    MEN. What if I am? He is the son of a
father who was dear to me.
    TY. You mean to say he is of *his* stock,
when he has turned out like this?

93

ΜΕ. πέφυκεν· εἰ δὲ δυστυχεῖ, τιμητέος.
ΤΥ. βεβαρβάρωσαι χρόνιος ὢν ἐν βαρβάροις.   485
ΜΕ. Ἑλληνικόν τοι τὸν ὁμόθεν τιμᾶν ἀεί.
ΤΥ. καὶ τῶν νόμων γε μὴ πρότερον εἶναι θέλειν.
ΜΕ. πᾶν τοὔξ ἀνάγκης δοῦλόν ἐστ᾽ ἐν τοῖς οοφοῖς.
ΤΥ. κέκτησό νυν σὺ τοῦτ᾽, ἐγὼ δ᾽ οὐ κτήσομαι.
ΜΕ. ὀργὴ γὰρ ἅμα σου καὶ τὸ γῆρας οὐ σοφόν.   490
ΤΥ. πρὸς τόνδ᾽ ἀγὼν τίς τοῦ σοφοῦ γ᾽ ἥκει πέρι,
    εἰ τὰ καλὰ πᾶσι φανερὰ καὶ τὰ μὴ καλά;
    τούτου τίς ἀνδρὸς ἐγένετ᾽ ἀσυνετώτερος,
    ὅστις τὸ μὲν δίκαιον οὐκ ἐσκέψατο
    οὐδ᾽ ἦλθεν ἐπὶ τὸν κοινὸν Ἑλλήνων νόμον;   495
    ἐπεὶ γὰρ ἐξέπνευσεν Ἀγαμέμνων βίον
    πληγεὶς θυγατρὸς κρᾶτα τῆς ἐμῆς ὕπο –
    αἴσχιστον ἔργον· οὐ γὰρ αἰνέσω ποτέ –
    χρῆν αὐτὸν ἐπιθεῖναι μὲν αἵματος δίκην,   500
    ὁσίαν διώκοντ᾽, ἐκβαλεῖν τε δωμάτων
    μητέρα· τὸ σῶφρόν τ᾽ ἔλαβεν ἂν τῆς συμφορᾶς,
    καὶ τοῦ νόμου τ᾽ ἂν εἶχετ᾽ εὐσεβής τ᾽ ἂν ἦν.
    νῦν δ᾽ εἰς τὸν αὐτὸν δαίμον᾽ ἦλθε μητέρι.
    κακὴν γὰρ αὐτὴν ἐνδίκως ἡγούμενος   505
    αὐτὸς κακίων μητέρ᾽ ἐγένετο κτανών.
       ἐρήσομαι δέ, Μενέλεως, τοσόνδε σε·
    εἰ τόνδ᾽ ἀποκτείνειεν ὁμόλεκτρος γυνή,
    χὠ τοῦδε παῖς αὖ μητέρ᾽ ἀνταποκτενεῖ,
    κἄπειθ᾽ ὁ κείνου γενόμενος φόνῳ φόνον   510
    λύσει, πέρας δὴ ποῖ κακῶν προβήσεται;
    καλῶς ἔθεντο ταῦτα πατέρες οἱ πάλαι·
    εἰς ὀμμάτων μὲν ὄψιν οὐκ εἴων περᾶν
    οὐδ᾽ εἰς ἀπάντημ᾽, ὅστις αἷμ᾽ ἔχων κυροῖ,
    φυγαῖσι δ᾽ ὁσιοῦν, ἀνταποκτείνειν δὲ μή.   515

---

485 ἐν βαρβάροις Π7 codd.: ἀφ᾽ Ἑλλάδος M^{γρ}V^{2γρ} Ps.-Apoll.Tyan.
491 τοῦ σοφοῦ γ᾽ West: σοφίας codd. Σ Greg. Cor.
497 κρᾶτα τῆς ἐμῆς ὕπο Willink: τῆς ἐμῆς ὑπὲρ κάρα fere
     codd. (τῆς ἐμῆς ante θυγατρὸς MA; ὑπαὶ Tricl.)
502 ἂν τῆς MBOVAΣ: ἀντὶ Pr Sa L: ἔλαβ᾽ ἂν ἀντὶ Bergk
506 ἐγένετο μητέρα codd. (γένετο VK): transp. Porson

MEN. He is; and if he is in misfortune, I
have obligations towards him.
TY. You have become barbarized, being so   485
long among barbarians.
MEN. It is Greek always to honour one's
kinsman.
TY. Aye, and also not to aim to be above
the law.
MEN. Everything based on compulsion is held
slavish among the intelligent.
TY. Well, you can keep that doctrine. I
won't adopt it.
MEN. Because your testy old age is not   490
intelligent.
TY. What has an intelligence-contest to do
with this fellow, if seemly and unseemly are
obvious to everyone? What man has ever behaved
more stupidly than he has? He paid no regard
to what was right and did not take recourse to
the standard Greek procedure. I mean, when   495
Agamemnon gave out his life-breath, smitten on
the head by my daughter - a most horrid deed,
I shall never condone it - he ought to have
imposed the just penalty for bloodshed,   500
certainly, while aiming for religious correctness, and thrown his mother out of the house.
He would have got credit for sanity out of the
calamity, he would be keeping to the law, and
he would be a righteous man. As it is, he has
come to the same plight as his mother; for while
he was justified in thinking her wicked, he   505
acted more wickedly himself in killing her.

I will just ask you this, Menelaus. Suppose
Orestes were one day to be killed by the wife
sharing his bed, and suppose his son in turn
is to kill his mother, and then *his* son pay   510
off that murder with another - how far will it
go till the end of the troubles? Our fathers
of old ordered these matters well: they were
not for allowing a man who had blood on his
hands to come into anyone's sight or meet them,
but for rehabilitating him by banishment, not   515

αἰεὶ γὰρ εἷς ἔμελλ᾽ ἐνέξεσθαι φόνῳ,
τὸ λοίσθιον μίασμα λαμβάνων χερός.
ἐγὼ δὲ μισῶ μὲν γυναῖκας ἀνοσίους,
πρώτην δὲ θυγατέρ᾽, ἣ πόσιν κατέκτανεν·
(Ἑλένην τε, τὴν σὴν ἄλοχον, οὔποτ᾽ αἰνέσω,520
οὐδ᾽ ἂν προσείποιμ᾽· οὐδὲ σὲ ζηλῶ, κακῆς
γυναικὸς ἐλθόνθ᾽ οὕνεκ᾽ εἰς Τροίας πέδον·)
ἀμυνῶ δ᾽, ὅσον περ δυνατός εἰμι, τῷ νόμῳ,
τὸ θηριῶδες τοῦτο καὶ μιαιφόνον
παύων, ὃ καὶ γῆν καὶ πόλεις ὄλλυσ᾽ ἀεί.   525
   ἐπεὶ τίν᾽ εἶχες, ὦ τάλας, ψυχὴν τότε,
ὅτ᾽ ἐξέβαλλε μαστὸν ἱκετεύουσά σε
μήτηρ; ἐγὼ μὲν οὐκ ἰδὼν τἀκεῖ κακά
δακρύοις γέροντ᾽ ὀφθαλμὸν ἐκτήκω τάλας.
ἓν γοῦν λόγοισι τοῖς ἐμοῖς ὀμορροθεῖ·   530
μισῇ γε πρὸς θεῶν, καὶ τίνεις μητρὸς δίκας
μανίαις ἀλαίνων καὶ φόβοις. τί μαρτύρων
ἄλλων ἀκούειν δεῖ μ᾽, ἃ γ᾽ εἰσορᾶν πάρα;
   ὡς οὖν ἂν εἰδῇς, Μενέλεως· τοῖσιν θεοῖς
μὴ πρᾶσσ᾽ ἐναντί᾽, ὠφελεῖν τοῦτον θέλων,   535
ἔα δ᾽ ὑπ᾽ ἀστῶν καταφονευθῆναι πέτροις.
[ἢ μὴ ᾽πίβαινε Σπαρτιάτιδος χθονός.]
   θυγάτηρ δ᾽ ἐμὴ θανοῦσ᾽ ἔπραξεν ἔνδικα·
ἀλλ᾽ οὐχὶ πρὸς τοῦδ᾽ εἰκὸς ἦν αὐτὴν θανεῖν.
ἐγὼ δὲ τἄλλα μακάριος πέφυκ᾽ ἀνήρ,   540
πλὴν εἰς θυγατέρας· τοῦτο δ᾽ οὐκ εὐδαιμονῶ.
ΧΟ. ζηλωτὸς ὅστις ηὐτύχησεν εἰς τέκνα
καὶ μὴ ᾽πισήμους συμφορὰς ἐκτήσατο.
ΟΡ. ὦ γέρον, ἐγώ τοι πρὸς σὲ δειμαίνω λέγειν,
ὅπου σὲ μέλλω σήν τε λυπήσειν φρένα.   545
ἀπελθέτω δὴ τοῖς λόγοισιν ἐκποδών   548
τὸ γῆρας ἡμῖν τὸ σόν, ὅ μ᾽ ἐκπλήσσει λόγου,
καὶ καθ᾽ ὁδὸν εἶμι· νῦν δὲ σὴν ταρβῶ τρίχα. 550

---

517 χερός MBV²A: χεροῖν OV
528 fort. κοὐκ
530 γοῦν Schaefer: οὖν codd.
537 (= 626) del. Brunck (cum 536), Hermann; non hic resp. Σ
543 καὶ μὴ ᾽πισήμοις συμφοραῖς ὠδύρατο Stob.
548-50 huc transp. Hartung

killing him in turn. Otherwise there would
always be one person guilty of homicide, taking
over the latest pollution on his hands. As for
me, I hate impure women, and in first place my
daughter, who killed her husband (Helen too,
your wife, I shall never commend and should   520
not care to speak to, and I am not impressed
by your going to Troy-land on a bad woman's
account); but I will defend the law as far as
I am able, to curb this animal butchery which
is always the ruin of land and community.   525
    I mean, what were you feeling, you devil,
when your mother put forth her breast as she
pleaded with you? As for me, although I did
not see that awful scene, my poor old eye runs
away in tears. One thing at any rate supports   530
my argument: you are hated by the gods, and
are paying your mother's price by rushing about
in fits of frenzy and panic. What need have I
to hear from other witnesses things that are
here to be seen? So to make it clear to you,
Menelaus: don't go against the gods by choosing   535
to help him, but leave him to be stoned to
death by the townspeople. [Or else do not set
foot on Spartan soil.] My daughter in dying
had her just deserts, but it was not fitting
that she should be killed by him. I have been
a fortunate man otherwise, except as regards   540
my daughters. In this respect I am ill-starred.
    CHORUS-LEADER. Lucky is the man who has
been successful with his children and not got
ones who are notorious disasters!
    OR. Grandfather, I must say I am afraid of
answering you in a situation where I am bound   545
to hurt and annoy you. Assume our debate is
not to be hampered by your age, which deters
me from speaking, and I will go ahead; but in
reality I am inhibited by your grey hair.   550

ἐγὼ δ' ἀνόσιός εἰμι μητέρα κτανών·   546
ὅσιος δέ γ' ἕτερον ὄνομα, τιμωρῶν πατρί.   547
τί χρῆν με δρᾶσαι; δύο γὰρ ἀντίθες δυοῖν· 551
πατὴρ μὲν ἐφύτευσέν με, σὴ δ' ἔτικτε παῖς,
τὸ σπέρμ' ἄρουρα παραλαβοῦσ' ἄλλου πάρα·
ἄνευ δὲ πατρὸς τέκνον οὐκ εἴη ποτ' ἄν.
ἐλογισάμην οὖν τῷ γένους ἀρχηγέτῃ   555
μᾶλλόν μ' ἀμῦναι τῆς ὑποστάσης τροφάς.
ἡ σὴ δὲ θυγάτηρ – μητέρ' αἰδοῦμαι λέγειν –
ἰδίοισιν ὑμεναίοισι κοὐχὶ σώφροσιν
εἰς ἀνδρὸς ᾔει λέκτρ'· ἐμαυτόν, ἢν λέγω
κακῶς ἐκείνην, ἐξερῶ· λέξω δ' ὅμως.   560
Αἴγισθος ἦν ὁ κρυπτὸς ἐν δόμοις πόσις·
τοῦτον κατέκτειν', ἐπὶ δ' ἔθυσα μητέρα,
ἀνόσια μὲν δρῶν, ἀλλὰ τιμωρῶν πατρί.
ἐφ' οἷς δ' ἀπειλεῖς ὡς πετρωθῆναί με χρή,
ἄκουσον ὡς ἅπασαν Ἑλλάδ' ὠφελῶ.   565
εἰ γὰρ γυναῖκες εἰς τόδ' ἥξουσιν θράσους,
ἄνδρας φονεύειν, καταφυγὰς ποιούμεναι
εἰς τέκνα, μαστοῖς τὸν ἔλεον θηρώμεναι,
παρ' οὐδὲν αὐταῖς ἦν ἂν ὀλλύναι πόσεις
ἐπίκλημ' ἐχούσαις ὅτι τύχοι· δράσας δ' ἐγώ   570
δεῖν', ὡς σὺ κομπεῖς, τόνδ' ἔπαυσα τὸν νόμον.
μισῶν δὲ μητέρ' ἐνδίκως ἀπώλεσα,
ἥτις μεθ' ὅπλων ἄνδρ' ἀπόντ' ἐκ δωμάτων
πάσης ὑπὲρ γῆς Ἑλλάδος στρατηλάτην
προύδωκε κοὐκ ἔσωσ' ἀκήρατον λέχος·   575
ἐπεὶ δ' ἁμαρτοῦσ' ᾔσθετ', οὐχ αὑτῇ δίκην
ἐπέθηκεν, ἀλλ', ὡς μὴ δίκην δοίη πόσει,
ἐζημίωσε πατέρα κἀπέκτειν' ἐμόν.
πρὸς θεῶν – ἐν οὐ καλῷ μὲν ἐμνήσθην θεῶν
φόνον δικάζων· εἰ δὲ δὴ τὰ μητέρος   580
σιγῶν ἐπῄνουν, τί μ' ἂν ἔδρασ' ὁ κατθανών;
οὐκ ἄν με μισῶν ἀνεχόρευ' Ἐρινύσιν;

---

546   ἐγὦδ'· Hermann
559   εἰς ἄλλ' ἐσῄει F.W.Schmidt
564   χρή MBA: δεῖ OV

My position is that I am outside the law in   546
having killed my mother, but also within it,   547
by an alternative title, as the avenger of my
father. What ought I to have done? I mean,   551
set two things against two others. My father
planted me, and your daughter bore me –
ploughland taking over the seed from another:
without the father there would never be a child.
So I reckoned I should rather take the side of   555
the author of my birth than of her who undertook
the fostering. And your daughter – I hesitate to
say my mother – in private nuptials, not the
sensible kind, was visiting a man's bed. If I
speak ill of her, I shall be proclaiming it   560
of myself, but I will speak it all the same.
Aegisthus was the secret husband in the house:
I killed him, and thereupon made sacrifice of
my mother, doing an unholy thing, but avenging
my father.
    As for the grounds on which you threaten me
with stoning, hear how I am the benefactor of   565
all Greece. I mean, if women are going to
have the effrontery to murder their men, taking
refuge with their children, angling for mercy
with their breasts, it would cost them nothing
to do away with their husbands when they have
a grievance of any kind; but I, by acting   570
monstrously (as you claim), have put a stop
to this practice.
    It was in justifiable loathing that I killed
my mother: she betrayed her husband when he was
away from home under arms, as commander for all
Greece, and she did not keep the marriage-bed   575
pure; and when she realized her mistake, she
did not punish herself, but, to avoid being
punished by her husband, she penalized my
father and killed him. In heaven's name – hardly
appropriate to mention heaven in judging murder,
but anyway – supposing I were condoning my   580
mother's conduct by saying nothing, what would
the victim have done to me? Would he not hate
me and be dancing me about with his Erinyes?

ἦ μητρὶ μὲν πάρεισι σύμμαχοι θεαί,
τῷ δ' οὐ πάρεισι, μᾶλλον ἠδικημένῳ;
　σύ τοι φυτεύσας θυγατέρ' ὦ γέρον κακὴν　585
ἀπώλεσάς με· διὰ τὸ κείνης γὰρ θράσος
πατρὸς στερηθεὶς ἐγενόμην μητροκτόνος.
ὁρᾷς; Ὀδυσσέως ἄλοχον οὐ κατέκτανεν
Τηλέμαχος· οὐ γὰρ ἐπεγάμει πόσει πόσιν,
μένει δ' ἐν οἴκοις ὑγιὲς εὐνατήριον.　590
　ὁρᾷς δ' Ἀπόλλων', ὃς μεσομφάλους ἕδρας
ναίων βροτοῖσι στόμα νέμει σαφέστατον·
[ᾧ πειθόμεσθα πάνθ' ὅσ'ἂν κεῖνος λέγῃ·]
τούτῳ πιθόμενος τὴν τεκοῦσαν ἔκτανον.
ἐκεῖνον ἡγεῖσθ' ἀνόσιον καὶ κτείνετε·　595
ἐκεῖνος ἥμαρτ', οὐκ ἐγώ. τί χρῆν με δρᾶν;
ἢ οὐκ ἀξιόχρεως ὁ θεὸς ἀναφέροντί μοι
μίασμα λῦσαι; ποῖ τις οὖν ἔτ'ἂν φύγοι,
εἰ μὴ ὁ κελεύσας ῥύσεταί με μὴ θανεῖν;
ἀλλ' ὡς μὲν οὐκ εὖ μὴ λέγ' εἴργασται τάδε,　600
ἡμῖν δὲ τοῖς δράσασιν οὐκ εὐδαιμόνως.
[γάμοι δ' ὅσοις μὲν εὖ καθεστᾶσιν βροτῶν,
μακάριος αἰών· οἷς δὲ μὴ πίπτουσιν εὖ,
τά τ' ἔνδον εἰσὶ τά τε θύραζε δυστυχεῖς.]
ΧΟ.　αἰεὶ γυναῖκες ἐμποδὼν ταῖς συμφοραῖς　605
ἔφυσαν ἀνδρῶν πρὸς τὸ δυσχερέστερον.
ΤΥ.　ἐπεὶ θρασύνῃ κοὐχ ὑποστέλλῃ λόγῳ,
οὕτω δ' ἀμείβῃ μ' ὥστε μ' ἀλγῆσαι φρένα,
μᾶλλόν μ' ἀνάψεις ἐπὶ σὸν ἐξελθεῖν φόνον·
καλὸν πάρεργον δ' αὐτὸ θήσομαι πόνων　610
ὧν οὕνεκ' ἦλθον, θυγατρὶ κοσμήσων τάφον.
μολὼν γὰρ εἰς ἔκκλητον Ἀργείων ὄχλον

586　τὸ κείνης γὰρ Triclinius: γὰρ τὸ κ. codd.: τὸ γὰρ Canter
588-90 del. Dindorf
591　fort. δ' Ἀπόλλω γ'
593　del. Nauck
602-4 del. Herwerden
604　θύρασι Herwerden
606　δυσχερέστερον recc. (codd. Thomani): δυστυχέστερον
　　HMBOVAΣ gnomol. Vatoped., -τατον Stob.
609　ἀνάψεις F (aut F²) Sa ξ: ἀνάξεις HMBOVA

Or is it that my mother has goddesses at hand
to fight for her but he, the more greatly
wronged, has none?

It was you, grandfather, who caused my   585
downfall by fathering a wicked daughter;
because of her temerity I lost my father, and
that made me a matricide. Do you see, Odysseus'
wife has not been killed by Telemachus; that's
because she did not go taking one husband after
another, and the bedchamber remains untainted   590
in the house.

And do you see Apollo, who dwells at the
central Navel and who gives out to mortals a
most sure voice: [whom we obey in everything
he says:] it was in obedience to him that I
killed my mother. Outlaw him, execute him, his 595
was the error, not mine. What should I have
done? Is the god not credit-worthy for me to
refer to him to clear my pollution? So where
else can one run, if he that told me to do it
will not save me from death?

No, do not say that this is not a good deed   600
done, only that for me, the doer, it was ill-
starred. [For men whose marriages are well
constituted, their lifetime is enviably happy;
but those whose marriages do not fall out well
are blighted both indoors and out.]

CHORUS-LEADER. Women always complicate men's
affairs in the more disagreeable direction.   606

TY. Since you are being insolent and do
not moderate your words, and give me such
answer that I feel pained, you will fire me
the more to go for your death. I shall reckon
it a nice extra to the task I came for, to   610
tend my daughter's tomb: I shall go to the
Argives' convocation and bring the city

101

ἑκοῦσαν οὐχ ἑκοῦσαν ἐπισείσω πόλιν
σοὶ σῇ τ' ἀδελφῇ, λεύσιμον δοῦναι δίκην.
μᾶλλον δ' ἐκείνη σοῦ θανεῖν ἐστ' ἀξία,   615
ἢ τῇ τεκούσῃ σ' ἠγρίωσ', εἰς οὓς ἀεί
πέμπουσα μύθους ἐπὶ τὸ δυσμενέστερον,
ὀνείρατ' ἀγγέλλουσα τἀγαμέμνονος
καὶ τοῦθ' ὃ μισήσειαν Αἰγίσθου λέχος
οἱ νέρτεροι θεοί· καὶ γὰρ ἐνθάδ' ἦν πικρόν·620
ἕως ὑφῆψε δῶμ' ἀνηφαίστῳ πυρί.
    Μενέλαε, σοὶ δὲ τάδε λέγω, δράσω τε πρός·
εἰ τοὐμὸν ἔχθος ἐναριθμῇ κῆδός τ' ἐμόν,
μὴ τῷδ' ἀμύνειν φόνον ἐναντίον θεοῖς,
ἔα δ' ὑπ' ἀστῶν καταφονευθῆναι πέτροις   625
ἢ μὴ 'πίβαινε Σπαρτιάτιδος χθονός.
τοσαῦτ' ἀκούσας ἴσθι, μηδὲ δυσσεβεῖς
ἕλῃ παρώσας εὐσεβεστέρους φίλους.
ἡμᾶς δ' ἀπ' οἴκων ἄγετε τῶνδε, πρόσπολοι.

ΟΡ. στεῖχ', ὡς ἀθορύβως οὑπιὼν ἡμῖν λόγος   630
    πρὸς τόνδ' ἵκηται, γήρας ἀποφυγὼν τὸ σόν.
        Μενέλαε, ποῖ σὸν πόδ' ἐπὶ συννοίᾳ κυκλεῖς,
    διπλῆς μερίμνης διπτύχους ἰὼν ὁδούς;
ΜΕ. ἔασον· ἐν ἐμαυτῷ τι συννοούμενος
    ὅπῃ τράπωμαι τῆς τύχης ἀμηχανῶ.   635
ΟΡ. μή νυν πέραινε τὴν δόκησιν, ἀλλ' ἐμούς
    λόγους ἀκούσας πρόσθε, βουλεύου τότε.
ΜΕ. λέγ'· εὖ γὰρ εἶπας. ἔστιν οὗ σιγὴ λόγου
    κρείσσων γένοιτ' ἄν, ἔστι δ' οὗ σιγῆς λόγος.
ΟΡ. λέγοιμ'ἂν ἤδη. τὰ μακρὰ τῶν σμικρῶν λόγων 640
    ἐπίπροσθέν ἐστι καὶ σαφῆ μᾶλλον κλυεῖν.
        ἐμοὶ σὺ τῶν σῶν, Μενέλεως, μηδὲν δίδου,
    ἃ δ'ἔλαβες ἀπόδος, πατρὸς ἐμοῦ λαβὼν πάρα.
    οὐ χρήματ' εἶπον· χρήματ', ἢν ψυχὴν ἐμήν

---

613 οὐχ ἑκοῦσαν Canter (cf. Σ): οὐκ ἄκουσαν codd.
     ἀνασείσω HVAʸᵖ (ἐκπείσω A): fort. ἐνσείσω
625 (= 536) del. Kayser
638 ἔστιν Kirchhoff: ἔστι δ' codd.

crashing down on you and your sister whether it
will or no, so that you pay the penalty of
stoning. She deserves to die more than you   615
do: she enraged you against your mother by
constantly sending tales to your ear to foment
hate, reporting her dreams of Agamemnon and
this adultery with Aegisthus - may the nether
gods' hatred fall upon it, for in this life   620
too it was galling - till she set the house
alight with a fire not of Hephaestus.
    To you, Menelaus, I say this, and I will
act on it too: if you hold my hostility in
any account, and my connexion with you, don't
protect Orestes' life in opposition to the gods,
but leave him to be stoned to death by the   625
townspeople, or else do not set foot on Spartan
soil. Let that be sufficient warning, and
don't choose the wicked as your friends,
pushing the righteous aside. As for me, take
me away from this house, servants.
    [*Exit Tyndareos and attendants. Menelaus paces
about in thought.*]
    OR. Go your way, so that what I have to   630
say next may reach my uncle without interruptions,
freed from your elderly presence. - Menelaus,
where are you going, circling about in thought,
treading the divided ways of divided concern?
    MEN. Let me be. I am thinking something
over in my mind, in doubt which course of   635
fortune to turn along.
    OR. Well, don't come to conclusions from
first impressions. First hear what I have to
say, and then consider your options.
    MEN. Say on; you're right - in some cases
silence may turn out preferable to speech, but
in others speech to silence.
    OR. Then I will have my say. Long speeches 640
put little ones in the shade, and are more
convincing to listen to.
    You need not offer me anything of yours,
Menelaus, only repay your debt, what you got
from my father. I don't mean assets: it *is*

σώσῃς, ἅπερ μοι φίλτατ' ἐστὶ τῶν ἐμῶν.   645
    ἀδικῶ· λαβεῖν χρή μ' ἀντὶ τοῦδε τοῦ κακοῦ
ἄδικόν τι παρὰ σοῦ· καὶ γὰρ Ἀγαμέμνων πατήρ
ἀδίκως ἀθροίσας Ἑλλάδ' ἦλθ' ὑπ' Ἴλιον
οὐκ ἐξαμαρτὼν αὐτός, ἀλλ' ἁμαρτίαν
τῆς σῆς γυναικὸς ἀδικίαν τ' ἰώμενος.   650
    ἓν μὲν τόδ' ἡμῖν ἀνθ' ἑνὸς δοῦναί σε χρή·
ἀπέδοτο δ', ὡς χρὴ τοῖς φίλοισι τοὺς φίλους,
τὸ σῶμ' ἀληθῶς, σοὶ παρ' ἀσπίδ' ἐκπονῶν,
ὅπως σὺ τὴν σὴν ἀπολάβοις ξυνάορον·
ἀπότεισον οὖν μοι ταὐτὸ τοῦτ' ἐκεῖ λαβών   655
μίαν πονήσας ἡμέραν, ἡμῶν ὕπερ
σωτήριος στάς, μὴ δέκ' ἐκπλήσας ἔτη.
ἃ δ' Αὐλὶς ἔλαβε σφάγι' ἐμῆς ὁμοσπόρου,
ἐῶ σ' ἔχειν ταῦθ'· Ἑρμιόνην μὴ κτεῖνε σύ·
δεῖ γάρ σ' ἐμοῦ πράσσοντος ὡς πράσσω τὰ νῦν   660
πλέον φέρεσθαι, κἀμὲ συγγνώμην ἔχειν·
ψυχὴν δ' ἐμὴν δὸς τῷ ταλαιπώρῳ πατρί·
[κἀμῆς ἀδελφῆς, παρθένου μακρὸν χρόνον·]
θανὼν γὰρ οἶκον ὀρφανὸν λείψω πατρός.
    ἐρεῖς· ἀδύνατον. αὐτὸ τοῦτο· τοὺς φίλους   665
ἐν τοῖς κακοῖς χρὴ τοῖς φίλοισιν ὠφελεῖν·
ὅταν δ' ὁ δαίμων εὖ διδῷ, τί δεῖ φίλων;
ἀρκεῖ γὰρ αὐτὸς ὁ θεὸς ὠφελεῖν θέλων.
    φιλεῖν δάμαρτα πᾶσιν Ἕλλησιν δοκεῖς
(κοὐχ ὑποτρέχων σε τοῦτο θωπείᾳ λέγω)·   670
ταύτης ἱκνοῦμαί σ' – ὦ μέλεος ἐμῶν κακῶν,
εἰς οἷον ἥκω. τί δέ; ταλαιπωρεῖν με δεῖ·
ὑπὲρ γὰρ οἴκου παντὸς ἱκετεύω τάδε.
ὦ πατρὸς ὅμαιμε θεῖε, τὸν κατὰ χθονός
θανόντ' ἀκούειν τάδε δόκει, ποτωμένην   675
ψυχὴν ὑπὲρ σοῦ, καὶ λέγειν ἁγὼ λέγω.
[ταῦτ' εἴς τε δάκρυα καὶ γόους καὶ συμφοράς]

---

654 ἀπολάβοις rec.: -βῃς MBOVA Eust.
663 del. Paley
667 δεῖ BˢV Arist. Plut.: χρὴ (666) MBOA gnomol. Vatoped.
672 δεῖ: χρὴ (sic) Mˠᵖ
677 susp. Wecklein, del. Biehl (677-9 Paley)

assets if you save my life, the most precious   645
ones I have.

I'm a wrongdoer. To balance this evil I
need to get a wrongdoing from you, just as
Agamemnon my father wrongfully mustered Greece
and went up to Ilion not from error of his own
but to put right the error and wrongdoing of   650
your wife.

That's one thing you should give me in return
for another. And then, as kinsmen should for
kin, he gave his body sincerely, exerting
himself at your shield-side so that you could
get your consort back: so repay me this same   655
thing that you were given there, by exerting
yourself just for one day, taking a stand for
my salvation, not making it ten whole years. As
for what Aulis took, the slaughter of my sister,
I'll let you have that, you needn't kill
Hermione. After all, when I am faring as I am   660
at present, you're bound to get the better of
the bargain, and I'm bound to concede it. But
grant my poor father *my* life [and my sister's,
who has long remained unwed], for if I die I
shall leave his house bereft.

You'll say "impossible". That's just it: 665
it's in time of trouble that people must help
their friends and family. When Fortune is being
generous, what need is there of human attachments? God is enough by himself when he
chooses to help.

You have the reputation in all Greece of
loving your wife, and I'm not trying to sneak   670
under your defences by flattery in saying so.
In her name I beseech you ... Oh, the plight
I am in, to have come to this! But what of it?
I shall have to endure it; after all, I am
making this entreaty for the sake of my whole
house. O uncle, same blood as my father, imagine
the dead man below to be listening to all this,   675
a soul hovering over you, and to be saying what
I am saying! [These things for my weeping and
wailing and woes] I have spoken, I have made my

105

εἴρηκα κἀπήτηκα, τὴν σωτηρίαν
θηρῶν, ὃ πάντες κοὐκ ἐγὼ ζητῶ μόνος.
ΧΟ. κἀγώ σ᾽ ἱκνοῦμαι καὶ γυνή περ οὖσ᾽ ὅμως   680
τοῖς δεομένοισιν ὠφελεῖν· οἷός τε δ᾽ εἶ.
ΜΕ. Ὀρέστ᾽, ἐγώ τοι σὸν καταιδοῦμαι κάρα
καὶ ξυμπονῆσαι σοῖς κακοῖσι βούλομαι·
καὶ χρὴ γὰρ οὕτω τῶν ὁμαιμόνων κακά
ξυνεκκομίζειν, δύναμιν ἣν διδῷ θεός,   685
θνῄσκοντα καὶ κτείνοντα τοὺς ἐναντίους.
τὸ δ᾽ αὖ δύνασθαι πρὸς θεῶν χρῄζω τυχεῖν·
ἥκω γὰρ ἀνδρῶν συμμάχων κενὸν δόρυ
ἔχων, πόνοισι μυρίοις ἀλώμενος
σμικρᾷ σὺν ἀλκῇ τῶν λελειμμένων φίλων.   690
μάχῃ μὲν οὖν ἂν οὐχ ὑπερβαλοίμεθα
Πελασγὸν Ἄργος· εἰ δὲ μαλθακοῖς λόγοις
δυναίμεθ᾽, ἐνταῦθ᾽ ἐλπίδος προήκομεν.
σμικροῖσι γὰρ τὰ μεγάλα πῶς ἕλοι τις ἂν
πόνοισιν; ἀμαθὲς καὶ τὸ βούλεσθαι τάδε.   695
ὅταν γὰρ ἡβᾷ δῆμος εἰς ὀργὴν πεσών,
ὅμοιον ὥστε πῦρ κατασβέσαι λάβρον·
εἰ δ᾽ ἡσύχως τις αὐτὸν ἐντείνοντι μέν
χαλῶν ὑπείκοι, καιρὸν εὐλαβούμενος,
ἴσως ἂν ἐκπνεύσει᾽· ὅταν δ᾽ ἀνῇ πνοάς,   700
τύχοις ἂν αὐτοῦ ῥᾳδίως ὅσον θέλεις·
ἔνεστι δ᾽ οἶκτος, ἔνι δὲ καὶ θυμὸς μέγας,
καραδοκοῦντι κτῆμα τιμιώτατον.
ἐλθὼν δὲ Τυνδάρεών τέ σοι πειράσομαι
πόλιν τε πεῖσαι τῷ λίαν χρῆσθαι καλῶς·   705
καὶ ναῦς γὰρ ἐνταθεῖσα πρὸς βίαν ποδί
ἔβαψεν, ἔστη δ᾽ αὖθις ἢν χαλᾷ πόδα.
μισεῖ γὰρ ὁ θεὸς τὰς ἄγαν προθυμίας,
μισοῦσι δ᾽ ἀστοί. δεῖ δ᾽ ἔμ᾽ - οὐκ ἄλλως λέγω -
σῴζειν σε σοφίᾳ, μὴ βίᾳ τῶν κρεισσόνων.   710
ἀλκῇ δέ σ᾽ οὐκ ἄν, ᾗ σὺ δοξάζεις ἴσως,

---

693 προήκομεν V: προσήκομεν ΜΒΟΑΣᵏ
694 γὰρ KSa: μὲν γὰρ ΜΒΟΝΣᵏ: μὲν Α
698 αὐτὸς ξ
700 ἐκνεύσει᾽ Wilamowitz
704 δὲ Τ. τέ σοι: δ᾽ ἐγώ σοι Τ. Μʸᵖ
705 πείσας Hermann, πείθων Weil

claim, in the pursuit of my survival, a thing
that all men, not I alone seek.
    CHORUS-LEADER. I too entreat you, woman   680
though I am, to help these in their need. You
have the power.
    MEN. Orestes, be assured that I respect you
and want to share the toil of your troubles;
for so one *should* share the burden of one's
kinsmen's troubles - if God provides the means - 685
fighting their enemies to the death. But then,
as to the means, I need to get it from the gods;
for I have come with spear-force deficient in
fighting men, a wanderer through countless
toils with small strength of remaining   690
supporters. So in battle we would not be able
to overcome Pelasgian Argos; but whether I
could do it with soothing words - that's the
area of hope I find myself in now. I mean, how
could one capture a great prize by small
efforts? It is stupid even to entertain the   695
ambition. For when the people turns angry and
is rampant, it is like having a raging fire to
put out. But if one gently slackens oneself
and gives way so long as it strains, taking
care with one's timing, it may well blow itself
out, and when it abates, you may easily get   700
all you want from it. There is compassion there,
there is also passion, a most valuable property
for him who waits and watches.
    I will go, then, and try to persuade both
Tyndareos and the city for you to direct their 705
vehemence wisely. For a ship too, if forcibly
strung tight by the sheet, dips under, but it
rights itself again if one slackens the sheet.
God, you see, abhors zealots, and so do the
citizens. So I must try to save you (yes, I
don't dispute that) by cleverness, not by   710
force in the face of superior strength. I
could not save you by valour, in the way you
perhaps imagine; it's no easy matter with one

σώσαιμ' ἄν· οὐ γὰρ ῥᾴδιον λόγχῃ μιᾷ
στῆσαι τροπαῖα τῶν κακῶν ἃ σοὶ πάρα.
οὐ γάρ ποτ' Ἄργους γαῖαν εἰς τὸ μαλθακόν
προσηγόμεσθα· νῦν δ' ἀναγκαίως ἔχει   715
δούλοισιν εἶναι τοῖς σοφοῖσι τῆς τύχης.

ΟΡ. ὦ πλὴν γυναικὸς οὕνεκα στρατηλατεῖν
τἄλλ' οὐδέν, ὦ κάκιστε τιμωρεῖν φίλοις,
φεύγεις ἀποστραφείς με, τὰ δ' Ἀγαμέμνονος   720
φροῦδ'; ἄφιλος ἦσθ' ἄρ' ὦ πάτερ πράσσων κακῶς.
οἴμοι, προδέδομαι, κοὐκέτ' εἰσὶν ἐλπίδες,
ὅπῃ τραπόμενος θάνατον Ἀργείων φύγω·
οὗτος γὰρ ἦν μοι καταφυγὴ σωτηρίας.
    ἀλλ' εἰσορῶ γὰρ τόνδε φίλτατον βροτῶν   725
Πυλάδην δρόμῳ στείχοντα Φωκέων ἄπο,
ἡδεῖαν ὄψιν· πιστὸς ἐν κακοῖς ἀνήρ
κρείσσων γαλήνης ναυτίλοισιν εἰσορᾶν.

ΠΥΛΑΔΗΣ
θᾶσσον ἢ μ' ἐχρῆν προβαίνων ἱκόμην δι' ἄστεως,
σύλλογον πόλεως ἀκούσας, τὸν δ' ἰδὼν αὐτὸς σαφῶς, 730
ἐπὶ σὲ σύγγονόν τε τὴν σήν, ὡς κτενοῦντας αὐτίκα.
τί τάδε; πῶς ἔχεις; τί πράσσεις, φίλταθ' ἡλίκων ἐμοί
καὶ φίλων καὶ συγγενείας; πάντα γὰρ τάδ' εἶ σύ μοι.
ΟΡ. οἰχόμεσθ', ὡς ἐν βραχεῖ σοι τἀμὰ δηλώσω κακά.
ΠΥ. συγκατασκάπτοις ἂν ἡμᾶς· κοινὰ γὰρ τὰ τῶν φίλων. 735
ΟΡ. Μενέλεως κάκιστος ἐς ἐμὲ καὶ κασιγνήτην ἐμήν.
ΠΥ. εἰκότως, κακῆς γυναικὸς ἄνδρα γίγνεσθαι κακόν.
ΟΡ. ὥσπερ οὐκ ἐλθὼν ἔμοιγε ταὐτὸν ἀπέδωκεν μολών.
ΠΥ. ἦ γὰρ ἔστιν ὡς ἀληθῶς τήνδ' ἀφιγμένος χθόνα;
ΟΡ. χρόνιος· ἀλλ' ὅμως τάχιστα κακὸς ἐφωράθη φίλοις. 740
ΠΥ. καὶ δάμαρτα τὴν κακίστην ναυστολῶν ἐλήλυθεν;

---

730 ὄντ' ἰδών τ' Cron (τ' ὄντ' ἰδών τ' Willink)

spear to claim the field from the ills that
beset you. For I never used to attempt to win
over the land of Argos to mollity; but now it   715
is unavoidable for the intelligent to take
orders from fortune. [*Exit.*]

OR. You good for nothing but to make war
for a woman, you most worthless when it comes
to succouring your kin, do you turn your back
on me and run away, is Agamemnon's cause   720
finished? So you are friendless after all,
father, when things go badly. Oh, I am
betrayed: there are no further prospects of a
way along which to turn to escape death from
the Argives. Menelaus was my refuge for survival.

[*Pylades is seen approaching at speed.*]

But stay, here I see my closest friend,   725
Pylades, coming at a run from Phocis - a welcome
sight! A trusty man in time of trouble is better
to behold than calm water for mariners.

PYLADES. I came faster than I had to through
the town, having heard of a gathering of the
citizens (and seen some of it distinctly   730
myself) against you and your sister - that they
mean to kill you directly. What is this? How
are you, what's your state of affairs, favourite
of my age-group, of my friends, of my relations,
for you're all these things to me?

OR. I am finished, to tell you my plight
in brief.

PYL. If that were so, you'd demolish me too. 735
Friends share everything.

OR. Menelaus is behaving very badly towards
me and my sister.

PYL. Only to be expected - that a bad woman
should turn out to have a bad husband.

OR. To me at any rate his coming has brought
the same benefit as if he had not come.

PYL. You mean he really has arrived in this
country?

OR. At long last - yet in no time he's been   740
shown up as false to his nearest.

PYL. And has he shipped home his disreputable
wife?

ΟΡ. οὐκ ἐκεῖνος, ἀλλ' ἐκείνη κεῖνον ἐνθάδ' ἤγαγεν.
ΠΥ. ποῦ 'στιν, ἢ πλείστους 'Αχαιῶν ὤλεσεν γυνὴ μία;
ΟΡ. ἐν δόμοις ἐμοῖσιν, εἰ δὴ τούσδ' ἐμοὺς καλεῖν χρεών.
ΠΥ. σὺ δὲ τίνας λόγους ἔλεξας σοῦ κασιγνήτῳ πατρός;   745
ΟΡ. μή μ' ἰδεῖν θανόνθ' ὑπ'ἀστῶν καὶ κασιγνήτην ἐμήν.
ΠΥ. πρὸς θεῶν, τί πρὸς τάδ' εἶπε; τόδε γὰρ εἰδέναι θέλω.
ΟΡ. ηὐλαβεῖθ', ὃ τοῖς φίλοισι δρῶσιν οἱ κακοὶ φίλοι.
ΠΥ. σκῆψιν εἰς ποίαν προβαίνων; τοῦτο πάντ' ἔχω μαθών.
ΟΡ. οὗτος ἦλθ' ὁ τὰς ἀρίστας θυγατέρας σπείρας πατήρ.   750
ΠΥ. Τυνδάρεων λέγεις· ἴσως σοι θυγατέρος
                                        θυμούμενος.
ΟΡ. αἰσθάνῃ. τὸ τοῦδε κῆδος μᾶλλον εἵλετ' ἢ πατρός.
ΠΥ. κοὐκ ἐτόλμησεν πόνων σῶν ἀντιλάζυσθαι παρών;
ΟΡ. οὐ γὰρ αἰχμητὴς πέφυκεν, ἐν γυναιξὶ δ' ἄλκιμος.
ΠΥ. ἐν κακοῖς ἄρ'εἶ μεγίστοις· καί σ'ἀναγκαῖον θανεῖν;   755
ΟΡ. ψῆφον ἀμφ' ἡμῶν πολίτας ἐπὶ φόνῳ θέσθαι χρεών.
ΠΥ. ἢ κρινεῖ τί χρῆμα; λέξον· διὰ φόβου γὰρ ἔρχομαι.
ΟΡ. ἢ θανεῖν ἢ ζῆν· ὁ μῦθος οὐ μακρὸς μακρῶν πέρι.
ΠΥ. φεῦγέ νυν λιπὼν μέλαθρα σὺν κασιγνήτῃ σέθεν.
ΟΡ. οὐχ ὁρᾷς; φυλασσόμεσθα φρουρίοισι πανταχῇ.   760
ΠΥ. εἶδον ἄστεως ἀγυιὰς τεύχεσιν πεφαργμένας.
ΟΡ. ὡσπερεὶ πόλις πρὸς ἐχθρῶν δῶμα πυργηρούμεθα.
ΠΥ. κἀμὲ νῦν ἐροῦ τί πάσχω· καὶ γὰρ αὐτὸς οἴχομαι.

---

750 σπείρων πατήρ ξ: κεκτημένος Σ^{γρ}
758 μῦθος VF: μῦθος δ' HMBOA
762 δῶμα Wecklein: σῶμα codd.

110

OR. It isn't he that has brought her, but she that has brought him.

PYL. Where is she, that has caused the most Achaean deaths for one woman?

OR. In my house – if one is to call this one mine.

PYL. And what did you say to your uncle?　　745

OR. That he should not stand by and see me and my sister killed by the citizens.

PYL. What in heaven's name did he say to that, I should like to know?

OR. He was cautious, as false friends are.

PYL. Taking his stand on what? When I hear this, I have it all.

OR. That father of champion daughters came　750 along.

PYL. You mean Tyndareos: angry at you about his daughter, I daresay.

OR. You have it. Menelaus preferred his connexion with him to that with my father.

PYL. And could not bring himself to take a personal share of your burdens?

OR. No. He is not a born warrior, only valiant among women.

PYL. Then you're in the direst trouble. Is　755 it inevitable you must actually die?

OR. The citizens have to cast their vote concerning us on the murder charge.

PYL. Vote to settle what? Tell me – I'm feeling afraid.

OR. Either life or death: it doesn't take long to say, but the things it refers to are long-lasting.

PYL. Then leave the house and flee with your sister.

OR. Can't you see? There are guard-posts　760 on the watch for us on every road.

PYL. I did see the city streets blocked with armour.

OR. Our house is besieged like a town by its enemies.

PYL. Now ask me in my turn what is happening

ΟΡ. πρὸς τίνος τοῦτ' ἂν προσείη τοῖς ἐμοῖς κακοῖς κακόν;
ΠΥ. Στροφίος ἤλασέν μ' ἀπ' οἴκων φυγάδα θυμωθεὶς πατήρ.   765
ΟΡ. ἴδιον ἢ κοινὸν πολίταις ἐπιφέρων ἔγκλημα τί;
ΠΥ. ὅτι συνηράμην φόνον σοι μητρός, ἀνόσιον λέγων.
ΟΡ. ὦ τάλας· ἔοικε καὶ σὲ τἀμὰ λυπήσειν κακά.
ΠΥ. οὐχὶ Μενέλεω τρόποισι χρώμεθ'· οἰστέον τάδε.
ΟΡ. οὐ φοβῇ μή σ' Ἄργος ὥσπερ κἄμ' ἀποκτεῖναι θέλῃ;   770
ΠΥ. οὐ προσήκομεν κολάζειν τοῖσδε, Φωκέων δὲ γῇ.
ΟΡ. δεινὸν οἱ πολλοί, κακούργους ὅταν ἔχωσι προστάτας.
ΠΥ. ἀλλ' ὅταν χρηστοὺς λάβωσι, χρηστὰ βουλεύουσ' ἀεί.
ΟΡ. εἶἑν. εἰς κοινὸν λέγειν χρή.
ΠΥ.   τίνος ἀναγκαίου πέρι;
ΟΡ. εἰ λέγοιμ' ἀστοῖσιν ἐλθών ...
ΠΥ.   ὡς ἔδρασας ἔνδικα;   775
ΟΡ. πατρὶ τιμωρῶν <γ'> ἐμαυτοῦ ...
ΠΥ.   μὴ λάβωσί σ' ἄσμενοι.
ΟΡ. ἀλλ' ὑποπτήξας σιωπῇ κατθάνω;
ΠΥ.   δειλὸν τόδε.
ΟΡ. πῶς ἂν οὖν δρῴην;
ΠΥ.   ἔχεις τιν' ἣν μένῃς σωτηρίαν;
ΟΡ. οὐκ ἔχω.
ΠΥ.   μολόντι δ' ἐλπίς ἐστι σωθῆναι κακῶν;
ΟΡ. εἰ τύχοι, γένοιτ' ἄν.   780
ΠΥ.   οὐκοῦν τοῦτο κρεῖσσον ἢ μένειν.
ΟΡ. ἀλλὰ δῆτ' ἔλθω;
ΠΥ.   θανὼν γοῦν ὧδε κάλλιον θανῇ.
ΟΡ. εὖ λέγεις· φεύγω τὸ δειλὸν τῇδε.
ΠΥ.   μᾶλλον ἢ μένων.   783
ΟΡ. καὶ τὸ πρᾶγμά γ' ἔνδικόν μοι.
ΠΥ.   τόδε δοκεῖν εὔχου μόνον.   782

---

770 θέλῃ: βίαν Mᵞᵖ (scil. -κτείνῃ βίᾳ)
776 γ' add. Kirchhoff
777 δειλὸν MOˢV: δεινὸν BOA
782 post.783 transp. Morell (et ita Σ?): post 785 Weil
     πρᾶγμά γ' ξ: πρᾶγμ' MBOVA
     τόδε Paley: τὸ MBOVA: τῷ KLξ: τοῦ δοκεῖν ἔχου Lenting

112

to me; for I too am finished.

OR. By whose hand might this woe be added
to those I have?

PYL. Strophius my father has banished me   765
from his house in anger.

OR. Bringing what complaint against you,
private or in common with his people?

PYL. That I helped you undertake your
mother's murder; he declares me an outlaw.

OR. Oh no! It looks as if my troubles are
going to irk you too.

PYL. My ways are not Menelaus'. I must put
up with it.

OR. Aren't you afraid Argos may want to   770
put you to death as well as me?

PYL. I don't belong to these people to
punish but to Phocis.

OR. The mob is a formidable thing when it
has knavish leaders.

PYL. But whenever they find good ones, they
keep good counsel.

OR. All right. We must plan jointly.

PYL. What needs to be done?

OR. Suppose I went and told the assembly ... 775

PYL. That you acted rightly?

OR. In avenging my father, yes –

PYL. They may welcome the chance to seize you.

OR. But am I to die cowering in silence?

PYL. That would be craven.

OR. What should I do, then?

PYL. Have you any chance if you stay here?

OR. No.

PYL. But if you go there's a hope of
deliverance?

OR. With luck there could be.   780

PYL. So that's better than staying.

OR. Well then, shall I go?

PYL. At least if you die you'll die more
nobly so.

OR. You're right, I avoid cowardice this way.

PYL. More than by staying.

OR. Besides, there's justice in my case.

ΟΡ. καί τις ἄν γέ μ'οἰκτίσειε ...
ΠΥ.   μέγα γὰρ ηὐγένειά σου.
ΟΡ. θάνατον ἀσχάλλων πατρῷον.
ΠΥ.   πάντα ταῦτ' ἐν ὄμμασιν.   785
ΟΡ. ἰτέον, ὡς ἄνανδρον ὀκλέως κατθανεῖν.
ΠΥ.   αἰνῶ τάδε.
ΟΡ. ἦ λέγωμεν οὖν ἀδελφῇ ταῦτ' ἐμῇ;
ΠΥ.   μὴ πρὸς θεῶν.
ΟΡ. δάκρυα γοῦν γένοιτ' ἄν.
ΠΥ.   οὔκουν οὗτος οἰωνὸς μέγας.
ΟΡ. δηλαδὴ σιγᾶν ἄμεινον.
ΠΥ.   τῷ χρόνῳ τε κερδανεῖς.
ΟΡ. κεῖνό μοι μόνον πρόσαντες ...
ΠΥ.   τί τόδε καινὸν αὖ λέγεις;   790
ΟΡ. μὴ θεαί μ' οἴστρῳ κατάσχωσ'.
ΠΥ.   ἀλλὰ κηδεύσω σ' ἐγώ.
ΟΡ. δυσχερὲς ψαύειν νοσοῦντος ἀνδρός.
ΠΥ.   οὔκ ἔμοιγε σοῦ.
ΟΡ. εὐλαβοῦ λύσσης μετασχεῖν τῆς ἐμῆς.
ΠΥ.   τὸ δ' οὖν ἴτω.
ΟΡ. οὐκ ἄρ' ὀκνήσεις;
ΠΥ.   ὄκνος γὰρ τοῖς φίλοις κακὸν μέγα.
ΟΡ. ἕρπε νυν οἴαξ ποδός μοι ...
ΠΥ.   φίλα γ'ἔχων κηδεύματα.   795
ΟΡ. καί με πρὸς τύμβον πόρευσον πατρός ...
ΠΥ.   ὡς τί δὴ τόδε;
ΟΡ. ὥς νιν ἱκετεύσω με σῶσαι.
ΠΥ.   τό γε δίκαιον ὧδ' ἔχει.
ΟΡ. μητέρος δὲ μηδ' ἴδοιμι μνῆμα.
ΠΥ.   πολεμία γὰρ ἦν.
ἀλλ'ἔπειγ', ὡς μή σε πρόσθε ψῆφος Ἀργείων ἕλῃ,
περιβαλὼν πλευροῖς ἐμοῖσι πλευρὰ νωχελῆ νόσῳ·   800
ὡς ἐγὼ δι' ἄστεώς σε, σμικρὰ φροντίζων ὄχλου,
οὐδὲν αἰσχυνθεὶς ὀχήσω. ποῦ γὰρ ὢν δείξω φίλος,
εἴ σε μὴ 'ν δειναῖσιν ὄντα συμφοραῖς ἐπαρκέσω;

_____

789 τε Herwerden: δὲ MA: γε V: γὰρ BO
800 προσβαλὼν F.W.Schmidt
803 εἴ γε ... ὄντι Reeve (εἴ τι ... ὄντι Blaydes)

PYL. Only pray for it to be thought so.

OR. And people may take pity on me ...

PYL. Your noble blood counts for a lot, after all.

OR. In indignation at my father's death.   785

PYL. All this is in prospect.

OR. I must go. It is unmanly to die ingloriously.

PYL. I approve.

OR. Shall we tell my sister, then?

PYL. For heaven's sake no.

OR. Certainly there would be tears.

PYL. Then that would be a serious omen.

OR. Obviously better to say nothing.

PYL. And you'll save time.

OR. Only one worry stands in my way ...   790

PYL. What now?

OR. That the goddesses may catch me with their frenzy.

PYL. But I'll be looking after you.

OR. It's unpleasant to be in contact with a sick man.

PYL. Not with you, for me.

OR. Beware of catching my insanity.

PYL. Oh, let it ride.

OR. So you won't be reluctant?

PYL. No. Reluctance is a great vice in friends.

OR. Be moving, then, helmsman of my steps...795

PYL. I will, with affection for my charge.

OR. And guide me to the tomb of my father ...

PYL. With what intention?

OR. So that I can appeal to him to save me.

PYL. Justice at least requires it.

OR. As for my mother's memorial, I don't even want to set eyes on it.

PYL. No, she was your enemy. Now hurry, in case the Argives' vote gets you first; let your side that's torpid with disease lie across   800 mine. I'll bear you through the town with little care for the crowd, quite unashamed. In what circumstances am I to show I'm your friend if I don't help you when you're in dire straits?

ΟΡ. τοῦτ' ἐκεῖνο, κτᾶσθ'ἑταίρους, μὴ τὸ συγγενὲς μόνον·
    ὡς ἀνὴρ ὅστις τρόποισι συντακῇ θυραῖος ὤν   805
    μυρίων κρείσσων ὁμαίμων ἀνδρὶ κεκτῆσθαι φίλος.

ΧΟ. ὁ μέγας ὄλβος ἅ τ' ἀρετά   str.
    μέγα φρονοῦσ'ἀν' Ἑλλάδα καὶ
      παρὰ Σιμουντίοις ὀχετοῖς
    πάλιν ἀνῆλθ' ἐξ εὐτυχίας Ἀτρείδαις   810
    παλαιπαλαιᾶς ἀπὸ συμφορᾶς δόμων,
    ὁπότε χρυσέας ἔρις ἀρ-
      νὸς ἤλυθε Τανταλίδαις,
    οἰκτρότατα θοινάματα καὶ
      σφάγια γενναίων τεκέων·   815
      ὅθεν φόνῳ φόνος ἐξαμεί-
      βων δι' αἵματος οὐ προλεί-
      πει δισσοῖσιν Ἀτρείδαις.

    τὸ καλὸν οὐ καλόν, τοκέων   ant.
    πυριγενεῖ τεμεῖν παλάμᾳ   820
      χρόα, μελάνδετον δὲ φόνῳ
    ξίφος ἐς αὐγὰς ἀελίοιο δεῖξαι.
    τὸ δ' εὖ κακουργεῖν ἀσέβεια ποικίλα
    κακοφρόνων τ' ἀνδρῶν παράνοι-
      α· θανάτου γὰρ ἀμφὶ φόβῳ   825
    Τυνδαρὶς ἰάχησε τάλαι-
      να· "τέκνον, οὐ τολμᾷς ὅσια
      κτείνων σὰν ματέρα· μὴ πατρῴ-
      αν τιμῶν χάριν ἐξανά-
      ψῃ δύσκλειαν ἐς αἰεί".   830

---

813 ἤλυθε Π7 codd., sed male respondet 825: ἐτεθάλει Willink
820 τεμεῖν Porson, cf. Σ: τέμνειν codd.
823 δ' εὖ Bothe, cf. Σ: δ' αὖ codd.: γὰρ gnomol. Vatoped.
     κακοῦργον Σ^{γρ}
     ποικίλα M^{γρ}Σ : μεγάλη MBOVA
825 θανάτου: τοῦδε Dindorf: δεινὰ Kirchhoff. Cf. ad 813
827 fort. τέκος (EL. 1215)
829 τίκων (cf. 453) Triclinius

OR.   There you are - get yourselves comrades,
not just family! An outsider who becomes fused   805
to you by his character beats ten thousand
relatives as a friend to possess.
    [*Exeunt, Pylades supporting Orestes. Music.*]

CH.   The great prosperity and noble rank
        that was proud throughout Greece and beside
        the channels of Simois
        has ebbed again from success for Atreus' line,
        a legacy from the old old misfortune   811
            of the house
        when the golden lamb dispute
        came upon the Tantalids -
        most tragic feastings and slaughters
            of trueborn children;   815
        since when murder with murder
        exchanging through blood has not run short
        for the double line of Atreus.

        That "good" is not good, to slice
        parents' flesh with fireborn handiwork   820
        and to display the sword
        dark-laced with killing to the light of
            the sun.
        Virtuous crime is sin sophistical,
        wrong-headed men's delusion.
        For pierced by fear of death   825
        Tyndareos' poor daughter shrieked
        "My child, you are braving no lawful venture,
        killing your mother! Do not
        in seeking to honour your father's sake
        tie infamy to yourself for evermore!"   830

117

τίς νόσος ἦ τίνα δάκρυα καὶ   epod.
  τίς ἔλεος μείζων κατὰ γᾶν
ἦ ματροκτόνον αἷμα χειρὶ θέσθαι;
οἷον ἔργον τελέσας
βεβάκχευται μανίαις,   835
Εὐμενίσι θήραμα, φόνον
δρομάσι δινεύων βλεφάροις
Ἀγαμεμνόνιος παῖς.
ὦ μέλεος, ματρὸς ὅτε
  χρυσεοπηνήτων φαρέων   840
μαστὸν ὑπερτέλλοντ' ἐσιδών
σφάγιον ἔθετο ματέρα, πα-
  τρῴων παθέων ἀμοιβάν.

ΗΛ. γυναῖκες, ἦ που τῶνδ' ἀφώρμηται δόμων
     τλήμων Ὀρέστης θεομανεῖ λύσσῃ δαμείς;   845
ΧΟ. ἥκιστα· πρὸς δ' Ἀργεῖον οἴχεται λεών,
     ψυχῆς ἀγῶνα τὸν προκείμενον πέρι
     δώσων, ἐν ᾧ ζῆν ἦ θανεῖν ὑμᾶς χρεών.
ΗΛ. οἴμοι· τί χρῆμ' ἔδρασε; τίς δ' ἔπεισέ νιν;
ΧΟ. Πυλάδης. – ἔοικε δ' οὐ μακρὰν ὅδ' ἄγγελος   850
     λέξειν τὰ κεῖθεν σοῦ κασιγνήτου πέρι.

ΑΓΓΕΛΟΣ
     ὦ τλῆμον, ὦ δύστηνε τοῦ στρατηλάτου
     Ἀγαμέμνονος παῖ, πότνι' Ἠλέκτρα, λόγους
     ἄκουσον οὕς σοι δυστυχεῖς ἥκω φέρων.
ΗΛ. αἰαῖ, διοιχόμεσθα· δῆλος εἶ λόγῳ.   855
     [κακῶν γὰρ ἥκεις, ὡς ἔοικεν, ἄγγελος.]
ΑΓ. ψήφῳ Πελασγῶν σὸν κασίγνητον θανεῖν
     καὶ σ', ὦ τάλαιν', ἔδοξε τῇδ' ἐν ἡμέρᾳ.
ΗΛ. οἴμοι· προσῆλθεν ἐλπὶς ἦν φοβουμένη
     πάλαι τὸ μέλλον ἐξετηκόμην γόοις.   860
     ἀτὰρ τίς ἀγών, τίνες ἐν Ἀργείοις λόγοι
     καθεῖλον ἡμᾶς κἀπεκύρωσαν θανεῖν;

---

836 φόνον Wilamowitz: φόνῳ codd.
838 Ἀγ- West: Ἀγ- codd.
839 ματρὸς: ματέρος Hermann: possis e.g. πάλλευκον
852 del. Paley, Haslam
856 del. Brunck

118

What disorder, what distress,
what tragedy is there greater in the world
than taking the blood of matricide on
   one's hand?
From doing such a deed
he has been driven wild with madness fits, 835
the Benign Ones' quarry, rolling bloodshed
in his roving eyeballs - Agamemnon's son.
Unhappy man! when from the gold-weave robes
he saw his mother's breast rise into sight, 841
yet made her his slaughter-victim,
requital for his father's fate.

[*Electra comes out of the house and looks about for
Orestes.*]
   EL. Ladies, I suppose poor Orestes has gone
away from the house overcome by his god-sent   845
madness?
   CHORUS-LEADER. Not at all; he has gone to
the people of Argos to face the fatal trial
that is at hand, in which it is fixed that
you and he live or die.
   EL. Oh no! Why did he do it, who persuaded
him?
   CH.-L. Pylades ... [*An excited old man is seen
approaching from the direction of the town.*] But it   850
looks as if this bringer of news will soon
give the report from there about your brother.
   OLD MAN. O unhappy one, o unfortunate, the
war-commander Agamemnon's daughter, lady
Electra, hear the tale of disaster I have come
to bring you.
   EL. Oh, we are done for! You are clear   855
enough in what you say. [For you have come,
as it seems, with bad news.]
   OLD MAN. By the Pelasgians' vote your
brother's death and yours, poor lady, was
decreed this day.
   EL. O woe! It has come, the prospect I
had long been fearing, dissolving in lament   860
over what was to come! But how was the trial?
What speeches among the Argives brought us
down and confirmed the sentence of death?

λέγ', ὦ γεραιέ· πότερα λευσίμῳ χερὶ
ἢ διὰ σιδήρου πνεῦμ' ἀπορρῆξαί με δεῖ,
κοινὰς ἀδελφῷ συμφορὰς κεκτημένην;   865
ΑΓ. ἐτύγχανον μὲν ἀγρόθεν πυλῶν ἔσω
βαίνων, πυθέσθαι δεόμενος τά τ' ἀμφὶ σοῦ
τά τ' ἀμφ' Ὀρέστου (σῷ γὰρ εὔνοιαν πατρί
ἀεί ποτ' εἶχον, καί μ' ἔφερβε σὸς δόμος,
πένητα μέν, χρῆσθαι δὲ γενναῖον φίλοις)·   870
ὁρῶ δ' ὄχλον στείχοντα καὶ θάσσοντ' ἄκραν
οὗ φασι πρῶτον Δαναὸν Αἰγύπτῳ δίκας
διδόντ' ἀθροῖσαι λαὸν εἰς κοινὰς ἔδρας.
ἀστῶν δὲ δή τιν' ἠρόμην ἄθροισμ' ἰδών·
"τί καινὸν Ἄργει; μῶν τι πολεμίων πάρα   875
ἄγγελμ' ἀνεπτέρωκε Δαναϊδῶν πόλιν;"
ὃ δ' εἶπ'· "Ὀρέστην κεῖνον οὐχ ὁρᾷς πέλας
στείχοντ', ἀγῶνα θανάσιμον δραμούμενον;"
ὁρῶ δ' ἄελπτον φάσμ', ὃ μήποτ' ὤφελον,
Πυλάδην τε καὶ σὸν σύγγονον στείχονθ'ὁμοῦ, 880
τὸν μὲν κατηφῆ καὶ παρειμένον νόσῳ,
τὸν δ' ὥστ' ἀδελφὸν ἴσα φίλῳ λυπούμενον,
νόσημα κηδεύοντα παιδαγωγίᾳ.
ἐπεὶ δὲ πλήρης ἐγένετ' Ἀργείων ὄχλος,
κήρυξ ἀναστὰς εἶπε· "τίς χρῄζει λέγειν,   885
πότερον Ὀρέστην κατθανεῖν ἢ μὴ χρεών
μητροκτονοῦντα;" κἀπὶ τῷδ' ἀνίσταται
Ταλθύβιος, ὃς σῷ πατρὶ συνεπόρθει Φρύγας·
ἔλεξε δ', ὑπὸ τοῖς δυναμένοισιν ὢν ἀεί,
διχόμυθα, πατέρα μὲν σὸν ἐκπαγλούμενος,   890
σὸν δ' οὐκ ἐπαινῶν σύγγονον, καλοῖς κακούς
λόγους ἑλίσσων, ὅτι καθισταίη νόμους
εἰς τοὺς τεκόντας οὐ καλούς· τὸ δ'ὄμμ'ἀεί
φαιδρωπὸν ἐδίδου τοῖσιν Αἰγίσθου φίλοις.
τὸ γὰρ γένος τοιοῦτον· ἐπὶ τὸν εὐτυχῆ   895
πηδῶσ' ἀεὶ κήρυκες· ὅδε δ' αὐτοῖς φίλος,
ὃς ἂν δύνηται πόλεος ἔν τ' ἀρχαῖσιν ᾖ.
ἐπὶ τῷδε δ' ἠγόρευε Διομήδης ἄναξ.
οὗτος κτανεῖν μὲν οὔτε σ' οὔτε σύγγονον
εἴα, φυγῇ δὲ ζημιοῦντας εὐσεβεῖν·   900

863-5 del. Herwerden

120

Tell me, old man: is it by stoning hand or by
way of iron that I must break off my breath,
sharing in all that happens to my brother?   865
     OLD MAN. I happened to be coming inside the
gates from the country, wanting to find out the
state of affairs about you and Orestes (for I
always used to be well disposed towards your
father, and your house fed me, a poor man but   870
honourable in service to my friends), and I
saw a crowd coming and taking seats on the
summit where they say Danaus, submitting himself
to judgment against Aegyptus, first assembled
the people to sit together. So seeing the
assembly I asked one of the townspeople, "What's
new with Argos? Has some report from an enemy   875
set Danaus' descendants in a flutter?" He said,
"Don't you see Orestes approaching over there,
about to run his death-trial?" And I saw an
unlooked-for apparition, which I wish I never
had: Pylades and your brother walking together,   880
the one downcast and drooping with sickness,
the other, like a brother to him, sharing his
friend's distress, caring for his sickness as
if supervising a schoolboy.
     Then when the assembly of Argives was full,
a herald stood up and said "Who wishes to   885
speak on whether Orestes should die or not as
a matricide?" And thereupon Talthybius stood
up, who was with your father when he devastated
the Phrygians. But, being always under those
in power, he spoke double talk, exalting your   890
father, but not commending your brother,
plaiting foul words with fair ones, saying that
he was establishing bad precedents towards
parents; and all the time he was giving the
glad eye to Aegisthus' supporters. The herald
breed is like that: they always jump to the   895
side of the successful, and count as their
friend whoever has influence over the community
and is one of the authorities.
     Next spoke lord Diomedes. He was not for
killing either you or your brother, but for the 900

121

ἐπερρόθησαν δ᾽ οἳ μὲν ὡς καλῶς λέγοι,
οἳ δ᾽ οὐκ ἐπήνουν. κἀπὶ τῷδ᾽ ἀνίσταται
ἀνήρ τις ἀθυρόγλωσσος, ἰσχύων θράσει,
Ἀργεῖος οὐκ Ἀργεῖος, ἠναγκασμένος,
θορύβῳ τε πίσυνος κἀμαθεῖ παρρησίᾳ·   905
[πιθανὸς ἔτ᾽ αὐτοὺς περιβαλεῖν κακῷ τινι·
ὅταν γὰρ ἡδὺς τοῖς λόγοις φρονῶν κακῶς
πείθῃ τὸ πλῆθος, τῇ πόλει κακὸν μέγα·
ὅσοι δὲ σὺν νῷ χρηστὰ βουλεύουσ᾽ ἀεί,
κἂν μὴ παραυτίκ᾽, αὖθίς εἰσι χρήσιμοι   910
πόλει. θεᾶσθαι δ᾽ ὧδε χρὴ τὸν προστάτην
ἰδόνθ᾽· ὅμοιον γὰρ τὸ χρῆμα γίγνεται
τῷ τοὺς λόγους λέγοντι καὶ τιμωμένῳ.]
ὃς εἶπ᾽ Ὀρέστην καὶ σ᾽ ἀποκτεῖναι πέτροις
βάλλοντας· ὑπὸ δ᾽ ἔτεινε Τυνδάρεως λόγους   915
[τῷ σφὼ κατακτείνοντι τοιούτους λέγειν].
    ἄλλος δ᾽ ἀναστὰς ἔλεγε τῷδ᾽ ἐναντία,
μορφῇ μὲν οὐκ εὔωπος, ἀνδρεῖος δ᾽ ἀνήρ,
ὀλιγάκις ἄστυ κἀγορᾶς χραίνων κύκλον,
αὐτουργός – οἵπερ καὶ μόνοι σῴζουσι γῆν –   920
ξυνετὸς δέ, χωρεῖν ὁμόσε τοῖς λόγοις θέλων,
ἀκέραιος, ἀνεπίπληκτον ἠσκηκὼς βίον·
ὃς εἶπ᾽ Ὀρέστην παῖδα τὸν Ἀγαμέμνονος
στεφανοῦν, ὃς ἠθέλησε τιμωρεῖν πατρί
κακὴν γυναῖκα κἄθεον κατακτανών   925
ἢ κεῖν᾽ ἀφῄρει, μήθ᾽ ὁπλίζεσθαι χέρα
μήτε στρατεύειν ἐκλιπόντα δώματα,
εἰ τἄνδον οἰκουρήμαθ᾽ οἱ λελειμμένοι
φθεροῦσιν, ἀνδρῶν εὐνίδας λωβώμενοι.
καὶ τοῖς γε χρηστοῖς εὖ λέγειν ἐφαίνετο.   930
    κοὐδεὶς ἔτ᾽ εἶπε· σὸς δ᾽ ἐπῆλθε σύγγονος,
ἔλεξε δ᾽· "ὦ γῆν Ἰνάχου κεκτημένοι,

---

901 λαοὶ δ᾽ ἐπερρόθησαν (ex *Hec.* 553) OA
906-13 del. Dindorf
906 ἀστοὺς Valckenaer
911 χρὴ: δεῖ H
916 del. Weil
922 ἀκέραιον FL Hesych.
929 φθεροῦσιν Wecklein: φθείρουσιν codd.

moral course of punishing you with exile; and
they murmured in response, some saying that he
spoke persuasively, while others disapproved.
  Next there stood up a man with no shutters
to his mouth, strong on audacity, an Argive but
no true one - pressurized - reliant on hectoring   905
and stupid abuse: [plausible enough to pitch
them on some disaster yet; for when a man
attractive in speech but wrong-headed is
persuasive to the majority, it is a calamity
for the city, whereas those who regularly
give good and sensible counsel are useful to   910
the state sooner or later. And one should view
the leader in this light, for much the same
applies to the orator and the holder of office.]
He said to kill Orestes and you by stoning;
but it was Tyndareos that had provided the   915
arguments [of this kind for the use of the
speaker who condemned you].
  Another stood up and spoke in the opposite
sense to him, not physically good-looking, but
a manly man, one who rarely impinges on the
town or the market circle, a working farmer (it
is these alone that ensure the land's survival), 920
but intelligent, willing to come to grips with
the arguments, uncorrupted, self-disciplined
to a life above reproach. He said to crown
Orestes the son of Agamemnon, for having had
the will to avenge his father by killing a
wicked and impious woman who threatened to   925
deprive us of all that - no more taking arms or
soldiering away from home, if those left behind
are to ruin domestic managements by violating
the men's bedfellows. And decent people, at
least, found him convincing.   930
  No one else spoke; and your brother came
forward and said, "Heirs to the land of Inachus,

[πάλαι Πελασγοί, Δαναΐδαι δὲ δεύτερον,]
ὑμῖν ἀμύνων οὐδὲν ἧσσον ἢ πατρί
ἔκτεινα μητέρ'. εἰ γὰρ ἀρσένων φόνος   935
ἔσται γυναιξὶν ὅσιος, οὐ φθάνοιτ' ἔτ' ἂν
θνῄσκοντες, ἢ γυναιξὶ δουλεύειν χρεών.
τοὐναντίον δὲ δράσετ' ἢ δρᾶσαι χρεών·
νῦν μὲν γὰρ ἡ προδοῦσα λέκτρ' ἐμοῦ πατρός
τέθνηκεν· εἰ δὲ δὴ κατακτενεῖτ' ἐμέ,   940
ὁ νόμος ἀνεῖται, κοὐ φθάνοι θνῄσκων τις ἄν,
ὡς τῆς γε τόλμης οὐ σπάνις γενήσεται."
ἀλλ' οὐκ ἔπειθ' ὅμιλον, εὖ δοκῶν λέγειν,
νικᾷ δ' ἐκεῖνος ὁ κακὸς ἐν πλήθει χερῶν
ὃς ἠγόρευε σύγγονον σέ τε κτανεῖν.   945
   μόλις δ' ἔπεισε μὴ πετρούμενος θανεῖν
τλήμων 'Ορέστης· αὐτόχειρι δὲ σφαγῇ
ὑπέσχετ' ἐν τῇδ' ἡμέρᾳ λείψειν βίον
σὺν σοί. πορεύει δ' αὐτὸν ἐκκλήτων ἄπο
Πυλάδης δακρύων· σὺν δ' ὁμαρτοῦσιν φίλοι   950
κλαίοντες, οἰκτίροντες· ἔρχεται δέ σοι
πικρὸν θέαμα καὶ πρόσοψις ἀθλία.
ἀλλ' εὐτρέπιζε φάσγαν' ἢ βρόχον δέρῃ,
ὡς δεῖ λιπεῖν σε φέγγος· ηὐγένεια δέ
οὐδέν σ' ἐπωφέλησεν, οὐδ' ὁ Πύθιον   955
τρίποδα καθίζων Φοῖβος, ἀλλ' ἀπώλεσεν.

[ΧΟ. ὦ δυστάλαινα παρθέν', ὡς ξυνηρεφές
πρόσωπον εἰς γῆν σὸν βαλοῦσ' ἄφθογγος εἶ,
ὡς εἰς στεναγμοὺς καὶ γόους δραμουμένη.]

ΧΟ. κατάρχομαι στεναγμόν, ὦ Πελασγία,   str.
     τιθεῖσα λευκῶν ὄνυχα διὰ παρηΐδων,   961
     αἱματηρὸν ἄταν,

---

933 del. Musgrave (noverant Σ Eust.)
     Δαναΐδαι δὲ KG: Δαναΐδαι HMBOVA
944 χερῶν Wecklein: λόγων O: λέγων Π18?(]εγ[),HMBVA
946 πετρούμενος Π7HMVˢ: -μένους BOVA
954 ὡς οὔ σ' ὁρᾶν δεῖ φέγγος Σʸᵖ
955 Πύθιον West: Πύθιος codd.
957-9 non in omnibus libris fuisse testatur Σ
960-81 choro tribuit Weil: Electrae codd. Σ
960 Πελάσγιαι Σʸᵖ
961 λευκῶν Hartung: λευκὸν codd. (λευκῶν ὀνύχωνΒ²ˢ)

124

[anciently Pelasgians, and Danaus' descendants later,] I was fighting for you just as much as for my father when I killed my mother. For if 935
murder of menfolk is to be permitted to women, you won't be able to die too quickly for them, or else we must be women's slaves. You will be doing the opposite of what you should do: as it is, she who was unfaithful to my father's bed is dead, but if you are going to put me to 940
death, established custom is undone, and people will be dying as soon as anything, since boldness won't be in short supply." But he was not persuading the crowd, good though his speech seemed, and victory went to the other scoundrel in the number of hands raised, the one who advocated killing your brother and you. 945

Poor Orestes just managed to persuade them that he should not be stoned: he gave an undertaking to depart from life slain by his own hand this day, together with you. Pylades, in tears, is bringing him back from the convocation, and his supporters are with them, crying, 950
lamenting. You have a painful spectacle coming, and seeing him will be distressing.

So be making swords ready, or a noose for your neck, as you have to depart from the light. Your noble birth has been no help to you, and 955
neither has Phoebus on his tripod-seat at Pytho - he has been your ruin.   [*Exit.*]

[CHORUS-LEADER. Poor unhappy woman, how shadowed the face you cast down to the earth, speechless, as though you will take quick recourse to wailings and laments.] [*Music.*]

CH.   I start the wailing, o Pelasgia,   960
      putting the fingernail through my
         white cheeks -
      a bleeding detriment -

κτύπον τε κρατός, ὃν ἔλαχ'ἁ κατὰ χθονός
νερτέρων πότνα, καλλίπαις θεᾴ.
ἰαχείτω δὲ γᾶ Κυκλωπία,   965
σίδαρον ἐπὶ κάρα τιθεῖσα κούριμον,
[τῶν 'Ατρειδῶν] πήματ' οἴκων.
ἔλεος ἔλεος ὅδ' ἔρχεται
τῶν θανουμένων ὕπερ,
στρατηλατᾶν 'Ελλάδος ποτ' ὄντων.   970

βέβακε γὰρ βέβακεν, οἴχεται τέκνων   ant.
πρόπασα γέννα Πέλοπος ὅ τ'ἐπὶ μακαρίοις
ζῆλος ὧν ποτ' οἴκοις·
φθόνος νιν εἷλε θεόθεν ἅ τε δυσμενής
φοινία ψῆφος ἐν πολίταις.   975
ἰὼ ἰώ, πανδάκρυτ' ἐφαμέρων
ἔθνη πολύπονα, λεύσσεθ' ὡς παρ' ἐλπίδας
    Μοῖρα βαίνει.
ἕτερα δ' ἕτερον ἀμείβεται
πήματ' ἐν χρόνῳ μακρῷ·   980
βροτῶν δ' ὁ πᾶς ἀστάθμητος αἰών.

ΗΛ.   μόλοιμι τὰν οὐρανοῦ   astroph.
μέσον χθονός <τε> τεταμέναν
αἰωρήμασιν
πέτραν ἀλύσεσι χρυσέαισι,
    φερομέναν δίναισι
    βῶλον ἐξ 'Ολύμπου,
ἵν' ἐν θρήνοισιν ἀναβοάσω
γέροντι πατέρι Ταντάλῳ,   985
ὃς ἔτεκεν ἔτεκε γενέτορας ἐμέθεν, δόμων
οἴας κατεῖδον ἄτας·

---

964 πότνα Herwerden: Περσέφασσα codd.
967 τῶν 'Ατρειδῶν (-δᾶν MVA) del. Musgrave
973 ζηλωτὸς ... οἶκος codd. Σ: corr. Musgrave
976 ἰὼ ὤ Hartung: ιῳῶω Π18: ἰώ μοι Diggle
979 ἕτερον West: ἑτέροις codd. Σ: ἕτερος Porson
982 τε add. Hermann
986 fort. δόμους
987 οἴας (vel ἃς) Madvig: οἵ codd. Σ

and the head-beating that falls to the
   infernal
mistress of all below, the fair-child
   goddess.
Let the Cyclopian land cry loud   965
the house's woes, setting the iron blade
to its shorn head!
Compassion, compassion comes forward here
for these who will die, who were once
war-leaders of Greece.   970

For passed away, passed away, gone
   is the whole line
of Pelops' children, and the felicity
that was once on his blest house:
the grudge of God has got it,
and the murderous vote of hate among the   975
   people.
Oyoy, tear-laden toilful tribes of mortals
that live for the day, behold how destiny
   transgresses expectations!
Different woes to different men by turns
pass in the fullness of time; imponderable 980
the whole of human life.

EL.   I wish I could go to that rock
      strung in suspense between sky and earth
      by golden chains, the whirlwind-borne
      glebe that came from Olympus,
      to cry in lamentation to old father Tantalus
      who sired, who sired my forbears   986
      what wounds to the house I have seen.

τὸ πτανὸν μὲν δίωγμα πώλων,
τεθριπποβάμονι στόλῳ Πέλοψ ὁπότε
  πελάγεσι διεδίφρευσε, Μυρτίλου φόνον   990
δικὼν ἐς οἶδμα πόντου,
λευκοκύμοσιν πρὸς Γεραιστίαις ποντίων σάλων
ἀϊόσιν ἁρματεύσας·
ὅθεν δόμοισι τοῖς ἐμοῖς   995
ἦλθ' ἀρὰ πολύστονος,
λόχευμα ποιμνίοισι Μαιάδος τόκου
τὸ χρυσόμαλλον ἀρνὸς ὁπότ'
  ἐγένετο τέρας
  ὀλοὸν Ἀτρέως ἱπποβώτα·   1000
ὅθεν Ἔρις τό τε πτερωτὸν
  ἀλίου μετέβαλεν ἅρμα
  τὰν πρὸς ἑσπέραν κέλευθον
οὐρανοῦ, προσαρμόσασα χιονόπωλον Ἀῶ,
ἑπταπόρου τε δράμημα Πελειάδος   1005
  εἰς ὁδὸν ἄλλαν [Ζεὺς μεταβάλλει].
τῶν δ' ἔτ' ἀμείβει θανάτους θανάτων
  τά τ' ἐπώνυμα δεῖπνα Θυέστου
λέκτρα τε Κρήσσας Ἀερόπας δολί-
  ας δολίοισι γάμοις· τὰ πανύστατα δ'   1010
εἰς ἐμὲ καὶ γενέταν ἐμὸν ἤλυθε
δόμων πολυπόνοις ἀνάγκαις.

ΧΟ. καὶ μὴν ὅδε σὸς σύγγονος ἕρπει
  ψήφῳ θανάτου κατακυρωθείς,
  ὅ τε πιστότατος πάντων Πυλάδης,
  ἰσάδελφος ἀνήρ, ἰθύνων <οἳ>   1015
  νοσερὸν κῶλον [Ὀρέστου],
  ποδὶ κηδοσύνῳ παράσειρος.

---

988 τὸ πτανὸν (-ῶν O) codd. Σ: ποτανὸν Porson
989 ὁπότε ΣV²L²: ὅτε MBOVA
1003 ἑσπέραν MVA: ἕσπερον BO Hesych. Phot. *Suda*
1004 προσαρμόσασα V², -σασ' (ante οὐρανοῦ) ξ: -σας MBOVAΣ
     χιονόπωλον West: μονόπωλον ἐς codd.
1006 Ζεὺς del. Weil, μεταβάλλει Biehl
1011 ἐμὲ συγγενέταν τ' Willink
1015 οἳ add. West
1016 Ὀρέστου om. F (rest. F²), del. Elmsley

128

There was that flying colt-chase
when Pelops with four-horsed equipage
rode over on the sea's expanses, hurling   990
Myrtilus to death in the swell of the waves,
driving his car
from the sea surge
by the white-surf strand of Geraestus.
Thence came upon my house   995
a curse fraught with woe,
when what the son of Maia brought to birth
    in the flocks,
that gold-fleeced prodigy of a lamb
appeared, ruinous thing
of Atreus breeder of horses.   1000
Hence Conflict turned the sun's winged
    car about
to the westward sky-course, yoking on
the snowy steeds of Dawn,
and turned the running of the
    seven-track Pleiad   1005
onto another path.
And for that affair, that death, it has
    yet brought deaths,
and the feast that bears Thyestes' name,
and the love-bed of Cretan Aërope,
deceiver in marriage deceitful; and to   1010
    end all
it has come at me and my father
by the toil-fraught law of the house.

[*Orestes and Pylades are seen returning.*]

    CH. But see, here comes your brother,
confirmed in sentence of death, and the truest
of all friends, Pylades, the equal of a
brother, guiding his infirm legs with caring 1015
step, as an outrunner.

129

ΗΛ.　οἲ 'γώ· πρὸ τύμβου γάρ σ' ὁρῶσ' ἀναστένω,
　　　ἀδελφέ, καὶ πάροιθε νερτέρων πύλης.
　　　οἲ 'γὼ μάλ' αὖθις· ὥς σ' ἰδοῦσ' ἐν ὄμμασιν　　1020
　　　πανυστάτην πρόσοψιν ἐξέστην φρενῶν.
ΟΡ.　οὐ σῖγ' ἀφεῖσα τοὺς γυναικείους γόους
　　　στέρξεις τὰ κρανθέντ'; οἰκτρὰ μὲν τάδ',
　　　　　　　　　　　　　　　　　　　　ἀλλ' ὅμως.
　　　[φέρειν σ' ἀνάγκη τὰς παρεστώσας τύχας.]
ΗΛ.　καὶ πῶς σιωπῶ; φέγγος εἰσορᾶν θεοῦ　　　1025
　　　τόδ' οὐκέθ' ἡμῖν τοῖς ταλαιπώροις μέτα.
ΟΡ.　σὺ μή μ' ἀπόκτειν'· ἅλις ἀπ' Ἀργείας χερός
　　　τέθνηχ' ὁ τλήμων· τὰ δὲ παρόντ' ἔα κακά.
ΗΛ.　ὦ μέλεος ἥβης σῆς, Ὀρέστα, καὶ πότμου
　　　θανάτου τ' ἀώρου. ζῆν ἐχρῆν σ', ὅτ' οὐκέτ' εἶ.
ΟΡ.　μὴ πρὸς θεῶν μοι περιβάλῃς ἀνανδρίαν,　　1031
　　　εἰς δάκρυα πορθμεύουσ' ὑπομνήσει κακῶν.
ΗΛ.　θανούμεθ'· οὐχ οἷόν τε μὴ στένειν κακά·
　　　πᾶσιν γὰρ οἰκτρὸν ἡ φίλη ψυχὴ βροτοῖς.
ΟΡ.　τόδ' ἦμαρ ἡμῖν κύριον· δεῖ δ' ἢ βρόχους　　1035
　　　ἅπτειν κρεμαστοὺς ἢ ξίφος θήγειν χερί.
ΗΛ.　σύ νύν μ', ἀδελφέ, μή τις Ἀργείων κτάνῃ
　　　ὕβρισμα θέμενος τὸν Ἀγαμέμνονος γόνον.
ΟΡ.　ἅλις τὸ μητρὸς αἷμ' ἔχω· σὲ δ' οὐ κτενῶ,
　　　ἀλλ' αὐτοχειρὶ θνῆσχ' ὅτῳ βούλῃ τρόπῳ.　　1040
ΗΛ.　ἔσται τάδ'· οὐδὲν σοῦ ξίφους λελείψομαι.
　　　ἀλλ' ἀμφιθεῖναι σῇ δέρῃ θέλω χέρας.
ΟΡ.　τέρπου κενὴν ὄνησιν, εἰ τερπνὸν τόδε
　　　θανάτου πέλας βεβῶσι, περιβαλεῖν χέρας.
ΗΛ.　ὦ φίλτατ', ὦ ποθεινὸν ἥδιστόν τ' ἔχων　　1045
　　　τῇ σῇ γ' ἀδελφῇ σῶμα καὶ ψυχὴν μίαν.
ΟΡ.　ἔκ τοί με τήξεις· καί σ' ἀμείψασθαι θέλω

1019　νερτέρων πύλης Jacobs: νερτέρου (-ων B³Sa) πυρᾶς codd.
1020　σ' ἰδοῦσ' ἐν Porson: ἰδοῦσά σ' ἐν MBO: ἰδοῦσά σ'
　　　MᵞᵖBᵞᵖV: ἰδοῦσ' ἐν AFPrSaG
1022　γόους MᵞᵖPrξ: λόγους MBOVA
1024　non legit Σ, del. Kirchhoff
1030　οὐκέτ' εἶ: οὐκέτι MᵞᵖO, Σ?
1032　ὑπομνήσει Musgrave: ὑπόμνησιν codd. Σ
1038　γόνον: δόμον Ar. Byz. ap. Σ
1046　τῇ σῇ γ' ἀδελφῇ West, σῶμα Willink: τῆς σῆς ἀδελφῆς
　　　ὄνομα codd. Σ

130

EL. O woe! I moan as I see you before your
tomb, brother, and before the gates of the
nether ones. O woe again! Seeing you before my 1020
eyes for the very last time, I go out of my
mind.

OR. Won't you be quiet, leave your womanish
wails and put up with what's been determined?
It's a sad business, but still. [You've no
choice but to endure the situation at hand.]

EL. How can I be quiet? The sight of this 1025
divine light is something we poor sufferers
may share in no longer.

OR. Don't bore me to death: I'm dead enough
from Argos' hand, damn it. Leave our troubles
be.

EL. O unhappy in your youth, Orestes, your
fate, your untimely death! You should be
living, now when you are no more.   1030

OR. For heaven's sake don't make me look
unmanly, bringing me to tears with your
reminders of our plight.

EL. We're going to die: it's impossible
not to cry, everyone finds it poignant, the
life that is dear to mortals.

OR. This is our appointed day. We must   1035
either tie hanging-nooses or sharpen a sword.

EL. *You* kill me, then, brother, don't let
any of the Argives do it and make a mockery
of Agamemnon's children.

OR. It's enough that I have my mother's
blood on my hands. I won't kill you. You must
die by your own hand, in whatever way you like. 1040

EL. Very well; I shall not be any slower
than you with the sword. Now I want to put
my arms round your neck.

OR. Enjoy the empty pleasure, if it is
enjoyable for people who stand close to death
to embrace.

EL. [*hugging him*] O my dearest, whose body   1045
is lovable and most delightful to your sister,
and whose life is one with hers.

OR. You'll melt me, you know. Now I want to

131

φιλότητι χειρῶν. τί γὰρ ἔτ' αἰδοῦμαι τάλας;
ὦ στέρν' ἀδελφῆς, ὦ φίλον πρόσπτυγμ' ἐμόν·
τάδ' ἀντὶ παίδων καὶ γαμηλίου λέχους   1050
προσφθέγματ' ἀμφοῖν τοῖν ταλαιπώροιν ἄρα.
ΗΛ. φεῦ·
πῶς ἂν ξίφος νὼ ταὐτόν, εἰ θέμις, κτάνοι
καὶ μνῆμα δέξαιθ' ἕν, κέδρου τεχνάσματα;
ΟΡ. ἥδιστ' ἂν εἴη ταῦθ'· ὁρᾷς δὲ δὴ φίλων
ὡς ἐσπανίσμεθ', ὥστε κοινωνεῖν τάφου.   1055
ΗΛ. οὐδ' εἶφ' ὑπὲρ σοῦ, μὴ θανεῖν σπουδὴν ἔχων,
Μενέλαος ὁ κακός, ὁ προδότης τοὐμοῦ πατρός;
ΟΡ. οὐδ' ὄμμ' ἔδειξεν, ἀλλ' ἐπὶ σκήπτροις ἔχων
τὴν ἐλπίδ' ηὐλαβεῖτο μὴ σῴζειν φίλους.
ἀλλ' εἶ' ὅπως γενναῖα κἀγαμέμνονος   1060
δράσαντε κατθανούμεθ' ἀξιώτατα.
κἀγὼ μὲν εὐγένειαν ἀποδείξω πόλει
παίσας πρὸς ἧπαρ φασγάνῳ· σὲ δ' αὖ χρεών
ὅμοια πράσσειν τοῖς ἐμοῖς τολμήμασιν.
Πυλάδη, σὺ δ' ἡμῖν τοῦ φόνου γενοῦ βραβεύς, 1065
καὶ κατθανόντοιν εὖ περίστειλον δέμας
θάψον τε κοινῇ πρὸς πατρὸς τύμβον φέρων.
καὶ χαῖρ'· ἐπ' ἔργον δ', ὡς ὁρᾷς, πορεύομαι.
ΠΥ. ἐπίσχες. ἓν μὲν πρῶτά σοι μομφὴν ἔχω,
εἰ ζῆν με χρῄζειν σοῦ θανόντος ἤλπισας.   1070
ΟΡ. τί γὰρ προσήκει κατθανεῖν σ' ἐμοῦ μέτα;
ΠΥ. ἤρου; τί δὲ ζῆν σῆς ἑταιρείας ἄτερ;
ΟΡ. οὐκ ἔκτανες σὺ μητέρ', ὡς ἐγὼ τάλας.
ΠΥ. σὺν σοί γε κοινῇ· ταὐτὰ καὶ πάσχειν με δεῖ.
ΟΡ. ἀπόδος τὸ σῶμα πατρί, μὴ σύνθηισκέ μοι.   1075
σοὶ μὲν γὰρ ἔστι πόλις - ἐμοὶ δ' οὐκ ἔστι δή -
καὶ δῶμα πατρὸς καὶ μέγας πλούτου λιμήν.

1051   ἀμφοῖν τοῖν ταλαιπώροιν Lobeck: ἀμφὶ τοῖς —οις codd.
ἄρα MBV: πάρα M²B³v¹OA: μέτα (ex 1026) Mʸᵖ
1064   βουλεύμασι(ν) Π11 VPrʸᵖ Saʸᵖ
1073   σὺ Pr+: σὴν MBOVA

132

respond with loving arms. Why go on feeling
inhibited, damn it? O sister's breast, o
beloved embrace of mine ... these endearments
take the place of children and the marriage   1050
bed for both of us poor creatures, as it
turns out.

EL. [*with a sigh*] Oh, if only the same sword
could kill us both, if that's allowed, and
one memorial receive us, crafted in cedar.

.OR. That would be nicest; but you see how
short we are of friends for sharing a burial.   1055

EL. But did Menelaus not speak for you
with concern to save your life, the scoundrel,
the betrayer of my father?

OR. He didn't even show his face. Having
his hopes on the sceptre, he was taking care
not to preserve his kin.

Now come on, let's make sure we do some-   1060
thing noble and fully worthy of Agamemnon
when we die! I'm going to prove my nobility
to the city by stabbing to my liver with a
sword; and you in turn must match my brave
efforts. Pylades, you must act as supervisor   1065
of our suicide. When we are dead, array our
bodies well and bury us together, taking us
to our father's grave-mound. And farewell -
as you see, I'm on my way to the task. [*He
moves towards the house.*]

PYL. Wait. One thing, to begin with, I hold
against you, if you thought I would want to   1070
go on living after your death.

OR. Why, what is fitting about your dying
with me?

PYL. Need you ask? What is fitting about
life without your companionship?

OR. You didn't kill a mother, as I did,
alas.

PYL. Yes I did, together with you: so I
must suffer the same fate too.

OR. Let your father have you back, don't   1075
die with me. You have a people - as I have no
longer - and a father's house and a secure base

133

γάμων δὲ τῆς μὲν δυσπότμου τῆσδ' ἐσφάλης,
ἣν σοι κατηγγύησ' ἑταιρείαν σέβων,
σὺ δ' ἄλλο λέκτρον παιδοποίησαι λαβών·   1080
κῆδος δὲ τοὐμὸν καὶ σὸν οὐκέτ' ἔστι δή.
ἀλλ', ὦ ποθεινὸν ὄμμ' ὁμιλίας ἐμῆς,
χαῖρ'· οὐ γὰρ ἡμῖν ἐστι τοῦτο, σοί γε μήν·
οἱ γὰρ θανόντες χαρμάτων τητώμεθα.
ΠΥ. ἦ πολὺ λέλειψαι τῶν ἐμῶν βουλευμάτων.   1085
μήθ' αἷμά μου δέξαιτο κάρπιμον πέδον,
μὴ λαμπρὸς αἰθήρ, εἴ σ' ἐγὼ προδούς ποτε
ἐλευθερώσας τοὐμὸν ἀπολίποιμι σέ.
καὶ συγκατέκτανον γάρ, οὐκ ἀρνήσομαι,   1089
καὶ πάντ' ἐβούλευσ' ὧν σὺ νῦν τίνεις δίκας·
καὶ ξυνθανεῖν οὖν δεῖ με σοὶ καὶ τῇδ' ὁμοῦ·
ἐμὴν γὰρ αὐτήν, ἧς <γε> λέχος ἐπήνεσα,
κρίνω δάμαρτα. τί γὰρ ἐρῶ καλόν ποτε
γῆν Δελφίδ' ἐλθὼν Φωκέων ἀκρόπτολιν\
ὃς πρὶν μὲν ὑμᾶς δυστυχεῖν φίλος παρῆ,   1095
νῦν δ' οὐκέτ' εἰμὶ δυστυχοῦντί σοι φίλος;
οὐκ ἔστιν· ἀλλὰ ταῦτα μὲν κἀμοὶ μέλει·
ἐπεὶ δὲ κατθανούμεθ', εἰς κοινοὺς λόγους
ἔλθωμεν, ὡς ἂν Μενέλεως συνδυστυχῇ.
ΟΡ. ὦ φίλτατ', εἰ γὰρ τοῦτο κατθάνοιμ' ἰδών.   1100
ΠΥ. πιθοῦ νυν, ἄμμεινον δὲ φασγάνου τομάς.
ΟΡ. μενῶ, τὸν ἐχθρὸν εἴ τι τιμωρήσομαι.
ΠΥ. σίγα νυν, ὡς γυναιξὶ πιστεύω βραχύ.
ΟΡ. μηδὲν τρέσῃς τάσδ', ὡς πάρεισ' ἡμῖν φίλαι.
ΠΥ. Ἑλένην κτάνωμεν, Μενέλεῳ λύπην πικράν.   1105
ΟΡ. πῶς; τὸ γὰρ ἕτοιμόν ἐστιν, εἴ γ' ἔσται καλῶς.
ΠΥ. σφάξαντες. ἐν δόμοις δὲ κρύπτεται σέθεν;
ΟΡ. μάλιστα· καὶ δὴ πάντ' ἀποσφραγίζεται.

1082 ὄμμ' Πι1 VA: ὄνομ' MBO gnomol. Vatoped.
1085 πολὺ M²OV: που BVᶜA
1092 γε add. Porson (λέχος γ' K, τὸ λ. Tricl.)

134

of wealth. As for marriage, you have lost it
with my ill-fated sister here, whom I promised
you in regard for our comradeship, but take
another love-bed and have children; the matri- 1080
monial link between us is no more.   Now,
beloved face of companionship to me, fare well:
it isn't possible for us, but it is for you -
we dead are deprived of all welfare.
     PYL. How far you are from catching my   1085
intentions. May the fruitful soil not accept
my blood nor the bright air my soul if ever I
betray you, letting myself go free while
deserting you.   I both killed with you, I shall
not plead innocent, and resolved with you all   1090
that you are now paying the penalty for; so I
must also die with you, and with her - having
agreed to marry her, I deem her my wife.   For
otherwise what fine words shall I ever have
to say when I go to the Delphian land, high
citadel of the Phocians, as one who stood by   1095
you in friendship before your misfortune,
but now you are in it am your friend no longer?
Impossible. This affair concerns me too; and
as we're going to die, let's confer together
with a view to making Menelaus suffer at the
same time.
     OR. Oh Pylades, if only I could see that   1100
before I die.
     PYL. Do as I say, then, and wait a while
longer for the sword-cut.
     OR. I will, if I'm to get some revenge
on my enemy.
     PYL. Hush, now: I don't trust women very far.
     OR. Have no fear of these, they're here
as our friends.
     PYL. Let us kill Helen - a bitter pain for   1105
Menelaus.
     OR. How? The readiness is there, if we
can make a good job of it.
     PYL. Butcher her. She's hidden in your house?
     OR. She certainly is, in fact she's sealing
everything off.

ΠΥ. ἀλλ' οὐκέθ', Ἅιδην νυμφίον κεκτημένη.
ΟΡ. καὶ πῶς; ἔχει γὰρ βαρβάρους ὀπάονας.   1110
ΠΥ. τίνας; Φρυγῶν γὰρ οὐδέν' ἂν τρέσαιμ' ἐγώ.
ΟΡ. οἵους ἐνόπτρων καὶ μύρων ἐπιστάτας.
ΠΥ. τρυφὰς γὰρ ἥκει δεῦρ' ἔχουσα Τρωϊκάς;
ΟΡ. ὡς Ἑλλὰς αὐτῇ σμικρὸν οἰκητήριον.
ΠΥ. οὐδὲν τὸ δοῦλον πρὸς τὸ μὴ δοῦλον γένος.   1115
ΟΡ. καὶ μὴν τόδ' ἔρξας δὶς θανεῖν οὐχ ἅζομαι.
ΠΥ. ἀλλ' οὐδ' ἐγὼ μήν, σοί γε τιμωρούμενος.
ΟΡ. τὸ πρᾶγμα δήλου καὶ πέραιν', ὅπως λέγεις.
ΠΥ. εἴσιμεν ἐς οἴκους δῆθεν ὡς θανούμενοι.
ΟΡ. ἔχω τοσοῦτον, τἀπίλοιπα δ' οὐκ ἔχω.   1120
ΠΥ. γόους πρὸς αὐτὴν θησόμεσθ' ἃ πάσχομεν.
ΟΡ. ὥστ' ἐκδακρῦσαί γ', ἐνδόθεν κεχαρμένην.
ΠΥ. καὶ νῶν παρέσται ταῦθ' ἅπερ κείνῃ τότε.
ΟΡ. ἔπειτ' ἀγῶνα πῶς ἀγωνιούμεθα;
ΠΥ. κρύπτ' ἐν πέπλοισι τοισίδ' ἕξομεν ξίφη.   1125
ΟΡ. πρόσθεν δ' ὀπαδῶν τίς ὄλεθρος γενήσεται;
ΠΥ. ἐκκλήσομέν σφας ἄλλον ἄλλοσε στέγης.
ΟΡ. καὶ τόν γε μὴ σιγῶντ' ἀποκτείνειν χρεών.
ΠΥ. εἶτ' αὐτὸ δηλοῖ τοὔργον οἷ τείνειν χρεών.
ΟΡ. Ἑλένην φονεύειν· μανθάνω τὸ σύμβολον.   1130

1114 ὡς gnomol. Scorial.: ὥσθ' codd.

136

PYL. Well not any more, now she's engaged
to Hades.
OR. But how? She has foreign attendants. 1110
PYL. What are they? *I* wouldn't be scared
of any Phrygian.
OR. Such as superintendents of mirrors
and perfumes.
PYL. You mean she's come *here* with the
comforts of Troy?
OR. Yes, she finds Greece restricted as a
living-space.
PYL. The slave breed is nothing as against 1115
the free.
OR. I must say, if I do this, I don't
mind dying twice over.
PYL. Nor I for that matter, when I'm
avenging you.
OR. Explain the business and go over it,
how you mean.
PYL. We'll go into the house pretending
we're going to kill ourselves.
OR. I've got that much, but not the rest. 1120
PYL. We'll cry and make moan to her of
our plight.
OR. Ha, so that she comes out in tears
though inwardly gleeful.
PYL. It will be the same for us as for her
at that point.
OR. After that how will we conduct our
endeavour?
PYL. Concealed in these robes we'll have 1125
swords.
OR. But first how will the attendants be
got rid of?
PYL. We'll shut them out in different parts
of the building.
OR. Right, and whoever doesn't keep quiet
we must kill.
PYL. After that the job itself makes clear
what we must aim for.
OR. Helen's murder: I can make that 1130
connexion.

ΠΥ. ἔγνως. ἄκουσον δ᾽ ὡς καλῶς βουλεύομαι.
εἰ μὲν γὰρ εἰς γυναῖκα σωφρονεστέραν
ξίφος μεθεῖμεν, δυσκλεὴς ἂν ἦν φόνος·
νῦν δ᾽ ὑπὲρ ἁπάσης ῾Ελλάδος δώσει δίκην,
ὧν πατέρας ἔκτειν᾽, ὧν [δ᾽] ἀπώλεσεν τέκνα,
νύμφας τ᾽ ἔθηκεν ὀρφανὰς ξυναόρων·   1136
ὀλολυγμὸς ἔσται, πῦρ τ᾽ ἀνάψουσιν θεοῖς,
σοὶ πολλὰ κἀμοὶ κέδν᾽ ἀρώμενοι τυχεῖν,
κακῆς γυναικὸς οὕνεχ᾽ αἷμ᾽ ἐπράξαμεν.
ὁ μητροφόντης δ᾽ οὐ καλῇ ταύτην κτανών,   1140
ἀλλ᾽ ἀπολιπὼν τοῦτ᾽ ἐπὶ τὸ βέλτιον πεσῇ,
῾Ελένης λεγόμενος τῆς πολυκτόνου φονεύς.
οὐ δεῖ ποτ᾽, οὐ δεῖ, Μενέλεων μὲν εὐτυχεῖν,
τὸν σὸν δὲ πατέρα καὶ σὲ κἀδελφὴν θανεῖν,
μητέρα τ᾽...ἑῶ τοῦτ᾽· οὐ γὰρ εὐπρεπὲς λέγειν·
δόμους δ᾽ ἔχειν σοὺς δι᾽ ᾽Αγαμέμνονος δόρυ 1146
λαβόντα νύμφην. μὴ γὰρ οὖν ζῴην ἔτι,
εἰ μὴ ᾽π᾽ ἐκείνῃ φάσγανον σπάσω μέλαν.
ἢν δ᾽ οὖν τὸν ῾Ελένης μὴ κατάσχωμεν φόνον,
πρήσαντες οἴκους τούσδε κατθανούμεθα.   1150
ἑνὸς γὰρ οὐ σφαλέντες ἕξομεν κλέος,
καλῶς θανόντες ἢ καλῶς σεσωμένοι.
ΧΟ. πάσαις γυναιξὶν ἀξία στυγεῖν ἔφυ
ἡ Τυνδαρὶς παῖς, ἣ κατῄσχυνεν γένος.
ΟΡ. φεῦ·
οὐκ ἔστιν οὐδὲν κρεῖσσον ἢ φίλος σαφής,   1155
οὐ πλοῦτος, οὐ τυραννίς· ἀλόγιστον δέ τι
τὸ πλῆθος ἀντάλλαγμα γενναίου φίλου.
σὺ γὰρ τά τ᾽ εἰς Αἴγισθον ἐξηῦρες κακὰ
καὶ πλησίον παρῆσθα κινδύνων ἐμοί,
νῦν τ᾽ αὖ δίδως μοι πολεμίων τιμωρίαν   1160
κοὐκ ἐκποδὼν εἶ ... παύσομαί σ᾽ αἰνῶν, ἐπεί
βάρος τι κἀν τῷδ᾽ ἐστίν, αἰνεῖσθαι λίαν.
ἐγὼ δὲ πάντως ἐκπνέων ψυχὴν ἐμήν
δράσας τι χρῄζω τοὺς ἐμοὺς ἐχθροὺς θανεῖν,

1135 δ᾽ (τ᾽ V+) del. West
1158 κακά: καλῶς Herwerden

138

PYL. You've got it. But hear how good my
plan is. If we were to let loose our swords at
a more right-thinking woman, it would be an
infamous killing; but as it is, she'll be
paying the penalty on account of all Greece,
those whose fathers she killed, whose children 1135
she destroyed and made brides bereft of their
husbands: there'll be a hallelujah, and they'll
light fires for the gods, praying for many
blessings to come to you and me for having
accomplished the slaughter of a bad woman. "The
matricide" won't be what you're called after 1140
killing her: you'll leave that behind and
take a turn for the better, being known as the
slayer of Helen the mass murderer. It must
never be, it must not, that Menelaus prospers
while your father and you and your sister had
to die, and your mother ... I won't pursue 1145
that, it's not seemly to speak of; and that
he has your house, when it's through Agamemnon's
spear that he has got his wife back. I'll be
damned indeed if I don't draw my dark sword
against her! But if after all we don't
achieve Helen's murder, we'll set fire to
these buildings before we die. In one or the 1150
other we won't fail: we shall be famous for
a glorious death or a glorious deliverance.
    CHORUS-LEADER. Tyndareos' daughter deserves
the abhorrence of all women: she has disgraced
her sex.
    OR. [*with a sigh*] Oh, there's nothing better 1155
than an unmistakeable friend - not riches, not
monarchy. Incalculable in amount is the
exchange value of a genuine friend. First you
devised the nastiness for Aegisthus and stood
by me close to danger, and now again you offer 1160
me revenge on my enemies and are not about to
make yourself scarce - I won't go on praising
you, for there's something burdensome even in
this, being over-praised. But as I'm breathing
out my life-soul in any case, I want to do
something to my enemies before I die, so that

ἵν' ἀνταναλώσω μὲν οἵ με προύδοσαν,　　　　1165
στένωσι δ' οἵπερ κἄμ' ἔθηκαν ἄθλιον.
'Αγαμέμνονός τοι παῖς πέφυχ', ὃς 'Ελλάδος
ἦρξ' ἀξιωθείς, οὐ τύραννος, ἀλλ' ὅμως
ῥώμην θεοῦ τιν' ἔσχ'· ὃν οὐ καταισχυνῶ
δοῦλον παρασχὼν θάνατον, ἀλλ' ἐλευθέρως　　1170
ψυχὴν ἀφήσω, Μενέλεων δὲ τείσομαι.
ἑνὸς γὰρ εἰ λαβοίμεθ', εὐτυχοῖμεν ἄν,
εἴ ποθεν ἄελπτος παραπέσοι σωτηρία
κτανοῦσι μὴ θανοῦσιν· εὔχομαι τάδε·
ὃ βούλομαι γάρ, ἡδὺ καὶ διὰ στόμα　　　　1175
πτηνοῖσι μύθοις ἀδαπάνως τέρψαι φρένα.
ΗΛ.　ἐγώ, κασίγνητ', αὐτὸ τοῦτ' ἔχειν δοκῶ,
　　σωτηρίαν σοὶ τῷδέ τ' ἐκ τρίτων τ' ἐμοί.
ΟΡ.　θεοῦ λέγεις πρόνοιαν. ἀλλὰ ποῦ τόδε;
　　ἐπεὶ τὸ συνετόν γ' οἶδα σῇ ψυχῇ παρόν.　　1180
ΗΛ.　ἄκουε δή νυν· καὶ σὺ δεῦρο νοῦν ἔχε.
ΟΡ.　λέγ'· ὡς τὸ μέλλειν ἀγάθ' ἔχει τιν' ἡδονήν.
ΗΛ.　'Ελένης κάτοισθα θυγατέρ'; εἰδότ' ἠρόμην.
ΟΡ.　οἶδ', ἣν <γ'> ἔθρεψεν 'Ερμιόνην μήτηρ ἐμή.
ΗΛ.　αὕτη βέβηκε πρὸς Κλυταιμήστρας τάφον...　1185
ΟΡ.　τί χρῆμα δράσουσ'; ὑποτίθης τίν' ἐλπίδα;
ΗΛ.　χοὰς κατασπείσουσ' ὑπὲρ μητρὸς τάφῳ.
ΟΡ.　καὶ δὴ τί μοι τοῦτ' εἶπας εἰς σωτηρίαν;
ΗΛ.　συλλάβεθ' ὅμηρον τήνδ' ὅταν στείχῃ πάλιν.
ΟΡ.　τίνος τόδ' εἶπας φάρμακον τρισσοῖς φίλοις;1190
ΗΛ.　'Ελένης θανούσης, ἤν τι Μενέλεώς σε δρᾷ
　　ἢ τόνδε κἀμέ – πᾶν γὰρ ἓν φίλον τόδε –
　　λέγ' ὡς φονεύσεις 'Ερμιόνην· ξίφος δὲ χρή
　　δέρῃ πρὸς αὐτῇ παρθένου σπάσαντ' ἔχειν.

1184　γ' add. West

140

I dispose of my betrayers and so that they   1165
groan who have made me suffer. I am after all
the son of Agamemnon, who became leader of
Greece on merit, not by royal succession, and
yet acquired a certain divine strength. I will
not disgrace him with a servile death: I will   1170
discharge my soul like a free man, and make
Menelaus pay. For if we could just get hold of
one thing, good fortune would be ours – if some
unexpected salvation were to drop down from
somewhere so that we killed without being
killed. That's my prayer; it's nice even to   1175
voice my desire in fleeting words and gratify
my mind at no cost.

    EL.   Brother, I think I have that very thing
– salvation for you and Pylades, and also for me.

    OR.   Divine providence, you mean. But ...
where is this salvation? For I know there's
intelligence in your make-up.   1180

    EL.   Listen, now; and you too, Pylades, pay
attention.

    OR.   Say on. There is a certain pleasure
in the prospect of good.

    EL.   You know Helen's daughter? Of course
you do.

    OR.   Yes, the one my mother brought up,
Hermione.

    EL.   She has gone to Clytaemestra's grave – 1185

    OR.   What to do? What hope are you
suggesting?

    EL.   To pour libations at the grave on her
mother's behalf.

    OR.   Well, and what do you tell me this
has to do with saving us?

    EL.   You must seize her as a hostage when
she comes back.

    OR.   What do you prescribe this as the   1190
remedy for, for us three allies?

    EL.   When Helen is dead, if Menelaus tries
to do anything to you or to any of us – this
is all one alliance – tell him you're going to
kill Hermione. You must draw your sword and
hold it right at the girl's throat. If he helps

κἂν μέν σε σῴζῃ μὴ θανεῖν χρῄζων κόρην   1195
'Ελένης Μενέλεως πτῶμ' ἰδὼν ἐν αἵματι,
μέθες πεπᾶσθαι πατρὶ παρθένου δέμας·
ἢν δ' ὀξυθύμου μὴ κρατῶν φρονήματος
κτείνῃ σε, καὶ σὺ σφάζε παρθένου δέρην·
καί νιν δοκῶ, τὸ πρῶτον ἢν πολὺς παρῇ,   1200
χρόνῳ μαλάξειν σπλάγχνον· οὔτε γὰρ θρασύς
οὔτ' ἄλκιμος πέφυκε. τήνδ' ἡμῖν ἔχω
σωτηρίας ἔπαλξιν. εἴρηται λόγος.
ΟΡ. ὦ τὰς φρένας μὲν ἄρσενας κεκτημένη,
τὸ σῶμα δ' ἐν γυναιξὶ θηλείαις πρέπον,   1205
ὡς ἀξία ζῆν μᾶλλον ἢ θανεῖν ἔφυς.
Πυλάδη, τοιαύτης ἄρ' ἁμαρτήσῃ τάλας
γυναικός, ἢ ζῶν μακάριον κτήσῃ λέχος.
ΠΥ. εἰ γὰρ γένοιτο, Φωκέων δ' ἔλθοι πόλιν
καλοῖσιν ὑμεναίοισιν ἀξιουμένη.   1210
ΟΡ. ἥξει δ' ἐς οἴκους 'Ερμιόνη τίνος χρόνου;
ὡς τἆλλα γ' εἶπας εἴπερ εὐτυχήσομεν
κάλλισθ' ἑλόντες σκύμνον ἀνοσίου πατρός.
ΗΛ. καὶ δὴ πέλας νιν δωμάτων εἶναι δοκῶ·
τοῦ γὰρ χρόνου τὸ μῆκος αὐτὸ συντρέχει.   1215
ΟΡ. καλῶς. σὺ μέν νυν, σύγγον''Ηλέκτρα, δόμων
πάρος μένουσα παρθένου δέχου πόδα·
φύλασσε δ' ἢν τις, πρὶν τελευτηθῇ φόνος,
ἢ ξύμμαχός τις ἢ κασίγνητος πατρός,
ἐλθὼν ἐς οἴκους φθῇ, γέγωνέ τ' εἰς δόμους,1220
ἢ σανίδα παίσασ' ἢ λόγους πέμψασ' ἔσω.
ἡμεῖς δ' ἔσω στείχοντες ἐπὶ τὸν ἔσχατον
ἀγῶν' ὁπλιζώμεσθα φασγάνῳ χέρας.
[Πυλάδη· σὺ γὰρ δὴ συμπονεῖς ἐμοὶ πόνους.]
    ὦ δῶμα ναίων Νυκτὸς ὀρφναίας πάτερ,   1225
καλεῖ σ''Ορέστης παῖς σὸς ἐπίκουρον μολεῖν.
[τοῖς δεομένοισι. διὰ σὲ γὰρ πάσχω τάλας
ἀδίκως· προδέδομαι δ' ὑπὸ κασιγνήτου σέθεν,
δίκαια πράξας· οὗ θέλω δάμαρθ' ἑλών   1229
κτεῖναι· σὺ δ' ἡμῖν τοῦδε συλλήπτωρ γενοῦ.]

1196 Μενέλεως (-λαος Tricl.) 'Ελένης codd.: transp. Hermann
1224 susp. Hermann
1227-30 del. Nauck; cf. Σ 1229 ἐν τῷ ἀντιγράφῳ οὐ φέρονται
    οὗτοι οἱ δ' ἴαμβοι

142

to save you because he doesn't want her to die, 1195
after seeing Helen lying in her own blood,
release the girl into her father's possession.
But if he can't control his temper and seeks
your death, you make as if to cut the girl's
throat, and I think that even if he blusters   1200
at first, in time he'll soften his spleen, as
he's not brave or tough by nature. This is the
defence I have for our salvation. End of speech.
     OR. Oh, you have the mind of a man, yet a
body outstanding among the female sex: how   1205
well you deserve to live rather than to die!
You see, Pylades, such is the woman whom you're
to lose, alas - or, if you survive, whose bed
you'll be fortunate to possess.
     PYL. If only that would come true, and she
come to my Phocian community acclaimed in   1210
fine wedding-songs.
     OR. But how soon will Hermione arrive home?
I mean, all you've said is excellent, provided
we can succeed in catching this cub of an
unholy father.
     EL. Already I imagine she's nearing the
house: the length of time agrees in itself.   1215
     OR. Good. You then, Electra, stay in front
of the house and receive the girl when she
comes; but keep a lookout in case before the
killing is finished someone, either our uncle
or some companion-in-arms, approaches the house
too soon, and make it known to us inside   1220
either by knocking on the door-panel or by
sending word in. As for us, let us go in and
equip our hands with swords for the final trial,
[Pylades, since you are sharing the task with
me].
     O father, dwelling in the house of impene-   1225
trable Night, Orestes thy son calls upon thee
to come in aid [to these in their need. It is
on thy account that I am suffering injustice;
and I have been betrayed by thy brother after
doing what was right. His wife I want to seize
and slay: be thou our accomplice in this].   1230

143

ΗΛ. ὦ πάτερ, ἱκοῦ δῆτ', εἰ κλύεις εἴσω χθονός
     τέκνων καλούντων, οἳ σέθεν θνήσκουσ' ὕπερ.
ΠΥ. ὦ συγγένεια πατρὸς ἐμοῦ, κάμὰς λιτάς,
     Ἀγάμεμνον, εἰσάκουσον· ἔκσωσον τέκνα.
ΟΡ. ἔκτεινα μητέρ' ...
ΗΛ.   ἡψάμην δ' ἐγὼ ξίφους ...   1235
ΠΥ. ἐγὼ δέ <γ'> ἐπεκέλευσα κἀπέλυσ' ὄκνου.
ΟΡ. σοί, πάτερ, ἀρήγων.
ΗΛ.   οὐδ' ἐγὼ προύδωκά σε.
ΠΥ. οὔκουν ὀνείδη τάδε κλυὼν ῥύσῃ τέκνα;
ΟΡ. δακρύοις κατασπένδω σ'.
ΗΛ.   ἐγὼ δ' οἴκτοισί γε.
ΠΥ. παύσασθε, καὶ πρὸς ἔργον ἐξορμώμεθα.   1240
     εἴπερ γὰρ εἴσω γῆς ἀκοντίζουσ' ἀραί,
     κλύει. σὺ δ', ὦ Ζεῦ πρόγονε καὶ Δίκης σέβας,
     δότ' εὐτυχῆσαι τῷδ' ἐμοί τε τῇδέ τε.
     τρισσοῖς φίλοις γὰρ εἷς ἀγών, δίκη μία·
     ἢ ζῆν ἅπασιν ἢ θανεῖν ὀφείλεται.   1245

ΗΛ. Μυκηνίδες ὦ φίλιαι,   str.
     τὰ πρῶτα κατὰ Πελασγὸν ἕδος Ἀργείων...
ΧΟ. τίνα θροεῖς αὐδάν, πότνια; παραμένει
     γὰρ ἔτι σοι τόδ' ἐν Δαναϊδῶν πόλει.   1250
ΗΛ. στῆθ' αἳ μὲν ὑμῶν τόνδ' ἀμαξήρη τρίβον,
     αἳ δ' ἐνθάδ' ἄλλον οἶμον, εἰς φρουρὰν δόμων.
ΧΟ. τί δέ με τόδε χρεός ἀπύεις;
     ἔνεπέ μοι, φίλα.
ΗΛ. φόβος ἔχει με μή τις ἐπὶ δώμασι   1255
     σταθεὶς ἐπὶ φοίνιον αἷμα
     πήματα πήμασιν ἐξεύρῃ.
ΗΜ.ᵃ χωρεῖτ', ἐπειγώμεσθ'. ἐγὼ μὲν οὖν τρίβον
     τόνδ' ἐκφυλάξω, τὸν πρὸς ἡλίου βολάς.
ΗΜ.ᵝ καὶ μὴν ἐγὼ τόνδ', ὃς πρὸς ἑσπέραν φέρει. 1260

1234 τέκνα: κακῶν F.W.Schmidt
1235b-6 ΗΛ. ... ΠΥ. Μ²: ΠΥ. ... ΗΛ. MBOVaA
1236 γ' add. Triclinius
      ἐπεκέλευσα BVa: ἐπεβούλευσα MOA
1246 φίλιαι Hermann: φίλαι codd.

EL. O father, come indeed, if inside the
earth thou hearest thy children calling, who
are dying for thy sake.
PYL. O kinsman of my father, o Agamemnon,
give ear to my prayers too: deliver thy children.
OR. I slew my mother –   1235
EL. I handled the sword –
PYL. And I urged him on and freed him from
his hesitation.
OR. – In thy defence, father.
EL. Nor did I betray thee.
PYL. Then hearing these reproaches wilt thou
not save thy children?
OR. With tears I make thee libation –
EL. And I with laments.
PYL. Stop now, and let us set out to the   1240
task, for if prayers do penetrate within the
earth, he hears us. O Zeus our ancestor and
Justice's holiness, grant success to Orestes
and me and Electra here; for this trio of
allies faces a single trial, a single settlement: one sentence for all of us, either life 1245
or death!
   [Orestes and Pylades stride into the house. Music.]

EL.   Dear women of Mycenae,
        first-ranking in the Argives' Pelasgian
           seat –
CH.   What speech would you voice, my lady? This
        title still remains with you in the city 1250
        of Danaus' children.
EL.   Take up positions, some of you on the
        carriage-way here, others here on the
        other path, to watch before the house.
CH.   But why do you cry me this need?
        Say, as I love you.
EL.   I am afraid lest anyone stop   1255
        by the house, at the deed of blood,
        and discover new woes upon old.
SEMICHORUS 1. Forward, let's make haste. I'll
        guard this road, then, the one towards
        the sun's shafts.
SEMICHORUS 2. And I this westward one.   1260

145

ΗΛ. δόχμιά νυν κόρας διάφερ' ὀμμάτων
ἐκεῖθεν ἐνθάδ', εἶτα πάλιν.
ΧΟ.   σκοπιάν
ἔχομεν ὡς θροεῖς.   1265

ΗΛ. ἐλίσσετέ νυν βλέφαρον,   ant.
κόραισι δίδοτε πάντα διὰ βοστρύχων.
ΗΜ.ᵃ ὅδε τις ἐν τρίβῳ· πρόσεχε· τίς ὅδ' ἄρ' ἀμφὶ μέλαθρον πολεῖ σὸν ἀγρότας ἀνήρ;   1270
ΗΛ. ἀπωλόμεσθ' ἄρ', ὦ φίλαι· κεκρυμμένους
θῆρας ξιφήρεις αὐτίκ' ἐχθροῖσιν φανεῖ.
ΗΜ.ᵃ ἄφοβος ἔχε· κενός, ὦ φίλα,
στίβος ὃν οὐ δοκεῖς.
ΗΛ. τί δέ; τὸ σὸν βέβαιον ἔτι μοι μένει;   1275
δὸς ἀγγελίαν ἀγαθάν τιν',
εἰ τάδ' ἔρημα τὰ πρόσθ' αὐλᾶς.
ΗΜ.ᵝ καλῶς τά γ' ἐνθένδ'· ἀλλὰ τἀπὶ σοῦ σκόπει,
ὡς οὔτις ἡμῖν Δαναϊδῶν πελάζεται.
ΗΜ.ᵃ εἰς ταὐτὸν ἥκεις· καὶ γὰρ οὐδὲ τῇδ' ὄχλος.1280
ΗΛ. φέρε νυν ἐν πύλαισιν ἀκοὰν βάλω.
τί μέλλεθ' οἱ κατ' οἶκον ἐν ἡσυχίᾳ
σφάγια φοινίσσειν;   1285

οὐκ εἰσακούουσ'· ὦ τάλαιν' ἐγὼ κακῶν.   epod.
ἆρ' εἰς τὸ κάλλος ἐκκεκώφηται ξίφη;
τάχα τις Ἀργείων ἔνοπλος ὁρμήσας
ποδὶ βοηδρόμῳ μέλαθρα προσμείξει.   1290
σκέψασθέ νῦν ἄμεινον· οὐχ ἕδρας ἀγών·
ἀλλ' αἳ μὲν ἐνθάδ', αἳ δ' ἐκεῖσ' ἐλίσσετε.
ΧΟ. ἀμείβω κέλευθον
σκοπεύουσα πάντα.   1295

(βοὴ ἔνδοθεν)
ἰὼ Πελασγὸν Ἄργος, ὄλλυμαι κακῶς.
ΗΛ. ἠκούσαθ'; ἄνδρες χεῖρ' ἔχουσιν ἐν φόνῳ.
ΧΟ. Ἑλένης τὸ κώκυμ' ἐστίν, ὡς ἀπεικάσαι.

1267 κόρας διάδοτε Canter | πάντα διὰ β. Triclinius:
διὰ β. πάντη(ι) fere codd. Σ (πάντα KSaˢGL)
1269 πρόσεχε Seidler: προσέρχεται codd.: τίς ὅδε Hermann
1278 τἀπὶ σοῦ fere MA: τἀπίσω M²BOVa: τοὐπίσω GᶜΞ
1285 σφαγίδα Σʸᵖ
1287 ἐκκεκώφηνται ΣʸᵖPr Sa Clem.: -ωνται Ar. Byz. ap. Σ

EL. Sideways now turn your sight about,
     from there to here, then back again.
CH. We're keeping watch obedient to your call.1265
EL. Be wheeling your eye, now,
     let your pupils take in everything
          through your hanging hair.
SEM. 1. Here's someone on the path! Attention:
     who is this moving about near your palace,
     this countryman?   1270
EL. We're lost, then, my dears; he will reveal
     the lurking sworded predators to our foes
     directly!
SEM. 1. Keep courage, dear mistress, the track
     is empty that you think otherwise.
EL. What about your side, is it still secure? 1275
     Give a report, of a good kind
     if it's all clear there on the approach
          to the courtyard.
SEM. 2. All's well from this side: just watch
     your sector, as none of Danaus' stock
     is coming towards us.
SEM. 1. The same result. No people about this 1280
     way either.
EL. All right, let me put my ear to the doors.
     You in the house, why so slow, when all's
     quiet, to stain the slaughter-victim red? 1285

     They're not listening. O misery me!
     Have their swords lost their edge in the
          face of that beauty?
     Soon someone from the Argives, speeding
     in arms on a rescue run, will engage the 1290
     palace. Take a better look now: it is not
     a test of sitting inactive. One group
     wheel here, the other there.
CH. I change tracks
     and keep watch   on each road.   1295
[Cry within] Oyé, Pelasgian Argos, I am
          perishing foully!
EL. Did you hear that? The men have their
     hands at a killing.
CH. It is Helen's scream, to judge by the

147

ΗΛ.　ὦ Διός, ὦ Διὸς ἀέναον κράτος,
　　　ἔλθ' ἐπίκουρος ἐμοῖσι φίλοισι πάντως.　　1300
(βοὴ ἔνδοθεν)
　　　Μενέλαε, θνήσκω, σὺ δὲ παρὼν μ'οὐκ ὠφελεῖς.
ΧΟ.ΗΛ.　φονεύετε καίνετε θείνετ'
　　　ὄλλυτε, δίπτυχα δίστομα φάσγαν'
　　　ἐκ χερὸς ἱέμενοι,
　　　τὰν λιποπάτορα λιπογάμετον, ἃ πλείστους　　1305
　　　ἔκανεν Ἑλλάνων
　　　δορὶ παρὰ ποταμὸν ὀλομένους,
　　　ὅθι δάκρυα δάκρυσιν
　　　ἔπεσε σιδαρέοισι βέλεσιν ἀμφὶ τὰς
　　　Σκαμάνδρου δίνας.　　　　　　　　　　　　1310

ΧΟ.　σιγᾶτε σιγᾶτ'· ᾐσθόμην κτύπον τινός
　　　κέλευθον εἰσπεσόντος ἀμφὶ δώματα.
ΗΛ.　ὦ φίλταται γυναῖκες, εἰς μέσον φόνον
　　　ἥδ' Ἑρμιόνη πάρεστι. παύσωμεν βοήν·
　　　στείχει γὰρ εἰσπαίσουσα δικτύων βρόχους.　1315
　　　καλὸν τὸ θήραμ', ἢν ἁλῷ, γενήσεται.
　　　πάλιν κατάστηθ', ἡσύχῳ μὲν ὄμματι,
　　　χροιᾷ τ' ἀδήλῳ τῶν δεδραμένων πέρι·
　　　κἀγὼ σκυθρωποὺς ὀμμάτων ἔξω κόρας,
　　　ὡς δῆθεν οὐκ εἰδυῖα τάξειργασμένα.　　　1320
　　　ὦ παρθέν', ἥκεις τὸν Κλυταιμήστρας τάφον
　　　στέψασα καὶ σπείσασα νερτέροις χοάς;
ΕΡΜΙΟΝΗ
　　　ἥκω, λαβοῦσα πρευμένειαν. ἀλλά μοι
　　　φόβος τις εἰσελήλυθ', ἥντιν' ἐν δόμοις

1295　σκοπεύουσα Nauck: σκοποῦσα codd.: σκοπεύς cod. Anecd.
　　　Studemund. p.226
1302　θείνετε Μ^{γρ} +: om. MBOVaA
1303　φάσγανα πέμπετε MBO^{ac}Va
1305　τὰν OKG: om. MBVaA
　　　λιπογάμετον West: λ(ε)ιπόγαμον codd.
1309　ἔπεσεν ἔπεσε σιδαρέοις Parker
1311　κτύπον K^s+: κτύπου MBOVaA
1313　μέσον βόλον Wecklein
1315　ἐσπαίσουσα Wecklein: εἰσπεσοῦσα codd.
　　　βρο]χοις Π13
1320　fin.]κακα Π13

sound of it.

EL.   O Zeus', Zeus' unfailing power,
       come to support my dear ones whatever   1300
          you do.
[*Cry within*]   Menelaus, I'm *DYING*, and you're not
       here to help me!
EL. and CH.   Slaughter her, slay her,
          smite her, finish her,
       darting the twofold, two-edged swords
       at grappling range -
       that deserter of father, deserter of
          husband, who brought   1305
       death to unparalleled numbers of Greeks
       spear-slain beside the river
       where tears upon tears were shed
       by dint of iron missiles round
       the waters of Scamander.   1310

    CHORUS-LEADER.   Quiet, quiet - I hear the
sound of someone who has got onto the path
near the house.
    [*Hermione is seen approaching.*]
    EL.   Oh my dears, here is Hermione arrived
in the middle of the killing. We must stop
our clamour, she is about to walk smack into   1315
the net. A lovely catch she'll make if
she's captured! Take up your stations again,
with faces calm and colour unrevealing about
what's been done, and I'll keep my eyes cast
down as though I don't know of these doings.   1320
    Hermione, have you come from adorning
Clytaemestra's tomb and pouring libations to
the nether ones?
    HERMIONE.   I have, and I got her benevolence.
But a certain fear has got into me, as to what

149

τηλουρὸς οὖσα δωμάτων κλύω βοήν.   1325
ΗΛ. τί δ'; ἄξι' ἡμῖν τυγχάνει στεναγμάτων.
ΕΡ. εὔφημος ἴσθι· τί δὲ νεώτερον λέγεις;
ΗΛ. θανεῖν 'Ορέστην κἄμ' ἔδοξε τῇδε γῇ.
ΕΡ. μὴ δῆτ', ἐμούς γε συγγενεῖς πεφυκότας.
ΗΛ. ἄραρ'· ἀνάγκης δ' εἰς ζυγὸν καθέσταμεν.   1330
ΕΡ. ἦ τοῦδ' ἕκατι καὶ βοὴ κατὰ στέγας;
ΗΛ. ἱκέτης γὰρ 'Ελένης γόνασι προσπεσὼν βοᾷ —
ΕΡ. τίς; οὐδὲν οἶδα μᾶλλον, ἢν σὺ μὴ λέγῃς.
ΗΛ. τλήμων 'Ορέστης, μὴ θανεῖν, ἐμοῦ θ' ὕπερ.
ΕΡ. ἐπ' ἀξίοισι τἄρ' ἀνευφημεῖ δόμος.   1335
ΗΛ. περὶ τοῦ γὰρ ἄλλου μᾶλλον ἂν φθέγξαιτό τις;
     ἀλλ' ἐλθὲ καὶ μετάσχες ἱκεσίας φίλοις,
     σῇ μητρὶ προσπεσοῦσα τῇ μέγ' ὀλβίᾳ,
     Μενέλαον ἡμᾶς μὴ θανόντας εἰσιδεῖν.
     ἄγ', ὦ τραφεῖσα μητρὸς ἐν χεροῖν ἐμῆς,   1340
     οἴκτιρον ἡμᾶς κἀπικούφισον κακῶν.
     ἴθ' εἰς ἀγῶνα δεῦρ', ἐγὼ δ' ἡγήσομαι·
     σωτηρίας γὰρ τέρμ' ἔχεις ἡμῖν μόνη.
ΕΡ. ἰδού, διώκω τὸν ἐμὸν εἰς δόμους πόδα.
     σώθηθ' ὅσον γε τοὐπ' ἔμ'.
ΗΛ.   ὦ κατὰ στέγας   1345
     φίλοι ξιφήρεις, οὐχὶ συλλήψεσθ' ἄγραν;
ΕΡ. οἲ 'γώ· τίνας τούσδ' εἰσορῶ;
ΗΛ.   σιγᾶν χρεών·
     ἡμῖν γὰρ ἥκεις, οὐχὶ σοί, σωτηρία.
     ἔχεσθ' ἔχεσθε· φάσγανον δὲ πρὸς δέρῃ
     βαλόντες ἡσυχάζεθ', ὡς εἰδῇ τόδε   1350
     Μενέλαος, οὕνεκ' ἄνδρας, οὐ Φρύγας κακούς
     εὑρὼν ἔπραξεν οἷα χρὴ πράσσειν κακούς.

1329 ἐμούς BVaA: ἐμοῦ ΜΟ
1340 αγ Π7 (coniecerat Weil): ἀλλ' codd.

crying it was in the house that I heard as I
was still a long way off.   1325
    EL. Why, things are coming our way that
justify groans.
    HER. Speak no evil. But what do you mean,
that's new?
    EL. Death for Orestes and me has been
decreed by the state.
    HER. God forbid - you are my relations.
    EL. It is fixed; so we have been set to   1330
the yoke of necessity.
    HER. And is this why there is clamour in
the house?
    EL. Yes, for fallen as suppliant at Helen's
knees there cries ...
    HER. Who? I am none the wiser if you don't
say.
    EL. Poor Orestes, that he should not die,
and also on my behalf.
    HER. It is for good reason, then, that the   1335
house wails aloud.
    EL. Yes, what else should anyone rather
make a noise about? Now, come and join your
cousins in their supplication, crouching
before your mother, that so fortunate lady,
so that she does not let Menelaus stand by and
see us die. Come, you were nursed in my   1340
mother's arms, have pity on us and give us
relief from our woes. Step forward to the
struggle, this way, I'll escort you - our
final salvation lies in you alone.
    HER. See, I'm hurrying my feet into the
house. Salvation be yours, so far as it rests
with me.   1345
    EL. [*just inside the doorway*] Ahoy, my sworded
comrades within, won't you seize the prey?
    HER. Oh! Oh! Who are these I see?
    EL. Silence! Your coming means salvation
for us, not for you. Hold her, hold her; set
the sword at her throat and take it easy - so   1350
Menelaus may know he has encountered men, not
worthless Phrygians, and fared as villains
ought to fare. [*They disappear inside. Music.*]

ΧΟ. ἰὼ ἰὼ φίλαι,   str.
κτύπον ἐγείρετε, κτύπον καὶ βοάν
πρὸ μελάθρων, ὅπως ὁ πραχθεὶς φόνος
μὴ δεινὸν ᾿Αργείοισιν ἐμβάλῃ φόβον   1355
βοηδρομῆσαι πρὸς δόμους τυραννικούς
πρὶν ἐτύμως ἴδω τὸν ῾Ελένας φόνον
καθαιμακτὸν ἐν δόμοις κείμενον,
ἢ καὶ λόγον του προσπόλων πυθώμεθα·
τὰ μὲν γὰρ οἶδα συμφορᾶς, τὰ δ᾿ οὐ σαφῶς. 1360
διὰ δίκας ἔβα θεῶν
νέμεσις ἐς ῾Ελέναν·
δακρύοισι γὰρ ῾Ελλάδ᾿ ἅπασαν ἔπλησεν
διὰ τὸν ὀλόμενον ὀλόμενον ᾿Ιδαῖον
Πάριν ὃς ἄγαγ᾿ ῾Ελλάδ᾿εἰς ῎Ιλιον.   1365

── ἀλλὰ κτυπεῖ γὰρ κλῆθρα βασιλείων δόμων,
σιγήσατ᾿· ἔξω γάρ τις ἐκβαίνει Φρυγῶν,
οὗ πευσόμεσθα τὰν δόμοις ὅπως ἔχει.
ΦΡΥΞ
᾿Αργεῖον ξίφος ἐκ θανάτου   astroph.
πέφευγα βαρβάροις ἐν εὐμάρισιν   1370
κεδρωτὰ παστάδων
ὑπὲρ τέραμνα Δωρικάς τε τριγλύφους,
φροῦδα φροῦδα, γᾶ γᾶ,
βαρβάροισι δρασμοῖς.
αἰαῖ·   1375
πᾷ φύγω, ξέναι,
πολιὸν αἰθέρ᾿ ἀμ-
πτάμενος ἢ πόντον, ᾿Ωκεανὸς ὃν
ταυρόκρανος ἀγκάλαις
ἑλίσσων κυκλοῖ χθόνα;
ΧΟ. τί δ᾿ ἐστίν, ῾Ελένης πρόσπολ᾿, ᾿Ιδαῖον κάρα;
ΦΡ. ῎Ιλιον ῎Ιλιον, ὤμοι μοι,   1381
Φρύγιον ἄστυ καὶ καλλίβωλον ῎Ι-
δας ὄρος ἱερόν, ὥς σ᾿ ὀλόμενον στένω
ἁρμάτειον ἁρμάτειον μέλος

─────────

1360 τὰ ... τὰ Μᶜ: τὰς ... τὰς (et συμφοράς) Π13 codd.
1366-8 damn. Σ: fort. 1366 solus delendus est
1381 ὤμοι μοι Π19 codd.: κ]ακων Π14

152

CH. Io, io, my dears,
     rouse stamping, dancing and song
     in front of the palace, so that this
        blood-deed
     may not strike dread alarm into the Argives
     to make them run to aid the royal house   1356
     before I truly see the slain Helen
     lying bloodied within,
     or else hear word from one of her attendants;
     for part of the drama I know, part not for sure.
     Justly the gods' disapprobation   1361
     has visited Helen,
     for she filled all Greece with tears
     because of that accursed, accursed Idaean
     Paris, who brought Greece to Ilion.   1365

     CHORUS-LEADER. But the bars of the palace
doors are clanking. Be quiet, one of the
Phrygians is coming out, from whom we'll hear
the state of things inside. [*A Phrygian has
appeared on the roof and is scrambling down.*]

PHRYGIAN. Out of death I have escaped
     the Argive sword in Asian moccasins   1370
     over the boudoir's
     cedared timbers and the Doric triglyphs –
     gone, gone, O land! O land! –
     in my barbarian flight.
     Woe is me!   1375
     Which way may I escape, ladies:
     by flying up unto the white heaven,
     or to the sea that Ocean the bull-headed
     winds in his arms as he rounds the earth?
CH.-L. What is it, O footman of Helen, Idaean
     soul?   1380
PHR. Ilion, Ilion, ah woe, woe!
     Phrygian city and fair-glebed holy mountain
     of Ida, how I moan your fall
     with barbarian cry, a chariot, chariot
        melody:

βαρβάρῳ βοᾷ, δι' ὀρνιθόγονον   1385
  ὄμμα κυκνόπτερον καλλοσύνας, Λήδας
σκύμνον, Δυσελέναν Δυσελέναν,
ξεστῶν περγάμων
'Απολλωνίων 'Ερινύν.
ὀττοτοῖ
ἰαλέμων ἰαλέμων·   1390
Δαρδανία τλάμων,
Γανυμήδεος ἱπποσύνα, Διὸς εὐνέτα.
ΧΟ. σαφῶς λέγ' ἡμῖν αὖθ' ἕκαστα τάν δόμοις.
     [τὰ γὰρ πρὶν οὐκ εὔγνωστα συμβαλοῦσ' ἔχω.]
ΦΡ. αἴλινον αἴλινον ἀρχὰν θανάτου   1395
    βάρβαροι λέγουσιν,
    αἰαῖ, 'Ασιάδι φωνᾷ,
    βασιλέων ὅταν αἷμα χυθῇ κατὰ γᾶν
    ξίφεσι σιδαρέοισιν "Αιδα.
ἦλθον εἰς δόμους,   1400
ἵν' αὖθ' ἕκαστά σοι λέγω,
λέοντες "Ελλανες δύο διδύμω·
τῷ μὲν ὁ στρατηλάτας πατὴρ ἐκλῄζετο,
ὁ δὲ παῖς Στροφίου, κακόμητις ἀνήρ
  οἷος 'Οδυσσεύς, σιγᾷ δόλιος,
  πιστὸς δὲ φίλοις· θρασὺς εἰς ἀλκάν,   1405
  ξυνετὸς πολέμου, φόνιός τε δράκων·
ἔρροι τᾶς ἡσύχου
προνοίας κακοῦργος ὤν.
οἵ δὲ πρὸς θρόνους ἔσω
μολόντες ἇς ἔγημ' ὁ τοξότας Πάρις
γυναικός, ὄμμα δακρύοις   1410
πεφυρμένοι, ταπεινοί
ἔζονθ', ὁ μὲν τὸ κεῖθεν, ὁ δὲ
  τὸ κεῖθεν, ἄλλος ἄλλοθεν δεδραγμένοι,

1385 δι' Porson: διὰ τὸ τᾶς Π19 codd. Σ
1387 Δυσελέναν rec. (semel tantum), Kirchhoff (bis): -νας
      bis fere HMBOVaA
1394 deest in Π19, deerat in multis libris teste Σ
1395 ἀρχᾶν θανάτῳ Kirchhoff: ἀρχὰν θρήνου Hartung (cf.Σ):
      an ἰαλέμων ἰαλέμων (1390) pro θανάτου ponendum?
1397 possis αἰαῖ αἰαῖ (Paley), 'Ασίδι
1413 δεδραγμένοι Shilleto: πεφραγμένοι codd. Σ

                   all because of the bird-born   1385
                   swan-plume vision of loveliness, Leda's
                   lion-cub, Ill-Helen, Ill-Helen,
                   the dressed Apolline battlements'
                   Vengeance incarnate.
                   Ottotoi, the dirges, the dirges!   1390
                   Unhappy land of Dardanus:
                   the riding of Ganymede, Zeus' concubine.
CH.-L.   Tell us plainly the exact details of
                   events indoors. [For what you said before
                   I have not been able to interpret with
                   certainty.]
PHR.   Ailinon, Ailinon barbarians say   1395
                   to inaugurate death, ah woe!
                   with Asian voice, when royal blood
                   is shed on earth by Hades-swords of iron.
                      There came into the house   1400
                   (to give you the exact particulars)
                   lions of Greece, a matching pair.
                   One was called the son of the Commander;
                   the other, Strophius' son, a man of
                      harsh resource
                   like Odysseus, silently cunning
                   yet true to his friends, bold in battle,   1405
                   skilled in fighting, and a deadly snake:
                   damn him for his calm
                   purposiveness, the villain.
                      They came in to the seat
                   of her whom Paris the bowman wed,
                   their faces blurred with tears,   1410
                   and crouched all humble, one this side,
                      one that,
                   clutching from different angles,

                                   155

περὶ δὲ γόνυ χέρας ἱκεσίους
ἔβαλον ἔβαλον ῾Ελένας ἄμφω.　　　　　　　1415
ἀνὰ δὲ δρομάδες ἔθορον ἔθορον
　ἀμφίπολοι Φρύγες·
προσεῖπεν δ᾽ἄλλος ἄλλον πεσὼν ἐν φόβῳ,
μή τις εἴη δόλος,
κἀδόκει τοῖς μὲν οὔ,　　　　　　　　　　1420
τοῖς δ᾽ ἐς ἀρκυστάτων
μηχανὰν ἐμπλέκειν
παῖδα τὰν Τυνδαρίδ᾽ ὁ
ματροφόντας δράκων.
ΧΟ. σὺ δ᾽ἦσθα ποῦ τότ᾽; ἦ πάλαι φεύγεις φόβῳ; 1425
ΦΡ. Φρυγίοις ἔτυχον Φρυγίοισι νόμοις
παρὰ βόστρυχον αὔραν αὔραν
῾Ελένας ῾Ελένας εὔπαγεῖ
κύκλῳ πτερίνῳ πρὸ παρηΐδος ἀΐσσων·
[βαρβάροισι νόμοισιν.]　　　　　　　　　1430
ἃ δὲ <χρυσέα> λίνον ἠλακάτᾳ
δακτύλοις ἕλισσεν -
νῆμα δ᾽ ἵετο πέδῳ -
σκύλων Φρυγίων ἐπὶ τύμβον ἀγάλ-
ματα συστολίσαι χρῄζουσα λίνῳ,　　　　1435
φάρεα πορφύρεα, δῶρα Κλυταιμήστρᾳ.
προσεῖπεν δ᾽ ᾽Ορέστας
Λάκαιναν κόραν· "ὦ
Διὸς παῖ, θὲς ἴχνος
πέδῳ δεῦρ᾽ ἀποστᾶσα κλισμοῦ　　　　　1440
Πέλοπος ἐπὶ προπάτορος ἔδρανα
παλαιᾶς ἑστίας,
ἵν᾽ εἰδῇς λόγους ἐμούς."
ἄγει δ᾽ ἄγει νιν, ἃ δ᾽ ἐφείπετ᾽
οὐ πρόμαντις ὧν ἔμελλεν·　　　　　　　1445
ὁ δὲ συνεργὸς ἄλλ᾽ ἔπρασσ᾽·
ἰὼν κακὸς Φωκεύς·

1421　ἀρκυστάτων Blomfield: -τάταν codd. Σ
1430　βαρβάροισι νόμοισιν del. Hartung
1431　χρυσέᾳ add. West: non habuit Π20
1433　νῆμα δ᾽ OL: νήμαθ᾽ ΗΑ: νήματα δ᾽ ΜΒVaΣ
1441　ἔδρανα Π20: ἕδραν codd. Σ

156

and flung, both flung their suppliant arms
round Helen's knees.   1415
    Up at a run they leapt, they leapt,
the Phrygian footmen;
and one spoke to another, fallen afraid
lest it should be some trick:
and some thought not,   1420
but some thought that the child
of Tyndareos was being entwined
in a device of hunting-nets
by that matricidal snake.
CH.-L. And where were you at that point? Or   1425
had you long since fled in panic?
PHR. I chanced in the Phrygian, Phrygian fashion
to be speeding a breeze, a breeze
past the tresses of Helen, of Helen,
    across her cheek
with a roundel of firm-set plumes
    [in Asian fashion];   1430
and she with <golden> distaff
was twisting yarn in her fingers,
the spun thread making for the floor,
for from the Phrygian spoils
she wanted to make up finery for the   1435
    grave-mound,
clothes of purple to offer Clytaemestra.
    Orestes   addressed then
the maid from   Laconia:
"O daughter of Zeus, set down your foot
on the ground, this way, away from your   1440
    chair,
to Pelops my forefather's
ancient hearth-seat
to learn what I have to say."
And he led her, led her, and she followed
with no presentiment of what he planned.   1445
His accomplice was going about other
    business,
the evil Phocian:

157

"οὐκ ἐκποδών ἴτ' ἄλλα, κακοὶ Φρύγες;"
ἔκλησεν δ' ἄλλον ἄλλοσ' ἐν στέγαισι,
τοὺς μὲν ἐν σταθμοῖσιν ἱππι-
κοῖσι, τοὺς δ' ἐν ἐξέδραισι,
τοὺς δ' ἐκεῖσ' ἐκεῖθεν, ἄλλον   1450
ἄλλοσε διαρμόσας ἀποπρὸ δεσποίνας.
ΧΟ. τί τοὐπὶ τῷδε συμφορᾶς ἐγίγνετο;
ΦΡ. 'Ιδαία μᾶτερ μᾶτερ
ὀβρίμα ὀβρίμα, αἰαῖ <αἰαῖ>
φονίων παθέων ἀνόμων τε κακῶν   1455
ἅπερ ἔδρακον ἔδρακον ἐν δόμοις τυράννων.
ἀμφιπορφύρων πέπλων
ὑπὸ σκότου ξίφη σπάσαντες ἐν χεροῖν
ἄλλοσ' ἄλλοθεν
δίνησαν ὄμμα, μή τις παρὼν τύχοι.
ὡς κάπροι δ' ὀρέστεροι
γυναικὸς ἀντίοι σταθέντες   1460
  ἐννέπουσι "κατθανῇ, κατθανῇ·
κακός σ' ἀποκτείνει πόσις,
κασιγνήτου προδοὺς
ἐν Ἄργει θανεῖν γόνον."
ἃ δ' ἀνίαχεν ἴαχεν "ὤμοι μοι"·   1465
λευκὸν δ' ἐμβαλοῦσα πῆχυν στέρνοις
κτύπησε κρᾶτα μέλεον πλαγάν·
φυγᾷ δὲ ποδὶ τὸ χρυσεοσάμβαλον ἴχνος
ἔφερεν ἔφερεν· εἰς κόμας δὲ
  δακτύλους δικὼν 'Ορέστας,
Μυκηνίδ' ἀρβύλαν προβάς,   1470
ὠμοῖς ἀριστεροῖσιν ἀνακλάσας δέρην
παίειν λαιμῶν ἔμελλεν εἴσω μέλαν ξίφος.

1447 ἄλλαι Aᵃᶜ?, Scaliger: ἀλλ'αἰεὶ M, ἀλλ'ἀεὶ H?BOVa,
      alterutrum A¹?
1454 αἰαῖ iteravit Weil
1457 ἀμφιπορφύρων Radermacher: ἀμφιπορφυρέων MFSa, ἀμφὶ
      πορφυρέων HBOVaA
1458 ἐν MᶜFKPrŞaGLξ: ἐκ HMᵃᶜBOVaA | ἄλλοσ' ἄλλοθεν
      δίνησαν Willink: ἄλλος ἄλλοσε δίνασεν codd.
1467 πλαγᾷ MA
1468 -σάμβαλον HʸᵖMᵃᶜB: -σάνδαλον HᶜMᶜB²OVaA
1469-70 rhythmus laborat, v. comm.

"Won't you clear off elsewhere, you
  Phrygian scum?"
And he shut us up in different parts of
  the buildings,
some in the stables, some in the verandahs,
some moved from here to there - in all   1450
  directions
setting us apart, well clear of our
  mistress.
CH.-L. What was the next phase of the episode?
PHR. Idaean Mother, Mother,
  terrible, terrible goddess! Oh, oh,   1455
the murderous ordeals, the outrageous evils
that I witnessed, witnessed in the royal
  house!
With swords in their hands drawn from
  the shadow
of purple-bordered robes,
they rolled their eyes from side to side
to see no one was there.
Like mountain boars they stood facing   1460
  the woman,
and said "You are to die, to die:
your vile husband is your cause of death,
who has betrayed his brother's
children to die - in Argos!"   1464
She screamed aloud, screamed "O woe, woe!",
and clapping her pale forearm to her chest
she beat her head a sorry blow;
then on her foot in flight bore off,
  bore off
her golden sandal-sole. Orestes,
flinging his fingers in her hair,
getting his Mycenaean boot ahead,   1470
bending her neck back to his left
  shoulder,
prepared to strike his dark sword in
  her throat.

ΧΟ. ποῦ δ᾽ ἦστ᾽ ἀμύνειν οἱ κατὰ στέγας Φρύγες;
ΦΡ. ἰαχᾷ δόμων θύρετρα καὶ σταθμούς
μοχλοῖσιν ἐκβαλόντες, ἔνθ᾽ ἐμίμνομεν,
βοηδρομοῦμεν ἄλλος ἄλλοθεν στέγης,   1475
ὃ μὲν πέτρους, ὃ δ᾽ ἀγκύλας,
ὃ δὲ ξίφος πρόκωπον ἐν χεροῖν ἔχων.
ἔναντα δ᾽ ἦλθεν Πυλάδης ἀλίαστος
οἷος οἷος Ἑκ-
τωρ ὁ Φρύγιος ἢ τρικόρυθος   1480
Αἴας, ὃν εἶδον εἶδον
ἐν πύλαισι Πριαμίσιν.
φασγάνων δ᾽ ἀκμὰς συνήψα-
μεν· τότε δὴ τότε διαπρεπεῖς ἐγένοντο
Φρύγες,
ὅσον Ἄρεος ἀλκὰν <ἀλκάν>
ἥσσονες Ἑλλάδος ἐγενόμεθ᾽ αἰχμᾶς,   1485
ὃ μὲν οἰχόμενος φυγάς, ὃ δὲ νέκυς ὤν,
ὃ δὲ τραῦμα φέρων,
ὃ δὲ λισσόμενος θανάτου προβολάν·
ὑπὸ σκότον δ᾽ ἐφεύγομεν,
νεκροὶ δ᾽ ἔπιπτον, οἳ δ᾽ ἔμελλον, οἳ δ᾽ ἔκειντ᾽·
ἔμολε δ᾽ ἁ τάλαιν᾽ Ἑρμιόνα δόμους   1490
ἐπὶ φόνῳ χαμαιπετεῖ ματρός, ἃ
νιν ἔτεκεν τλάμων·
ἄθυρσοι δ᾽ οἷά νιν
δραμόντε Βάκχαι σκύμνον ἐν χεροῖν
ὀρείαν ξυνήρπασαν.
πάλιν δὲ τὰν Διὸς κόρας
ἐπὶ σφαγὰν ἔτεινον· ἃ δ᾽ ἀπὸ θαλάμων
ἐγένετο διαπρὸ δωμάτων ἄφαντος,   1495
ὦ Ζεῦ καὶ Γᾶ καὶ Φῶς καὶ Νύξ,
ἤτοι φαρμάκοισιν ἢ μάγων
τέχναισιν ἢ θεῶν κλοπαῖς.
τὰ δ᾽ ὕστερ᾽ οὐκέτ᾽ οἶδα· δρα-
πέτην γὰρ ἐξέκλεπτον ἐκ δόμων πόδα.

1473 δ᾽ἦτ᾽ (F²+) vel δῆτ᾽ codd.: corr. West
1474 ἐμβαλόντες HMBA
1484 ἀλκάν iteravit West
1493 κόρας Rauchenstein: κόραν codd.
1494 ἀπὸ Weil: ἐκ codd.

CH.-L. And where were you to defend her, you
      Phrygian domestics?
PHR. With a yell, using crowbars, we cracked
      out the door-posts
      and frames of the rooms in which we were
        detained,
      and ran to the rescue from different   1475
        parts of the building,
      one with stones, another with slings,
      another with drawn sword in his hands.
      But against us came Pylades, unflinching
      as Hector the Phrygian, or triple-helmèd   1480
        Ajax,
      whom I saw, I saw at Priam's gates.
      So we joined sword-points: then indeed
        the Phrygians
      showed up outstandingly
      how far in martial prowess we were born
      inferior to Greek arms,   1485
      one fled, another dead, another wounded,
      another begging to protect his life.
      So we were seeking refuge in the shadows,
      some falling slain, some soon to fall,
        some fallen,
      when the unhappy Hermione arrived,   1490
      just as the mother who had the
        misfortune to bear her
      was being killed and sinking to the ground.
      Like Bacchants at a mountain cub (lacking
        only the thyrsus)
      they ran and seized her in their grip,
      then reached again toward the slaughtering
      of Zeus' daughter - but she from the
        chambers
      had vanished out through the house,   1495
      O Zeus, O Earth, O Light and Dark!
      either by magic drugs or sorcerers' arts
      or gods' deceits.
      What followed, I know not; I was smuggling
      out of the building my runaway legs;

πολύπονα δὲ πολύπονα πάθεα Μενέλας   1500
ἀνασχόμενος ἀνό-
νατον ἀπὸ Τροίας ἔλαβε
τὸν 'Ελένας γάμον.
ΧΟ. καὶ μὴν ἀμείβει καινὸν ἐκ καινῶν τόδε·
ξιφηφόρον γὰρ εἰσορῶ πρὸ δωμάτων
βαίνοντ' 'Ορέστην ἐπτοημένῳ ποδί.   1505
ΟΡ. ποῦ 'στιν οὗτος ὃς πέφευγεν ἐκ δόμων τοὐμὸν ξίφος;
ΦΡ. προσκυνῶ σ', ἄναξ, νόμοισι βαρβάροισι προσπίτνων.
ΟΡ. οὐκ ἐν 'Ιλίῳ τάδ' ἐστίν, ἀλλ' ἐν 'Αργείᾳ χθονί.
ΦΡ. πανταχοῦ ζῆν ἡδὺ μᾶλλον ἢ θανεῖν τοῖς σώφροσιν.
ΟΡ. οὔ τί που κραυγὴν ἔθηκας Μενέλεῳ βοηδρομεῖν;   1510
ΦΡ. σοὶ μὲν οὖν ἔγωγ' ἀμύνειν· ἀξιώτερος γὰρ εἶ.
ΟΡ. ἐνδίκως ἡ Τυνδάρειος ἄρα παῖς διώλετο;
ΦΡ. ἐνδικώτατ', εἴ γε λαιμοὺς εἶχε τριπτύχους θενεῖν.
ΟΡ. δειλίᾳ γλώσσῃ χαρίζῃ, τἄνδον οὐχ οὕτω φρονῶν.
ΦΡ. οὐ γάρ, ἥτις 'Ελλάδ' αὐτοῖς Φρυξὶ διελυμήνατο;   1515
ΟΡ. ὄμοσον – εἰ δὲ μή, κτενῶ σε – μὴ λέγειν ἐμὴν χάριν.
ΦΡ. τὴν ἐμὴν ψυχὴν κατώμοσ', ἥν ἂν εὐορκοῖμ' ἐγώ.
ΟΡ. ὧδε κἀν Τροίᾳ σίδηρος πᾶσι Φρυξὶν ἦν φόβος;
ΦΡ. ἄπεχε φάσγανον· πέλας γὰρ δεινὸν ἀνταυγεῖ φόνον.
ΟΡ. μὴ πέτρος γένῃ δέδοικας, ὥστε Γοργόν' εἰσιδών;   1520
ΦΡ. μὴ μὲν οὖν νεκρός· τὸ Γοργοῦς δ' οὐ κάτοιδ' ἐγὼ κάρα.

1501 Μενέλας Willink: Μενέλαος codd.
1510 Μενέλεων HGPrSaξ, cf. Σ
1512 διώλλυτο vel διόλλυται West
1513 θενεῖν F.W.Schmidt: θανεῖν codd.
1519 ἄπαγε Μ^{γρ}

162

but after enduring toilsome, toilsome   1500
ordeals, Menelaus has got from Troy
his consort Helen all to no avail.

[*Orestes barges out of the house, sword in hand.*]
CH. Look, here is another novel situation
succeeding previous ones: I see Orestes, armed
with his sword, coming out to the house-front
with excited step.   1505
OR. Where's this fellow who's escaped out
of the house from my sword?
PHR. I make obeisance to you, my lord,
prostrating myself according to the barbarian
procedure.
OR. We are not in Ilion now, but in Argive
country.
PHR. Everywhere life is sweeter than death
to men of sound mind.
OR. You haven't been shouting for people   1510
to aid Menelaus, have you now?
PHR. Not me, no, rather to support you –
you are worthier.
OR. So it was right that Tyndareos'
daughter perished?
PHR. Rightest of all if she had a triple
set of throats to stab.
OR. You're using your tongue to please,
from cowardice, without thinking the same
inwardly.
PHR. Without thinking it, when she has
ravaged Greece, Phrygians and all?   1515
OR. Swear – or I'll kill you – that you're
not speaking to please me.
PHR. I swear on my life, which you can
expect me to keep an oath by.
OR. Was it like this at Troy too, was iron
the terror of every Phrygian? [*He holds the
sword still nearer the Phrygian's throat.*]
PHR. Keep your sword off – close up it has
a dreadful glint of death.
OR. Are you afraid of turning into a
stone, as if you'd got sight of the Gorgon?   1520
PHR. No: of turning into a corpse. The

163

ΟΡ.   δοῦλος ὢν φοβῇ τὸν "Αιδην, ὅς σ' ἀπαλλάξει κακῶν;
ΦΡ.   πᾶς ἀνήρ, κἂν δοῦλος ᾖ τις, ἥδεται τὸ φῶς ὁρῶν.
ΟΡ.   εὖ λέγεις· σῴζει σε σύνεσις. ἀλλὰ βαῖν' εἴσω δόμων.
ΦΡ.   οὐκ ἄρα κτενεῖς μ';
ΟΡ.   ἀφεῖσαι.   1525
ΦΡ.   καλὸν ἔπος λέγεις τόδε.
ΟΡ.   ἀλλὰ μεταβουλευσόμεσθα.
ΦΡ.   τοῦτο δ' οὐ καλῶς λέγεις.
ΟΡ.   μῶρος, εἰ δοκεῖς με τλῆναι σὴν καθαιμάξαι δέρην·
       οὔτε γὰρ γυνὴ πέφυκας οὔτ' ἐν ἀνδράσιν σύ γ' εἶ.
       τοῦ δὲ μὴ στῆσαί σε κραυγὴν οὕνεκ' ἐξῆλθον δόμων·
       ὀξὺ γὰρ βοῆς ἀκοῦσαν "Αργος ἐξεγείρεται·   1530
       Μενέλεων δ' οὐ τάρβος ἡμῖν ἀναλαβεῖν εἴσω ξίφους·
       ἀλλ' ἴτω ξανθοῖς ἐπ' ὤμων βοστρύχοις γαυρούμενος.
       εἰ γὰρ 'Αργείους ἐπάξει τοῖσδε δώμασιν λαβών,
       τὸν 'Ελένης φόνον διώκων, κἀμὲ μὴ σώσει θανεῖν
       σύγγονόν τ' ἐμὴν Πυλάδην τε τὸν τάδε ξυνδρῶντά μοι, 1535
       παρθένον τε καὶ δάμαρτα δύο νεκρὼ κατόψεται.

ΧΟ.   ἰὼ ἰὼ τύχας·   ant.
       ἕτερον εἰς ἀγῶν', ἕτερον αὖ δόμος
       φοβερὸν ἀμφὶ τοὺς 'Ατρείδας πίτνει.
       τί δρῶμεν; ἀγγέλλωμεν εἰς πόλιν τάδε;
       ἢ σῖγ' ἔχωμεν; ἀσφαλέστερον, φίλαι.   1540
       - ἴδε πρὸ δωμάτων ἴδε προκηρύσσει
       θοάζων ὅδ' αἰθέρος ἄνω καπνός·
       ἅπτουσι πεύκας, ὡς πυρώσοντες δόμους
       τοὺς Τανταλείους, οὐδ' ἀφίστανται πόνου.
       τέλος ἔχει δαίμων βροτοῖς,   1545
       τέλος ὅπα θέλῃ·

1527 μῶρος εἶ· δοκεῖς ... δέρην; Σ^{γρ} : εἶ, δοκῶν rec.
1534 σώσῃ(ι) θανεῖν Μ^{γρ}Β^{γρ}V (σώσει Blaydes): σώζειν θέλῃ ΗΜ,
       σώζειν θέλει ΒΟΑ
1535 del. Paley
1537 τύχας Elmsley: τύχα codd.
1544 πόνου PrSa: φόνου ΗΜΒΟVΑ

Gorgon's head I've no knowledge of.

OR. You're a slave, yet you fear Hades who will deliver you from misery?

PHR. Every man, even if he's a slave, enjoys seeing the light of day.

OR. Well said! You're saved by your intellect. Go indoors.

PHR. You're not going to kill me, then?   1525

OR. You're discharged.

PHR. I like it.

OR. Wait, I'm going to reconsider.

PHR. This, on the other hand, I don't like.

OR. You're an idiot, if you see me bringing myself to bloody your neck: you're neither a physical woman, nor to be reckoned among men. The reason I came out was to stop you raising a hue and cry - when Argos hears the call, it   1530 rouses itself sharp. But I'm not afraid to get Menelaus back within sword-range. Let him come, with his dandy blond shoulder-locks. For if he's going to get the Argives and lead them against this house in prosecution of Helen's killing, and not deliver me from death together with my sister and Pylades my accom-   1535 plice in this business, he is going to see two dead bodies - his daughter as well as his wife.

[The Phrygian scuttles off to find Menelaus; Orestes goes back into the palace. Music, the same as at 1353.]

CH. Io, io, how it falls!
Into another ordeal, another again, the house
plunges, a dread one, concerning Atreus'
line.
What do we do? Report it to the town?
Or hold silent? Safer so, my dears.   1540
— See, at the palace-front, see, this
smoke swifting
high in the air makes its own proclamation:
they're lighting torches, ready to fire
the house
of Tantalus, persevering in their struggle!
God controls the outcome for men,   1545
controls it the way he wants;

165

μεγάλα δέ τις ἁ δύναμις καὶ ἀλάστωρ·
ἔπεσ' ἔπεσε μέλαθρα τάδε δι' αἱμάτων
διὰ τὸ Μυρτίλου πέσημ' ἐκ δίφρου.

— ἀλλὰ μὴν καὶ τόνδε λεύσσω Μενέλεων δόμων πέλας
ὀξύπουν, ᾐσθημένον που τὴν τύχην ἢ νῦν πάρα.   1550
οὐκέτ' ἂν φθάνοιτε κλῇθρα συμπεραίνοντες μοχλοῖς,
ὦ κατὰ στέγας 'Ατρεῖδαι. δεινὸν εὐτυχῶν ἀνήρ
πρὸς κακῶς πράσσοντας, ὡς σὺ νῦν, 'Ορέστα, δυστυχεῖς.

ΜΕ. ἥκω κλυὼν τὰ δεινὰ καὶ δραστήρια
διssοῖν λεόντοιν· οὐ γὰρ ἄνδρ' αὐτὼ καλῶ.   1555
ἤκουσα γὰρ δὴ τὴν ἐμὴν ξυνάορον
ὡς οὐ τέθνηκεν, ἀλλ' ἄφαντος οἴχεται,
κενὴν ἀκούσας βάξιν, ἥν φόβῳ σφαλείς
ἤγγειλέ μοί τις. ἀλλὰ τοῦ μητροκτόνου
τεχνάσματ' ἐστὶ ταῦτα καὶ πολὺς γέλως.   1560
ἀνοιγέτω τις δῶμα. – προσπόλοις λέγω
ὠθεῖν πύλας τάσδ', ὡς ἂν ἀλλὰ παῖδ' ἐμήν
ῥυσώμεθ' ἀνδρῶν ἐκ χερῶν μιαιφόνων
[καὶ τὴν τάλαιναν ἀθλίαν δάμαρτ' ἐμήν
λάβωμεν, ᾗ δεῖ ξυνθανεῖν ἐμῇ χερί   1565
τοὺς διολέσαντας τὴν ἐμὴν ξυνάορον].

ΟΡ. οὗτος σύ, κλῇθρων τῶνδε μὴ ψαύσῃς χερί·
Μενέλαον εἶπον, ὃς πεπύργωσαι θράσει·
ἢ τῷδε θριγκῷ κρᾶτα συνθραύσω σέθεν
ῥήξας παλαιὰ γεῖσα, τεκτόνων πόνον.   1570
μοχλοῖς δ' ἄραρε κλῇθρα, σῆς βοηδρόμου
σπουδῆς ἅ σ' εἴρξει, μὴ δόμων εἴσω περᾶν.

ΜΕ. ἔα, τί χρῆμα; λαμπάδων ὁρῶ σέλας,
δόμων δ' ἐπ' ἄκρων τούσδε πυργηρουμένους,

1546 καὶ ἀλάστωρ West, cf. Σ τις ... φονικὸς δαίμων: δι'
      ἀλαστόρων codd.
1564-6 susp. Wecklein

but a mighty power is that of the vengeance-
   demon.
These halls have fallen, fallen amid
   blood-deeds
because of that fall of Myrtilus from
   the car.

[*Menelaus is seen approaching in haste with armed
attendants and Argives.*]
Well, now I can also see Menelaus here nearing
the house at a sharp pace; he must have become 1550
aware of the latest turn of events. You can't
bolt the staples too soon now, you Atridae in
the building! A man enjoying success is a
formidable force against those who are doing
badly, as you, Orestes, are now.
   MEN. I have come upon hearing the monstrous,
drastic deeds of a pair of lions - I do not   1555
call them men. What I have heard is that my
consort is - not dead, but vanished away: an
empty rumour that someone deluded by terror
told me. No, this is the matricide's trickery,
quite ridiculous.   1560
   Someone open the house. I bid my attendants
press through the doors here, so we may at
least rescue my daughter from murderers' hands
[and take possession of my poor unhappy wife,
with whom must perish by my hand those who   1565
have done away with my consort].
   [*He and his henchmen are approaching the doors when
Orestes and Pylades appear on the roof. Orestes is
holding Hermione and has his sword at her throat;
Pylades is holding smoking torches.*]
   OR. You there, don't lay a finger on those
fastenings - Menelaus I mean, with your towering
brazenness - or I shall smash your head in with
this coping-stone, breaking the ancient   1570
parapet that masons toiled on. The hasps are
made fast with bolts, and will check you in
your urgent rescuing and stop you entering
the house.
   MEN. How now, what's this? I see a blaze of
torches, and on the house-top these people

167

```
        ξίφος δ' ἐμῆς θυγατρὸς ἐπίφρουρον δέρῃ.        1575
ΟΡ.    πότερον ἐρωτᾶν ἢ κλύειν ἐμοῦ θέλεις;
ΜΕ.    οὐδέτερ'· ἀνάγκη δ', ὡς ἔοικε, σοῦ κλύειν.
ΟΡ.    μέλλω κτενεῖν σου θυγατέρ', εἰ βούλῃ μαθεῖν.
ΜΕ.    'Ελένην φονεύσας ἐπὶ φόνῳ πράσσεις φόνον;
ΟΡ.    εἰ γὰρ κατέσχον μὴ θεῶν κλεφθεὶς ὕπο.         1580
ΜΕ.    ἀρνῇ κατακτάς κἀφ' ὕβρει λέγεις τάδε;
ΟΡ.    λυπράν γε τὴν ἄρνησιν· εἰ γὰρ ὤφελον -
ΜΕ.    τί χρῆμα δρᾶσαι; παρακαλεῖς γὰρ εἰς φόβον.
ΟΡ.    τὴν 'Ελλάδος μιάστορ' εἰς "Αιδου βαλεῖν.
ΜΕ.    οὐκ ἤρκεσέν σοι τὸ παρὸν αἷμα μητέρος;        1589
ΟΡ.    οὐκ ἂν κάμοιμι τὰς κακὰς κτείνων ἀεί.         1590
ΜΕ.    ἀπόδος δάμαρτος νέκυν, ὅπως χώσω τάφῳ.        1585
ΟΡ.    θεοὺς ἀπαίτει.   παῖδα δὲ κτενῶ σέθεν.
ΜΕ.    ὁ μητροφόντης ἐπὶ φόνῳ πράσσει φόνον;
ΟΡ.    ὁ πατρὸς ἀμύντωρ, ὃν σὺ προύδωκας θανεῖν.    1588
ΜΕ.    ἦ καὶ σύ, Πυλάδη, τοῦδε κοινωνεῖς φόνου;      1591
ΟΡ.    φησὶν σιωπῶν· ἀρκέσω δ' ἐγὼ λέγων.
ΜΕ.    ἀλλ' οὔ τι χαίρων, ἤν γε μὴ φύγῃς πτεροῖς.
ΟΡ.    οὐ φευξόμεσθα· πυρὶ δ' ἀνάψομεν δόμους.
ΜΕ.    ἦ γὰρ πατρῷον δῶμα πορθήσεις τόδε;           1595
```

1589-90 post 1584 transp. West

beleaguered, and a sword on guard at my   1575
daughter's throat.
     OR. Which do you want, to ask the questions
or to listen to me?
     MEN. Neither; but it looks as if I'm forced
to listen to you.
     OR. I'm intending to kill your daughter,
if you're interested.
     MEN. After murdering Helen you're compounding
that murder with another?
     OR. If only I had achieved that, without
being robbed by the gods.   1580
     MEN. You deny having killed her, you say
that to mock me?
     OR. Painful though the denial is. If only
I had ...
     MEN. Done what? You're inviting me to be
afraid.
     OR. Struck that polluter of Greece into
the house of Hades.
     MEN. Weren't you content with your mother's
blood that is on your hands as it is?   1589
     OR. I don't expect to tire of killing
bad women.   1590
     MEN. Give me back my wife's body, so that
I can cover her in a grave-mound.   1585
     OR. Ask the gods for her. But your child
I _will_ kill.
     MEN. The mother-killer seeks to compound
one murder with another?
     OR. The father-supporter, whom you betrayed
to die.   1588
     MEN. Are you too involving yourself in
this murder, Pylades?   1591
     OR. He says yes in silence. It will be
sufficient if I do the talking.
     MEN. But you'll regret it - that is, unless
you escape on wings.
     OR. We shan't be escaping. We shall be
setting fire to the house.
     MEN. You mean to say you'll lay waste this
your father's palace?   1595

169

OP. ὡς μή γ' ἔχῃς σύ, τήνδ' ἐπισφάξας πυρί.
ME. κτεῖν'· ὡς κτανών γε τῶνδέ μοι δώσεις δίκην.
OP. ἔσται τάδ'.
ME.   ἆ ἆ, μηδαμῶς δράσῃς τάδε.
OP. σίγα νυν, ἀνέχου δ' ἐνδίκως πράσσων κακῶς.
ME. ἦ γὰρ δίκαιον ζῆν σέ;
OP.   καὶ κρατεῖν γε γῆς. 1600
ME. ποίας;
OP.   ἐν "Αργει τῷδε τῷ Πελασγικῷ.
ME. εὖ γοῦν θίγοις ἂν χερνίβων –
OP.   τί δὴ γὰρ οὔ;
ME. καὶ σφάγια πρὸ δορὸς καταβάλοις.
OP.   σὺ δ' ἂν καλῶς;
ME. ἁγνὸς γάρ εἰμι χεῖρας.
OP.   ἀλλ' οὐ τὰς φρένας.
ME. τίς δ' ἂν προσείποι σ';
OP.   ὅστις ἐστὶ φιλοπάτωρ. 1605
ME. ὅστις δὲ τιμᾷ μητέρ';
OP.   εὐδαίμων ἔφυ.
ME. οὔκουν σύ γ'.
OP.   οὐ γὰρ ἁνδάνουσιν αἱ κακαί.
ME. ἄπαιρε θυγατρὸς φάσγανον.
OP.   ψευδὴς ἔφυς.
ME. ἀλλὰ κτενεῖς μου θυγατέρ';
OP.   οὐ ψευδὴς ἔτ' εἶ.
ME. οἴμοι, τί δράσω;
OP.   πεῖθ' ἐς 'Αργείους μολών 1610
ME. πειθὼ τίν';
OP.   ἡμᾶς μὴ θανεῖν αἰτοῦ πόλιν –
ME. ἦ παῖδά μου φονεύσεθ';
OP.   ὧδ' ἔχει τάδε.
ME. ὦ τλῆμον 'Ελένη …
OP.   τἀμὰ δ' οὐχὶ τλήμονα;
ME. †σοὶ σφάγιον ἐκόμισ' ἐκ Φρυγῶν …
OP.   εἰ γὰρ τόδ' ἦν.

1607 γάρ μ' recc.   ἁνδάνουσί(ν) μ' MKᵃᶜ
1608 δ' ἔφυς West
1614 σὲ σφάγιον Canter: ὡς σφ. … Φρυγῶν σ' Diggle: σφ.
ἐκόμισά σ' Willink

170

OR. Yes, to stop you having it; and I'll
slaughter this girl over the flames.
MEN. Kill her: once you've done it you'll
pay me for all this.
OR. [*making to do so*] So be it.
MEN. Oh, oh, don't do it, don't!
OR. Shut up then, and endure the bad time
you deserve.
MEN. You mean *you* deserve to live?   1600
OR. And to rule the land.
MEN. What land?
OR. This one, Pelasgian Argos.
MEN. Well, it would be fine to have you
touching lustral vessels -
OR. Of course, why not?
MEN. And felling sacrificial victims before
battle.
OR. Whereas you'd be suitable?
MEN. Yes, my hands are pure.
OR. But not your heart.
MEN. But who would speak to you?   1605
OR. Anyone who loves his father.
MEN. What about anyone who respects his mother?
OR. Lucky man.
MEN. You're not, then.
OR. That's because I don't care for bad women.
MEN. Raise your sword from my daughter.
OR. You are false.
MEN. But you'll kill my daughter?
OR. Now you speak truth!
MEN. Oh, what am I to do?
OR. Go to the Argives and argue -   1610
MEN. What argument?
OR. Ask the city that we should not die -
MEN. Or else you'll murder my child?
OR. That's the position.
MEN. O unhappy Helen ...
OR. And isn't my situation unhappy?
MEN. I brought you back from Phrygia only to
be slaughtered -
OR. If only it were so.

171

ΜΕ. πόνους πονήσας μυρίους.
ΟΡ.   πλήν γ'εἰς ἐμέ.   1615
ΜΕ. πέπονθα δεινά.
ΟΡ.   τότε γὰρ ἦσθ' ἀνωφελής.
ΜΕ. ἔχεις με.
ΟΡ.   σαυτὸν σύ γ'ἔλαβες κακὸς γεγώς.
   ἀλλ' εἶ', ὕφαπτε δώματ', Ἠλέκτρα, τάδε·
   σύ τ', ὦ φίλων μοι τῶν ἐμῶν σαφέστατε,
   Πυλάδη, κάταιθε γεῖσα τειχέων τάδε.   1620
ΜΕ. ὦ γαῖα Δαναῶν ἱππίου τ'Ἄργους κτίται,
   οὐκ εἶ' ἐνόπλῳ ποδὶ βοηδρομήσετε;
   πᾶσαν γὰρ ὑμῶν ὅδε βιάζεται πόλιν
   ζῆν, αἷμα μητρὸς μυσαρὸν ἐξειργασμένος.
ΑΠΟΛΛΩΝ
   Μενέλαε, παῦσαι λῆμ' ἔχων τεθηγμένον -   1625
   Φοῖβός σ'ὁ Λητοῦς παῖς ὅδ'ἐγγὺς ὤν καλῶ -
   σύ θ' ὃς ξιφήρης τῇδ' ἐφεδρεύεις κόρῃ,
   Ὀρέσθ', ἵν' εἰδῇς οὓς φέρων ἥκω λόγους.
      Ἑλένην μέν, ἣν σὺ διολέσαι πρόθυμος ὤν
   ἥμαρτες, ὀργὴν Μενέλεῳ ποιούμενος,   1630
   ἥδ' ἐστιν, ἣν ὁρᾶτ' ἐν αἰθέρος πύλαις,
   σεσωμένη τε κού θανοῦσα πρὸς σέθεν·
   ἐγώ νιν ἐξέσωσα χὑπὸ φασγάνου
   τοῦ σοῦ κελευσθεὶς ἥρπασ' ἐκ Διὸς πατρός.
   Ζηνὸς γὰρ οὖσαν ζῆν νιν ἄφθιτον χρεών,   1635
   Κάστορί τε Πολυδεύκει τ'ἐν αἰθέρος πτυχαῖς
   σύνθακος ἔσται, ναυτίλοις σωτήριος.
   ἄλλην δὲ νύμφην εἰς δόμους κτῆσαι λαβών,
   ἐπεὶ θεοὶ τῷ τῆσδε καλλιστεύματι
   Ἕλληνας εἰς ἓν καὶ Φρύγας συνήγαγον   1640
   θανάτους τ'ἔθηκαν, ὡς ἀπαντλοῖεν χθονὸς
   ὕβρισμα θνητῶν ἀφθόνου πληρώματος.
      τὰ μὲν καθ''Ἑλένην ὧδ'ἔχει· σὲ δ'αὖ χρεών,
   Ὀρέστα, γαίας τῆσδ' ὑπερβαλόνθ' ὅρους
   Παρράσιον οἰκεῖν δάπεδον ἐνιαυτοῦ κύκλον·   1645

1622 οὐκ εἶ' Musgrave: οὐχὶ MBOVA: οὔκουν ΚΞ
1623 ὑμῶν Brunck: ἡμῶν codd. Σ
1631-2 susp. Paley
1631 πύλαις M²: πτύχαις (vel -αῖς) Π20 codd.
1633 κἀπὸ Π20 VAᵞᵖ

172

MEN. After I'd toiled endlessly.   1615
OR. Except where it concerned me.
MEN. I have been treated outrageously.
OR. Because you were no help *then*.
MEN. You've got me.
OR. You caught yourself, by being a swine.
- Ahoy there, Electra, set fire to the palace
from below, and you, my surest friend, Pylades,
burn the parapets of the walls here!   1620
MEN. O land of the Danaans, settlers of
knightly Argos, come on now, won't you run with
weapons to the rescue? Here is a man forcing
his way against your whole community to stay
alive when he has wrought the pollution of his
mother's blood!
[*The Argives form up and are about to storm the palace,
when suddenly Apollo and Helen appear on high.*]
APOLLO. Menelaus, take the edge off your   1625
temper - I am Phoebus, Leto's son, that hails
you here close at hand - and you that equipped
with sword beset this girl, Orestes, likewise,
to learn the message I bring.
As for Helen, whom you were eager to destroy
in your rage against Menelaus, but failed, here 1630
she is, this figure you see at the gates of
heaven, safe and well and not killed by you:
I rescued her and snatched her from beneath
your sword, at my father Zeus' bidding. For,
being Zeus' daughter, she is to live immortal, 1635
and with Castor and Polydeuces in the vales
of heaven she will sit enthroned as a saviour
for sailors. Take another wife to your house
to keep, Menelaus, for this one's supreme
beauty was the gods' instrument to bring the
Greeks and Phrygians face to face and cause   1640
much death, to clear out Earth's oppressive,
unlimited complement of mortals.
That is the position with Helen. As for
you, Orestes, you must pass beyond this
country's frontiers and live on Parrhasian
ground for a year's full circle; and the place 1645

173

κεκλήσεται δὲ σῆς φυγῆς ἐπώνυμον
['Αζᾶσιν 'Αρκάσιν τ''Ορέστειον καλεῖν].
ἐνθένδε δ' ἐλθὼν τὴν 'Αθηναίων πόλιν
δίκην ὑπόσχες αἵματος μητροκτόνου
Εὐμενίσι τρισσαῖς· θεοὶ δέ σοι δίκης βραβῆς   1651
πάγοισιν ἐν 'Αρείοισιν εὐσεβέστατην
ψῆφον διοίσουσ'· ἔνθα νικῆσαί σε χρή.
    ἐφ'ᾗ δ'ἔχεις, 'Ορέστα, φάσγανον δέρῃ,
γῆμαι πέπρωταί σ''Ερμιόνην· ὃς δ'οἴεται
Νεοπτόλεμος γαμεῖν νιν, οὐ γαμεῖ ποτε·   1655
θανεῖν γὰρ αὐτῷ μοῖρα Δελφικῷ ξίφει,
δίκας 'Αχιλλέως πατρὸς ἐξαιτοῦντά με.
Πυλάδῃ δ'ἀδελφῆς λέκτρον, ᾧ ποτ'ᾔνεσας,
δός· ὁ δ'ἐπιών νιν βίοτος εὐδαίμων μένει.
    "Αργους δ''Ορέστην, Μενέλεως, ἔα κρατεῖν,   1660
ἐλθὼν δ' ἄνασσε Σπαρτιάτιδος χθονός
φερνὰς ἔχων δάμαρτος, ἥ σε μυρίοις
πόνοις διδοῦσα δεῦρ' ἀεὶ διήνυσεν.
τὰ πρὸς πόλιν δὲ τῷδ' ἐγὼ θήσω καλῶς,
ὅς νιν φονεῦσαι μητέρ' ἐξηνάγκασα.   1665
ΟΡ. ὦ Λοξία μαντεῖε, σῶν θεσπισμάτων
οὐ ψευδόμαντις ἦσθ'ἄρ', ἀλλ'ἐτήτυμος.
καίτοι μ' ἐσῄει δεῖμα, μή τινος κλύων
ἀλαστόρων δόξαιμι σὴν κλύειν ὄπα·
ἀλλ'εὖ τελεῖται. πείσομαι δὲ σοῖς λόγοις·   1670
ἰδού, μεθίημ' 'Ερμιόνην ἀπὸ σφαγῆς,
καὶ λέκτρ'ἐπήνεσ', ἡνίκ'ἂν διδῷ πατήρ.
ΜΕ. ὦ Ζηνὸς 'Ελένη χαῖρε παῖ· ζηλῶ δέ σε
θεῶν κατοικήσουσαν ὄλβιον δόμον.
'Ορέστα, σοὶ δὲ παῖδ' ἐγὼ κατεγγυῶ,   1675
Φοίβου λέγοντος· εὐγενὴς δ'ἀπ'εὐγενοῦς
γήμας ὄναιο καὶ σὺ χὠ διδοὺς ἐγώ.

1647 del. Paley
1653 ἐφ'ἧς ξ
1658 ᾧ Π20ᶜΜΒ: ὡς Π20ᵃᶜΟΑ: ὃ V (in ras.?)
1674 κατοικήσουσαν Weil: -σασαν codd.

174

will be called after your exile [for Azanes and Arcadians to call it Oresteion]. From there you must go to the city of the Athenians and stand trial for matricidal bloodshed against the three Benign Ones; and gods as judges of your 1650 case on the Hill of Ares will divide their vote most righteously; wherein you are to win.

And her against whom, Orestes, you are holding your sword at her neck - Hermione - you are destined to marry. The man who thinks he is going to marry her, Neoptolemus, never 1655 will, for it is his fate to die by Delphian sword when petitioning me for compensation for Achilles his father. Give your sister to Pylades, to whom you had agreed to give her: the future life that awaits him will be happy.

As for Argos, leave Orestes to rule it, 1660 Menelaus; you go and be lord of the Spartiate land, enjoying the dowry from your wife, who has finished committing you to countless toils as always hitherto. Orestes' relations with the city I shall set aright, I who made him murder his mother. 1665

OR. O Loxias, prophetic one, in those oracles of yours you were no false prophet after all, but truthful! Though indeed the fear was getting into me that I had imagined I was hearing your voice when I was hearing some vengeance-demon. But it is turning out well at the end. I will do as you say: see, 1670 I release Hermione from slaughter, and agree to the marriage as soon as her father will give her.

MEN. O daughter of Zeus, Helen, hail and farewell! I congratulate you on going to live in the gods' blessed home. To you, Orestes, I betroth my daughter as Phoebus 1675 ordains. Noble, and marrying from a noble house, may you do well out of it, both you and I who give her.

175

ΑΠ.　χωρεῖτέ νυν ἕκαστος οἷ προτάσσομεν,
　　νεῖκός τε διαλύεσθε.
ΜΕ.　　　　　　　πείθεσθαι χρεών.
ΟΡ.　κἀγὼ τοιοῦτος· σπένδομαι δὲ συμφοραῖς,　　1680
　　Μενέλαε, καὶ σοῖς, Λοξία, θεσπίσμασιν.
ΑΠ.　ἴτε νυν καθ' ὁδόν, τὴν καλλίστην
　　θεῶν Εἰρήνην τιμῶντες· ἐγὼ δ'
　　Ἑλένην Δίοις μελάθροις πελάσω,
　　λαμπρῶν ἄστρων πόλον ἐξανύσας·　　1685
　　ἔνθα παρ' Ἥρᾳ τῇ θ' Ἡρακλέους
　　Ἥβῃ πάρεδρος θεὸς ἀνθρώποις
　　ἔσται, σπονδαῖς ἔντιμος ἀεὶ
　　σὺν Τυνδαρίδαις τοῖς Διός, ὑγρᾶς
　　ναύταις μεδέουσα θαλάσσης.　　1690
ΧΟ.　ὦ μέγα σεμνὴ Νίκη, τὸν ἐμὸν
　　βίοτον κατέχοις
　　καὶ μὴ λήγοις στεφανοῦσα.

1684　Δίοις Nauck: Διὸς fere codd. Tzetzes: Ζηνὸς ξ
1689　ὑγρᾶς Μᵞᵖ : υἱοῖς codd. Tzetzes
1691-3 Euripidi abiudicavit Matthiae

AP. Proceed, then, each of you, toward the
destinations I enjoin upon you, and end your
quarrel.
MEN. One can only obey.
OR. I feel so too, and I make my peace   1680
with this affair, Menelaus, and with your
oracles, Loxias.

[*Orestes, Hermione, and Pylades descend into the
house. Menelaus and his retinue begin to march out,
followed by the chorus. Music.*]

AP. Go on your ways, then, honouring
that fairest of deities, Peace, while I
take Helen to the halls of Zeus
across the shining starry vault.   1685
There, throned next Hera and Heracles'
wife Hebe, she will be to men
a goddess, ever honoured in libations
together with the Tyndarids, Zeus' sons,
queen of the restless sea for mariners.   1690
CH. O Victory, august goddess,
may you fill my life, and never cease
from crowning it with garlands.

177

COMMENTARY

The Hypotheses. Many plays have a Hypothesis or two prefixed to them in the manuscripts. The first of those before us is a straightforward narrative summary of the play, taken from an ancient book of Euripidean Hypotheses attributed to the Peripatetic Dicaearchus. In this book each Hypothesis was headed by the title and first line of the play. Several fragments are found in papyri, including remnants of the *Orestes* Hypothesis (P. Oxy. 2455, 2nd century A.D.). On this book, and reasons for doubting that it really goes back to Dicaearchus, see J. Rusten, *GRBS* 23 (1982), 357-67.

The second Hypothesis is ascribed in the heading to Aristophanes of Byzantium. This ascription is valid, but (as Dindorf saw) only as far as "The play has a dénouement – comic type". The highly concentrated synopsis, the reference to other treatments of the story (none in this case), and the statements about the scene, the chorus and the opening speech are characteristic of Aristophanes' Hypotheses; the remark about the dénouement recurs verbatim in that to *Alcestis*. Originally there would also have been information about the date of production and how the prizes were awarded. See Page's *Medea*, liii-lv; Pfeiffer, *History of Classical Scholarship* i. 192-6.

What follows is not part of Aristophanes' Hypothesis but apparently from a more discursive introduction to the play, possibly Didymus'. The anti-Euripidean tone of the final sentence would suit him (cf. Pfeiffer 277). It may have been through Didymus that Aristophanes' Hypotheses were preserved.

[*Orestes lies on a bed*.] Greek plays sometimes open with characters in positions in which they are supposed to have been for some time. The audience must have seen them taking up these positions; see Taplin (1977) 134-6. Possibly there was then some visual or audible signal to mark the start of the play. In Euripides these opening tableaux "always depict the helplessness and typically the isolation of the character(s) involved" (Halleran 80).

No explanation is given for Orestes' bed being out of doors. Contrast *Medea*, where the heroine initially lies distraught in her bedroom indoors (24, 141, 152), and leaves it to come out on stage (214). In *Hipp.* 170 ff. Phaedra has her bed brought out for a change of air. Here Orestes seems to have been camping out for five days (39), and Euripides expects no questions asked. He likes scenes with characters sitting, kneeling or lying, cf. Shisler 379–82.

Orestes will remain inert till 211. This of itself creates some suspense: when will he ever say or do something? It is akin to the famous prolonged silences of some Aeschylean characters, discussed by Taplin, *HSCP* 76 (1972), 57–97.

–70 Euripides' plays regularly open with an expository monologue. It is sometimes spoken by a supernatural figure who does not appear again, sometimes by a character who plays a part in the drama, depending on how much Euripides wants the audience to know in advance. Often, especially in the later plays, no attempt is made to disguise the expository function, and the speaker addresses no one but the audience and speaks without dramatic motivation. So here.

The structure is clear and purposeful. Electra begins by giving her genealogy (a common feature of Euripidean prologues). This enables her to recall some of the many misfortunes of the Tantalid house, to which the events of this play will be seen as adding a final chapter (807–18, 971–1012, 1544). The series leads directly to Orestes' matricide and so to the explanation of his present condition (34–45). Then we are told of two offstage factors that make the situation more dramatic and critical – the hostility of Argos (mortal danger) and the return of Menelaus (hope of salvation) – and of two further essential facts in preparation for the following scenes, that Helen is already in the house, and that Hermione is living there. With this the initial exposition is complete, and the final lines 67–70 look forward to dramatic action.

There is no thing: to begin a discourse by stating a universal truth and going on to a particular illustration of it is a procedure familiar from Homer on (see my n. on Hes. *Op.* 11–46), though few tragedies start in this way. Electra's observation applies not only to Tantalus but to the whole family down to Orestes.

179

3   humankind: lit. a man's *physis*, i.e. "man, being what he is".

4   I am not being sarcastic: she is referring to the time when he was the gods' favourite (8-9), contrasting it with his later plight (6-7). *Oneidizō* bears an unusual sense here and in 85. Note the parenthetic style of the whole passage (5, 8, 16, 17).

5   Zeus' offspring, as they say: Euripidean characters elsewhere express reserve towards stories of gods fathering mortals: *HF* 353-4, *Hel.* 17-21, *IA* 794-800. They might, after all, be invented by unmarried or adulterous mothers (cf. *Ion* 338-41, 1523-7, *Ba.* 26-31, 242-5). But Euripides does not mean to suggest that all such stories are false. For his dramatic purposes, at least, they are usually true, as in this play Helen is eventually shown to be truly Zeus' daughter.

6-7   hovers in mid air in dread of a rock: in *Od.* 11.582-92 he is "tantalized" by fruit and water that he cannot reach, but "the stone of Tantalus" is already proverbial in Archilochus (91.14) for a looming threat. The idea that Tantalus himself hovers aloft is new; cf. 982 ff. and n. there.

8-9   so they say: another expression of reserve regarding something both unverifiable and outside normal experience; cf. *El.* 737 f., *IT* 386 f.
a mortal enjoying equal status with gods at the shared table: cf. *Nostoi* fr. 10, Pind. *O.* 1.39, 54 f., 60 f., Diod. 4.74.2.

10   an unchecked tongue: perhaps alluding to the story in the *Nostoi* that Zeus granted Tantalus a wish, and he rashly asked to have everything the gods have (Zeus conceded this but, by suspending the stone over him, prevented him from enjoying it); or to the later-attested version (Diod. l.c. and others) that Tantalus divulged the gods' secrets to men. But the story that he declared the sun to be a mass of solid matter (schol. Pind. *O.* 1.91a) appears to derive from an interpretation of Euripides (*pace* Willink, *CQ* 33 [1983], 32 f.). There are several alternative accounts of Tantalus' error that do not involve his tongue.

11   Pelops: his story (987-94) is passed over here, as the emphasis is on sufferings.

12-13 the goddess ... spun strife: in Homer Moira (Fate) or

180

Zeus or the gods collectively spin men's destinies for
them at their birth. Spinning is an excellent symbol for
making the indefinite definite. The scholiast's variant
reading "the goddess Strife ... spun that he should make
quarrel" is inferior: the spinning should be done by a
universal deity, and strife is the particular result in
Atreus' case.
raking out her wool-coils: carding the loose tufts of wool
in preparation for spinning. A drastic activity with
overtones of tribulation; cf. Page on *Med.* 1030.
4 Why need I recount: again passing over the details of a
story of which more will be heard later (811 ff., 995 ff.).
A golden lamb was found in Atreus' flocks, and he
claimed the throne on the strength of it. But Thyestes
got possession of the lamb after seducing Atreus' wife.
The sun and stars changed direction; Atreus was
confirmed in power and banished his brother. When he
returned Atreus invited him to dinner and served him
meat which turned out to be that of his children. The
earliest known sources are the epic *Alcmaeonis* fr. 6
Kinkel and Pherecydes *FGrH* 3 F 133; Aeschylus alludes
to part of the story in *Ag.* 1096, 1193, 1583 ff., etc.,
and it may have formed the subject of Sophocles' *Atreus*.
Other Euripidean references: *El.* 699-736, *IT* 812-6, fr.
861.
5 Anyway – children: Di Benedetto deletes this line as
containing the chief of the "obscenities" which Electra has
just indicated she does not wish to recount. But she says
"why need I recount those obscenities?" precisely so that
she can mention the grim climax of the story without the
detail of what led up to it. The question would be feeble
as a way of leaving the subject, and 16 would read
awkwardly as the next line.
6 I say nothing of intervening events: these cannot be the
same as the ones referred to in 14, as Di Benedetto
supposes. (If they were, it would be better to delete
12-15 with Klinkenberg.) The reference is most likely to
the story told in Sophocles' *Thyestes in Sicyon* of
Thyestes' incest with his daughter Pelopia, who gave
birth to Aegisthus. The parenthesis is then equivalent to
"for I say nothing further of Thyestes".
if glorious he be: his death and funeral were ignominious
(Aesch. *Cho.* 429-50), and so long as he remained

unavenged he was, in heroic terms, in a state of dishonour.

18 Aërope: a central figure in Euripides' *Cretan Women* (438 B.C.). There (as in [Hes.] fr. 194 + 195.3-7) she was given in marriage to Pleisthenes, and bore Agamemnon and Menelaus to him. But in *Hel.* 390 f. (and Soph. *Aj.* 1291-5) she is Atreus' wife, as here, and it was she whom Thyestes seduced (1009). She was by all accounts a lady of lax morals.

19 her whom the gods abhor: it turns out in the end that this is not so.

21 a notable marriage: *IT* 208 suggests a story that Agamemnon won her against much competition.

23 Chrysothemis, Iphigeneia ... Electra: Homer names Agamemnon's daughters as Chrysothemis, Laodice, and Iphianassa (*Il.* 9.145; Electra first in Xanthus *PMG* 700, [Hes.] fr. 23a.16). Sophocles took Chrysothemis to serve as a foil to Electra in his *Electra* (like Ismene in *Antigone*), and this is no doubt why Euripides recognizes her existence. But he does not mention her again or explain what has become of her.

myself, Electra: this identifies the speaker to the audience. Only in *El.* does Euripides make them wait longer.

25 in an endless cloth: an all-enveloping thing which he let her put over him after his bath, taking it to be a robe, and then found no way out for his head and arms. It is described in vague terms in the *Oresteia*, more clearly in other sources, for which see Fraenkel on *Ag.* 1382. It was held up for everyone to see at *Cho.* 980 ff. In a fine vase-painting of c.470 B.C. (reproduced in Taplin [1978] pl. 10; A.J.N.W. Prag, *The Oresteia. Iconographic and Narrative Tradition* (1985) pls. 3-4) it is depicted as a filmy, stretchy envelope in which the naked Agamemnon stands helpless between his murderers.

26-7 not seemly for an unwed woman to say: cf. *El.* 945. The emphasis is on Clytaemestra's adulterous love for Aegisthus to the exclusion of things that were Agamemnon's fault (his sacrifice of Iphigeneia and his bringing Cassandra into the house; cf. *El.* 1018 ff.).

for public consideration: she speaks as if acknowledging the presence of the audience. See 128 n.

28 how should Phoebus be accused of wrong?: she is

tempted to do so, but reluctant to believe that a god could be unrighteous. This is the first of many aspersions in the play on Apollo's role in the killing. They must not be read as "Euripides criticizing the gods", for in the end it turns out that everything was for the best after all. Similarly in *Ion*, where Creusa at the end (1609) retracts her previous reproaches of Apollo.

0   **not in everyone's eyes:** in Homer (*Od.* 1.298, etc.) Orestes' deed is regarded as wholly admirable, though there the emphasis is on his killing Aegisthus, and Clytaemestra's death is scarcely mentioned (3.310, not in all ancient editions). In this play the situation is the complete opposite. The present line mediates between the two scenarios.

2   **I too took part:** this needs to be stated, because the plot requires the Argives' sentence to fall on her as well as Orestes. For what she actually did see 284, 616–21, 1235 (n.).

3   **[And so did Pylades – with us]:** clearly interpolated in anticipation of Pylades' later role in the play (cf. Introduction VI). The Argives are not concerned with him (cf. 50 "the pair of us"), and he should stay out of the picture for the moment. The name is padded out to make a whole line.

4–5 **poor Orestes here:** identifying the other visible figure.
    is sick ... with a savage sickness: an echo of Soph. *Phil.* 173; cf. Introduction III.

6   **his mother's blood:** the shed blood itself is seen as the source of madness (338, *HF* 966, Aesch. *Cho.* 1055 f.); it calls for an avenging Erinys (*Cho.* 400-2). On the connection of murder with madness cf. Parker 129.
    bowls him along: the image (also in *El.* 1253, *IT* 82) is not, I think, of driving a chariot (despite *trochēlatēs* "charioteer") but of whipping a hoop along (LSJ *trochos* II). So in later verse of Love, Tibull. 1.5.3, Anacreont. 31.

8   **the Benign Ones:** like Menelaus in 409 (and the chorus of Soph. *OC* 129), she will not name the Erinyes, but the euphemism *Eumenides* serves to remove any doubt about who is meant, as *semnai* does in 410 (n.). The parallel supports the line against those who delete it as a gloss incompatible with "I am shy of naming the goddesses".

183

terror: a feature of Orestes' affliction, cf. 255 ff., 270, 532, Aesch. *Cho*. 1024, 1052, *Eum*. 88.

40 became cleansed: a corpse is unclean until disposed of by the proper ritual. See Collard on *Supp*. 1211-2; Parker 34 ff.

41-2 he has swallowed no food, not given his skin a wash: classic forms of self-neglect. Cf. N. Hopkinson on Call. *H*. 6.12.

43-5 when his body gets relief etc.: as in *IT*, Euripides represents Orestes' madness as intermittent, so that for most of the play he can speak and act coherently.
like a colt from under the yoke: a conventional simile; cf. *Il*. 6.506 ff., and Barrett *ap*. R. Carden, *The Papyrus Fragments of Sophocles* (1974) 217.

46 This city of Argos: such an indication of place is a regular item in prologue speeches: *Med*. 10 "this land of Corinth", etc. It comes unusually late in this case.
has decreed: the phrasing suggests the official Attic formula "the Council and the People has decreed" (*edoxe tēi boulēi kai tōi dēmōi*). The democratic assembly which has made this decision, and which will presently pass sentence on the matricides, seems to meet only for special crises, cf. 874-6. We must remember that there is an interregnum: Orestes will eventually assume his father's sceptre (1660, cf. 437). See further on 612.

47 hospitality of ... fire: that is, give us a light from their fires; cf. Hdt. 7.231, [Dem.] 25.61, Din. 2.9, and the Roman "interdict upon (sharing) water and fire" (*aquae et ignis interdictio*). For the excommunication as a whole see also Aesch. *Cho*. 294, Soph. *OT* 236 ff., Hdt. 3.52.1; MacDowell 25 f.; Parker 194. It isolates the polluted man and prevents him from harming others by contagion. In practice it would force him into exile.

48 matricides that we are: the present participle expresses their continuing status. Cf. 887, 1535.
this is the appointed day: for the programmatic motif "today will be decisive" in prologues cf. Aesch. *Sept*. 21ff., Eur. *Alc*. 20, 27, *Hipp*. 22, *Hec*. 44; later in the play, Soph. *Aj*. 753 ff., *OT* 438, Eur. *Alc*. 105.

50 by stoning: the traditional form of communal execution of an abominated criminal, where everyone and no one takes responsibility for the killing. See Fraenkel on *Ag*. 1616.

51 [or sharpen - at our necks]: interpolated on the basis of

953, cf. 864, 1062. Death by the sword is not an alternative to be debated by the Argives (cf. 442) but a suicide option which Orestes in the event persuades them to concede in lieu of stoning (946 ff.).

52 But we do have some hope: in other Euripidean prologues where a bad situation is set out, hope rests only in the gods. Here we have a more elaborate (misleading) preparation for what is to come.

54 Filling the harbour of Nauplia: this may sound like a fleet, but Menelaus probably returns with a single ship, as in *Helen*. Cf. 242 (v.l.), 688-90. Nauplia was the port of Argos, about seven miles distant.

56 went wandering astray: as related in *Od*. 3.276-312, 4.81-9, 351-586.

57-60 Note Euripides' ingenuity in arranging that Helen is already at hand for the next scene while Menelaus is still awaited and his response to the situation unknown.

58 below Ilion: Troy stands on an elevation overlooking the plain where the fighting took place. Cf. *Il*. 2.216 etc. *hypo Ilion ēlthe*, "went to (fight) below Ilion".

59 throwing stones: cf. above on 50.

60 She is indoors: in several Euripidean prologues the audience is informed that a certain person is indoors, in anticipation of a later appearance: *Alc*. 19, *Andr*. 41, *Tro*. 32-4, *Phoen*. 66.

61 weeping for her sister: this prepares for her sending grave-offerings.

63-4 the daughter Menelaus left ... Hermione: this much was given by older tradition (*Od*. 4.3-14, *Il*. 3.175, Sapph. 16.10, [Hes.] fr. 204.94, etc.), but her lodging with Clytaemestra seems to be invented for the purposes of this play. She should now be seventeen or eighteen.

66 and puts her troubles out of mind: in re-using a line from an earlier play (*Hec*. 279) Euripides has overlooked the contradiction with 61.

67 I am watching every road: the monologue ends with a transition from narrative to live drama; cf. *Med*. 46, *Hcld*. 48, *IT* 61, *Hel*. 63, *Ba*. 55, etc. Electra explains what she is doing now out of doors (but she is also looking after her brother, 93). It would have been sufficient to watch the road from Nauplia, but "every road" gives a greater sense of anticipation.

In Soph. *OT* 73 ff. and 287 ff. anxiety about when a

character will arrive is the cue for his appearance; cf. Aesch. *Sept.* 36 ff., Eur. *El.* 759 ff., *Ba.* 1211 ff., *IA* 1098 ff.; Taplin (1977) 137 f. This time Euripides uses a more sophisticated technique: it is a different character who will appear, and not by either of the visible roads. Cf. Taplin 94-6 on "false preparation"; Halleran 40-2.

70   It is a helpless thing, a house in ill fortune: as often, the long speech is concluded with a general reflection. The use of *chrēma* is perhaps colloquial (Stevens 20).

71-125   Dialogue with Helen. Following an opening soliloquy it is common for a second character to appear and conduct dialogue with the first. The scene serves to show us something of Helen, who, though important to the plot in a passive way, will not be seen again until her final apotheosis; and it sets Hermione off on her errand, preparing long in advance for later developments. In moving the story forward before the chorus appears, this goes beyond what is usual.

71   Child of Clytaemestra and Agamemnon: vocative phrases opening an address were sometimes expanded by interpolation, as M.W. Haslam has shown for Soph. *El.* 1-2 and Eur. *Phoen.* 1-3 (*GRBS* 16 [1975], 149-74). This might be another example, but 72 would be abrupt on its own.

72   so long unwed: bringing out the contrast with Helen's own state. Aegisthus prevented Electra from marrying because any son she had would be a threat to him (Soph. *El.* 963-6, cf. Eur. *El.* 40-2). The early lyric poet Xanthus (*PMG* 700) connected *Ēlektrā* with *alektros* "bedless", and her spinsterhood is often alluded to in tragedy; cf. 26, 206. It will be remedied at the end of the play.

74   became: *ephȳ* is used as in Soph. *Tr.* 36, 489, *OC* 1444, with no reference to *physis*.

75   does not affect me with pollution: if everyone shared the Argives' horror of speaking to the matricides (47), it would be hard to write a play. Euripides feels it necessary for Helen (but not others later) to justify herself. "I am polluted" and "I feel polluted" are nearly synonymous; cf. *HF* 1233 f.

76   Phoebus: cf. 28 n. Similarly in *El.* 1296 Castor allows

186

Electra to speak to him, with the justification "I will attribute the bloody deed to Phoebus".

the misdeed: *hamartiā* implies bad judgment as well as bad consequences. It may spring from factual ignorance, sensual weakness, or moral blindness.

8 **my sister**: confirming the speaker's identity, which the audience will already have guessed.

9 **as I did**: a formula for veiling distasteful details. We might say "you know how". See Fraenkel on *Ag.* 1171. The story of Helen's transfer to Egypt, used in *El.* 1280-3 and *Helen*, is here discarded.

from the heaven-sent madness: for this too she puts the blame on the gods – rightly, as we learn in 1639-42.

82 **Agamemnon's children**: or *gonos* may refer to Orestes alone, as in 326. There is a hint of "what a come-down for a glorious family".

84 **for a corpse is what he is**: justifying what might have sounded a rude expression (cf. Stevens 12). Similarly the next line "I am not being sarcastic" (cf. 4 n.).

86 **you the fortunate one**: she has come home, if not to popular acclaim, at least unharmed and laden with riches, and Menelaus has succeeded in his venture.

90 **and his mother too**: Helen maintains her concern for Clytaemestra; we are coming to her request. Electra responds only to "O pitiable" (Orestes).

93 **Well, I am rather occupied**: lit. "Yes, at any rate (so far as I can) as one who is occupied".

5 **My mother's**: reminding us of the relationships, and of the difference between Electra's attitude to Clytaemestra and Helen's.

you want me to: or "suggest I should". "Order" is often too strong a translation of *keleuō*.

6 **To take**: the construction continues from 94.

an offering of hair: cutting the hair, the easiest form of self-mutilation, was in itself an act of mourning, and it was natural to lay the cut hair solemnly upon the body or grave of the person for whom it had been given, not just throw it away. But Euripides may have known the practice only from literature (*Il.* 23.135-52, and especially Aesch. *Cho.* 7, 168, etc. of Orestes' hair-offering for Agamemnon) and certain hero-cults (*Hipp.* 1425 f.). Cf. Burkert (1985) 374 n.29.

libations: liquid offerings poured on the earth reach the dead directly; see further on 115. Again *Choephoroe* (15, 23, 84–164) provides Euripides' most obvious source of inspiration.

100 the you speak truly: she accepts the reproach; she did behave badly, although it was Aphrodite who caused her to do so. So in the *Iliad* she blames herself freely (3.173, 6.344, 356) as well as the gods (3.400, 6.349, 357).

101 the Mycenaeans: in the original saga Agamemnon ruled from Mycene, six miles north of the town of Argos, but his territory as a whole is often called "Argos" in Homer (*Il.* 2.108 etc.). Argos as a town had surpassed Mycene in importance since the eleventh century, and finally destroyed it in about 463. Aeschylus always calls the site of Agamemnon's palace Argos. Euripides sometimes speaks of Mycene, without distinguishing it from Argos. Usually Argos can be taken as the region, but in *El.* 641 it must be the town (= Mycene in 963), and so in this play, 46, 872 ff., etc.

108 It is not seemly for girls: this consideration had not inhibited Helen from suggesting that Electra should go. It is a rule more applicable to Athens than to the epic world, though acknowledged in Euripidean tragedy in *Hcld.* 43, 474, *Phoen.* 89–95, 1275 f., and extended to married women in *Tro.* 648 f., *IA* 735, 1029–32. Cf. Dover 98; P. Walcot, *Greek Drama in its Theatrical and Social Context* (1976) 90 f.

109 repaying Clytaemestra for bringing her up: any service performed for or expected by a parent or other provider of livelihood – especially looking after parents in old age – tended to be so interpreted. Cf. e.g. *Il.* 4.478, Hes. *Op.* 188, Aesch. *Sept.* 477, 548, *Ag.* 728 f., Eur. *Phoen.* 45, Lys. 6.49, Isoc. 6.108.

112 [*Hermione appears*]: all three speaking actors are already on stage, and Hermione must on this appearance be played by a non-speaking extra. In 1321 ff. she will be played by the actor now playing Helen.

114 to the edge: *amphi* can mean "in or to the area surrounding". Clytaemestra's cremated remains are imagined as covered by a substantial round barrow, like Agamemnon's in *Choephoroe* (and Darius' in *Persians*). Cf. 402–4.

115 the milk honey-mix (i.e. milk and honey mixed) and the sprinkle of wine: traditional libations to the dead, cf.

Od. 10.519, Aesch. *Pers.* 610 ff., Eur. *IT* 159 ff.;
Burkert (1985) 71.

16 **stand on top of the mound:** as Orestes does to address
his dead father in Aesch. *Cho.* 4, and Neoptolemus to
address his in Eur. *Hec.* 523 f.

19-20 **to keep a kindly attitude:** dead persons, especially
those who were powerful in life, are often represented in
tragedy as able to exercise great influence on local affairs
for good or ill: Agamemnon (Aesch. *Cho.* 130 ff. etc.,
Soph. *El.* 453 ff.; *Or.* 1225 ff.), Orestes (Aesch. *Eum.*
767 ff.), Oedipus (Soph. *OC* 389 ff., 576 ff., etc.),
Achilles (Eur. *Hec.* 538 ff.). They are not called *hērōes*,
but the ideology is that of the hero cults of the archaic
age; see E. Rohde, *Psyche*, chapter 5; Burkert (1985)
203-8. Clytaemestra is accommodated to the pattern *ad
hoc*; there is no further suggestion in the play that she
is an active force, except as mistress of the Erinyes that
beset Orestes.

21 **and this unhappy pair:** so Hermione's errand becomes
ostensibly relevant to the main plot.
whom a god has ruined: 28 n.

24 **my child:** this use of the dative *moi* is a Euripidean
idiom.

25 **mind you come back as quickly as you can:** natural
motherly concern, and at the same time a signal that we
can expect to see Hermione returning later.

The dialogue scene has fulfilled its purposes and is
not prolonged; Helen goes indoors without further words
to Electra.

26 **O Nature:** adverse comment on someone's conduct or
attitude often begins from an exclamation of more
universal import; see Barrett on *Hipp.* 616 ff. (p. 275),
Stevens on *Andr.* 319. For rhetorical apostrophizing of
abstractions cf. Soph. *OT* 380, Eur. *Andr.* l.c., *Ion*
1512 (all beginning speeches), *Supp.* 1108, and 213
below. The point here is that time and Troy have not
altered Helen's vanity, which is clearly congenital – a bad
trait, yet one that has seen her through many
difficulties.

28 **Did you notice:** tragedy never explicitly recognizes the
existence of the spectators (as comedy does); cf. D.
Bain, *CQ* 25 (1975), 13-25. But occasionally in
expostulations we find a second person plural (or

189

singular) which cannot be related to anyone present on stage. See Soph. *Aj.* 1028, *El.* 1384, Eur. *Hipp.* 943; Taplin (1977) 131, and for a slightly different type Stevens on *Andr.* 622-3. In some cases we may say that the address is to "the world at large", but in the present passage it seems pedantic to deny that it is to the audience.

The variant *idete* (imperative) is unsuitable now that Helen has gone, and *eidete* is supported by *Phoen.* 1676. along the edge: *trichas* is to be understood again with *par' akrās*.

132-3 here they are: the chorus always arrives within 200 lines of the start of a tragedy. One way of integrating this obligatory element into the drama is for a character already on stage to descry and describe the approaching group: so also in Aesch. *Cho.*, Soph. *OC*, Eur. *Phoen.* Here they are identified as singers; cf. 850 n.

again: if this is the right translation, it is a unique suggestion of previous songs which the audience has not heard, and this may anyway be implied by "my friends who sing with me". Alternatively *au* may mean "here's another interruption".

my friends who sing with me: or perhaps "to sing with me". The phrase prepares us for a lyric dialogue. As often, the chorus consists of local women, sympathetic to the heroine but, as women, devoid of political influence.

133-5 They will soon shift him - in his frenzy: again anticipating what actually happens, though not exactly.

136-9 Dearest women - calamity: these lines have been suspected as duplicating 140-1. But those lines belong to the chorus (see below), and must be a response to Electra's plea. Her friends lack the wit to keep quiet without being told.

his rousing: lit. "(for anyone) to rouse him".

140-207 Parodos (choral entry). The chorus is further integrated into the main action by making its first performance a lyric dialogue shared with the character already on stage. This technique appears in many of Euripides' and Sophocles' later plays. In some of them Euripides gives his chorus-women a suitable everyday-life occupation to act out: in *Ion* they are sightseers at

190

Delphi, in *Helen* they have just been drying their washing, in *Phaethon* they are the palace cleaning women, and here they are visitors to a sickbed. Interest is focussed for the moment entirely on Orestes' medical condition, with no reference to the danger he and Electra are in from the Argives. As in the parodoi of a number of Sophoclean and Euripidean plays, the chorus expresses its sympathy and concern for the plight of the hero or heroine, asking questions and making comments. The presence of the sleeper who must if possible not be awakened gives the dialogue a special character: the singing and dancing are exceptionally quiet, and there is anxiety from moment to moment. Euripides had written a very similar scene in *HF* 1042 ff., where Heracles is sleeping off his madness; cf. also Soph. *Tr.* 962 ff. and *Phil.* 839 ff. The naturalistic effects in the interplay between Electra and the chorus make it a delightful entertainment.

The metre is mainly dochmiac (appropriate to nervous tension), with occasional iambo-trochaic and in 181-4 enoplian cola. We have a few scraps of information about the music. Dion. Hal. *Comp.* 63 f., commenting on non-agreement of melody and word accents, refers to 140-2 (the first bit of song in the best known of tragedies), and tells us that the first three words were all sung on one note, *arbylēs* and *tithete* each had their third syllables on the same note as the second and their first syllables on lower ones, *ktypeit'* had both syllables on the same note, and *apopro bāte* had *bā* as its highest note. (As he passes over *ichnos*, we can infer that here the melody did agree with the accent, the first syllable being the higher.) The same relationships must hold for all the corresponding syllables in 153-5. Then a scholiast on 176 says "This song is sung on the top notes and is very high. It is implausible that Electra should use a high voice, especially when upbraiding the chorus [182 ff.], but she has to, because it is proper to people lamenting. And it is all as quiet as possible."

140-3 Quietly – of the bed: Dionysius and other ancient writers attribute all of this to Electra, and presumably heard it sung by her in productions of their time. It was a natural error for producers to make, but the division of parts should match that in the antistrophe, according to

191

the normal rule (for which see Page, *CQ* 31 [1937], 94–9).

After "do not stamp" the manuscripts (but not Dionysius or Π 16) repeat "let there be no clatter" from 137, and in 154 an extra dochmius has been interpolated in an attempt to restore responsion.

Keep well clear, that way: Electra directs the dance, as in 1251 ff.

144 **There:** colloquial (Stevens 35).

145 **panpipe:** the simplest and slightest of Greek wind instruments, mainly a herdsman's plaything. See D. Paquette, *L'Instrument de musique dans la céramique de la Grèce antique* (1984) 63–71. The theatre aulete will have done his best to imitate it at this point.

147 **as if indoors:** where one need not raise one's voice so much to be heard. Or perhaps "as if I were in there and you were hearing me from outside", cf. *El.* 1166.

149 **Draw in, draw in:** probably nautical language. One can imagine these imperatives guiding a ship to a gentle meeting with the quay. The verbal repetitions in this line are matched in the antistrophe (162). Resolution of dochmiacs here gives a sequence of 35 short syllables, which is easily a record (27 in *Hel.* 695 f.).

154 **[what his plight]:** the deletion of this phrase (cf. 140–3 n.) leaves a hiatus not justified by period-end, which is remarkable but not entirely unparalleled in dochmiacs, cf. West (1982) 110.

155 **with shallow groan:** for the weakness of his breathing cf. 84. Amphitryon listens to Heracles' breathing in *HF* 1060, and doctors recognized it as a useful indicator in sickness (many passages in G. Maloney & W. Frohn, *Concordance des oeuvres hippocratiques* [1984] iv.3638 ff.).

157 **You'll finish me:** the colloquialism *apoleis* (Stevens 11) is "poeticized" (Willink) by omitting the prefix.

160 **his horrible god-sent acts:** even the friendly chorus has no word of praise for Orestes' deed; but it too puts the blame on Apollo.

162 **his oracle, oracle:** *laskō* (lit. "scream") often in tragedy of prophetic utterance; see Easterling on Soph. *Tr.* 824–5.

163 **on Themis' tripod:** Themis was said to have been the goddess of the Delphic oracle before Apollo (Aesch. *Eum.* 2, Eur. *IT* 1259, etc.). This implied that every oracle

given was a right and proper ordinance (*themis*), and the point of the present reference is that her successor has not maintained her standards.

54 Loxias: a common name of Apollo in the 5th century, usually in connection with oracles. The popular derivation from *loxos* "slanting" (taken to stand for "ambiguous") is very doubtful.

that murder be followed by murder: *apophonos phonos* and the similar phrase in 192 are usually understood to mean "unnatural murder", on the analogy of expressions like *potmos apotmos* "abnormal fate" (for which see Barrett on *Hipp.* 1142-4). Hermann took it as "a murder that would not count as murder", i.e. that would be exempt from guilt. Both interpretations involve difficulties of language, and I prefer "murder to follow murder", as if *phonos apo phonou*. This is a recurrent theme in the play (510, 816, 1579, 1587).

66 Do you see – he stirs: a false alarm, for extra excitement; cf. 1268-74, and in the prior sleep-scene *HF* 1069-71.

69 I think: *edoxa* is a "momentary" aorist, reporting the new impression just formed. So e.g. *El.* 644 *xynēka* "I understand".

71 retrace your steps: the phrase is appropriate to dancing without actually signifying it. It is a dance from the audience's viewpoint, but not from Electra's.

74 O mistress, mistress Night: this poetic invocation was probably suggested by Soph. *Phil.* 827 ff., where the chorus prays to Sleep to come and bring relief to Philoctetes. Electra, however, is praying for oblivion for herself as much as for Orestes. He is asleep already, she must wait for the day to end. Night existed as a goddess only in cosmogonic myth, not in cult.

76 the cosmic dark: *erebos* in Hesiod and Homer is the realm of darkness, not precisely located but sometimes associated with Hades or Tartarus. Erebos and Night are named side by side in Hes. *Th.* 123, Acusilaus DK 9 B 1, Ar. *Birds* 693.

77 on thy wings: in *Birds* 695 "black-winged Night" lays an egg in Erebos.

78 to the house that was Agamemnon's: in Greek prayers the deity called upon for assistance is usually asked to come to the spot; cf. 1226 n. The use of an adjective

193

Agamemnonios to represent a genitive is an archaism preserved in epic (*Il.* 10.326 etc.) and in Lesbian (cf. D.L. Page *Sappho and Alcaeus* [1955] 165).

181 <u>we are lost, are lost:</u> when a compound verb is repeated, the prefix is often omitted. Cf. 149 *prosithi* ... *ithi*, 1101 f., 1465; J. Diggle, *GRBS* 14 (1973), 265 and *Studies* 18. <u>Oh!:</u> the division of *oichometha* into *oichometh'. ā!* is a distinct improvement; cf. 145, *HF* 1052. Electra is brought abruptly down to earth.

184-5 <u>careful to avoid clamorous voice:</u> as in the corresponding lines of the antistrophe (206), the text is suspect; *ana* is hard to account for. Metrically 185 consists (as transmitted) of three resolved cretics.

191 <u>Sacrificial victims Phoebus made of us:</u> a unique and violent metaphor for the normal "destroyed us" (i.e. sealed our fate). It suggests physical slaughter of the chosen victim, the most savage and immediate form of destruction in Greek everyday life.

192 <u>sequential murder:</u> see on 164. <u>father's murderer:</u> "father-killer" in Greek does not invariably mean "killer of one's own father", cf. *Od.* 1.299, Aesch. *Cho.* 909, Soph. *Tr.* 1125.

194 <u>It *was* just – But *not good*:</u> a startling antithesis, since justice is normally taken to be self-evidently good. "Every man who is *dikaios* is *agathos*" (Thgn. 148). But what is good in one way may be bad in another, cf. 819. In *El.* 1244 Castor says that what Clytaemestra suffered was just, but not what Orestes did to her. In *Ba.* 1249 Cadmus cries that "Dionysus has destroyed us justly, but too severely". The division of the line between the chorus and Electra (guaranteed by the strophe) does not imply that they take contrasted views of the matter: the two phrases are complementary. This is typical of the style of antiphonal laments, cf. Aesch. *Pers.* 1002 ff., *Sept.* 961 ff., Eur. *Tro.* 1302 ff.

195 <u>You slew and were slain:</u> the apostrophe of Clytaemestra balances that of Night in the strophe, with the jingle *ekanes ethanes* (cf. Aesch. *Sept.* 962) corresponding to the repetition *potnia potnia* in 174.

200 <u>as good as dead:</u> justifying the preceding statement that Clytaemestra has destroyed both Agamemnon (who is literally dead) and her children. *Isonekys* is formed like *isopais, isopresbys, is-oneiros* (Aesch. *Ag.* 75, 78, *PV* 549).

01   for you are among the dead: this should refer to Orestes
     (cf. 83 f., 385) to complete the argument. But the
     unsignalled change of addressee is odd, and "you" should
     perhaps be changed to "he".
02-7 my life is gone etc.: as to why she herself is "as good
     as dead", we might have expected a mention of the death
     sentence that may be impending. But that remains
     completely out of sight at this stage of the play. Instead
     Euripides draws on motifs that properly belong to the
     time when she was ruled by Aegisthus and her mother:
     cf. Soph. *El.* 86 ff., 164 ff., and especially 185 ff.
     ("much of my life has now passed away from me without
     hope ... I who waste away without children"); Eur. *El.*
     54-9, 112 ff. True, her earlier cause for weeping has
     been succeeded by another one, but protracted
     spinsterhood should not now be among her prime worries,
     since (*a*) she has been promised to Pylades (1079), and
     (*b*) there is some likelihood that she will be stoned to
     death before the day is out. These points are made not to
     fault Euripides but to make it clear where his mind was
     focussed.
08-10 The music stops, the dancers become still; Orestes
     has slept safely through it. But now the final twist of
     suspense. Is he dead? Just as we are wondering, he
     surprises us by waking up, apparently happy and
     refreshed.
     I don't like the look of him: a colloquial idiom, cf. Ar.
     Thesm. 406, *Wealth* 353.
     he's too limp: lit. "with his too-relaxed quality". On this
     substantival use of the neuter participle (an Attic
     development) see Moorhouse 257 f.

1-315 Dialogue of Orestes and Electra. In *Trachiniae, Medea*
     and *Hippolytus* a parodos in which the chorus expresses
     its concern about someone is followed by that person's
     appearance on stage. The present case is analogous. The
     touching scene has two main purposes: to display the
     selfless mutual devotion of brother and sister, and to let
     us see a bout of Orestes' madness, which, once we have
     seen it, will fade out as a theme of the play. The
     portrayal of madness and other kinds of frenzy had long
     been part of the tragedians' stock-in-trade. See B.

Simon, *Mind and Madness in Ancient Greece* (1978) 108-13; R. Padel in P. Heelas & A. Lock (ed.), *Indigenous Psychologies* (1981) 105-31.

The scene is composed in four clearly marked sections: 211-36, Orestes wakes and receives nursing; 237-52, he is given the news of Menelaus' return (preparing for his dialogue with Menelaus in the next episode); 253-76, he suffers a fit of insanity; 277-315, he recovers, and he must now comfort Electra as she comforted him in the first section. Her role as his nurse is now finished, and she is sent indoors so that the actor can change costume for another part.

213 O mistress Oblivion: Hesiod had listed Lēthē as a goddess (*Th.* 227), but Euripides has no tradition in mind; *ad hoc* deification was a stock device for formulating reflections on the powers of abstract entities. Cf. 126 n.; Dodds on *Ba.* 370-2; West (1966) 33 f.

how clever you are: *sophos* is a common term of praise in Euripides' vocabulary. Cf. 397 n.

215 Wherever did I come here from?: Heracles is similarly puzzled in *HF* 1094-1105 and Soph. *Tr.* 984.

216 my former mind has deserted me: whatever state of consciousness he was in before he fell asleep has gone and he cannot recapture it. The expression "former *phrenes*" recurs in *Ba.* 947, 1270; cf. Archil. 172.2-3.

217-67 Distichomythia (alternation of two-line utterances) is first found in the *Oresteia*, and is not uncommon in Sophocles and Euripides. One can see that some replies have been padded out from one line to two (230, 234, etc.).

218 Would you like me to deal with you (lit. touch you, lay hands on you): a strong echo of Soph. *Phil.* 761, "would you like me to take hold of you and touch you at all?" Hence also "take hold" in Orestes' answer.

219 sticky foam: on this motif (of Orestes also at *IT* 308) see Bond on *HF* 930-1009.

221 The menial task is a pleasure: cf. Soph. *El.* 1145.

223 Support my side: he is too weak to sit up without support. Cf. 800.

224 I can't see very well: lit. "I am seeing fragmentedly", or "my seeing is reduced".

226 how unkempt you are: "you" may either be the head or Orestes himself. The verb looks like another borrowing

from *Philoctetes* (226, and *ēgriōsai* in another sense 1321).

230   a nuisance of a thing to have: the article before *ktēma* is abnormal, and Soph. *Phil.* 81 may support Kirchhoff's *ti*. But perhaps the construction is influenced by a mental *aniāron esti to ktēma*.

232   There's no pleasing the sick: more extended use of this motif in *Hipp.* 176 ff.

233   set your feet down on the ground: he will remain sitting, but with his feet down he will be in position for springing about in 255 ff. The Ephesian mural mentioned in the Introduction (I) shows him sitting on the bed with Electra standing behind.

234   A change is always nice: as a general axiom this may echo Heraclitus, who wrote that "it (the cosmic fire?) finds relief by changing" (fr. 56 Marcovich = DK 22 B 84). Euripides echoes him also in fr. 638/833 (Hclt. 47 M. = DK 22 B 62), and perhaps *Med.* 410 f.

235   by all means: a colloquial use of *malista*, as in modern Greek (Stevens 16).

236   better to have the semblance: another semi-philosophical remark. The distinction between appearance and reality had been a fruitful topic since Parmenides. For the importance of appearances cf. 314 f. and 782. Taken out of context, the present line sounds like a shocking preference of appearance to truth (the converse of Amphiaraus' famous preference in Aesch. *Sept.* 592); but in fact Orestes is only saying that if he cannot have real health, the semblance is better than nothing.

238   while the Erinyes are letting you think straight: a clear hint of the coming fit. Euripides was probably remembering Aesch. *Cho.* 1026, where Orestes, aware that his mind is starting to go, makes a declaration about his deed "while I am still sane".

242   his galley: most MSS. give the plural, but after *selmata*, *neōs* was more likely to be changed to the plural than vice versa. Cf. 54 n.

243   light of deliverance: a common poetic metaphor from Homer on.

244   who owes gratitude to: lit. "who has got favours from". The whole Trojan war was fought for Menelaus' sake, so he owes a large debt to Agamemnon, which Agamemnon's heirs will now claim. Cf. 453, 642 ff.

197

246 bringing Helen home: the cue for Orestes to condemn
her, which helps to prepare the ground for the later plot
to assassinate her.
248 If he comes with wife: the line is so phrased as to be
readily quotable about anyone who marries (agetai, lit.
"brings home", is often used of marrying a woman). It is
meant to be heard as a variant of the commonplace that
wives or women generally are an evil (Hes. Th. 592,
Sem. 7.96 ff., Susarion 1, etc.; in Euripides, Hipp.
664-8, Andr. 181 f., 269-72, 353, Or. 605 f., etc.; many
passages collected in Stob. 4.22.136 ff.).
249-50 a notable brood of daughters: there were three,
Timandra, Clytaemestra, and Helen, and they all
abandoned or betrayed their husbands ([Hes.] fr. 176,
cf. Stes. PMG 223). Cf. 541. Euripides says nothing of
the older poets' explanation that Aphrodite caused it all
out of malice - according to Stesichorus, at least, because
Tyndareos had accidentally left her out of a sacrifice to
all the gods.
such censure: the condemnation of women implied in 248.
251 You be different: Electra's married life is still in the
future.
253-79 The mad scene is characterized by heightened poetic
style.
253 your eye is becoming disturbed: rolling eyes are
regularly mentioned as a symptom of mental disturbance,
see Page on Med. 1174-5. As they cannot actually be
shown by a masked actor, they always have to be
reported, whether by the sufferer himself (PV 882, Soph.
Aj. 447) or by a witness. Here the announcement
mitigates the abruptness of Orestes' outburst. His fit
perhaps comes at this point simply because it is the next
item on Euripides' programme. The idea that it is
precipitated by the thought of Clytaemestra is
psychologically sound but may be too subtle. If that is
what the poet intended, he probably directed that
Orestes' last utterance (251-2) should be delivered with a
note of hysteria; otherwise no one could have taken the
point.
254 you were sane: a present participle may correspond to an
imperfect indicative. Cf. Moorhouse 210.
255-7 Mother etc.: the breach of regular distichomythia by
the three-line utterance contributes to the sense that

198

things are going awry. Cf. 1047-51; Dodds on *Ba.* 927-9. As in Aesch. *Cho.* 1048 ff. and Eur. *IT* 285 ff., Orestes sees the Erinyes, the agents of his mother's wrath, coming to get him. In *IT* 289 one of them threatens to hurl Clytaemestra upon him like a great rock; here she is behind them.

threaten me with: *episeie* probably means "(hold as if to) hurl down upon"; cf. 613, and the image in *IT* l.c. In Homer the verb is used of Zeus shaking his aegis at the Trojans with terrifying effect (*Il.* 4.167, cf. 15.230).

blood-eyed: see Stevens on *Andr.* 978. The bloodshot eyes of the madman himself (836, *HF* 933; Fraenkel on *Ag.* 1428) are transferred to the goddesses of madness.

snaky: they were imagined with snakes growing from their heads in place of hair, like Gorgons (Aesch. *Cho.* 1049 f.), or with snaky arms (Eur. *El.* 1345, vase paintings); cf. *IT* 286 f., Aesch. *Eum.* 128.

"Longinus" *Subl.* 15.2 picks these lines out for praise: "Here the poet himself has seen the Erinyes; and what he has imagined, he has almost made the audience see".

259 You're not seeing etc.: so in Aesch. *Cho.* 1051 ff. the chorus tells Orestes that what he sees are mere fancies arising from mental disorder.

260 O Phoebus: the god who has promised to see him through; cf. 268 ff., 419 f.

They'll kill me: cf. *IT* 291. In fact their habit is to hound their victims to death over a long period, cf. Aesch. *Cho.* 288-96, *Eum.* 264-75, 334-40.

bitch-faced: so at *El.* 1252. They snarl at him like the hunting-hounds they metaphorically are (*Cho.* 924, 1054, cf. *Eum.* 111-3, 131-2, 246).

261 fierce-eyed: another feature of the madman, *HF* 868.

priestesses of the nether ones: i.e. they slaughter victims in honour of the angry dead. Cf. Aesch. *Ag.* 735 and Eur. *Alc.* 25 with 74-6.

262 I'll not let go: various transpositions have been prompted by the conviction that this should be the response to Orestes' "Let go". But it is her attempt to grasp him more tightly that makes him think an Erinys has got hold of him.

I'll thread my arm in: round his body, under his arms.

265 you're getting a grip on my waist: a well-known

wrestling hold from which there was no escape. See R.G.
Ussher on Ar. *Eccl.* 260; M. Poliakoff, *Studies in the
Terminology of Greek Combat Sports* (1982) 40 ff.

Tartarus: in Homer and Hesiod a place into which
discredited gods are thrown; later sometimes identified
with Hades ([Hes.] *Sc.* 255, Anacr. *PMG* 395.8 f.), but
usually suggesting a specially dark and horrific region;
cf. *Hipp.* 1290, *Phoen.* 1604, Soph. *OC* 1389. It is where
the Erinyes themselves belong (Aesch. *Eum.* 72, cf. *HF*
870).

268 Give me my horn-drawn bow: Orestes calls to an imagined
attendant. The high-flown ornamental epithet refers to
the composite type of bow made from wood, horn
(keratin) and sinew. Its construction and virtues are
explained by H.L. Lorimer, *Homer and the Monuments*
(1950) 276 f.

Loxias' gift: Apollo's own weapon was the bow, and in
Aesch. *Eum.* 179 ff. he himself drives the Erinyes from
his temple by threatening them with it. The idea that he
gave Orestes a bow for this purpose comes from
Stesichorus (*PMG* 217). But clearly no one actually hands
Orestes a bow at this point, and we must assume that it
has no existence outside his imagination. The scholiast
records that "modern actors" use no bow, but wrongly
infers from Stesichorus that they should.

271 a deity: for the menacing use of the indefinite pronoun
see Bond on *HF* 747 f.

273-4 the feathered shafts speeding out: more high-flown
language, with an echo of *Eum.* 182. "Far-shooting bow"
is also Aeschylean.

276 with your wings: cf. 317, 321 f., *IT* 289. In Aeschylus
they fly without wings (*Eum.* 250, cf. 51).

Phoebus' oracles: the imagined shooting from Apollo's bow
and this explicit laying of responsibility at Apollo's door
combine to banish the Erinyes, which are after all an
emanation from Orestes' conscience (396).

277 But stay: on this favourite Euripidean interjection *eā* see
Page on *Med.* 1004, Fraenkel iii.580 n.4, Stevens 33.
Heracles uses it on waking up after his madness in *HF*
1089.

out of breath: cf. *HF* 1093 with Bond's notes.

279 the surge: a similar image (*klydōn*) in *HF* 1091. Cf.
341-4 n.

I see calm water: Hegelochus, the actor playing Orestes at the original performance, pronounced *galēn'* with a falling instead of a rising intonation on *-lē-*, so turning it into "I see a weasel" (Ar. *Frogs* 303 with schol., and other comedians cited by schol. *Or.*). Perhaps a mere slip (cf. S.G. Daitz, *CQ* 33 [1983], 294 f.), but actors have been known to do such things from high spirits.

280 **why are you crying:** she must have been doing this since he broke free from her at 265.

with your head inside your dress: concealment of tears was common, cf. *Od.* 4.115, 8.84, Aesch. *Cho.* 81, Eur. *Hipp.* 243-6, *Supp.* 111, 286, *IA* 1122 f., Pl. *Phd.* 117c; Shisler 385.

282 **being a bother:** colloquial (Stevens 56 f.). The stylistic level is no longer so grand.

284 **you agreed:** her part in the murder varies somewhat with the needs of different contexts (cf. 32 n.), but it is never equal to Orestes'.

288-93 **I think my father etc.:** this utilitarian argument runs quite contrary to the tradition (which is followed in 579-84). In Aeschylus Apollo instructs Orestes (and no one subsequently doubts) that Agamemnon's wrath would persecute him if he failed to avenge him (*Cho.* 271-96, cf. 925, *Eum.* 466 f.). Throughout it is assumed that Agamemnon will be gratified by the killing of Clytaemestra and will be likely to lend his support to the enterprise, and similarly in the two *Electras*, especially Euripides' (e.g. 677 ff., 976-8).

290 **reached for my chin with many an appeal:** lit. "extended many appeals from my chin", a reduction of "made many an appeal by extending his hand to make it depend from my chin". See 383 n.

291 **into the neck:** anatomically *sphagai* are the hollows above the collar-bone, where the subclavian arteries run close to the surface (Thuc. 4.48.3, Arist. *HA* 493b7, 511b35; Hippocratica). This is where Clytaemestra was struck (*El.* 1223).

294 **dear sister head:** elsewhere (237, *IT* 983) this is an elevated equivalent of "dear sister/brother"; cf. Barrett on *Hipp.* 651-2. Here the focus is on the actual head.

296-300 **When you see etc.:** just as you have been helping me in my low periods, so I must now comfort you. The roles are reversed (Electra's crying corresponds to Orestes' described in 44); cf. 303 n.

shrink: in medical writers of reducing a swelling, by incision or other means; hence metaphorically *PV* 380, *IA* 694, Ar. *Frogs* 941, Call. *Epigr.* 46.3 Pfeiffer = 1049 Gow-Page. It is interesting to see mental illness conceived in such physical terms.

301   **Now go into the house:** this necessary exit (211-315 n.) is well motivated by Orestes' recognition that his sister is exhausted from attending him.

303   **take food, and wash yourself:** Orestes' self-neglect (41-2) is now attributed to her.

304   **through sitting with me:** by failing to take care of herself, not by catching his malady from him.

305   **I am lost:** brother and sister (309) each affirm at the end of the scene that they are helpless without the other.

306   **as you see, I am without any others:** he may mean "it is obvious from my circumstances that the gods are doing nothing for me".

307   **Impossible:** she insists that there is no question of her leaving his bedside, whatever the consequences to her own health. The ethics of the scene call for this noble attitude to be struck, but dramaturgical necessity calls for it to be abandoned three lines later.

308   **It comes to the same:** lit. "they (living and dying) have the same within them"; or "it (dying) has the same within it (as living)".

310   **brotherless, fatherless, friendless:** such rhetorical accumulations of three negative adjectives are common in tragedy. See Fraenkel on *Ag.* 412, Stevens on *Andr.* 491. With "friendless", Menelaus is excluded from the picture.

313   **be none too receptive:** implying that his illness is at least partly related to his mental attitude. Cf. Thuc. 2.51.4 on psychological resistance to the plague.
    stay on the comfortable bed: Orestes is to remain resting (perhaps dozing) through the choral song that follows, ready for the next episode.

314   **even if one is not ill, but fancies one is:** a perceptive comment on the power of auto-suggestion. It recalls Protagoras' famous doctrine that truth is subjective, except that Electra recognizes "real" illnesses as well as imagined ones. She is hinting that Orestes' illness may be all in his mind, though even so, care must be taken of it. This interpretation of his condition - very different from her references to objective Erinyes in 37 f. and 238

- is admirably suited to the stage we have now reached, as Orestes, though remaining physically weak for several more scenes, is to suffer no more hallucinations.

315 ṛatigue: or "indisposition".

316-47 The chorus' act-dividing song represents, as often, a lyrical counterpiece to the preceding dialogue. Reverting to the poetic view of the Erinyes as external deities, they pray to them for an end to Orestes' madness, thus further smoothing over its actual disappearance from the play. They go on to comment on Orestes' piteous situation and the piteous deed that led to it, not omitting to mention the fatal oracle, and they end with reflections on the vulnerability of human fortune as exemplified by the house of Tantalus.

    The metre is dochmiac, as in the parodos. Some fragments of music to lines 338-44 are preserved in a papyrus of about 200 B.C. (Π6). The same music is to be assumed for the corresponding words of the strophe (322-8). The vocal melody appears to be based on an archaic form of scale, the pre-Platonic Phrygian scale described by Aristides Quintilianus 1.9 (pp. 18 f. Winnington-Ingram), and there is no reason to doubt that it is Euripides' original music. Here is a version in modern notation, at an approximation to the original pitch. (The sign ⱱ flattens the note by a quarter-tone.)

8va bassa   katolo]phȳromai - māteros [haima sās ho s'anab]accheuei?

8va bassa   Ho megas [olbos ou monimo]s em brotois: ana [de laiphos hōs

8va bassa   ti]s akatou thoās tina[xās daimōn] kateklysen d[einōn

203

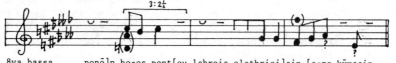

8va bassa   ponō]n ho-os pont[ou labrois olethrioi]sin [e-ng kȳmasin.

The notes in brackets are played on the shawm only, and their duration is uncertain. They are written in the papyrus (in the special instrumental notation) as if they preceded the vocal notes, but to avoid a disruption of rhythm it is better to assume that they sounded simultaneously, the two shawm-pipes diverging at these points. There are some irregular rhythmic groupings where the equivalent of four quavers is fitted into the time of three, or six into the time of five. The reading of some notes is doubtful, and there are considerable gaps. Line 339 of the text wrongly appears before 338 in the papyrus, but it may be that the sequence of musical notes is correct, i.e. that the notes appearing over -*phȳromai māteros* ... *b]accheuei* really belong to *b]accheuei katolo[-* ... *-]phȳromai*. For discussion of the fragment see J.F. Mountford in J.U. Powell & E.A. Barber (ed.), *New Chapters in the History of Greek Literature* ii (1929) 146–69; D.D. Feaver, *AJP* 81 (1960), 1–15. For a photograph see *GRBS* 18 (1977), facing p. 81, or E.G. Turner, *Greek Manuscripts of the Ancient World* (1971) 71.

317–8 <u>Ye wild-running wingèd frenzying</u>: the invocation follows a typical structure (here doubled), with a cluster of epithets developed by a relative clause which states the god's characteristic activities. *Dromades ... potniades* is an echo of *Phoen.* 1124 f., where *potniades* refers to mares frenzied by drinking the water of Potniae in Boeotia. The association seems to have led Euripides to modify the Erinyes' older epithet *potniai* and interpret it as "frenzied" or "frenzying", and later in *Ba.* 664 to transfer it to bacchants.

319 <u>who have been assigned</u>: the gods' individual functions and privileges are conceived as having been allotted to them when Zeus came to power (Hes. *Th.* 74, 885), or in some cases earlier. The Erinyes claim to have received theirs from Moira in Aesch. *Eum.* 334, cf. 208, 347 ff., 385, 392 ff.

an unbacchanal coven: *thiasos* generally stands for a Bacchic troupe (see Dodds on *Ba.* 56-57). The Erinyes have the savage frenzy of bacchants without having undergone Bacchic initiation. The phrase is of a common type in which a paradoxical, negative adjective serves to show that the noun is being used metaphorically; cf. 621, 1492, and my n. on Hes. *Op.* 525.

321 dark-hued: cf. 408, Aesch. *Sept.* 977, *Ag.* 462, *Eum.* 52, Eur. *El.* 1345.

324 I beseech you, beseech you: the repetition intensifies, as in "please, please". Cf. Alc. fr. 374 "Accept my visit, accept it, I pray you, I pray".

328 you ... poor man: this kind of apostrophe is common in Euripidean choruses, e.g. *Med.* 989, 996, *Andr.* 789. The fact that Orestes is visible is not essential.

330 Phoebus' oracle, oracle: a rather mechanical echo of 162. The whole strophe contains a number of verbal reminiscences of earlier passages.
precinct: on the word *dapedon* see Barrett on *Hipp.* 230.

331 where, they say, the central Navel lurks: lit. "where the mid-navel out-of-the-way places are said (to be)". The "Navel" of the Earth, marking its central point, was claimed to be at Delphi. This curious concept seems to be of oriental origin, cf. A.J. Wensinck, *The Ideas of the Western Semites concerning the Navel of the Earth* (1916); M. Eliade, *Shamanism* (1964) 268, 272. "They say" does not express scepticism but makes the Navel a romantic, faraway place.

333-8 What tragedy - drives you wild: this complicated sentence needs some unravelling. "What is the meaning of this lamentable, bloody ordeal of which Orestes is in the throes?" The further clauses added to this initial question (the rambling construction is typical of Euripidean lyric) serve to answer it. Some demon, no doubt established in the house by ancient crimes, has caused the shedding of Clytaemestra's blood by Orestes, and thus brought him tears (cf. 44) which merge with the tears of those previously afflicted; the bloodshed itself is the source of his frenzy. For choruses asking "what is behind this strange situation?" cf. Soph. *Aj.* 172 ff., *OT* 151 ff., 1098 ff., Eur. *Med.* 151 ff., *Hipp.* 141 ff., etc.

333 tragedy: *eleos* is usually "compassion" (one of the main emotions that Tragedy arouses, in Aristotle's view); here of its object. Similarly in 832.

205

336-7 demon: or "wrathful spirit" (alastōr). See Fraenkel on
Ag. 1501; Parker 108 f. In Ag. l.c. it is the avenging
demon incurred by Atreus, and Clytaemestra says that as
murderer of Agamemnon she is its incarnation. Euripides
similarly wants to link Orestes' deed with its antecedents,
but avoids being specific.
tears in stream with tears: a variation on the "murder
upon murder" motif (164 n.).
channelling into: odd imagery, generated by the
preceding "stream of tears".

339 I grieve for you, grieve for you: the repetition matches
"seeking justice - seeking payment" at the corresponding
place in the strophe (323), while being formally modelled
on 324.

340 Great prosperity ... is not lasting: the archaic poets'
doctrine is that ill-gotten wealth is not lasting; see my n.
on Hes. Op. 320. The gods always can reverse fortunes
(e.g. Archil. 130, Sol. 13.65-70, Thgn. 662-4, Simon.
PMG 521), but the idea that prosperity never lasts does
not appear before the 5th century: e.g. Hdt. 1.5.4,
207.2, Bacchyl. fr. 54, Eur. Hcld. 610 f., Supp. 269 f.,
331, Tro. 1203-6, HF 103, IA 161 f., frr. 45, 273, 420,
1073 f.. Trag. adesp. 1(f), 368a. See also on 974.

341-4 upsetting it - of the sea: the hazards of seafaring, so
familiar to Greeks, made it a natural field of metaphor in
relation to fortune, success, sudden disaster, etc.
"Waves" of trouble e.g. Alc. fr. 6, Aesch. Sept. 758,
and often.
some higher power: daimōn is the divine agent responsible
for one's fortunes at any given time; see my n. on Hes.
Op. 122-3.

345 For what other house: the general sense is "for if the
Tantalids cannot be looked up to as dependable, I don't
know who can, and now they are brought low", but the
last clause is unexpressed. A rhetorical question is fairly
common at the end of a strophe or song.

346 marriage of holy stock: Tantalus was the son of Zeus (5)
and a nymph. Pelops' wife Hippodamea was a
granddaughter of Ares.

48-724 Dialogue of Orestes and Menelaus (with intervention of Tyndareos 456-631), followed in 725-806 by a scene between Orestes and Pylades. This abnormally long act prepares the ground for the Argive assembly-meeting which is then to take place off stage. Menelaus' arrival cannot be further delayed, because Orestes and Electra are counting on his help in the debate. As the debate itself cannot be shown on stage, Euripides wants us to hear the issues argued out between persons who will be involved in it, and to represent the prosecution case he brings in the old Tyndareos. He is chosen above all because he is particularly well placed to exert pressure on Menelaus. (Euripides may also have been influenced by Hellanicus' story of a prosecution of Orestes at Athens by "persons from Sparta" [*FGrH* 323a F 22], who presumably included Tyndareos.) At the end of the argument it becomes clear that Menelaus' expected support for Orestes will not be forthcoming. Finally Orestes must leave to attend the debate. But he is too weak to get there unaided. Pylades' appearance solves this problem, as well as introducing a note of optimism into the situation to keep the audience in uncertainty about the outcome.

48 But see now: the high promise of Menelaus' arrival contrasts effectively with the despair the chorus has just been expressing. Entrances following strophic songs are normally unannounced, but exceptions occur where, as here, the entry is notably stately or impressive, and anapaests are used in such cases. See Hourmouziades 141, Taplin (1977) 73, Halleran 11-14. On the question whether such anapaests were recited to a musical accompaniment see *DFA*² 162. Menelaus looks dashing (1532 n.).

49-51 [And by his elegance – Tantalids' blood]: I delete this sentence, because it is silly (Menelaus' elegance, whether of gait or apparel, cannot be evidence of his descent) and because *poly* cannot be used to mean "very" in classical Greek where there is no sense of measurement. (The variant *pollēi* is metrically impossible, and no emendation fully convincing.) The interpolation was probably made for a production in which the pomp of the returning conqueror was exaggerated, cf. Introduction VI. Its author manufactured a crude connection with 347, perhaps at the expense of some words now lost.

52 O thou who launched: choral greetings of this sort are

207

found only with majestic entries (especially by chariot); see Taplin (1977) 74, 287.

a thousand-vessel horde: after Aesch. *Ag.* 45; similarly *Andr.* 106, *IT* 141. The figures in Homer's catalogue of ships add up to 1186.

354 with Success you consort for your own part: i.e. I need not use the salutation *eutychei* as well as *chaire*.

356 O palace: ignoring the chorus' greeting, Menelaus addresses the house he has not seen for so long. Cf. *HF* 523, Aesch. *Ag.* 518 and Fraenkel on 503; Taplin (1977) 299. This enables him to explain to us, before he notices Orestes, how much he already knows of the situation. On this technique of making a new arrival express his existing feelings before he notices what is to be seen on the stage (with exclamation of surprise, leading to dialogue) see D.J. Mastronarde, *Contact and Discontinuity* (1979) 25.

361 and by what a death etc.: rightly deleted by Dindorf; "fate and death" is a feeble coupling, and 372 f. is hardly compatible with any previous explicit mention of Clytaemestra as the murderess.

362 Malea: the cape at the SE. tip of the Peloponnese, associated with Menelaus' homeward voyage in *Od.* 3.287 and Agamemnon's in 4.514. If Menelaus is to be thought of as coming from Egypt, Malea would be his first sight of mainland Greece; but nothing is said in this play of where he has been since leaving Troy, and Euripides' geography is often negligent.

363 the soothsayer for sailors: in the *Odyssey* (4.512-37) Menelaus learns of Agamemnon's murder from another prophetic sea-god, Proteus, in Egyptian waters. But in *Helen* Euripides had transformed Proteus into a mortal king of Egypt, and here he makes use of Glaucus, a figure of fishermen's superstition (see Paus. 9.22.7, schol. Pl. *Rep.* 611c) whose story had been dramatized by Aeschylus (*Glaucus Pontius*).

364 the prophet of Nereus: Glaucus' mantic knowledge is here derived from the greater sea-god Nereus, for whom see my nn. on Hes. *Th.* 233. Similarly in *Rhes.* 972 f. Lycurgus, who like Glaucus was formerly a mortal, is now "the prophet of Bacchus" while himself divine.

367 his last ablutions: if the verse is genuine, Menelaus must have taken this (despite the strange "met", *peripesōn*) to

refer only to the washing of the corpse (the ordinary
sense of the phrase), whereas in fact it referred at the
same time to the fatal bath (cf. *El.* 157). But the
clumsily-worded line may belong with [361].

68 filled me ... with tears: after *Od.* 4.538 ff.

70 already on her way here: he sent her before he knew
that her sister was not there to receive her. Willink is
wrong to delete this line.

73 harbour salts: lit. "sea-beaten ones". For the device of
the casual off-stage informant cf. 471 n.

75 tell me where he is, young ladies: new arrivals often ask
choruses for directions. Most similar is *Supp.* 1044: Iphis
asks if the chorus has seen Evadne, and Evadne herself
answers from the high rock where he has not noticed
her. *Hec.* 484 is another case where the person sought is
present (lying on the ground) but not immediately seen.

80 Here I am: Orestes must leave his bed here. Even if he
could reach Menelaus' knees from it, he cannot stay in
bed throughout the act, and there is no later opportunity
for him to get up. Whether the bed is removed by
stagehands at any point, we do not know.

82 As a first offering: Orestes feels the need for Menelaus'
help so urgently that he makes an immediate appeal for it
before explaining the whole situation. The following
stichomythia is primarily expository, and culminates in a
renewal of the initial appeal at 449-55.
I touch your knees: on supplication see Shisler 379 f.; J.
Gould, *JHS* 93 (1973), 74-103; Collard on *Supp.* 8-11; on
knee-touching in particular, W. Burkert, *Structure and
History in Greek Mythology and Ritual* (1979) 44-7.

83 making contact in prayer uttered without foliage: lit.
"fastening to them (your knees) pleas from a leafless
mouth". It is actually himself that he fastens to Menelaus'
knees (cf. *IA* 1216 f.), but the act of fastening creates
his plea; hence "pleas" can appear as the object of the
verb. Cf. 290. A properly prepared suppliant would
carry a leafy olive-bough with some wool round it; see
Collard l.c., Friis Johansen & Whittle on Aesch. *Supp.*
22, and for an explanation Burkert, op. cit. 44. In
Aesch. *Supp.* 354 the boughs are described as "shading"
the suppliants, and hence ibid. 656 their mouths are
"shaded".

84 the very man: a somewhat doubtful use of *autos*, and

auton is a tempting correction.

388   disfigure me: or "make me unseemly".

389   wasted: lit. "dried out".

390   my name has not deserted me: I am the Orestes you were looking for, even if no longer a viable human being.

393   Be sparing in mentioning evils: the corollary of the proverb "good things stand repeating two or three times", for which see Dodds on Pl. *Gorg.* 498e11.

395-411 Menelaus interrogates Orestes in the manner of a doctor, the sort described in Pl. *Laws* 720d, who asks how the ailment began and developed and who learns from the patient as well as advising him as best he can.

396   My intellect etc.: a famous line. It has already been hinted that Orestes' madness comes from within (314 n.). Now he himself gives a sophisticated interpretation of it as arising from his sense of guilt. He uses a striking formulation in identifying his *xynesis* (normally an admirable thing) as his sickness. The definite article particularizes; its use with abstracts in general propositions is not relevant here.

Greek did not yet have a word for "conscience" (*syneidēsis* is Hellenistic), but the concept was beginning to be familiar. See Dodds 36 f.; V.A. Rodgers, *GRBS* 10 (1969), 241-54; Dover 220-3; Parker 252-4. For the debilitating anguish caused by a bad conscience see especially *Andr.* 802 ff., Antiphon 5.93. Note, however, that Menelaus finds Orestes' answer obscure.

397   It's intelligent: Menelaus repeatedly judges things in terms of *sophiā* (415, 417, 488, 490, 695, 716, cf. 710). Cf. Introduction IV.

399   she is formidable, that one: lit. "the goddess is formidable". As a power affecting human life, anguish can readily be treated as a deity (cf. 213 n.), but how little this means is shown by the continuation "but still curable".

402   The day I was building up: the "doctor" will need to know how many days ago that was, but this essential supplementary question does not appear till 421. Euripides' first draft may have had these lines together, and the introduction of another line of enquiry (403-10) caused the thread to be broken.

404   in the night: appropriate for an experience of the supernatural, see my n. on Hes. *Th.* 10. The Greeks

counted the night as belonging to the following day, so
this was part of the day on which, after recovering the
bones from the dying pyre, he was to raise the barrow
over them. Euripides may have been thinking of *Il.*
23.217 ff., where Patroclus' pyre burns through the
night till dawn, and Achilles remains grieving beside it;
the collecting of bones and the raising of the mound
follow.

5 keeping you upright: i.e. are you sure you weren't
asleep? The main point of the question is to allow Pylades
to be mentioned, as he had to be somewhere in
preparation for his later appearance. (The mention in 33
is interpolated.)

7 from what kind ... are you being disordered by: the bad
grammar is Euripides'. Cf. Soph. *Tr.* 1160 and Moorhouse
97, 130.

8 three: so also 1650, *Tro.* 457, and Orphic theogonies.
Collectivities of gods are often crystallized into trinities
(Moirai, Charites, etc.); cf. West (1966) 36 n.2.
that looked like Night: being black (321 n.) and winged
(177 n., 276 n.). In Aesch. *Eum.* 321 etc. Night is their
mother. Apollo looks like Night when he comes on his
deadly mission in *Il.* 1.47.

9 I don't care to name them: cf. 38 n. We have reverted to
recognition of the Erinyes as objective realities.

0 they are awesome: a regular epithet of the Erinyes
(Aesch. *Eum.* 1041, Soph. *Aj.* 837, *El.* 112), and the
"Awesome Goddesses" of Athenian cult (Ar. *Knights* 1312,
Thuc. 1.126.11, etc.; L.R. Farnell, *Cults of the Greek
States* v [1909] 440-2, 471-3) were identified with them at
least from the time of Aeschylus.
Turn to politer matters: most editors read *apetrepou*
(Hermann), "you showed good breeding in avoiding
naming them", but that would require an aorist.

3 be suffered by those who have done them: a
commonplace. See Pearson on Soph. fr. 229, and my n.
on Hes. *Op.* 265-6.

5 death: many tragic characters overcome by despair or
shame contemplate or commit suicide.
that isn't intelligent: similarly fr. 1070. In *HF* 1248-54
Theseus rejects Heracles' talk of suicide as unheroic and
foolish; cf. Bond's n.

7 rather backward: this same oracle is called foolish by

211

Orestes in *El.* 971 and even by Castor in 1246, 1302; cf. also (of Apollo) *Andr.* 1165, *Ion* 916 (dub.), and of other gods *HF* 347, *Ion* 1313, fr. 645.

418 We are slaves to the gods: god's relationship to man is analogous to that of master to slave, cf. *Hipp.* 88; he controls his destiny as he pleases.

whatever "the gods" are: a Euripidean cliché (after Aesch. *Ag.* 160), cf. *HF* 1263, *Tro.* 885, *Hel.* 1137, *Ba.* 894, fr. 480. We are governed by powers we do not understand.

420 Divinity is like that: it was a commonplace that divine punishment of sinners, though certain, was sometimes long delayed (Dodds on *Ba.* 882-7, adding Thgn. 201 ff., 731 ff.). Here the idea takes a more ironic form.

423 How soon: by contrast with the dilatory Apollo.

424 God may not be intelligent: answering Menelaus' other criticism of Apollo (417). I suspect that the line was originally written to follow 417, and that 418-23 is an expansion by Euripides. This assumes the validity of my emendation *ephȳ theos* for the nonsensical *ephȳs kakos* of the MSS.; a reference to Apollo seems indispensable. See my discussion in *BICS* 28 (1981), 69. Many editors read *ephȳn philos* (Brunck, comparing Soph. *Ant.* 99): "I may not be clever (like you), but I am true to my own (my father)".

he is true to his own: i.e. he will help me eventually.

425 help you at all: this could mean (*a*) do you find it a comfort, or (*b*) does Agamemnon's spirit show any sign of helping, or (*c*) are you benefiting from public approval? Against (*c*), Orestes' standing with the city is raised as a fresh question in 427. In favour of (*b*) is the suggestion of "failure to act" in 426 *aprāxiāi*, and the parallelism between 426 and 420.

429 the blood on your hands: lit. "your blood-of-hands". We should expect "your" to agree with "hands", but cf. Jebb on Soph. *Ant.* 794, Barrett on *Hipp.* 333-5, Bond on *HF* 468.

in the prescribed way: he would have had to sit as a suppliant at someone else's hearth, and his host would have to sacrifice a sucking pig and let its blood run down on the murderer's hands. See Parker 370-4. According to Aesch. *Eum.* 282 f., 449-52, Orestes received this purification at Delphi.

212

1   which of them ... want to run you out: the refusal of
purification locally will force him to leave; cf. 47 n.
Menelaus correctly assumes that certain influential
individuals are behind the city's attitude.

2-3 Oeāx ... the killing of Palamēdēs: alluding to a
favourite story of the tragedians, which Euripides had
referred to in his *Philoctetes* of 431 and dramatized in his
Palamedes of 415. Palamedes, son of Nauplius, was put to
death on a false charge of treason, having been framed
by Odysseus. Oeax was his brother. According to one
version (Dictys 6.2, Hyg. *Fab*. 117) it was Oeax who
prompted Clytaemestra to murder Agamemnon, and Paus.
1.22.6 describes a 5th-century painting on the Acropolis
which showed Pylades killing "the sons of Nauplius" as
they came to Aegisthus' aid.

4   at two removes: lit. "across three" (inclusive reckoning).
Similarly in musical terminology the interval A to C is *dia
triōn*.

5   Aegisthus' party: the *apo* signifies "from Aegisthus'
direction", "on his side"; *pros* with genitive would be
more usual. Aegisthus' friends are mentioned in the
report of the debate (894); Oeax, surprisingly, is not.

6   abuse: *hybrizō* = "behave outrageously towards" by
unwarranted speech or action.

    against me: Orestes has been using the first person
plural intermittently (394, 414, 428, 438), clearly in the
sense of the singular, and I continue to treat it so here,
although the vote is to be about Electra too. She is left
out of the picture throughout the conversation. In saying
"against", Orestes anticipates the verdict.

    I am encircled: a new detail, not altogether rational.
There should be no objection to Orestes' leaving. But the
drama requires this option to be closed, and Euripides
re-uses a motif already seen in *HF* 82 f. and *Hypsipyle*
p.36 Bond.
    My hope runs to you: now that Menelaus knows
everything, Orestes resumes the appeal begun in 382.
    your near ones: not "me and my sister" but "me because
I am in the category of your near ones". Cf. 453, Soph.
OC 813; Barrett on *Hipp*. 49; Moorhouse 7.
    debts of gratitude: 244 n.

-5   The name etc.: "a friend in need is a friend indeed".
The unreliability of friends in misfortune is a

213

commonplace, cf. Thgn. 79-82, 299, 697 f., 857-60, 929 f., Democr. DK 68 B 101, 106; in Euripides, *Med*. 561, *El*. 605-7, 1131, *HF* 57-9, etc.

The sententious close (70 n.) rounds off the section. The appeal to Menelaus is complete. Just as we are awaiting his response - he has given no indication of his attitude so far - there is an unexpected interruption as Tyndareos arrives on the scene. We had not even heard that he was at Argos. There will now be three generations of the family on stage together. As usual in three-character scenes, the dialogue does not circulate freely among all three. It is at first between Tyndareos and Menelaus, afterwards between Tyndareos and Orestes.

456-8 See now etc.: the entrance announcement is, as often, given to the chorus-leader. This is especially suitable when the preceding dialogue contains no pointers towards the new arrival.

on aged legs the Spartiate struggles: Euripides likes to stress the difficulties old men have with the uphill slope of the *eisodos* and/or the steps up onto the stage, cf. *El*. 489 ff., *HF* 119 ff., *Ion* 738 f., and also Ar. *Lys*. 286 ff.

dark-robed and shorn: entrance announcements often contain descriptive elements. As he wrote his play the poet had nowhere to note such specifications but in the text. He also tells us *why* Tyndareos is dressed as he is, and so warns us that he is unlikely to be sympathetic towards Orestes. Dark robes for mourning: Aesch. *Cho*. 11, Eur. *Alc*. 427, *Hel*. 1088.

459 I am lost etc.: for other cases of speech or dialogue after an approaching character has been sighted but before he can hear it see Hourmouziades 145, Taplin (1977) 73. The most similar is *HF* 1155 ff., where Heracles is ashamed to be seen by Theseus and wonders how he can hide - clearly the model for this passage.

462 He even took care of me when I was small: this seems to be not tradition but invention to make the situation more poignant. Sentimental reminiscences of childhood care are quite common, cf. *Il*. 9.485 ff., *Od*. 15.363 ff., 16.442 ff., Aesch. *Cho*. 749 ff., 896 ff., Eur. *Tro*. 1180 ff., Ar. *Clouds* 861 ff., 1380 ff.

465 the Zeus-twins: their own sons, Castor and Polydeuces,

whose real father was Zeus.

66 <u>o my wretched heart and soul</u>: people address their own heart from Homer on (*Od.* 20.18 *kradiē; thȳme* is commoner), but their *psȳchē* not before the 5th century (Adesp. eleg. 28.3 = Simonides, Pind. *P.* 3.61; in Euripides, *IT* 839, 882, *Ion* 859, frr. 308.1, 924.1). Orestes is no longer talking to Menelaus but thinking aloud.

67 <u>What darkness can I find</u>: Heracles finds darkness by veiling his head, *HF* 1159. Orestes would like to become invisible, and thinks of concealing himself in cloud like a Homeric god.

70 <u>Where, oh where</u>: the old servant in *El.* 487 makes a similar excited entry, "where, oh where is my young mistress?" (Primitive reduplication: similarly Sanskrit, *kva kva?*) Tyndareos' arrival is well motivated; he has come specially to see Menelaus.

71 <u>I was at Clytaemestra's tomb</u>: explaining (to the audience, not to anyone on stage) why he is in Argos at all. The motif of pouring libations at Clytaemestra's tomb was readily suggested by Hermione's errand. In real life he could not have avoided meeting her, but she is ignored here. When he says "I heard" we understand that his informant was some passer-by; cf. 373, 730, 874, *Ba.* 1222, 1230.

74 <u>Take me to him</u>: it is only from such occasional orders (cf. 629) that the presence of attendants is confirmed, but it is probable that they normally accompanied important personages such as kings and seers.

76 <u>whose pillow was also Zeus'</u>: Castor, Polydeuces and Helen were born to Leda from Zeus; her children by Tyndareos were Clytaemestra and Timandra (249-50 n.), and according to [Hes.] fr. 23(a).10 Phylonoe. Tyndareos is ennobled by Zeus' use of his wife. Similarly Amphitryon in *HF* 1, 149, 339.

78 <u>[What a plague – what is coming]</u>: the exclamation *eā*, standing outside the metre, has been filled out into a complete trimeter by someone who understood it as a cry of distress (as in *IA* 1132, which is probably not by Euripides) rather than simply surprise (as elsewhere). The banal remark adds nothing of value. See Fraenkel iii.580 n.4.

79 <u>the matricide-serpent</u>: Clytaemestra herself dreamed of mothering a snake (Aesch. *Cho.* 527 ff., cf. 928). Conversely she is a "snake" to him, ibid. 994 (cf. 249, 1047). The same metaphor Aesch. *Supp.* 895, Soph. *Ant.* 531, Eur. *Ion* 1262 f.

480 glinting: from his eyes. If his mask had allowed, we might imagine Orestes looking guilty as well as sick.
my bête noire: "my shudder-object". *Stygēm' emon* is coined under the influence of *kēdeum' emon* in 477, just as the *karā* phrase in 481 is influenced by that in 476.

481 the unholy creature: Willink takes this as vocative, but Tyndareos' disgust is focussed on Orestes.

485 You have become barbarized: or "adopted foreign values". For Tyndareos the basis of Greek culture is a community-oriented system of law; cf. 495, 512 ff., and *Med.* 536-8. Menelaus rightly points out that kinship obligations are no less important to a Greek. We recall the conflict of issues in *Antigone*.

487 to be above the law: cf. *Ba.* 890-2 with Dodds' n.

488 Everything based on compulsion: as hinted by "among the intelligent", this echoes contemporary sophists' arguments. Cf. Democr. DK 68 B 181 (conviction a better guarantor of morality than law/compulsion; cf. Critias *TrGF* 43 F 11, 19.5 ff.); Pl. *Gorg.* 483b ff. (law an artificial curb on nature); *Rep.* 338e ff., Xen. *Mem.* 1.2.40-6 (law = compulsion by the stronger).

490 your testy old age: Menelaus regards enlightened thinking as the prerogative of younger men, implying its equation with modern thinking. Cf. Ar. *Clouds* 129 f.

492 if seemly – everyone: most editors attach this conditional clause to the next sentence, but the sense is "we have no need of any special *sophiā* in this case, because the issues are as plain as daylight; anyway, Orestes himself has not shown any".

There follows a typical *agōn*, a scene in which the two sides of an argument are set out in lengthy speeches separated by brief and non-committal comments from the chorus-leader, and which ends with the original disagreement exacerbated. On this form in Euripides cf. Collard (1975) ii.132-5.

493 behaved: *gignomai* often means not "become" but "turn out to be" (when put to the test), "show oneself to be".

494 what was right: he runs the idea of *dikē* together with that of law. But from another point of view the killing of

Clytaemestra was *dikaion* (194, 572, 775, Aesch. *Cho.* 988, 1027, etc.).

95 the standard Greek procedure: each city had its own laws, but it was possible to generalize about certain widely established usages which were regarded as no less binding and indeed acquired a higher status from their universality. Cf. Eur. *Telephus* fr. 148.8 Austin, *Andr.* 693, *Supp.* 311, 526, 538, 671, *Hel.* 1241, 1561, fr. 853.3, Thuc. 3.59.1, 4.97.2. Tyndareos thinks that Clytaemestra should have been treated as an ordinary murderer, and that exile (515) would have been the correct measure. This is in accord with both Homeric and Attic practice (see Barrett on *Hipp.* 34-7, Parker 114, 116-8), and it is the chorus's first thought at Aesch. *Ag.* 1410.

97 smitten on the head: so Stes. *PMG* 219, Soph. *El.* 99. In this version the weapon is an axe (so also Eur. *Hec.* 1279, *El.* 160, 279, 1160, *Tro.* 361), whereas in Homer and Aeschylus it was a sword. See T.G. Tucker, *The Choephori of Aeschylus* (1901) 263-6; Fraenkel iii.806-9.

01 while aiming for religious correctness: others take *hosiān* as adj. with *dikēn* and *diōkonta* as "in prosecuting the case", but the participle is then redundant and the emphasis not that suggested by the word order in 500. *Hosiā* = a state of affairs that will satisfy the gods, see Parker 330.

thrown his mother out of the house: to avoid sharing it with her. See Parker 122 f. But the tragedians all represent Clytaemestra as having too firm a grip on the house to be turned out. Electra (except in Eur. *El.*) does live with her, very much under her thumb.

02 out of the calamity: ablatival genitive, cf. *Med.* 534. The variant *anti*, "instead of calamity", is less well attested and necessitates the emendation *elab' an* (a type of elision found mainly in emendations).

03 righteous: from "showing proper deference, respectful" (towards the gods), *eusebēs* comes to mean generally "moral" with no particular religious overtone.

04 plight: on the non-personal use of *daimōn* see Fraenkel on *Ag.* 1341 f., Stevens on *Andr.* 98.

08-11 Suppose Orestes – end of the troubles: at the close of *Choephoroe* the chorus, reviewing the chain of killings in the house, ask "where will it end?" The answer in

217

Orestes' case is in fact purification abroad followed by a judicial absolution at Athens. But in principle Tyndareos has a good point, given the assumption that a vendetta-killing is never free from guilt or acceptable to everyone.

511 pay off: as if absolving a debt.
how far will it go etc.: lit. "how far will the end of the troubles go on?", a mixture of "how far will the troubles go?" and "where will they reach an end?" (*Hipp.* 936-7).

512 ordered these matters well: when they established our traditions.

515 rehabilitating him by banishment: *hosioun* "conveys the idea of restoring religious normality" (Parker 121), and Attic authors "commonly treat exile itself as a form of purification" (ibid. 114). Infinitive as if *ouk ekeleuon* had been written in 513; similarly in 900, *Phoen.* 1218, etc.

517 pollution on his hands: lit. (reading *cheros*) "hand-pollution"; and *cheroin* if preferred will be genitive rather than dative. Cf. 429.

518-25 As for me etc.: he stresses that he condemns Orestes' actions not out of any sympathy for his daughter but strictly as a matter of principle.

519 my daughter: here he has only the one daughter in mind; the parenthesis about Helen in 520-2 looks like an afterthought on Euripides' part.

523 defend the law: this expression also Thuc. 3.67.6. Cf. Heraclitus 103 Marcovich = DK 22 B 44 "the people should fight on behalf of the law no less than for a city wall", and Soph. *Ant.* 677.

524 this animal butchery: Hes. *Op.* 276-80 contrasts the savagery of the animal world with the justice which is proper to the human. Fifth-century sophists (perhaps first Protagoras) developed a theoretical account of man's gradual rise from a primitive "animal-like" state; Archelaus (DK 60 A 1, 2, 4.6) laid emphasis on law as a human invention. Cf. Eur. *Supp.* 201 f. (*thēriōdes*), Critias *TrGF* 43 F 19.1-8, and in general W.K.C. Guthrie, *History of Greek Philosophy* iii.60-84; E.R. Dodds, *The Ancient Concept of Progress and Other Essays* (1973) 1-25.

526 ff. The last part of Tyndareos' speech is bitty. For eight lines he addresses Orestes directly. We should not say that "he has forgotten" the embargo on doing so, but

that Euripides waives it in the interests of the drama. Cf. 75 n. Similarly at *Hipp.* 946: Theseus has been avoiding speaking at Hippolytus, but in the end we must see him attacking him directly. He excuses himself by saying "since I am in the presence of pollution anyway".

26 <u>I mean:</u> taking up the theme of the inhumanity of Orestes' deed.

27 <u>put forth her breast:</u> an established feature of the story (Aesch. *Cho.* 896-8, Eur. *El.* 1206 f.), perhaps going back to epic accounts. Hecuba does the same in pleading with Hector at *Il.* 22.80 ff., and Stesichorus *SLG* S 13 may be another early parallel. In *Phoen.* 1568 Euripides extends the motif to Jocasta. According to the earlier tragic passages, Orestes was deeply disturbed by his mother's gesture.

30 <u>supports:</u> *homorrhotheō* was perhaps originally "murmur in agreement", of an assembly (see my n. on Hes. *Op.* 220).

31 <u>you are hated by the gods:</u> Orestes' madness is evidence that the gods are against him, and this confirms Tyndareos' arguments that he is in the wrong.

32-3 <u>What need have I – to be seen:</u> forestalling the question who has told Tyndareos about Orestes' madness. He alluded to his unhealthy appearance in 480, and the bed is probably still there as evidence at least of some sort of disorder. Alternatively "witnesses" may stand for "proofs" of Orestes' guilt: the visible signs of divine wrath are all Tyndareos needs.

36-7 <u>but leave him – Spartan soil:</u> these two lines recur at 625 f., and it is very unlikely that they are both genuine in both places. The scholiast comments on the second line only at 626, and the threat is more effective if it comes only as Tyndareos' parting shot. Brunck deleted 536-7; but 536 is guaranteed by 564, and one expects a positive injunction to complement the negative in 535. Following 536, 537 was a natural interpolation from the parallel passage.

Tyndareos earlier spoke of exile as the correct sentence for murderers. But in 538 he allows that Clytaemestra deserved her death, and he can hardly take a more lenient view in Orestes' case.

38-9 <u>My daughter – killed by him:</u> a brief final recapitulation of the main argument. No defence can be made for Clytaemestra, but Orestes was not entitled to do what he did. If she was to be put to death, it should presumably have been by communal stoning (cf. Aesch. *Ag.* 1118).

540-1 **I have been a fortunate** etc.: as in 519, the thought of the one bad daughter leads to the other. These lines too may have been an afterthought. But it is good that we should be reminded of Helen from time to time.

542-3 **Lucky is the man** etc.: the convention of making the chorus-leader say a brief nothing (normally of two lines) between opposing speeches perhaps allowed the second speaker to step forward and take up a more prominent position, while the first stepped back.

544-50 Orestes begins, as forensic orators (especially in defence cases) often do, with a deprecatory preface explaining what a handicap he is under (cf. Stevens on *Andr.* 184 ff.). At the same time he shows that he has a proper sense of deference towards a much older man. 546-7 do not belong in this preface but constitute the starting proposition of the main argument, re-stated at the end of the first section (563). Hartung's transposition of the two lines to follow 550 is necessary. They presuppose that Tyndareos' age, the obstacle to Orestes' speaking, has indeed been discounted as proposed in 548-50.

546 **My position is:** a typical use of *egō de* following the prefatory remarks, cf. *Med.* 526, *Phoen.* 473, 503, Denniston 170 f. Hermann's articulation as *egōid'* is mistaken.
outside the law: that is, the moral law underwritten by the gods.

547 **but also within it:** this paradox is in the spirit of the *Dissoi Logoi* (DK 90), a work of *c*.400 B.C. which elaborates on the Heraclitean and Protagorean idea that opposite qualities can be predicated of a thing when it is considered from different viewpoints.

551 **What ought I to have done?:** he has been told in 500; but the question is a standard rhetorical one, cf. Dem. 18.28, 62, 190, 301.
set two things against two others: the first thing is the father's claim on his son's loyalty; it is set against the mother's, and found to be superior. The second point is Clytaemestra's adultery, which lessened her claims

220

further, and this is set against the unholiness of matricide.

553 ploughland: an ancient metaphor (Aesch. *Sept.* 753, Soph. *OT* 1211, 1257, etc.), reflected in the Attic betrothal formula "I give you my daughter for the sowing (*ep' arotōi*) of legitimate children" (see Gomme – Sandbach on Men. *Pk.* 1010). The point here is that the child grows from the father's seed alone. Euripides' immediate source is Aesch. *Eum.* 658 ff. (Apollo's defence of Orestes), but the belief was common: Hippon DK 38 A 13, Anaxagoras DK 59 A 107, Diog. Apoll. DK 64 A 27, Pl. *Tim.* 91d. Cf. G.E.R. Lloyd, *Science, Folklore and Ideology* (1983) 86 ff.

555-6 I reckoned I should rather take: an unusual construction; the result of my reckoning was the idea of taking my father's side.
the fostering: of the seed.

558 private nuptials: i.e. not arranged in the proper way by her family. "Nuptials" is metaphorical, as there was clearly not even an unofficial ceremony.

560 I shall be proclaiming it of myself: it does no one credit to be the son of an adulteress.

562 I killed him: Attic law allowed the killing of an adulterer caught with one's wife, mother, sister, daughter, or concubine (Lys. 1.30, Dem. 23.53). In Aesch. *Cho.* 989 f. the killing of Aegisthus is regarded in this light and as in no need of justification, and Orestes is never criticized for it.
and thereupon made sacrifice: as if to solemnize the first killing. The verb suggests both that the killing of Clytaemestra was of secondary importance and that it was almost a ritual duty. She speaks of her murder of Agamemnon as a sacrifice in Aesch. *Ag.* 1433, 1504 (cf. 1118). See further Denniston on Eur. *El.* 1222; Burkert, *GRBS* 7 (1966), 116–21.

563 doing an unholy thing etc.: returning to the starting-point of the paragraph.

565 hear how I am the benefactor: the *Rhetorica ad Alexandrum* (pseudo-Aristotle, perhaps the earliest surviving treatise of rhetoric) teaches that the defendant who cannot deny his action should try to argue that it was lawful, right, and for the public good (1427a25).

566 to have the effrontery: a phrase constantly used by the

orators of their opponents' behaviour.

569 <u>it would cost them nothing</u>: if I had not changed the odds. The argument is far-fetched. Clytaemestra's grievances were not trivial; and no one has suggested that she should have gone unpunished.

574 <u>as commander for all Greece</u>: in Aesch. *Eum.* 625 f. /637 Agamemnon's royal eminence is represented as making his murder all the more culpable.

576 <u>realized her mistake</u>: her conscience was inert, by all accounts, so this presumably means "realized that she was in an unsustainable position" or "that the game was up".

579 <u>hardly appropriate to mention heaven</u>: it is a mannerism of Euripides to insert a reflective comment upon an ordinary idiom that would normally pass without remark. Cf. 1083, *Hipp.* 88, *Hel.* 560. The point is that murder is polluting and abhorrent to the gods.

580 <u>in judging murder</u>: he has passed from defending himself to trying Clytaemestra.

582 <u>be dancing me about with his Erinyes</u>: see on 288-93. Erinyes can be considered indifferently either as self-sufficient goddesses who have been operating almost since the beginning of the world (319 n.) or as the personal agents of individuals (*Od.* 11.280, 17.475, Aesch. *Cho.* 924, Eur. *Med.* 1389, etc.). It is not clear why Agamemnon's would have persecuted Orestes rather than Clytaemestra. *Anechoreue* suggests the "coven" (319) or wild band of revellers (Aesch. *Ag.* 1189 *kōmos*) that seizes the reluctant victim and forces him to dance with them against his will.

585 <u>It was you</u>: from blaming Clytaemestra he progresses to blaming her father for begetting her. The scholiast compares *Il.* 5.875, where Ares blames Zeus for having fathered such a goddess as Athena. For Greek orators attack was an essential part of defence.

588 <u>Do you see</u>: Penelope is known to be waiting faithfully for Odysseus. Her conduct and Clytaemestra's are already contrasted in *Od.* 11. 405-61, 24.192-202, and it may have been this association that led genealogists to make them cousins (West [1985] 157). The contrast is rather oddly dragged in here – that Clytaemestra was killed because she was bad is not controversial – and some editors delete the sentence. However, it seems presupposed by 591 (assuming that paragraph to be

genuine, see below), because *horāis* is less naturally used there and would hardly have been used at all if it were not following on from 588-90. For *horāis?* pointing to facts not immediately present to the senses cf. Soph. *Ant.* 712, Eur. *Ba.* 319, 337, fr. 794; pointing to things that are, *Hipp.* 313 etc. (Stevens 36 f.).

89 taking one husband after another: normally the man *gamei*, the woman *gameitai*. The active here underlines the extent to which Clytaemestra took the initiative (558 n.). Cf. Trag. adesp. 194 (Helen seducing Paris), and the jest in Anacr. fr. iamb. 7 = *PMG* 424.

90 the bedchamber: the word may signify Penelope herself (cf. *Andr.* 446, *bouleutēria* = the Spartans), in which case translate "she abides at home, an unflawed bedfellow".

91-9 And do you see Apollo – save me from death: these lines were condemned by J. Oeri, but it is hardly credible that Orestes should fail to use the Apollo argument. However, it does have the appearance of an afterthought. Cf. 605-6 n.

93 [whom we obey]: this second relative clause is redundant and clumsily phrased. The sequence 592, 594 looks authentic: he speaks with a most certain voice, and I obeyed him.

95 Outlaw him, execute him: the imperatives are plural, "all of you".

96 What should I have done?: i.e. in response to Apollo's instruction. Not a mere repetition of 551.

99 if he that told me etc.: there is no real parallel in drama for the synechphonesis *mē͜ ho*, though *kai ho* (*chō*) is common, and cf. Pind. *I.* 7.8-9 *ē͜ hot'* (dub.), Bacchyl. 3.22 *aglaïzetō͜ ho*. Porson deleted the article, but it is essential; Herwerden deleted the line, but an amplification of "where else" is desirable.
save me from death: by arranging for the blame to be laid at his own door.

00-1 No, do not say – ill-starred: Orestes ends by reasserting that what he did was good. The couplet parallels Tyndareos' closing couplet (540-1); both complain of having been denied fortune's favour. For a similar clausular echo cf. *El.* 1050/1096.

02-4 For men whose marriages etc.: these reflections are irrelevant here and ruin the perfect ending of the speech at 601. They no doubt originated in some other play and were added here by someone who was reminded of them by the reference above to Penelope. On this and some similar interpolations see E. Fraenkel, *Kleine Beiträge* (1964) i.416-22.

605 Women always complicate men's affairs: lit. "get in the way of the things that happen to men". Adverse comments on womankind are common in Euripides (248 n.), although many of his female characters are as good as or better than the males. This one may strike us as oddly unrelated to the last part of Orestes' speech (leaving the spurious 602-4 out of account). But this would not have been so in the first draft if, as suggested above, 591-9 was an afterthought. The choral comment would then have arisen from 585-90, and would have been separated from it only by 600-1.

608 that I feel pained: as Orestes anticipated in 545.

609 you will fire me: the future tense is illogical but looks forward to the debate. The variant *anaxeis* is better attested, but could not bear the required sense. Another possibility is *anazeis*, "you set me boiling".

612 convocation: *ekklētos ochlos* is a poetic paraphrase of *ekklēsiā*. Euripides is not imagining an exact counterpart to the Athenian ekklesia. The term originally denoted an assembly that met not routinely but as and when summoned; that is what it remained in some monarchical and oligarchic states, and what is assumed in this play (cf. 46 n.). Euripides does not specify who besides the king (872-3) might have had power to call a meeting in normal times, but in the present interregnum Oeax and Aegisthus' friends (432-6) have evidently taken the initiative. In real life Tyndareos, as a non-citizen, could only have attended by invitation. As it is, he does not personally speak in the debate but gets an Argive to present his point of view (915).

613 bring the city crashing down: or perhaps "lash it on at you" as if with reins. Cf. 255.
whether it will or no: this emended reading agrees with the scholiast's paraphrase. The MSS have "it being willing, not unwilling", an expression that normally emphasizes cases of unexpected willingness and that does not seem very fitting here. Tyndareos should not prejudge the Argives' inclination to pass the death

sentence; he is claiming that his own intervention will overcome all opposition. *Hekousan ouk hekousan* is like *hekousin te kai ākousin* (Pl. *Phil.* 14c, *Laws* 632b), with forceful asyndeton, as in *anō katō;* cf. Aesch. *Supp.* 862 *theleos atheleos,* Latin *uelit nolit,* and our "willy nilly".

615 **She deserves to die** etc.: the plot requires Electra to be in the same mortal danger as Orestes, though the grounds for sentencing her to death were clearly much slighter. These lines offer some justification.

617 **sending tales:** before his return to Argos. Soph. *El.* 170, 319, 1155 speaks of messages sent by him to her.

618 **her dreams of Agamemnon:** presumably he had appeared to her and called for vengeance. In Aeschylus and Sophocles it is only Clytaemestra who has a dream (as earlier in Stesichorus, *PMG* 219), but in *IT* 151 Euripides had used the motif with Iphigeneia.

619-20 **may the nether gods' hatred fall upon it:** a normal curse invokes the (Olympian) gods' hate, which may be expected to bring some kind of punishment. But the adulterers are dead, so only "the nether gods" (Hades and Persephone, if they have to be specified) can reach them. "For in this life too it was galling" implies that the affair is likely to be similarly judged in the other world.

621 **a fire not of Hephaestus:** i.e. a metaphorical fire, not a physical one. See 319 n.

622 **To you, Menelaus, I say this:** the mechanical function of the Tyndareos scene is to determine Menelaus' response to Orestes' supplication. This is one of the two ways in which Tyndareos materially affects the course of events, perhaps more decisive than his briefing a speaker in the debate. His threat to Menelaus therefore appears as the culmination of his final speech, and as soon as he has delivered it he departs, leaving Menelaus to ponder his options.

623 **my connexion with you:** as father-in-law. *Kēdos* and other words from this root are often used of connexion by marriage.

625-6 **but leave him – Spartan soil:** cf. 536-7 n. The threat to exclude Menelaus from Sparta is what was meant in 622 by "I will act on it too".

627-8 **don't choose the wicked – aside:** taking one side or another in a legal dispute tended to be interpreted as committing oneself to friendship or enmity; see Dover 181.

It had long been a commonplace that one should prefer good men to bad as friends, e.g. Hes. *Op*. 716, Thgn. 101 ff., 113 f., Eur. *Hcld*. 177 f.

630-1 Go your way etc.: the old man's exit will take a few moments, and this couplet addressed to his departing back fits in well. It allows Orestes to show that he is unabashed, and Menelaus to start his pacing about. Lines addressed to departing characters are necessarily of a sort that do not call for an answer, and most often they are insults, taunts, etc.; see Taplin (1977) 221 f.

632 circling about: the parallel of *El*. 561, where the same phrase *kyklein poda* is used of the old man prowling round Orestes to take a good look at him, shows that the scholiast is mistaken in thinking that Menelaus stands still and doodles with one foot. Cf. also Ar. *Birds* 1379.

633 the divided ways: a dilemma was sometimes portrayed as a choice between two roads (Hes. *Op*. 287-92, Thgn. 910 ff., Prodicus DK 84 B 2). Orestes sees in Menelaus' movements the reflection of his mind, and explains them for the audience.

634 I am thinking something over: Medea gives a similar answer at *Med*. 925 when Jason suddenly notices she is upset and asks why.

635 which course of fortune: his response to Orestes' supplication will have consequences for his own future.

636 don't come to conclusions from first impressions: lit. "don't go through with your impression", "don't take it to a conclusion"; *peraino* as in *Med*.341, *Andr*. 1062, *Phoen*. 1703.

640 Then I will have my say: a polite opening formula (Fraenkel on *Ag*. 838, Barrett on *Hipp*. 336). The new *agōn* (492 n.) begins with an unusually explicit announcement that a long speech is coming. The exaltation of long speeches reads almost like a riposte to Soph. *Phil*. 12 "this is no time for a long speech", which in its turn is surely a dig at Euripides' lengthy opening monologues. Cf. Jebb on Soph. *El*. 1289 ff. and *OC* 1116.

641 put little ones in the shade: or "eclipse", "upstage" them, lit. "are in front of" them.

644 I don't mean assets: the scholiast criticizes actors who made Orestes raise a hand as he said this, to forestall a protest by Menelaus that Agamemnon had not lent him any money. "But it is silly for Menelaus to suspect Orestes of

meaning that. If he did not know the speaker's identity or what he wanted, the gesture might have some plausibility, but as he does know, what they do is uncalled for and not viable."

it *is* assets if you save my life: Hes. *Op*. 686 had said "assets are (on a par with) life for mortals", i.e. their concern for assets is such that they risk their lives for them. Euripides inverts the striking equation: "life is the most important form of assets". *Psȳchē* is the regular word for "life at risk", cf. e.g. 847, 1034, 1517.

46 I'm a wrongdoer: the present tense of *adikeō* is often used of someone who has committed a wrong and not so far been punished. With Menelaus Orestes does not argue about the justice of his act; the issue is Menelaus' duty to help regardless of the rights and wrongs of the case.

47 a wrongdoing from you: the argument is sophistical and formulated in a more provocative way than it need have been. It may be paraphrased: "your wife did wrong when she left you. To put that right, Agamemnon was prepared to commit another wrong by making war on Troy, and you are indebted to him for that. Now I have done wrong, and you should be prepared to commit a wrong for me, by intervening in the processes of justice and saving me from the due punishment."

52-3 he gave his body sincerely: the second aspect of the debt is that Agamemnon put himself to personal risk and exertion on Menelaus' behalf.

at your shield-side: Euripides thinks in terms of classical hoplite warfare in which each man depended partly on the protection of his neighbour's shield and thus on his holding firm in his place in the line.

56 exerting yourself just for one day: Orestes probably hopes for a show of arms (cf. 691, 711), but his language is not explicit. In any case it will only be a one-day affair, not a ten-year war such as Agamemnon fought. In Soph. *Phil*. 83 f. Odysseus urges Neoptolemus to suspend his moral principles (cf. 647 above) "just for a short part of a day"; cf. *Med*. 1248.

58 what Aulis took: this way of referring to the sacrifice of Iphigeneia minimizes Agamemnon's responsibility for it. It might well be considered his largest contribution to Menelaus' cause, and it must remain without a counterpart in the present calculation. (The idea of threatening to kill

Hermione emerges only later, and then for quite different reasons and without reference to Iphigeneia.)

662 *my* life: he sacrificed a daughter, don't let his son be taken away from him too.

663 [and my sister's - unwed]: Orestes has spoken throughout of his own salvation, without mentioning Electra. (If he escapes, of course she will too.) 664 shows that here too he is speaking only of himself. The important thing for Agamemnon is that his (male) line should not die out. Someone with a broader view of things interpolated 663, possibly for consistency with 746 (a consistency which should not be forced on Euripides). To fill out his line he made a banal and irrelevant reference to Electra's spinsterhood, drawing on 72.

665 You'll say "impossible": anticipating likely objections was regular oratorical technique. Cf. Collard on *Supp.* 184-5. Orestes expects that Menelaus will find the prospect of standing up to Argos too daunting. A Thucydidean general would have argued that the prospects of success were better than they appeared; Orestes continues the theme of Menelaus' obligations.

That's just it: a colloquial idiom (Stevens 27). It is precisely because it is a "hopeless" and not an easy situation that Menelaus has a duty to help.

667 When Fortune - attachments?: Aristotle criticizes this idea in *EN* 9.9, pointing out that it is based on a limited concept of *philoi* as those who are of use to one. *Eu* in the phrase *eu didonai* is still recognizable as the neuter of the old adjective *eüs*. Cf. the Homeric *theoi dōtēres eāōn*, and Fraenkel on *Ag.* 121.

669-76 You have the reputation etc.: the more rational arguments have been presented, and the speech culminates in an emotional appeal to what Menelaus is known to hold dear. In principle a standard gambit, but really Helen is brought in for the sake of the aside in which Orestes laments at finding himself reduced to invoking her name.

673 my whole house: i.e. the survival of Agamemnon's line. This leads naturally to the next sentence.

675 imagine: Orestes is not claiming that his father's soul is actually present. It is in Hades. But he wants Menelaus to consider his appeal *as if* Agamemnon himself were making it and were going to hear his answer.

76 over you: in *Il.* 23.68 Patroclus' soul stands over the sleeping Achilles to address him; but so would any Homeric dream-figure. More relevant perhaps is Eur. *Hec.* 30, where Polydorus' ghost says it is flitting about over Hecuba, while she dreams of him (70 ff.).

77 [These things – and woes]: no satisfactory sense can be got out of this line, whether it is taken with 676 or with 678. It seems to have been interpolated to provide an object for the following verbs. 678-9 make a typical two-line quiet close, cf. 454 f., 540 f., 600 f., 627 f.

78 I have spoken: this absolute use of *eirēka*, "I have said my say" (*dixi*), is paralleled in Men. *Ep.* 352, cf. 292 f. More usual in tragedy is *eirētai logos* (1203, etc.).
I have made my claim: lit. "demanded back (what I am owed)", the verb being used absolutely by analogy with *eirēka; tēn sōtēriān* has to be taken as the object of *thērōn.*

80 I too entreat you: the chorus' spokesman is unusually decisive in support of the matricides. The audience is clearly not expected to feel dubious about the merits of Orestes' appeal.
woman though I am: Menelaus cannot be expected to pay so much attention to a woman.

81 You have the power: similarly in prayers to gods, *Il.* 16.515, Pind. *N.* 7.96, etc.; cf. my n. on Hes. *Th.* 420.

85 if God provides the means: this harmless-sounding, pious caveat is Menelaus' let-out.

88 spear-force: less likely "ship". Now that Menelaus is here, his ship (or ships, 54 n.) is no longer a focus of interest.

91 we: or "I".

92 Pelasgian Argos: the Pelasgians were a pre-Hellenic people of whom remnants survived in classical times in Chalcidice and south of the Propontis (Hdt. 1.57, Thuc. 4.109). They crop up variously in Greek antiquarian tradition and construction. In Homer they are associated especially with central Thessaly (*Il.* 2.840-3, if the Thessalian Larisa is meant; others in Crete, *Od.* 19.177), and *to Pelasgikon Argos* is part of Achilles' kingdom (*Il.* 2.681, cf. 16.233), probably what was later called Pelasgiotis. In the Hesiodic *Catalogue* Pelasgus headed an Arcadian genealogy. Aeschylus makes him the king of Argos before the arrival of Danaus (*Supp.* 251,

cf. fr. 46 Radt), and Euripides follows his account (*Archelaus* fr. 1.7 f. Austin). Inopportune recollection of Homer's *Pelasgikon Argos* doubtless reinforced the notion that Argos had a special connection with the Pelasgians. In the present passage the epithet is used to suggest "Argos with its proud and ancient traditions".

694-5 by small efforts: i.e. those a small force would be capable of making.
stupid: cf. 397 n.

696-703 Menelaus assumes the face of the skilful politician who knows how to ride the waves of popular feeling. "This passage doubtless gives the results of Euripides' own observation of the Athenian democracy" (Wedd).

697 a raging fire to put out: Alcaeus (fr. 74) compared a threat of tyranny to an incipient fire that should be put out before it took hold, and Heraclitus (102 M.= DK 22 B 43) wrote "hybris is more to be extinguished than a conflagration".

698-9 slackens oneself and gives way: the image is now of slackening sail before a storm.
taking care with one's timing: Menelaus' "being careful" (*eulabeia*) is later reported with contempt (748, 1059). Orestes wants unhesitating, decisive action, not circumspect waiting for the right moment. On *eulabeia* and its ambivalence see Bond on *HF* 166.

700 it may well blow itself out: Wilamowitz's *ekneuseien* would mean "he may well come safely through". But in this context *ekneō* (lit. "swim out") would convey an unfortunate suggestion of shipwreck.

703 a most valuable property: probably the passion, a force that the politician can exploit so long as he waits to see which way it is directing itself. It is harder to refer the phrase to the further noun (even though compassion is the more relevant of the two to Orestes' needs) or to both together.

704-5 try to persuade ... to direct their vehemence wisely: Hermann's *peisās* is attractive, "try to persuade them *and* to turn their vehemence to advantage". This accords better both with the preceding lines and with what follows. See next n.

706 For a ship too: the nautical imagery implicit in 698 f. now receives explicit statement. From both 698 f. and 708 f. it appears that it is Menelaus who must avoid

"stringing the ship too tight", that is, confronting the city with emphatic demands. The ship does not correspond to the city itself, as in the conventional "ship of state" metaphor, but to Menelaus' enterprise (cf. Alc. fr. 6): that is what is in danger of capsizing.

'08 God ... abhors zealots: i.e. they do not succeed.

'09 yes, I don't dispute that: reassuring much as in *Hec.* 302.

10 by cleverness: cf. 397 n.

14 I never used to attempt - to mollity: it is no use fighting, because the Argives are tough; in the old, pre-war days I never tried to soften them by rhetoric, but now it must be attempted.

16 to take orders from fortune: "everything based on compulsion is held slavish among the intelligent", Menelaus had said in 488.

17 You good for nothing: although Menelaus has promised help of a kind - perhaps the only kind that it was realistic to offer - he has done so in a cautious, doubting spirit. His parting words underline his lack of enthusiasm for the task. Orestes at once diagnoses his commitment as worthless (cf. 748-54), and this turns out to be a correct assessment: Menelaus will say nothing at the assembly. For the technique of addressing a departing character in words which he is treated as not hearing, see on 630-1.

8 succouring: not "avenging" (Agamemnon), the more usual sense of *tīmōreō*. See LSJ s.v. II.1.

20 Agamemnon's cause: cf. 662-4, 673.

21 So you are friendless: Greek idiom says "so you were friendless", the imperfect referring to the time before the realization. The particle *ara* is regular in this idiom. See Stevens 62 f.

22 betrayed: or "forsaken", "left in the lurch".

25 But stay, here I see: a stereotyped formula in Euripides for introducing a new character, see Bond on *HF* 138. Pylades' unexpected arrival marks a turning-point. The hope that Orestes and Electra have clung to from the beginning of the play has just faded, and all seems lost. With Pylades a true friend and ally appears, one with real spirit, and although no solution is yet in sight, the mood is transformed.

6 at a run: the speed of his approach adds to the dramatic effect, generating excitement even before he speaks. Cf. Taplin (1977) 147.

from Phocis: lit. from the Phocians. The name of a people occasionally serves as a geographical term, e.g. *Delphoi*, *Lokroi*, *Ēastseaxe* (East Saxons = Essex). After assisting in the killing of Clytaemestra and Aegisthus, Pylades had gone home. The reason why he has now come back is explained at 763 ff.

728   calm water: cf. 279, 341-4 n.; *Andr.* 891 f., Aesch. *Ag.* 899. Theognis 77 says that "a trusty man in time of discord is worth his weight in gold and silver".

729-806   For this final scene in the present act the metre changes to trochaic tetrameters. In all his late tragedies (from *Troades* on) Euripides has at least one scene in this metre, which up to then had been little used since Aeschylus' time. Such scenes – never as long as 100 lines – were perhaps delivered in recitative, with musical accompaniment; see *DFA²* 158-60. At any rate the metre was associated with heightened excitement. It was especially suitable for a running entry (cf. also 1506, 1549, *Ion* 1250, Soph. *OC* 887), as the rhythm itself suggested running and was called *trochaïkos* for that reason. So the change of metre, besides affording variety, reinforces the dramatic change of mood.

729   faster than I had to: usually taken as "faster than I should have", "at unseemly speed". But although Chrysothemis in Soph. *El.* 872 apologizes for her running as unladylike, it is not clear that a man in a hurry would have felt any such selfconsciousness. Theseus in Soph. *OC* 890 only says that he has come "faster than my legs enjoyed". And *echrēn* would hardly have been used for a mere matter of decorum.

730   some of it: *ton de* is used as if *ton men* had preceded; cf. *Hec.* 1162, Soph. *Tr.* 117, *OT* 1229, *El.* 1291; Denniston 166.

731   that they mean to kill you: the verdict is again anticipated (440 n.).

732   What is this? etc.: a lively "tricolon" (three phrases of increasing length) formed by colloquial questions (see Stevens 31, 41, 57). "How are you" refers to Orestes' whole situation, not to his health in particular.

733   of my relations: see 765 n.

735   If that were so: I have inserted this for clarity. As in

764, the potential optative is used to avoid admitting the unwelcome idea into the realm of actual fact.

demolish: a forceful metaphor; *kataskaptō* is normally to destroy a wall, a city, etc., by digging it up.

Friends share everything: this was or became proverbial, cf. *Andr.* 376 f., Pl. *Lys.* 207c, *Rep.* 424a, *Phdr.* 279c, Arist. *EN* 1159b31, Men. fr. 10, etc.

36 Menelaus is behaving very badly: Orestes speaks first of what has happened most recently, and works back from there to the essence of the danger facing him, so that this comes as a climax in 758.

37-44 These lines are particularly rich in pointed effects. The long tetrameter verse allows the poet a little more scope in stichomythia than the iambic trimeter.

37 turn out to have: cf. 493 n.

42 It isn't he that has brought her: the idea is that he allows himself to be led by her instead of showing a proper manly independence. Cf. 589 n. Euripides perhaps remembers (as in *Andr.* 627-31) the story in the *Little Iliad* and Ibycus that when Menelaus caught up with Helen at Troy he was going to kill her but changed his mind when she gave him a sight of her breast. Cf. 1287 n.

43 Where is she: Helen's presence in the house is included in Pylades' briefing because crucial to the plot.

47 in heaven's name ... I should like to know: padding out the question to fill a whole line. Cf. 749.

48 He was cautious: see 698-9 n.

49 Taking his stand on what?: *skēpsis* is what one figuratively leans on for support, an excuse or justification. It is never used of a physical support, but here the phrasing suggests a feature of the terrain that Menelaus had to go and occupy, as we say "taking up a position".

50-2 As quite often in stichomythia, the answer is too complex to be contained in one line, so it has to be spread over three, with the questioner helping it along in the second of them. Cf. 432-6, 440-2, 756-8, 1332-4.

That father of champion daughters: Orestes held Tyndareos to blame for Clytaemestra in 585. Cf. also 249 f., 540 f.

Menelaus preferred his connexion with him: so Orestes interprets· his uncle's reserved response, and indeed it was clear in 632-5 that he was affected by Tyndareos' warnings. Nothing emerges later to alter this assessment.

to that with my father: *kēdos* (623 n.) is strictly applicable only to the in-law relationship. Here we must understand "kinship".

754 not a born warrior: again the assumption is that Menelaus ought to intervene with force. His valour is generally suspect in tragedy; see Fraenkel on *Ag.* 115 (end), Stevens on *Andr.* 456-7.

valiant among women: there is probably no further allusion than to his attachment to Helen. If so, it is an ill-focussed jibe, a blurred version of 717.

755 Is it inevitable: this second half of the line is best taken as a question, to maintain the forward movement of the dialogue. The *kai* is connective, asking for additional information (cf. 741, 753), and at the same time emphasizes "die".

757 I'm feeling afraid: lit. "I am passing through fear". Pylades has a fair idea of the answer (cf. 731), but wants to know definitely. His apprehension heightens the effect of the next line; cf. Soph. *OT* 1169 f.

759 leave the house and flee: Pylades makes the same suggestion as Menelaus did in 443.

760 Can't you see?: see the n. on *horāis* at 588. The road-blocks are not imagined as being visible from the house.

762 Our house: the MSS reading "body" may be just possible, but it seems strange, and *dōma* for *sōma* is a very easy emendation.

763 Now ask me in my turn: the exposition of Orestes' situation is complete, and before the two go on to discuss what is to be done, we are given the explanation (an *ad hoc* invention) of why Pylades has returned to Argos. He too has become an outlaw as a result of the killing of Clytaemestra. This binds him all the closer to Orestes.

764 might this woe be added: see on 735.

765 Strophius: often mentioned as Pylades' father (Pind. *P.* 11.35, Aesch. *Ag.* 881, etc., and no doubt already in the *Nostoi*). Orestes was sent to him at the time of Agamemnon's murder – or according to Aeschylus even before – and there his friendship with Pylades developed. In Pindar, Aeschylus and Sophocles Strophius is just a family friend of Agamemnon, but Euripides in *IT* 918 has him married to a daughter of Atreus (later sources

identify her as Anaxibia, Cydragora, or Astyochea),
which makes Orestes and Pylades cousins. Cf. 733, 1233
n.

'68   Oh no!: ō talās probably refers to Pylades, but it could
refer to Orestes himself, afraid that even Pylades will
now turn against him.

'71   I don't belong to these people to punish: an unreliable
theory (as Orestes points out). If the Argives take a
more lenient view of Pylades than of Orestes it is not
because he is an alien but because it was not his mother,
and he was only an accessory (1236). But what matters is
not legal nicety but dramatic convenience. We want
Pylades to stay and help. It will not actually affect the
plot if the Argives do decide to include him in their
sentence; on the other hand it would be an unnecessary
complication to alter the terms of their debate at this
stage.

72   when it has knavish leaders: such as Oeax and the
friends of Aegisthus (432-6). The proposition was no
doubt meant to be perceived as relevant to Athenian
politics, at least in a general way. The scholiast's
suggestion that there is a specific reference to Cleophon,
who had been responsible for the rejection of a Spartan
peace offer two years before, is unverifiable. But one has
to admire the ancient scholar responsible: scenting a
topical allusion, he checked the exact date of the play
and investigated the history of the immediately preceding
years in search of the answer. The scholia to
Aristophanes reflect much learning of this sort. See also
903 n.

73   But whenever – good counsel: the effect of this answer
is to settle the argument. Pylades will stay and not be
afraid of the Argives. His logic leaves something to be
desired. He can hardly think it is an open question
whether the Argive demagogues are good or bad, so that
his chances are even. Willink proposes the excision of
772-3. But 772 at least seems well in place, and it is hard
to see what Euripides could have done after it but to
counter the one generalization with another, giving a
gnomic ending to this section of the dialogue.

74-98   For the deliberative section the tempo is increased by
dividing each line between speakers. Such division, in
trimeters or tetrameters, is found in PV (980 only) and in

nearly all plays of Sophocles and Euripides, more freely in the later ones. It is often called *antilabē*, though strictly speaking it is the half-lines themselves that were called *antilabai* (Hesychius s.v.). The present example is exceptionally long.

774 All right: the use of *eihen* is fully illustrated by Stevens 34. Here it marks the turning of attention to a new object.

775-6 The division of a single proposition between the speakers (750-2 n.) now gives the effect of both minds running along in close harmony.

They may welcome: *mē* with subjunctive in an independent clause is often used to express something the speaker is afraid of, or a possibility the hearer ought to bear in mind, just as if a main verb such as *phoboumai* or *horā* were present.

783 cowardice: he probably means both *being* and *being thought* cowardly.

782 pray for it to be thought so: the reality is useless here without the appearance; cf. 236 n. The variant *tōi dokein*, "pray to Appearance", is probably only a Byzantine conjecture for the unmetrical transmitted reading *to dokein*. An abstract idea expressed as an infinitive can have divinity predicated of it (Aesch. *Cho.* 59 f., Eur. *Hel.* 560), but does not thereby become a deity that can be prayed to. I have preferred Paley's *tode dokein* to Lenting's *tou dokein echou* ("hold fast to seeming so").

784 your noble blood: not just in itself, but the fact that he is the son of Agamemnon; cf. the next line.

785 All this: summing up the three arguments in 783 ff. This is against Weil's placing of 782 after 785.

787 Shall we tell my sister: a reminder that Electra is in the house; she will reappear in the next scene. Orestes' question may be seen as the reflection of one that Euripides asked himself. It would have served no useful dramatic purpose to bring Electra on here and further prolong this outsize act.

788 a serious omen: the expression *megas oiōnos* recurs in Xen. *Anab.* 6.1.23; cf. *Il.* 2.308 *mega sēma*, 324 *teras mega*.

789 you'll save time: the debate is impending, there is some urgency; cf. 799.

791   That the goddesses may catch me: the reminder of Orestes' affliction provides the opportunity for Pylades to demonstrate the strength of his friendship.

792   Not with you, for me: cf. 221, and Theseus' attitude to Heracles in *HF* 1220, 1234, 1400. There is no more touching depiction of affection in Greek art than the cup by the Brygos Painter which shows a girl tenderly holding a young man's head while he vomits over her feet (P.E. Arias - M. Hirmer - B.B. Shefton, *A History of Greek Vase Painting* [1962], pl.XXXIII).

793   of catching my insanity: association with a polluted man may be dangerous, but this is the only place where it is suggested that madness caused by blood-guilt may be contagious. Cf. Parker 129, 309.

   let it ride: Pylades shows the same magnificent disregard of risk to himself as those who persisted in visiting their sick friends during the plague, Thuc. 2.51.5.

795   helmsman: an unexpectedly high-flown metaphor. *Oiāx* (lit. "steering-oar") may either be vocative or a nominative predicate.

797   So that I can appeal to him: *Choephoroe* began with Orestes arriving at his father's grave-mound and praying to him, and prayers to Agamemnon there or from other locations are a recurring motif in Orestes-plays: *Cho.* 130-63, 315-71, 479-509, Soph. *El.* 453-8, Eur. *El.* 677-84, and below, 1225-39.

   Justice ... requires it: that Agamemnon should save Orestes.

798   As for my mother's memorial: the father's tomb recalls the mother's, of which we have heard earlier. Orestes built it (402), but now he will keep well away from it; his path and Hermione's are not to cross yet. The "memorial" (*mnēma*) is properly the stone stele at the top of the mound, cf. *El.* 328, *Il.* 11.371, 16.457, 17.434, *Od.* 12.14; Burkert (1985) 193 f.

800   let your side ... lie across mine: lit. "put it round". It is his arm rather than his side that will go round Pylades as he drapes himself over him. Cf. 223.

802   unashamed: at being seen on such close terms with the abhorred matricide.

804   There you are: a colloquial exclamation to the effect that something previously indicated, or familiar in principle, is here confirmed. See Stevens 31 f.

get yourselves comrades: advice to the world in general; see Stevens on *Andr.* 622–3, and cf. 128 n.

805   **An outsider:** Pylades' family relationship to Orestes (733, 765 n.) is here forgotten.
who becomes fused to you: the metaphor harmonizes with the spectacle of the linked bodies.

806   **beats ten thousand relatives:** cf. *IA* 1394, Soph. *OC* 498. Heraclitus is the first to reckon things on this scale, fr. 98 M.= DK 22 B 49 "one man is worth ten thousand to me provided he is of the highest quality". In *Early Greek Philosophy and the Orient* (1971) 194 f. I quoted examples from eastern texts.

The gnomic ending sums up the contrasted outcomes of the scene with Pylades and the preceding one with Menelaus. Cf. also Thuc. 3.82, quoted in Introduction IV.

807–43 This short choral interlude covers a much longer period of dramatic time, embracing Orestes' visit to his father's tomb, his arrival at the assembly, and the entire debate. This is normal tragic convention.

The chorus is untouched by Orestes' new optimism. It starts from where it left off in its last song, with the theme of the instability of fortune as illustrated by the Tantalids. This time some of the earlier troubles of the house are mentioned, with the implication that they are all connected. In the antistrophe and epode the focus is on Orestes' killing of Clytaemestra, the crime for which he is even now being judged. The chorus' attitude is initially condemnatory, but in the epode this is toned down to a kind of horrified pity more like what they have shown before. They make no reference to Apollo's part in the business. The metre is aeolic.

807   **noble rank:** *aretā* here keeps its old sense of "being (acknowledged as) a person of quality", "social standing" resulting from established wealth. Cf. *Andr.* 766–76. It therefore has an intimate connection with *olbos*; cf. *h.Hom.* 15.9, 20.8, Hes. *Op.* 313 with my n., and West (1985) 8; Denniston on *El.* 253. When a family's material prosperity collapses, its prestige wanes. Orestes' good birth may still attract sympathy (784), but he is practically dispossessed of his father's estate (437 f.,

744), and his stock has sunk low.

08 that was proud: present participle representing an imperfect (254 n.).

09 beside the channels of Simois: at Troy.

10 has ebbed again: lit. "gone back up again". From thinking of the Trojan river Euripides found himself imagining the prosperity itself as a stream coming down from a source, to which it is now retreating. Cf. 336-7 n. (end).

11 a legacy from: the Greek has simply "from", as vague an expression of relationship as it could be. (In 995 ff. Euripides speaks more explicitly of a curse.) 807-10 form a shapely, potentially self-sufficient sentence; it is now extended by a series of additional clauses loosely tagged on – the rambling style noted in 333-8 n.

the old old misfortune: reduplication is the most primitive means of intensification. We say "long long ago", and Greek could say *palai palai dē* (Ar. *Birds* 921, where it sounds paratragic; cf. *Knights* 1155, which sounds colloquial). For tragedy cf. *IT* 1406 "more and more", Soph. *Phil.* 1197 "never never", *OC* 210 "don't, don't". In *palaipalaiās* we must recognize an adjectival formation corresponding to *palai palai*. The *palai* cannot be taken separately with *anēlthe*, because that is a comment on what has happened in the last few days.

2 the golden lamb dispute: see 14 n.

3 came upon: the sense is satisfactory, but the verb may be corrupt, as the metre disagrees with (and is less plausible than) that of the antistrophe (825). Conjectures are· legion; Hermann's *eporeuse* "brought upon" (after 337) has the attraction of eliminating the surprising apposition "– most tragic feastings" etc.), though it leaves the assumed corruption unaccounted for.

8 the double line of Atreus: *dissoi Atreidai* usually means Agamemnon and Menelaus. The killings here in question are all on Agamemnon's side (Iphigeneia, Agamemnon, Clytaemestra). Euripides is using *Atreidai* to mean Atreus' descendants, as in 810, and he appends the conventional *dissoi* although Menelaus and his family do not come into account.

9 That "good" is not good: the paradox "it was just – but not good" (194 n.) is re-stated in a still more pointed form, closely followed in *Ba.* 395, "that 'wise' is not

239

wisdom" (see Dodds' n.). Our modern quotation-marks help us to see through the riddle: other people may call it good (Homer, for instance: 30 n.), but we don't. This inverted-commas use of *to kalon* is also seen in *Hel.* 952, *IA* 21. Euripides is fond of "X = not-X" formulations, cf. 904 n.

820   fireborn handiwork: forged iron; cf. Aesch. *Sept.* 207, Eur. *Hipp.* 1223.

821-2 display the sword ... to the light of the sun: the feeling that disgraceful and polluting things should be kept out of sight tended to be projected onto the sun itself. Cf. Hes. *Op.* 727 with my n., Soph. *OT* 1426 f., Eur. *HF* 1231, *IT* 1207, and van der Horst on pseudo-Phocylides 100 f. Euripides doubtless has in mind the scene at Aesch. *Cho.* 983 ff. where Orestes appeared standing over his victims; he displayed to the public the old robe with which they had killed Agamemnon, and he called on the sun to take note of it as evidence that he was justified in killing his mother. Cf. also Eur. *El.* 1175 ff.

dark-laced: the original meaning of this Homeric epithet of a sword is obscure. Euripides had used it before (*Phoen.* 1091, fr. 373.2), but this time he gives it the novel sense of "streaked with drying blood". *Melās* does not mean specifically "black", but covers all dark colours.

823   Virtuous crime: another oxymoron. Bothe's excellent *eu* for *au* is supported by the scholiast's paraphrase, "to do wrong with a plausible rationale", and by *IT* 559, where Iphigeneia says of the matricide "how well he did to accomplish a just evil" (*hōs eu kakon* ...).

sophistical: justifiable only with elaborate, clever arguments against straightforward moral perceptions. Cf. *Med.* 298-301, *Phoen.* 469 f., Soph. *OC* 762.

824   wrong-headed men's delusion: cf. *Ba.* 399-401, 887, 997-1000. The association of morality with sanity (implying that immorality does not pay) can be traced from Homer onward, e.g. *Od.* 2.231, 3.266, 16.278, 17.233, 24.457.

825   For: the two-stage depiction of the scene (825-30 + 840-3), by its very pathos, is taken as support for the chorus' moral assessment. They have said it was not *kalon*, strictly "good to contemplate, attractive"; many Greek value terms (*kalos*, *aischros*, *prepōn*, etc.) have an aesthetic basis.

240

27   My child etc.: Euripides likes to finish a strophe with a
      piece of reported speech.
      no lawful venture: the chorus put their own judgment
      into Clytaemestra's mouth.
30   infamy: cf. 30.
31-2 What disorder, what distress, what tragedy: again
      Euripides draws inspiration from the previous stasimon:
      333 "what tragedy, what trial" (see n. there on *eleos*),
      335 Orestes' tears, 338 his frenzy; and 834-9 are closely
      related to 316-28.
33   taking - on one's hand: for *haima thesthai*, "take
      blood(-guilt) upon oneself", see Dodds on *Ba*. 837. *Cheiri*
      is strictly instrumental, not locative, and emphasizes the
      idea of deliberate action.
35   he has been driven wild: they speak as if he were still
      suffering from his madness as much as ever.
36-7 rolling bloodshed in his roving eyeballs: cf. 253 n.,
      255-7 n. The blood with which his eyes are suffused is
      seen as a manifestation of the blood he has shed. *Dromasi*
      is borrowed from the address to the Eumenides in 317.
39   Unhappy man! when etc.: a similar exclamation over
      Agamemnon at *El*. 1160. These lines complement 825-30;
      Clytaemestra's exposure of her breast (527 n.) and her
      verbal entreaty were simultaneous. Like Tyndareos in
      526, the chorus is thinking of the effect of her gesture
      upon Orestes. See *El*. 1206-20.
40   the gold-weave robes: the royal gold is a picturesque
      new detail. Such touches of colour and splendour are
      typical of Euripides' later lyric style.
43   requital: the so-called "accusative in apposition to the
      sentence" - accusative because a product of the action
      just described. Cf. 1105; Moorhouse 45 f.

44-956 Report of the Argive debate and its outcome.
      Important offstage developments are normally narrated by
      a nameless subordinate character whom it is conventional
      to call a "messenger", though no one has sent him with a
      message. Euripides regularly makes these scenes into
      self-contained acts, framed by song. If the events related
      concern a major character in the play, he or she usually
      appears or reappears on stage later (if not dead, and
      sometimes even then): Orestes and Pylades will duly

                              241

return in the following act. On Euripidean messenger speeches in general see Collard on *Supp.* 634-777.

    It is Electra who must receive the news. She comes out of the house to look for Orestes, and the newsbringer arrives almost at once. He is a loyal old retainer of the house, a common type of minor figure in tragedy.

844   For the unannounced entrance cf. 348 n. Often a character appears with a question to the chorus, especially to ask where someone else is. Cf. 375 n.

848   to face: this is clearly the general sense, but *dōsōn* is very difficult. It might just be explained by the analogy of *dikēn didonai* "submit to judgment"; cf. also *Ba.* 715. But the text may be corrupt.

849   who persuaded him?: these preliminaries to the arrival of the newsbringer are very perfunctory, but Euripides does make sure, by putting this question in Electra's mouth, that she gets to hear of Pylades' appearance, if only from a one-word answer.

850   this bringer of news: Euripides cuts a corner by allowing the chorus-leader to presume without enquiry where the new arrival has come from and what his dramatic function will be. It is as if she knows she is in a tragedy; we remember how Electra in 132 more or less says "here comes the chorus", having four lines earlier addressed the audience as spectators. Cf. Halleran 46 on *El.* 759 f.

    soon: *ou makrān* ("not far off") has this sense also at *Tro.* 460.

852ff O unhappy one etc.: the news is delivered in three stages: first the general announcement "I bring terrible news", then (857-8) the short statement giving the essential point of what has happened, and finally the detailed account. This is a typical scheme, cf. *Hipp.* 1157 ff., *Andr.* 1070 ff., *HF* 910 ff., etc. In some plays the first stage is omitted or combined with the second, but the second is nearly always found.

    Paley deleted 852, and if it were an interpolation it would be very like that at Soph. *El.* 1 (71 n.); 853-4 may be compared with *IT* 238-9. But here the elaborate address is perhaps in place as an expression of the old man's emotion: cf. *Ba.* 1024-6, Aesch. *Pers.* 249 f. The title given to Agamemnon at once suggests the old man's devotion to the house.

855   Oh, we are done for: the nature of the bad news is

anticipated; cf. *Andr.* 1072, *Phoen.* 1336. These one-line interjections support the deletion of the flatly otiose 856. *Phoen.* 1075 seems a comparable interpolation.

58 was decreed: 46 n. Apart from "poor lady", this whole distich has the tone of an official proclamation.

50 dissolving in lament: the phrase is given an accusative object by analogy with verbs meaning "lament (over)". Such constructions are quite common in tragedy. See Page on *Med.* 206, Dodds on *Ba.* 1288; Moorhouse 37 f.

51 But how was the trial?: it is common for a newsbringer to be led on by questions.

53-5 Tell me – my brother: the further question, in high-flown language, prepares for the final part of the old man's report, about the practical details of the execution. Up to now only stoning has been in question (50 [without 51], 442, 536, 564, 625). Logically Electra has no reason to anticipate an alternative, but like Homer (*Il.* 23.857), Euripides goes beyond logical expectations in working his way towards what is actually going to happen. "By way of iron" could apply equally to suicide (a possibility not yet in view) or to execution.
break off my breath: an Aeschylean phrase (*Pers.* 507). It does not imply cutting through the windpipe but simply means "die".

56 from the country: he was no doubt recognizable as a peasant by his dress. By making him a countryman Euripides puts him in a class to be viewed with approval (cf. 920), dissociates him from the hostile townspeople, and enables him to describe the whole assembly as an outsider who was present only by accident.

70 a poor man but honourable: a favourite Euripidean motif. Cf. *El.* 253 with Denniston, frr. 232 N. = 6 Austin, 362.27 = 53 Au., 527, 739.

71-3 the summit where they say Danaus etc.: according to schol., Aegyptus prosecuted Danaus following the mass murder of his sons by their brides, Danaus' daughters, and the trial took place on the large hill-top known as the Hāliaiā (Hāliā), "Assembly(-place)". Some have conjectured that this was represented in Aeschylus' *Danaids* (see A.F. Garvie, *Aeschylus' Supplices* [1969] 208 ff.). Phrynichus' *Egyptians* or *Danaids* is also a possible source, as he is known to have brought Aegyptus to Argos (cf. Eur. fr. 846). In any case we

243

can assume Euripides to be following a literary and probably a tragic source.

first assembled the people: in the tradition as reported by schol., it was Inachus who first assembled the people on the hill, but that was not for a trial. Euripides is thinking in terms of trials and so looks back only as far as Danaus.

875-6 Has some report etc.: similar guesses at the reason for public meetings being called in *Od.* 2.30, Bacchyl. 18.5.

879 apparition: Orestes' spectral appearance (385) and his dependence upon Pylades made them a disconcerting sight.

882 like a brother: cf. 1015, *IT* 497 f. A man's brother is in theory his closest comrade; cf. *Il.* 24.46 f., *Od.* 8.546 f., 585 f., Hes. *Op.* 184, 707, Thgn. 97-9. Hence stories of brothers who quarrelled, like Atreus and Thyestes or Polynices and Eteocles, made a deep impression.

883 supervising a schoolboy: the same metaphor in *Hcld.* 729, *Ba.* 193. The *paidagōgos*, first heard of in 5th-century Athens, was a slave who superintended his master's sons to and from school. See F.A.G. Beck, *Greek Education 450-350 B.C.* (1964) 105-9.

884-945 The debate is constructed according to a rather obvious scheme. There are four speakers, alternately opponents and supporters of Orestes, and finally Orestes speaks for himself. The first pair of speakers are persons well known from epic tradition but not otherwise mentioned in the play. The second pair are not named and represent character-types. It is surprising that nothing is said by any of those we have been led to expect will take an active part. Menelaus' silence is understood, and Tyndareos is presumably not entitled to speak; but Oeax (432) is ignored, and Aegisthus' friends merely look on (894). The arguments and viewpoints reported have all been heard already in the scene with Tyndareos.

885 Who wishes to speak: a variant of the formula used in the Athenian Assembly, *tis agoreuein bouletai?* See Sommerstein on Ar. *Ach.* 45, Collard on *Supp.* 438-41.

888 Talthybius: he appears several times in the *Iliad* as Agamemnon's herald, doing whatever is required of him with unobtrusive efficiency. In *Hecuba* and *Troades* Euripides had portrayed him favourably. Vase painters

244

show him assisting at the killing of Aegisthus. So his failure to support Orestes is quite unexpected, though the cynical explanation given is in line with other Euripidean passages where heralds are criticized with some asperity (*Hcld.* 292 f., *Tro.* 424-6, fr. 1012).

the Phrygians: in tragedy the Trojans are freely called Phrygians (probably so already in Alc. fr. 42.15). In Homer the Trojans have Phrygian allies, but these come from the Sangarius valley, over a hundred miles to the east of Troy, and speak a different language from the Trojans (*h.Aphr.* 111-6). The historical Phrygians, an Indo-European people speaking a tongue with some similarities to Greek, seem to have moved into Asia Minor from Europe only in the tenth or ninth century. They established a powerful state in Anatolia for a time, but by the classical period it had lost its independence, and Phrygians were regarded by Greeks with a contempt that extends to the Trojan "Phrygians" of tragedy.

889 under those in power: Aegisthus' supporters are now the most influential party (436).

892 plaiting: *helissōn* suggests something not straightforward, difficult to unravel. Cf. *Andr.* 448, *Supp.* 141.

establishing bad precedents: cf. 571 for the danger of an individual occurrence becoming a *nomos* if condoned.

897 has influence over: genitive as after *krateō* or *archō*.

898 lord Diomedes: in Homer this brave and splendid hero is king of Argos. Euripides' confusion of Argos and Mycene (101 n.) leaves him without a throne, though still titled *anax*. To bring him into the Orestes story even as a marginal figure was quite original, so far as our knowledge goes.

900 the moral course: similarly it would have been *eusebes* for Orestes to banish his mother (503). For exile as a penalty for murder, and for the construction of the infinitive here, cf. 515 n.

903-5 For the technique of describing a character by means of a series of phrases in asyndeton cf. 918-22, and Headlam-Thomson on Aesch. *Ag.* 737-49.

903 a man with no shutters to his mouth: the image goes back to Theognis 421, while the compound adjective has its closest parallel in Soph. *Phil.* 188 *athyrostomos*. This ranter recalls Homer's Thersites with his voluble but ill-considered speechifying (*Il.* 2.212 ff., 246). Euripides

245

had criticized mob orators before (*Hec.* 254 ff., *Supp.* 243, 411-25, cf. fr. 1029.3). Speculation that he here intended a contemporary reference has a long history. Our Alexandrian commentator (772 n.) refutes a suggestion that Cleon was meant, pointing out that Cleon had died years before, and again proposes that there is an allusion to Cleophon.

904 an Argive but no true one: lit. "an Argive not Argive", a typically Euripidean oxymoron. The man is "not Argive" in that he is not true to Argive traditions and standards, and "pressurized" by others (Tyndareos). The ancient commentator finds support here for his Cleophon theory, quoting *Frogs* 679-82 as evidence that Cleophon had Thracian blood and was thus "an Athenian not Athenian". (He apparently had a Thracian mother: Plato Com. fr. 60 Kock; cf. also Aeschin. 2.76 for his allegedly irregular citizenship registration.)

906-13 [plausible enough – holder of office]: this political disquisition cuts off the relative pronoun in 914 from its antecedent, and 907-13 at least are evidently interpolated. 906 is more debatable. The danger that this man may some day lead Argos into disaster is unreal and irrelevant to the play; if the verse is genuine, it can only be read as a warning against Cleophon or others of his sort.

906 pitch them on: like a ship on a reef (Thuc. 7.25.7); not "surround them with".

909 give good ... counsel: the line-end is borrowed from 773.

915 but it was Tyndareos: this speaker is the only one of the five who actually advocates stoning. So Tyndareos was really the person responsible for the city's decision to pass the death sentence – fulfilling his threat in 612-4.

916 [of this kind – condemned you]: this thoroughly redundant line is no doubt an interpolation of the common type intended to supplement an elliptical construction (cf. Introduction VI). Its author wanted at least "for him" after "provided (the) arguments".

918-22 not physically good-looking etc.: this is the antithesis of the previous speaker, a sterling yeoman, not a regular performer in the assembly, intelligent, not suborned by anyone else. Obviously he will talk good sense.

919 the market circle: Euripides is thinking in Athenian terms. See Jebb on Soph. *OT* 161.

246

923   **to crown Orestes**: for a city to award a crown or wreath (often of gold) was the ancient equivalent of conferring a medal for some outstanding service. In the summer of 409 Athens had awarded a gold crown to the murderer of Phrynichus (ringleader in the 411 revolution) as a public benefactor. Orestes himself, in arguing that he had done the city a service by deterring future Clytaemestras (564-71), did not go as far as to claim that he should be rewarded: this is the rustic philosopher's contribution, breaking away from the question of whether Orestes should be punished by death or only by exile to reach a provocative new valuation. Nine years later Socrates, on trial for his life, argued (according to Plato, *Apol.* 36d) that he deserved to be honoured with free dinners in the prytaneum.

the son of Agamemnon: this is how he would be designated in the proposed honorary decree.

925   **impious**: already in Aesch. *Cho.* 46 and 525 she is branded as *dystheos*.

926-9   **no more taking arms** etc.: Euripides has divided the public-benefit argument between the farmer and Orestes (934-42). The farmer only gets the part relating to Clytaemestra's adultery, leaving the more substantial issue, the murder of Agamemnon, for Orestes to take up.

932   **Inachus**: the eponym of the Argive river. He headed the mythical genealogy of Argive kings; cf. West (1985) 76 f.

933   **[anciently Pelasgians - later]**: an interpolator saw fit to pad out the mention of Inachus with a feeble further piece of antiquarianism, for which cf. 692 n. Orestes addresses his audience as what they are; the eras of their past history are irrelevant.

936   **you won't be able to die too quickly**: a colloquial idiom, not in Aeschylus or Sophocles; illustrated by Stevens 24 f. Again in 1551.

938   **You will be doing**: "if you condemn me" is understood from the preceding "if murder of menfolk is to be permitted for women".

943   **good though his speech seemed**: understand "to some of us", cf. 901, 930. The audience might have been reminded of Antiphon's brilliant but unsuccessful speech in defence of his life in 411 (Thuc. 8.68.2, Arist. *EE* 1232b8). We ourselves might have judged Orestes' speech a better one if it had included some of the other arguments

that he used earlier (551-6, 572-84, 591-5). But Euripides is concerned to get on with the story, and we may forgive him for being somewhat perfunctory here.

944 in the number of hands raised: we need a reference to the voting, and Wecklein's *cherōn* restores it convincingly. The MSS *legōn* gives no clear sense and is evidently affected by *legein* at the end of 943. For voting by show of hands (*cheirotonein*) cf. Aesch. *Supp.* 607 f., Ar. *Eccl.* 264-7 with Ussher's nn.

946 just managed to persuade them: further speeches and another vote are implied, but the outcome is all we need to hear. The option of suicide before the end of the day, as an alternative to immediate stoning, is an unexpected twist. It will give time in which to form the plan of killing Helen. The dramaturgical device has a precedent in *Med.* 336 ff., where Medea, sentenced to exile, secures a stay of execution till the end of the day. But she already has plans for killing her enemies; Orestes and Electra have none as yet.

949-50 Pylades ... is bringing him back: advance notice of their reappearance in the next act. Cf. *El.* 855-7, etc.; Halleran 22.

convocation: 612 n.
and his supporters are with them: a naturalistic detail here, but the supporters clearly do not appear at 1012, where they would be a useless encumbrance.

952 a painful spectacle ... seeing him: *prosopsis* is an emotional seeing someone, a more personal word than *theāma*.

953 swords ... or a noose: two traditional means of suicide, both familiar in tragedy. Characters thinking of suicide often mention this pair of alternatives, or attempt them (see Stevens on *Andr.* 811, adding *Alc.* 228-30, *Ion* 1064 f., *Erechtheus* fr. 53.26 Austin); for other methods cf. Bond on *HF* 1148-52.

956 he has been your ruin: now that their fate is sealed (as it seems), it is an appropriate moment to recall Apollo's responsibility for the affair, last mentioned in 599. The motif will now lie dormant until the god's epiphany in the final scene.

Having delivered this judgment the old man departs (like most tragic newsbringers) without further ado. He had to change himself back to Pylades (or less probably Orestes).

957-9 [Poor unhappy woman - laments]: the scholiast records
that these lines were absent from some ancient copies.
Such cases might arise from accidental omission, but
mostly they arise from interpolation; see M.D. Reeve,
GRBS 13 (1972), 253-6. The present lines were clearly
intended to introduce a solo lament by Electra. It is
ridiculous for the chorus to utter them and then start
singing a lament itself. Now the MSS attribute the whole
of 960-1012 to Electra. But as Weil saw, this is a mistake:
she sings only the astrophic lyrics beginning at 982. (See
below.) 957-9 must have been composed for a production
in which the chorus' lyrics were either given to Electra
or (more likely, perhaps) omitted.
how shadowed: probably not by a veil (cf. 280 n.) but
simply by brow and hair, from being cast down; or
metaphorically "clouded". On heads bowed in sorrow in
tragedy cf. Shisler 381.

960-81 Following a Euripidean newsbringer's speech it is
normal for the chorus to be the first to utter, in
trimeters or (less often) in anapaests or lyrics; cf.
Reeve, l.c. 254 n.25. Here they launch into a lament of
traditional formal type with ritual elements
(cheek-scratching, head-beating, and see below on 960),
a *kommos* in the strict sense (cf. M. Alexiou, *The Ritual
Lament in Greek Tradition* [1974] 103; Collard [1975] ii.391
f.). This was already a conventional feature of
Aeschylean tragedy. Sophoclean laments are less formal
and ritualistic, but Euripides shows a liking for the old
type (e.g. *Andr.* 1197 ff., *Supp.* 798 ff., 1123 ff., *Tro.*
1216 ff., 1287 ff.). The iambic rhythms used here are
typical.
    That it is the chorus singing, not Electra, is clear
at least in 968 f. (cf. *Phoen.* 1286), and the moralizing in
976-81 is typically choral. Willink suggests giving Electra
the first part of each strophe, 960-4 and 971-5. Certainly
many laments are antiphonal, but this is usually clearly
marked. Here nothing in the text indicates an alternation
of voices, and the connectives at 965 and 971 point the
other way. Electra's contribution is her long solo at 982
ff.
960 I start the wailing: *katarchesthai* is especially used of

making the formal beginning of a ritual; of laments, *Hec.*
685, cf. *Andr.* 1199, *HF* 889.

o Pelasgia: addressing the whole country, inviting it to
mourn; cf. 965.

961-3　the fingernail ... the head-beating: for these practices
see Denniston on *El.* 146-9. *Ktypon* may be governed
either by *katarchomai* or by *titheisa*.

that falls to the infernal etc.: Persephone "had it allotted
to her" (cf. 319 n.), i.e. it is the proper thing to do
when someone is on the way to her realm. In Aesch.
Sept. 856-60 it is conceived as a rhythmic "rowing" which
conducts the ship of the dead across Acheron.

964　the fair-child goddess: this may mean either "who is the
fair child (of Demeter)" (for this sense of *kallipais* cf.
Dodds on *Ba.* 519-20, Bond on *HF* 689) or "who has a
fair child", alluding to Iacchus. If the latter, the
adjacence of *iācheitō* will not be coincidental.

965　the Cyclopian land: the massive walls of Mycene and
Tiryns were said to have been built by Cyclopes.
Euripides extends the epithet to the place as a whole, cf.
HF 15, *IT* 845, *IA* 265; on the Mycene-Argos confusion
cf. 101 n. For the idea of the land itself mourning and
cutting its hair cf. Aesch. *Pers.* 548, 683, [Simon.]
Epigr. 45.7 Page, Eur. *Hel.* 370-4.

970　who were once war-leaders of Greece: Agamemnon and his
children are mentally run together as "the Atridae". Cf.
810, 818 n., *El.* 876; perhaps *Tro.* 1217.

971　gone is the whole line: Menelaus is ignored.

974　the grudge of God: at its height, human felicity seems to
match that of the gods. But the gods will not tolerate
rivalry. It is in the 5th century that *phthonos* is first
explicitly ascribed to them (Pind. *P.* 10.20, *I.* 7.39,
Aesch. *Pers.* 362, *Ag.* 135, Hdt. 1.32.1, 3.40.2, 7.46.4,
Eur. *Alc.* 1135, *Supp.* 348, etc.), though some earlier
myths and narratives imply it, especially in cases where a
mortal spoke or acted as if a god's equal. Cf. Dodds 30
f.; H. Lloyd-Jones, *The Justice of Zeus* (1971) 3 f., 69
f.; P. Walcot, *Envy and the Greeks* (1978) 22 ff. Cf. 340
n.

975　and the murderous vote: in Greek poetry an event may
be attributed to divine and to human agency
simultaneously, cf. *Il.* 16.849 f.; Dodds 7, 16, 30 f.

976-8　tear-laden toilful tribes: the tone is lofty, as if from a

superhuman level of perception; cf. *h.Dem.* 256 ff. with Richardson's n. In tragedy only a chorus or a god could speak like this. Cf. especially Soph. *OT* 1186 ff.
that live for the day: not "only for a day" but "from day to day" without being able to see ahead. See H. Fränkel, *TAPA* 77 (1946) 131–45; M.W. Dickie, *Illinois Class. Studies* 1 (1976), 7–14. For the use of the word in apostrophizing mankind cf. Ar. *Clouds* 223 with Dover, *Birds* 687, Pl. *Rep.* 617d.
behold how: similar choral invitations to draw a moral from the events of the play in *Ion* 1090 ff., Soph. *OT* 1524–30, *El.* 1384 f.
destiny transgresses expectations: the fallibility of hope is a commonplace. See Collard on *Supp.* 479–80, my n. on Hes. *Op.* 96, and the tailpieces at the end of *Alcestis*, *Medea*, etc. The idea is naturally emphasized by a dramatist who deals in surprises, and we should bear in mind that the chorus' and the audience's present expectations are still to be upset.

979 Different woes to different men by turns pass: cf. Archil. 13.7–9, *Alc.* 893 f., *Hipp.* 1108, *Ba.* 905 f. The sound of the verse echoes its counterpart in the strophe (968).

980 in the fullness of time: "anything can happen in the fullness of time" (Hdt. 5.9.3), especially reversals (e.g. Soph. *Aj.* 646 ff., *OC* 607 ff.).

982–1012 Electra's monody. In Aeschylus actors sing only in dialogue with the chorus. The extended solo aria is found in *Prometheus* and Sophocles and is especially developed by Euripides. More often than not it is sung by a female character, and in the later plays it is always astrophic, which meant that the music could be shaped throughout to express all the emotional nuances of the words. The singer must have had to be something of a virtuoso. See A.S. Owen in *Greek Poetry and Life* (Essays presented to Gilbert Murray, 1936) 148–54; Collard (1981) 24 f. and on *Supp.* 990–1033.

Electra develops the chorus' lament on the fall of the Pelopids, and its previous reference to their history (807–18), into a cursory review of the whole family saga, told in a loosely additive, allusive style: no one who did

251

not know the stories already would understand them from this account. The metre is still mainly iambic, but more freely flowing than in the chorus' solemn *kommos*, and with a dactylic section near the end.

982 **I wish I could go to that rock:** in several Euripidean plays a singing female character or chorus expresses the wish to take wing and fly away to some distant place, usually to escape from a distressing situation (*Hipp.* 732 ff. with Barrett; cf. *IT* 1138 ff., *Ba.* 402 ff.). Here the motif is ingeniously used to create the fantasy of the last member of the family finding her way to the first and reciting to him the tale of his descendants.

983-4 **strung in suspense ... by golden chains:** for the legend of the rock cf. 6-7 n., 10 n. Euripides invents a part-poetic, part-scientific explanation of what keeps it aloft. The golden chain is derived from *Il.* 8.19 ff. (a passage much allegorized later; cf. my *Orphic Poems* [1983] 237-9), and we should imagine the other end of it fastened to the peak of Olympus as in *Il.* 8.25.

985 **the whirlwind-borne glebe:** *bōlos* is a detachable lump of earth. The gods must have broken a piece off Olympus. *Dīnē*, representing a natural rotatory motion in the cosmos, was a favourite word of 5th-century cosmologists; cf. *PV* 1052, *Alc.* 245, Dover on *Clouds* 380. The idea is probably not just that the rock is blown about by winds but that it flies round in a circular orbit with Olympus at the centre, like a celestial body. Tantalus is also airborne (6 f.), somewhere close to the rock, presumably attached to another chain. Anaxagoras (DK 59 A 42, 71) had taught that the heavenly bodies were stones torn off from the earth and held up against the firmament by centrifugal force. Euripides by using this principle has succeeded in explaining how a rock could hover perpetually over Tantalus' head. Possibly Anaxagoras himself had rationalized the myth in these terms; he did believe in certain invisible bodies revolving between the earth and the moon. In *Phaethon* Euripides had called the sun a golden *bōlos* (fr. 783 N.= inc. sed. 5 Diggle), and ancient commentators recognized Anaxagorean influence there. They were wrong, however, to identify that *bōlos* with this one and to interpret Tantalus' rock as the sun.

986 **who sired, who sired:** the repeated verb is here merely a stylistic mannerism, lacking the effect that it has for instance in 971.

252

987   I have seen: or perhaps "they (my forbears) have seen",
      or, emending to *domous*, "the house, what wounds it has
      seen". But Electra might claim to "see" events of before
      her time, as Pindar says "I have seen from afar
      Archilochus mostly in difficulties" (*P*. 2.55).

988   that flying colt-chase: Euripides follows a tradition
      probably derived from Pherecydes (*FGrH* 3 F 37–8)
      according to which Tantalus lived in Lydia and Oenomaus,
      the king whose daughter Pelops wanted, in Lesbos (cf.
      West [1985] 158). Oenomaus' habit was to pursue his
      daughter's suitors in a chariot and kill them if he caught
      them. His chariot-man Myrtilus was induced to sabotage
      his chariot, and he was killed, Pelops escaping with the
      girl and Myrtilus. He crossed the Aegean – he had
      winged horses – and threw Myrtilus out near Geraestus in
      southern Euboea; he then arrived and settled in the
      Peloponnese, which came to be named after him. The
      commoner version locates Oenomaus in the region of
      Olympia (so *IT* 824). Euripides wrote an *Oenomaus*,
      perhaps about the time of *Orestes*.

990   hurling Myrtilus to death: "Myrtilus' death" is in the
      accusative as being effected by the throwing action.

996   a curse fraught with woe: Myrtilus cursed Pelops and his
      descendants. Soph. *El*. 504–15 also traces the woes of the
      house to this, whereas Aeschylus had only traced them
      back to the curse of Thyestes (*Ag*. 1584–1602, *Cho*.
      1068). For Aeschylus, however, the curse is a real
      abiding force through which the past bleeds into the
      present: for Euripides it is merely a convenient
      justification for filling up songs with mythical retrospects.
      Cf. on 336–7 and 811.

997   the son of Maia: Hermes was Myrtilus' father. The
      multiplication of livestock was one of his functions (Hes.
      Th. 444). For the lamb story see 14 n.

1000 ruinous thing of Atreus: the genitive apparently depends
      on *teras oloon*. One would prefer to attach it to "the
      flocks", but this would probably require the transposition
      of *poimnioisi* to follow *hopote*.
      breeder of horses: the epithet marks him as a noble
      landowner. Argos was traditionally "horse-rearing" (*Il*.
      2.287 etc., Eur. *Supp*. 365, *Tro*. 1087).

1001 Conflict: the conflict of Atreus and Thyestes (812) brings
      this goddess into action, and she remains the subject

253

down to the end of the song. She already appears as a divine entity in Hesiod (*Th.* 225 f., cf. *Op.* 11 ff.) and Homer (*Il.* 4.440-5).

1002 turned the sun's winged car about: it may have been Sophocles' *Atreus* that made this myth well known. There were different versions and interpretations, but in the present passage and in *El.* 727-42 (cf. also *IT* 193, 816; Pl. *Polit.* 269a) the story appears to be that the sun and stars had their courses permanently changed: previously they had not risen in the east, culminated in the south, or set in the west. (Presumably they had done the opposite, but this is not spelt out – Oenopides DK 41 A 10 had a theory that the Milky Way marks the sun's earlier course.) *El.* 742 "on account of a mortal rights-dispute" implies the version that Zeus effected the miracle in support of Atreus' claim to the throne, after Thyestes, having stolen the lamb, said he would cede it only if the sun changed direction (cf. Plato l.c., Apollod. *Epit.* 2.12). Others say that the sun turned back in horror at the Thyestean feast; but in Euripides the feast comes afterwards (1008). See further A.C. Pearson, *The Fragments of Sophocles* (1917) i.92 f. and iii.5 f.

1003 to the westward sky-course: this accusative expresses the result of the change; cf. *IA* 343, 363.

1004 yoking on: to the sun's car.

the snowy steeds of Dawn: lit. "snow-colted Dawn". The MSS give "(yoking the car) to single-colted Dawn", with problematic metre and a dull epithet out of accord with poetic and artistic tradition. My emendation is an improvement on both scores. The idea is that "Dawn" is a goddess of the east not previously associated with the sunrise.

1005 the seven-track Pleiad: i.e. the Pleiades which go along as a group of seven. They stand for the stars in general, cf. *El.* 468, *Hel.* 1489, *Phaethon* 66, *Rhes.* 530. The words "Zeus changes" which the MSS give at the end of this sentence seem to have been added (from *El.* 728 v.l.?) by someone who had lost the thread. The historic present is extremely rare in lyric narrative (*ameibei* in 1007 is not an example; it refers to what is still happening).

1007 for that affair, that death: the demonstrative *tōn* is initially unspecific, then given definition by "deaths for

254

death". *Thanatōn* though plural, refers to the single death of Myrtilus.

008 that bears Thyestes' name: being notorious as "the feast of Thyestes" (*Ag.* 1242 and later writers).

009 Aërope: 18 n. Her adultery is brought in, out of historical sequence, as another scandal associated with Thyestes.

011 me and my father: one certainly expects "my brother", and Willink's *syngenetān t'* is attractive. On the other hand it would be surprising if Agamemnon's death were not mentioned. Cf. 1144 for the coupling of his death with his children's.

013-1245 This scene – the only one in which Orestes, Electra, and Pylades are all on stage together – begins where an Aeschylean tragedy might have ended, with the return of the hero on whom disaster has fallen and a general mood of sorrow and resignation. But from the start Orestes appears in a more heroic light than before, tight-lipped, disgusted by Electra's abandoned grief, and determined to show unflinching courage in his suicide. Then successive brainwaves of Pylades and Electra transform the position, first to one in which death is to be preceded by a satisfying act of vengeance, and finally to one in which there is a hope of escaping death, and even winning glory, by carrying out a dangerous coup. The play is turned onto a new track.

The three-actor scene is, as usual, largely compounded from duologues. In 1018-64 we have an emotional interchange between brother and sister, differentiated from that in 211-315 by Orestes' new strength and self-reliance, but otherwise comparable. In 1065-1176 Pylades becomes Orestes' interlocutor, making clear his fidelity and his determination to share his friend's fate, and then propounding his plan for the murder of Helen. In 1177-1224 Electra chips in with her further idea and the dialogue is again between her and Orestes, apart from a single remark by Pylades in response to an aside addressed to him (1209 f.). Finally in 1225-45 all three take part in a set-piece invocation of Agamemnon.

013-17 But see, here comes etc.: for the anapaestic

255

announcement cf. 348 n. It focusses attention on the "painful spectacle" of which Electra was forewarned at 952. So with other entries of persons condemned to death at *Andr*. 494, *HF* 442, *IT* 456. Cf. Taplin (1977) 73; Halleran 13 f.

1015 the equal of a brother: cf. 882 n., and for the formation *isadelphos*, 200 n.

1016 his infirm legs: this is the last reference to Orestes' illness.

1017 as an outrunner: i.e. like a trace-horse who helps the yoked horses to go faster by taking some of the weight of the chariot off them. See Jebb on Soph. *El*. 721 f. For various figurative uses cf. Alcm. 1.92, Aesch. *Ag*. 842, Soph. *Ant*. 140, Eur. *HF* 446.

1019 the gates of the nether ones: cf. Aesch. *Ag*. 1291, Eur. *Hipp*. 1447. The MSS absurdly have "your nether pyre" or "the pyre of the nether ones".

1020 O woe again: the double cry of pain, the second accompanied by "again", is something of a tragic formula, at least since Aesch. *Ag*. 1343-5 (where it corresponds to two separate blows).

1021 I go out of my mind: momentary aorist, cf. 169 n.

1022-59 Distichomythia (217-67 n.), interrupted at 1047-51.

1022 Won't you be quiet: the brusqueness is quite unexpected. The contrast in this passage between the tight-lipped man and the distraught woman recalls that between Eteocles and the Theban women in Aesch. *Sept*. 182 ff.

1024 [You've no choice – at hand]: the scholiast did not have this line, it spoils the distichomythia, and it is clearly an interpolation of the type described on 916. For other cases where a line has been added to "complete" a sentence that ended with the idiomatic "but still" cf. Bond on *HF* 1366.

1025 this divine light: lit. "god's light", the god being the sun. Cf. Page on *Med*. 352, Diggle on *Phaethon* 6. Any god can be called "the god" when the context makes his or her identity clear.

1027 bore me to death: a colloquial use of *apokteinō*, see Stevens 11 f.

1031 unmanly: Heracles in Soph. *Tr*. 1071-5 feels that his inability to endure without crying out loud makes a woman of him; cf. Dover 101.

1035-6 hanging-nooses ... a sword: 953 n. In what follows

(1041, 1052, 1063) the sword is assumed (the nobler instrument according to *Hel.* [299–301]).

039 It's enough etc.: similarly in *IT* 1007 f., where Iphigeneia has suggested sacrificing her own life so that Orestes can escape, he says "I won't cause your death as well as my mother's; her blood is enough".

041 Very well: Electra now shows that she too has the heroic resolve appropriate to a child of Agamemnon.
any slower than you with the sword: *sou xiphous* is probably not "your sword" but a double genitive. "I shall not be left behind by you, fall short of you, in connexion with the sword."

042–51 For the motif of the last embrace before death or separation cf. *Med.* 1069 ff., *El.* 1321 ff., *Tro.* 761 ff., Soph. *OT* 1466 ff., etc.; Shisler 384.

046 to your sister: the MSS text of this line is unintelligible. This dative (instead of the transmitted genitive) goes well with "most delightful" and restores sense to "whose life is one" (dative with *heis* as in *Phoen.* 156, Thgn. 300). I also accept Willink's *sōma* for *onoma*.
whose life: or "soul". Cf. 307 f., 865, 1052 f. The embrace is the physical and visible expression of their unity.

047–51 The temporary breakdown of the distichomythia corresponds to the breakdown of Orestes' tough male stance. Cf. 255–7 n.

048 being inhibited: about being "unmanly".

049 beloved embrace of mine: *prosptygm' emon*, "my embrace-object", "the person I embrace", is like *stygēm' emon* in 480.

050 children and the marriage bed: in Greek eyes no life was complete without these, and a young man who died before marriage was the object of especial sorrow. The continuation of Agamemnon's line was certainly not a matter to go by default. In fact both Orestes and Electra will have marriages fixed up by the end of the play.

053 one memorial receive us: "memorial" (798 n.) here stands for the tomb as a whole; but what is "crafted in cedar" is the coffin. Achilles promises Patroclus that their bones will be united in one urn (*Il.* 23.82 ff.), and Admetus in *Alc.* 365–7 intends to have himself interred in the same coffin as Alcestis.

054–5 how short we are of friends: there is Pylades, but

Orestes is thinking more of sympathetic relatives; the Argives may have other ideas about the disposal of the bodies. The sentence is designed to lead on to Electra's question about Menelaus.

1056-7 did Menelaus not speak: Euripides could have made the old man who reported the debate comment on Menelaus' failure to contribute to it. Instead he brings it up here to prepare the air for Pylades' anti-Menelaus scheme.

1058 the sceptre: Menelaus, it is anticipated, will be taking over Agamemnon's house (1108 n., 1146, 1596), and if he avoids alienating the Argives now, he can reasonably expect to be acknowledged as king. In the end Apollo directs otherwise (1660 f.).

1059 he was taking care: cf. 698-9 n.

1063 stabbing to my liver: in tragedy (not earlier) the liver sometimes appears as the centre of life and emotion; see R.B. Onians, *The Origins of European Thought* (1951) 84-9. For stabbing it in suicide cf. Soph. *Ant.* 1315, Eur. *HF* 1149, *Hel.* 983; in murder, *Med.* 379, *HF* 979.

1068 And farewell: such farewells are common in Euripides. See Bond on *Hypsipyle* fr. 64.67 (p.126).
I'm on my way: Pylades' intervention comes at the last possible moment.

1069 One thing ... I hold against you: *momphēn echō* takes a further accusative as if it were *memphomai*. Cf. 860 n.

1070 if you thought – after your death: Pylades had made a similar declaration in *IT* 674 ff. Euripides adapts several motifs from that scene in the dialogue that follows here.

1074 Yes I did – the same fate too: *IT* 675 "I sailed together with you, and I must die together with you too".

1075-7 Let your father – a father's house: *IT* 699 "No, go and stay alive and dwell in your father's house". It is perhaps the influence of this earlier passage that leads Euripides to forget or ignore Pylades' banishment (765); but in any case that would not be permanent.
a secure base: lit. "a big harbour". The phrase derives from Aesch. *Pers.* 250. Generally *limēn* as a metaphor signifies a place of refuge or reception (Aesch. *Supp.* 471, Soph. *Aj.* 683, *OT* 1208, *Ant.* 1000, 1284, Eur. *Med.* 769).

1078 As for marriage: cf. 1050 n. In *IT* 695 f. (cf. 915) Pylades is already married to Electra, and Orestes urges him to have children by her; here this has to be modified. The marriage is first mentioned in *El.* 1249, but may go back to the *Nostoi*. According to Hellanicus (*FGrH* 4 F 155) the couple had sons named Medon and Strophius.

081 the matrimonial link between us is no more: Orestes releases Pylades from all obligation in this respect. At the end of the play the link will be restored.

083-4 it isn't possible – welfare: Euripides several times follows the salutation *chaire* (lit. "be glad") with a remark about the difficulty of doing so, cf. *Alc.* 510, *Hec.* 426, *El.* 1357, *Phoen.* 618, *Ba.* 1380. It is a particular instance of the habit noted at 579.

086-8 May the fruitful soil etc: this affirmation of sincerity by means of a grave curse which is to take effect on the speaker if he is insincere resembles *Hipp.* 1028-31; cf. also Thgn. 869-72, 1089 (both of loyalty to friends), and my nn. on Hes. *Th.* 231, *Op.* 281, 284.

not accept my blood: the idea of rejection by the cosmic elements is paralleled in Empedocles DK 31 B 115 (of gods who shed blood or commit perjury), Soph. *OT* 1427 f. (Oedipus' pollution), Eur. *HF* 1295-8 (Heracles'). In saying "blood" rather than "body" Pylades alludes to the idea that the blood of the dead enriches the soil and so contributes to new life (Archil. 292, Aesch. *Sept.* 587; Nisbet & Hubbard on Hor. *Odes* 2.1.29).

nor the bright air my soul: "my soul" is not in the Greek, but must be what is meant. The idea that at death, while the body returns to earth, the soul or breath (*psȳchē* or *pneuma*) goes to its kindred air had been fashionable at Athens at least since 432 (civic epitaph for those fallen at Potidaea, *CEG* 10.6). In his *Erechtheus* of *c.*422 (fr. 65.71 ff. Austin) Euripides treats this as the special fate of Erechtheus' heroic daughters, but elsewhere he applies it to men in general. See Collard (1975) ii. 251 f.

092 I deem her my wife: explaining why it is fitting that he should join *her* in death (on her own account, not just accidentally on Orestes'); and at the same time declaring that he sticks by his agreement to marry her and does not wish to be released from it.

093 For otherwise: for this elliptical type of *gar* cf. Denniston 62 f.

what fine words: similar rhetorical questions are noted by

259

Bond on *HF* 578. The present passage adapts *IT* 676-9. It reflects the heroic "shame culture", which was by no means superseded in the classical period: Pylades' nobility is inseparable from his concern for his public esteem.

1094 the Delphian land: Pylades' home is generally given just as Phocis; for the more precise location cf. Pind. *P.* 11.36 and Eur. *Andr.* 1000. "Land" = city.

high citadel: an unofficial *ad hoc* designation to connect "Delphian" and "Phocian".

1096 but now you are in (misfortune) am your friend no longer: for this commonplace cf. 454-5 n.

1098 let's confer together: the sentence does not suggest that Pylades has already thought of a plan, but very soon it is assumed that he has. For the use of stichomythia in working out a plan of action cf. *IT* 1020 ff., *Ion* 970 ff., *Hel.* 813 ff.

1100 if only - before I die: Thgn. 339 f. "I would think myself (fortunate as) a god if I get revenge before I die"; Aesch. *Cho.* 438, Soph. *Aj.* 391, Eur. *El.* 281, 663, Call. fr. 591. But in these passages the speaker is not actually facing death, only saying that revenge is his single ambition in life. On the Greek principle of harming one's enemies wherever possible see Dover 180-3; Bond on *HF* 585 f. (Earlier references: *Od.* 6.184, Archil. 23.15, 126, Thgn. 872, 1090, Sappho 5.7, Sol. 13.5 f., Pind. *P.* 2.84, *I.* 3/4.66, Aesch. *Cho.* 123, *PV* 1041 f.)

1103 I don't trust women: during dialogue scenes with more than one actor on stage, the presence of the chorus is generally ignored. But when something is said that must be kept confidential, the chorus must be sworn to secrecy or at least, as here, given security vetting. See Barrett on *Hipp.* 710-2. It is perfunctorily done: Pylades continues in 1105 without so much as a particle to acknowledge the digression. On the untrustworthiness of women cf. Hes. *Op.* 375, Eur. *Med.* 421 f., *IT* 1298, fr. 440, Trag. adesp. 543, Antiphanes fr. 251, Men. frr. 584-5, 591.

1105 a bitter pain for Menelaus: for the syntax cf. 843 n. Medea kills her children to pain Jason.

1107 She's hidden in your house?: he asks for confirmation of what he was told in 744; the discussion has to be focussed on the scene of the planned action. Helen is "hidden", from Pylades' viewpoint, as the quarry not yet sighted, and indeed she is deliberately avoiding public appearances (57 ff., 98).

108 she's sealing everything off: setting her own seal (or Menelaus') on storeroom doors, chest lids, etc., as if she were sole mistress of the house. On the use of seals for internal security see Diggle on *Phaethon* 223.

109 engaged to Hades: she will soon be moving to other premises. As marriage is a woman's usual reason for moving house, a woman on her way to the house of Hades is sometimes poetically represented as going to marry him, cf. Soph. *Ant.* 654, 816, Eur. *Med.* 985, *HF* 484, *Tro.* 445, *IA* 461.

110 foreign attendants: these are mentioned in preparation for the scene with the Phrygian at 1369 ff.

111 *I* wouldn't be scared of any Phrygian: cf. 888 n.

112 mirrors: for Helen's collection of expensive mirrors cf. *Tro.* 1107.

113 the comforts of Troy: Homer does not characterize Troy by any special Asiatic luxury. This may first be seen in Sappho 44, perhaps, though there it is an elegance like that of Sardis, in no way deprecated. In Aesch. *Ag.* 935 f., however, Trojan pomp is imagined in terms of Persian – un-Greek, excessive, immodest. In *Tro.* 991-7 Helen's head is represented as having been turned by the wealth and luxury of Troy, so much greater than what she had in Argos.

115 The slave breed: *genos* can mean "class" with no genetic implication. But here there is a suggestion that barbarians are naturally slaves and Greeks naturally free, for which cf. *Telephus* fr. 127 Austin, *Andr.* 665 f., *Hel.* 276, *IA* 1402. The reason is that barbarians live under monarchs (*Hel.* l.c.). But slave characteristics can be inherited, according to Thgn. 535-8. Elsewhere in Euripides (e.g. *Ion* 854-6, frr. 511, 831) more enlightened ideas about slaves are expressed.

116 I don't mind: lit. "I'm not in awe about". The point is not quite the same as in 1100, but that death – even a second death besides the one Orestes is anticipating anyway – is a small price to pay for this satisfaction. Cf. *h.Aphr.* 149-54.

118 Explain the business: returning to the main question (1106, 1110) after the digression.

122 inwardly gleeful: it is not clear that they are justified in

assuming Helen's hostility. Cf. Introduction IV. But if the statement in 1108 is true, she is at least losing no time in adjusting to the expected deaths of Orestes and his sister.

1128 whoever doesn't - kill: preparation for 1506-36. "Doesn't keep quiet" means "tries to raise the alarm".

1129 the job itself makes clear: an adaptation of a familiar saying, "the event itself will show"; see Dodds on *Ba.* 973-6.

aim: lit. "stretch" (as if a bow).

1130 I can make that connexion: lit. "I understand the matching-piece", the meaning that Pylades' oblique expression fits. *Symbola* in the concrete sense are tokens that fit together with each other alone, and so serve as credentials. For this and the various derived senses see LSJ; sections III.2 and 5 are the most relevant here.

1131 hear how good my plan is: the initial phase of planning being complete, the stichomythia ends, and Pylades now argues that besides hurting Menelaus, the killing of Helen will (a) be just in itself and (b) earn the conspirators gratitude and glory. He does not go so far as to suggest that the sentence of death will be rescinded; Euripides holds that idea in reserve, because it is to be the great virtue of Electra's later proposal. (Cf. however 1152 n.)

1133 it would be: *an ēn* (instead of *an eiē*) suggests that the killing has already become a definite fact, not just a possibility.

1137 a hallelujah: *ololygmos* is ritual ululation by women, especially at the climax of a sacrifice (*Od.* 3.450, Aesch. *Ag.* 494 f., 1118, etc.; Burkert [1983] 5, [1985] 56, 74), but also to set the seal on a prayer (*Il.* 6.301, *Od.* 4.767, Aesch. *Sept.* 268, *Eum.* 1043, 1047), and in general when the presence of divinity is manifested (*h.Ap.* 445, Eur. *Med.* 1173, *Ba.* 24). Less clearly religious *ololygmoi* are uttered on occasions of emotional release such as successful childbirth (*h.Ap.* 119, Paus. 9.11.3 with Frazer) or triumph over enemies (*Od.* 22.408, Aesch. *Sept.* 825, *Ag.* 28, etc.; Fraenkel on *Ag.* 1236), but here too there would be at least a contingent association with acts of worship and thanksgiving to the gods. So in the present case.

they'll light fires: cf. Aesch. *Ag.* 88-96, *Cho.* 863, Eur. *El.* 714 f.

262

1145 and your mother: added for completeness, though her
death was not so regrettable. "Agamemnon and his whole
household."
1147 I'll be damned: lit. "may I not go on living"; colloquial
expression, see Stevens 17. The particle *oun*, "indeed",
"in reality", acknowledges the fact that Pylades is
expecting to die anyway.
1148 dark sword: cf. 821-2 n.
1149 if ... we don't achieve Helen's murder: he has no real
reason to anticipate failure, but Euripides knows they will
fail. Burning the house down (threatened at 1541 ff. but
not carried through) will prevent Menelaus from having
it.
1152 a glorious death or a glorious deliverance: standard
alternatives embraced by desperate heroes, cf. Soph. *Aj.*
479 f., *El.* 1320 f., Eur. *Cycl.* 201 f. (Glorious death
preferred to inglorious life: *BICS* 31 [1984], 171.) But
the cliché is not perfectly suited to this context. The
glorious death must correspond to the house-burning
alternative (1150 "before we die"; only it is not obvious
what is so glorious about it). The glorious deliverance
therefore corresponds to success in killing Helen; but
Pylades has not predicted that this will save their lives
(1131 n.), nor does Orestes in what follows anticipate
survival unless some further means of escape, outside
present calculation, should offer itself.
1153-4 Tyndareos' daughter etc.: the typical distich between
a pair of long speeches (542-3 n.). While not commenting
on the morality of the proposed action, the chorus makes
it clear that it is not going to stick up for Helen.
she has disgraced her sex: the context gives *genos* this
meaning. For the idea cf. *Od.* 11.432-4 (of Clytaemestra).
1155-76 Orestes' speech has, as it happens, the same number
of lines as Pylades', but usually equivalence is only
approximate (e.g. 491 ff. Tyndareos 49 lines, Orestes 57;
640 ff. Orestes 39, Menelaus 35).
1155-6 there's nothing better – monarchy: cf. *HF* 1425 with
Bond's n., Soph. *Phil.* 672 f., Men. *Dysc.* 811 f. Denial
of wealth and monarchy as the highest goods goes back to
Archil. 19, cf. Sol. 24, 33, Eur. *Med.* 599 f., *Hipp.* 1013
ff., *Ion* 621-32, *Phoen.* 549 ff., etc.
1158 you devised the nastiness for Aegisthus: we have no
earlier version in which this was Pylades' idea (contrast
Eur. *El.* 618 ff.).

1161 about to make: or "making", if *ei* is from *einai* and not *ienai*.

1162 something burdensome even in ... being over-praised: cf. *Hcld*. 202-4, *IA* 979 f.

1168 on merit, not by royal succession: Agamemnon had an important kingdom in the Argolid, but no sovereignty beyond his own borders. Traditionally he led the expedition against Troy because it was his brother who had been wronged, and he had the greater power of the two; the other Greeks joined in to do him honour (*Il*. 1.158 f., 174 f.) or because they were bound by oath to punish any abductor of Helen ([Hes.] fr. 204.78 ff., Stes. *PMG* 190, Eur. *IA* 57 ff.). The idea that they *chose* Agamemnon to lead them already appears at *El*. 1082; cf. *Hel*. 395 f., *IA* 84 f., 337 ff.

1169 acquired a certain divine strength: his stature as war-leader was such that he seemed something more than a local king, as if he were indeed sovereign of all Greece by divine authority.

1172 For if: another reason why this is a good course of action. It only needs one further element - some way in which we might avoid death ourselves - to convert it from a glorious ending to a state of good fortune. But that missing factor is only a dream.

1175 to voice: the construction is compressed. Euripides puts *dia stoma* as if an infinitive such as "send out" were to follow, or a participle as subject of *terpsai*, but he then proceeds as if this phrase by itself sufficiently expressed the idea of "voicing".

1176 fleeting words: lit. "flying", a variation on Homer's "winged words" with the new pointed sense of "fugitive". What exists only in spoken form does not stay to be enjoyed.

1177 I think I have: Iphigeneia uses the same modest phrase to introduce her stratagem at *IT* 1029.

1179 Divine providence: almost "a *deus ex machina*, which we are not allowed to expect in advance". Then he realizes that she must mean something more concrete, because she is not stupid.

1181 Listen, now: similarly in introducing a plan at *Hel*. 1049 and especially *Ion* 987 in a sequence like this one, "Ah, now I have an effective trick" ... "Listen, now. You know the battle of the sons of Earth?" "Yes, the one ..."

1182 there is a certain pleasure in the prospect: less likely "what pleasure is there in the delaying" (Willink). Cf. 239 f.

1183 You know Helen's daughter?: this kind of question is a convenient device for breaking things down into smaller elements for stichomythia. See Dodds on *Ba*. 462-3.

1184 Yes, the one: the addition of *ge* is an improvement because Orestes is adding a reason why he certainly should know; cf. *IT* 518, Soph. *Tr*. 1192.

my mother brought up: 63-4 n.

1190 us three allies: hitherto Orestes and Electra have been considered as a pair (as the condemned ones), or Orestes and Pylades (as the ones who will make the attempt on Helen). Electra's plan for saving all three (1178) binds them into a trio acting in concert; cf. 1192, 1244 f.

1195 helps to save you: by using his influence with the Argives, cf. 1610 f. "Saves you" would need an aorist; the present expresses "act in a way tending towards saving". Cf. *drāi* in 1191, *kteinēi* and *sphaze* in 1199, none of which can refer to definitive action.

1200 blusters: for this use of *polys* see LSJ s.v., I.2c.

1201 in time: as the threat to Hermione is maintained.

he's not brave: cf. 754 n.

1203 End of speech: perhaps a slightly naughty translation of what was an established formula (Aesch. *Eum*. 710, Eur. *Phoen*. 1012; similar phrases in Aesch. *Ag*. 582, Soph. *Aj*. 480, etc.) meaning in effect "I have come to the end of what I had to say".

1204 the mind of a man: i.e. tough, disposed to bold action, cf. Aesch. *Ag*. 11, Soph. fr. 943, Lys. 2.4; somewhat differently in Xen. *Oec*. 10.1. See further Dover 99-102.

210 wedding-songs: sung by friends as the bridegroom brought the bride to his house and after he had taken her into the bridal chamber; see Jebb on Soph. *Ant*. 813 ff. Praise of the couple and their pedigree qualities was a conventional element, cf. *Alc*. 920 f., Theoc. 18.53; travestied perhaps in Thgn. 193-6.

211 how soon: genitive of time within which, as e.g. Soph. *El*. 478; Moorhouse 58 f.

213 cub: various words denoting the young of animals are used metaphorically of young persons, *moschos*, *pōlos*, *poris*, *portis*, *damalis*, *neossos*. *Skymnos* is apt here (*a*) because she is to be hunted (cf. 1315 f.) and (*b*)

because her father is a formidable and fierce-tempered hero (cf. *Hcld.* 1006, *Andr.* 1107). Having used the word once, Euripides re-uses it less appositely at 1387; cf. also 1492.

1215 <u>the length of time ... agrees:</u> the length of time that has elapsed agrees with the supposition that she is nearly back. For *syntrechei* cf. *Ion* 547 and Hdt. 1.116.1; for the dramatic technique, Soph. *OT* 73 ff., where Creon's return from a mission is expected imminently because of the length of time he has been away. But Sophocles rather crudely makes him appear the next instant. Cf. 67 n. The length of Hermione's absence is of course determined by the needs of the plot; it appears excessive if measured by what Orestes has been through since she left.

1218-20 <u>keep a lookout in case etc.:</u> no one but Hermione will in fact come, but this precaution creates the entertaining song and dance scene 1246-96.
<u>some companion-in-arms:</u> one of those who have returned from Troy with Menelaus. Orestes is not afraid of casual visitors from the town (who would anyway be likely to support the killing of Helen) but of those able-bodied men who owe especial allegiance to Menelaus.

1220-1 <u>make it known:</u> until 1221 is added, *gegōne* is naturally taken as "call out loud enough for your voice to carry into the house" (see LSJ). The verb does not suit either of the methods of communication suggested in 1221. Possibly we should understand "call out, or (let us know) by banging on the door or by sending one of these women in". G.A. Longman, *CR* 8 (1958), 122, deletes 1221, but no motive for interpolation is apparent.

1224 <u>[Pylades, since – with me]:</u> this poor appendage has the hallmarks of interpolation – one word providing superfluous clarification of what precedes, the rest of the line mere padding. The change of addressee at 1222 does not demand the vocative (cf. 1181), and it comes unnaturally late in the sentence. See also 1227-30 n.

1225-45 The formal invocation of Agamemnon, Zeus, and Dike as a prelude to the assassination attempt is modelled on those in Aesch. *Cho.* 479-509 and Eur. *El.* 671-84. There, however, Agamemnon is asked to assist an act of revenge for his own murder, and in *Choephoroe* the prayer is logically made at his tomb (cf. *Or.* 797), by his

two children alone. In *Electra* Euripides had made a
third person participate in a supporting role, much as
here; cf. already *Cho*. 456-65. Another passage of *Electra*
is echoed at 1235-6, see below.
This section was probably added as an afterthought.
The arrangements for the end of the scene are made in
1216-23, and after 1222 f. we expect to see Orestes and
Pylades going indoors at once.

1225 the house of impenetrable Night: Hesiod locates the house
of Hades close to that of Night (*Th*. 746-73), but
Euripides is simply thinking of the darkness of death and
of the underworld. Cf. *Alc*. 269, 437, *HF* 46, 353, *Hel*.
177, etc.

1226 to come in aid: prayers for assistance usually ask the god
or hero to come in person, as if he could not act from a
distance. See my n. on Hes. *Op*. 2. So with Agamemnon
at *Cho*. 456-60.

1227-30 [to these in their need – accomplice in this]: the
first two lines of the prayer were solemn and weighty; in
these four Orestes just chatters on. They destroy the
symmetry which otherwise prevails between the different
speakers' utterances (as in *Cho*. 479-502, *El*. 671-83).
Electra's "come indeed" in 1231 echoes the appeal in 1226,
passing over the one in 1230. Given these suspicious
features, the scholiast's remark on 1229 that four lines in
this vicinity were absent from part of the tradition is
damning evidence (see 957-9 n.). Finally, 1230 and the
already condemned 1224 show a common dependence on *IT*
95 which indicates that both lines were composed
together. I suspect that the interpolator first took *IT* 95
to stand unaltered after 1223; then, adding 1227 ff. (he
felt, perhaps, that Orestes ought to explain the situation
to Agamemnon), he decided to transfer the high-flown
toude sylleptor to the prayer, and to substitute an
alternative (inferior) phrase in 1224. In 1227, "to these
in their need" is taken from 681; it fits more awkwardly
here.

1231 if inside the earth thou hearest: for the difficulty of
reaching the ears of the dead cf. Aesch. *Pers*. 633-9,
Cho. 315-22.

1233 kinsman of my father: if Euripides assumes the same
genealogy as in *IT* (see 765 n.), Strophius was connected
with Agamemnon only by marriage. According to an

alternative mentioned by schol., it was Strophius' father Crisus who married the daughter of Atreus. Perhaps the truth is that Euripides, having referred to Orestes' *syngeneia* with Pylades at 733, now unreflectingly projects the relationship back onto their fathers.

1235-6 <u>I slew – his hesitation:</u> adapted from *El.* 1221-6 (where Electra speaks both of urging Orestes on and of handling the sword). The MSS (apart from M²) make Pylades the second speaker, but he should clearly be the third, as throughout. It is not significant that Electra's role is represented as hortatory in 616-21 (cf. 32, 284). In Pylades' mouth 1236 is fully justified by *Cho.* 899-902.

<u>I urged him on:</u> this reading is favoured both by the following phrase and by the *Electra* parallel. The variant "I plotted" is probably a reminiscence of 1090.

1238 <u>these reproaches:</u> adapted from *Cho.* 495, where Orestes and Electra have been reminding their father of the disgraceful manner of his death to arouse him to action. Here the reproach is more an implied one: we have done a terrible deed on your behalf, we are even dying on your behalf (1232), and you have not yet demonstrated your gratitude.

1239 <u>I make thee libation:</u> as if they were at his tomb. This is not just a metaphor for "I weep". Libations would be appropriate with the prayers (115 ff., *Cho.* 87 ff., etc.), but in this case tears take their place.

1240 <u>Stop now:</u> as in *Cho.* 510 and *El.* 684, the third party calls an end to the prayer and says it is time for action. Pylades uses his last line in the symmetrical pattern for this purpose. In assuring the others that their prayers are heard he follows the old man in *Electra*.

1241 <u>penetrate:</u> lit. "lance". The verb is sometimes used of "discharging" words spiritedly, but here the idea of reaching a distant target is uppermost.

1242 <u>Zeus our ancestor:</u> the influence of the *Electra* passage is still discernible (671 "O Zeus paternal"). Zeus was Orestes' ancestor (5) and also Pylades' (not only through his mother, Atreus' daughter, but also in the male line, Zeus – Aeacus – Phocus – Crisus – Strophius). The fact is mentioned as strengthening their claim on him.

<u>Justice:</u> treated as an active goddess, closely associated with Zeus, in Hes. *Op.* 220-4, 256-62, and later especially in tragedy; addressed in Aesch. *Eum.* 511, 785, Eur. *Med.* 764, *El.* 771.

1244 settlement: the affair is imagined as a kind of lawsuit in which Zeus and Justice will adjudicate between the opposing claims. Cf. Fraenkel on *Ag*. 41.
1245 one sentence: lit. "debt". The judge decides what the claimant owes or is owed. Cf. LSJ *opheilō* I.3.

1246-1310 Preparation has been made for a murder. The conventional sequence, now that the murderers have gone into the house, would be a choral song followed by death-cries from inside and then the appearance of some servant or other to relate what has happened. Here there is the added complication of Hermione's return and capture to be fitted in, and apart from this, Euripides produces interesting and entertaining variations on the expected pattern. The first is that instead of a moody stasimon we get a lively lyric dialogue between Electra and the chorus, accompanying a performative dance. This is well set up: killing is men's work, and Electra may suitably stay to receive Hermione. (Contrast Soph. *El*. 1384 ff., where Electra goes in with the murderers and then after a short stasimon comes out again to watch for Aegisthus while the murder of Clytaemestra takes place.) If receiving Hermione were her only task, it would provide little material for song, but the extension of her brief to keeping a lookout for all comers (1218) creates the conditions for a nice exercise in music and movement.

The characterization of the chorus in the parodos has not been sustained since then – this is a phenomenon common to many tragedies – but now it is thrown into relief again. The interlude shares a number of features with the parodos: the easy and familiar relationship between Electra and her friends, among whom, however, she is the dominant figure; dance movements which she directs; an atmosphere of anxiety and suspense, with a false alarm in the middle; nervous emotional reactions from Electra; a feminine grace pervading the whole. The rhythms are mainly dochmiac (as in the parodos), but with some enoplian cola, and some admixture of spoken iambic trimeters (a feature of Euripides' later lyric dialogues).
1247 first-ranking: we have not been told before that Electra's friends come from the leading families of the city, though

it was a natural assumption. For the neuter *ta prōta* cf. Aesch. *Eum.* 487, Soph. *Phil.* 434, Eur. *Med.* 917, etc.; also in Hdt. (6.100.3, 9.78.1).

1251-2 <u>Take up positions</u> etc.: the chorus is to divide into two groups and watch the two roads that lead out on opposite sides of the orchestra. Compare Soph. *Aj.* 803 ff., where the chorus is sent right out of the theatre in each direction to search for Ajax; the two semichoruses return at 866 singing of their failure. There (805) as here (1239 f.), the two directions are identified as east and west. As the chorus numbered fifteen, the division must have been slightly unequal. On other cases of divided choruses cf. Dale on *Alc.* 77-135, Collard on *Supp.* 271-85; Taplin (1977) 190.

1257 <u>new woes upon old:</u> cf. 336-7 n.

1258-60 These trimeters were probably spoken by individual leaders of the two semichoruses.
<u>the one towards the sun's shafts:</u> "the sun" stands for the rising sun, cf. *Il.* 12.239, *Od.* 9.26, 13.240, and *antēlios*. The east was to the audience's left.

1263 <u>from there to here:</u> they do not just gaze fixedly down the *eisodoi*; there is evidently a good deal of dramatic prowling and peering about.

1264 <u>We're keeping watch:</u> the division of 1261-5 between Electra and the chorus is not matched in the antistrophe (1281-5), against the normal rule. Cf. Page, *CQ* 31 (1937), 95. Wilamowitz's attempt to evade the anomaly by giving the chorus 1263-5 ("From there to here - your call") and 1283-5 ("You in the house - red") seems to me to produce unnaturalness in both places. It should be Electra who specifies from where to where the chorus' eyes sweep, and who is so anxious about what those in the house are doing, calling to them from the door.

1267 <u>through your hanging hair:</u> i.e. even at the edges of your field of vision.

1268-70 <u>Here's someone</u> etc.: Willink assigns these lines and 1273-4 to the whole chorus, who are all wheeling their eyes in all directions. But this makes their disposition between the two roads pointless, and entails a less natural interpretation of 1275 (n.).

1270 <u>this countryman:</u> presumably seen or imagined on the side away from the town. The audience would not expect a countryman to turn out a real danger, cf. 866 n.

272 predators: lit. "wild animals", cf. 1401, 1459. But there is some attraction in Weil's *kekrymmenās* (M^{ac}) *thērās*, "the secret hunting"; cf. 1213 n., 1315 f., 1346.

273 Keep courage: *aphobos eche* is a poetic variant of the idiomatic *ech' hēsychos*, for which see Stevens 34 f.

275 What about your side: if 1268-70 and 1273-4 belong to the whole chorus, this line has to mean "How now? Can I still count on you?" (after this muddle). But it is naturally read as a turning from the one semichorus to the other; and *tade* in 1277 indicates a particular direction to be checked.

277 on the approach to the courtyard: the orchestra is apparently equated with the courtyard area.

278 your sector: addressed to the leader of the other semichorus.

280 The same result: lit. "you arrive at the same conclusion" (by asking me), or perhaps (as I do). Cf. *Hipp.* 273 (with Barrett), *Hec.* 748, *IA* 1002.

281-2 let me put my ear to the doors: so Phaedra does in *Hipp.* 567 ff.; but she hears things.

283-5 You in the house: on the attribution of these lines see 1264 n.

stain the slaughter-victim red: the variant "sacrificial knife" is inferior. Verbs meaning "to bloody" regularly have the victim's flesh as their object: *(kat)haimassō, (kat)haimatoō, phoinīssō*. In daily life a slaughter was normally a sacrifice, and in tragedy murder is sometimes portrayed in terms of sacrifice (562 n.), but *sphazō, sphagē* etc. do not in themselves have sacrificial implications. See e.g. 947, 1107, 1199, 1494, 1671.

286 They're not listening: she will not have called very loudly.

287 Have their swords - beauty: like Menelaus' at Troy (742 n.). The variant with plural verb arose because "have they become deaf" looked plausible after 1286. But a man cannot be "*kōphos* as to his sword": *xiphē* must be the subject.

292 sitting inactive: they are not really sitting down, but "sit" is often used to express or emphasize inactivity, cf. my n. on Hes. *Th.* 622.

293 One group wheel here etc.: the chorus cannot be left divided and stranded at the sides of the orchestra at the end of the song. It looks as if Electra directs the

semichoruses to change places, and while they are crossing over in the middle the manoeuvre is interrupted by Helen's cries, leaving the chorus reunited.

1296 Oyé, Pelasgian Argos: the audience will take this line and 1301 as the typical pair of last cries uttered by a character being killed behind the scenes (like Aesch. *Ag.* 1343/45, Soph. *El.* 1415/16, Eur. *HF* 749/54). In fact they are cries for help, of a type which may indeed serve as death-cries (*HF* 754) but may also precede them (Soph. *El.* 1404 f., 1409). We learn later that the killing was never accomplished. Similarly in *Antiope* (also a late play) Lycus utters cries for help and complains of being killed, but shortly afterwards is saved by the intervention of Hermes (fr. 48.50 ff. Kambitsis).

In real-life emergencies one shouted for neighbours and fellow-demesmen (Ar. *Clouds* 1321 ff. etc.; M. Davies, *ZPE* 48 [1982], 74); in tragedy for the whole city, cf. *Hcld.* 69, *Hec.* 1089, *HF* 754, *Antiope* l.c., etc.

1297 Did you hear that?: a typical reaction to the first cry, cf. *Med.* 1273, *Hec.* 1036, *El.* 747, 1166, etc. The rest of the line is similar to *Antiope* fr. 48.52 K. The MSS give this line and the next to Electra, 1299 f. to a semichorus. Electra should certainly sing 1299 f., and probably speak 1297 (cf. Soph. *El.* 1406), with the chorus-leader answering in 1298. Alternatively the chorus-leader might have both trimeters.

1299 Zeus' unfailing power: equivalent to "Zeus unfailingly powerful" (as e.g. 1242 *Dikēs sebas = semnē Dikē*), and so followed by masc. *epikouros*.

1301 Menelaus - help me: Clytaemestra shouts similarly for Aegisthus ("where are you?") at Soph. *El.* 1409.

1302-10 MSS ascribe to Electra or a semichorus. Probably all sing together, cf. 1311 and 1314.

1302 Slaughter her, slay her: bloodthirsty encouragement of the action inside, cf. Soph. *El.* 1415 f.; but the style, with the series of imperatives, is more like that of comic choruses on the warpath, Ar. *Ach.* 281-3, *Knights* 247 ff., *Birds* 365. (In tragedy also at *Rhes.* 675 f.) Cf. Dover on *Clouds* 1508.

1303 twofold: i.e. two. They dwell gleefully on the number of cutting edges.

1304 at grappling range: see LSJ *cheir* II.6e.

305 deserter of father: Sappho 16.10 "and she did not think
at all of her daughter or her dear parents". Cf. *II*.3.140.
deserter of husband: my *lipogameton* for MSS *lipogamon*
("deserter of marriage") improves the metre and gives a
better match with *lipopatora*. Stesichorus *PMG* 223.5 called
Tyndareos' daughters "bigamous, trigamous, deserters of
their men".
308 tears upon tears: 336-7 n.
309 iron missiles: spears and arrows. Only the heads were of
metal.

311-52 Hermione's return. Scenes in which a character for
whom a trap has been prepared in the house arrives and
is guided into it are sometimes quite short: Aesch. *Cho*.
838-54, *HF* 701-62, *Antiope* fr. 48 K. Longer examples
are *Hec*. 953-1022, *El*. 998-1146.
311 Quiet: the song is ended by a call for silence, as in
Hipp. 565, *Cycl*. 82, 624, Soph. *Phil*. 865.
313 in the middle of the killing: reinforcing the audience's
misconception.
314 our clamour: i.e. singing; the plot is about to advance,
and we must use spoken dialogue.
315 to walk smack into: a special sense of *eispaiō*, cf. *Rhes*.
560 and the analogous *emplēssō* (Pfeiffer on Call. fr.
75.37).
317-9 faces calm ... colour unrevealing ... eyes cast down:
as they all had masks on, changes of expression could be
registered only by deportment.
322 adorning: for *stephō* of offerings to the dead see Tucker
or Garvie on Aesch. *Cho*. 94.
323 her benevolence: for which she was told to pray, 119 f.
Hermione naively assumes that a prayer properly made is
automatically granted. Almost every line that she speaks
conveys her simplicity.
326 things are coming our way: deliberately ambiguous.
327 Speak no evil: see Bond on *HF* 1185 (p.368).
330 the yoke of necessity: a familiar metaphor, see Fraenkel
on *Ag*. 218, Barrett on *Hipp*. 1389-90. Again Electra
expresses herself ambiguously. She says nothing that is
not true, or almost true.
332 as suppliant at Helen's knees: Orestes has indeed been
doing this (1414), though Electra knows that things have

already gone further. The suggestion is that it was his cries that Hermione heard.

1333 Who? I am none the wiser if you don't say: doubtless the model for Housman's parody in his *Fragment of a Greek Tragedy*, "A shepherd's questioned mouth informed me that –" "What? For I know not yet what you will say." "Nor will you ever, if you interrupt." Cf. 750-2 n.

1335 wails aloud: *aneuphēmeō* (Soph. *Tr*. 783, Pl. *Phd*. 60a) is wrongly explained in LSJ. It means to break out in inauspicious or uncontrolled cries, to be *an-euphēmos*; it is not an *ana*- compound like *anaboaō* etc.

1342-3 to the struggle ... salvation lies in you: more double meanings.

I'll escort you: Electra has to leave the stage at the end of this scene on order to change into the Phrygian. She will not be seen again.

1344 I'm hurrying my feet: an Aeschylean phrase.

1347-8 Oh! Oh! – not for you: Willink deletes these lines; he thinks that Hermione disappears inside at 1345, Electra staying outside to deliver the remaining lines unheard by the victim or her captors (he compares *El*. 1139-46, *HF* 726-33). But in 1342 Electra said she would go in with Hermione, and she should not lag behind at 1345. If Hermione had completed her exit, she ought to have completed her exit line: the change of speaker in mid-line strongly suggests the actual sudden coup (cf. Soph. *Phil*. 974). The scene ends much more dramatically with 1347-8 retained. The MSS ascribe "Silence! – not for you" to Orestes, but it is implausible that he should either pop into view for a moment or be heard shouting this sentence from within. It is also unlikely that the audience was meant to see anything of the capture through the doorway.

1351 not worthless Phrygians: as at Troy.

1353-65 A short choral intermezzo before the events indoors are explained in full. Satisfaction at the justice of Helen's presumed death is an expected theme; cf. Aesch. *Cho*. 935 ff., Eur. *El*. 1147 ff., *HF* 735 ff. But the chorus is more aware than usual that it does not yet know the facts for certain. Until it is proved that Helen is dead, it feels there is still danger from Argos, and its lively dancing is not motivated by joy (as in *Cho.* and *HF* ll.cc., *El.* 859 ff.) but by the desire to avert public suspicion that anything untoward is going on – an idea borrowed from *Od.* 23.133 ff., though scarcely appropriate at a house whose owners are supposed to be committing suicide. And any passer-by who listened to the words of their song would know the very thing they wish to conceal. Metre: mainly dochmiac, alternating with iambic trimeters.

353 stamping: *ktypos* generally signifies percussive noise. At *Hec.* 1113 it may be used of purely vocal clamour, but here it is likely to refer to vigorous dancing. Cf. 137, 141, 182, *IA* 438, Tim. *Pers.* 200, and perhaps Soph. *OC* 1500.

354 this blood-deed: the model of *Od.* 23.137 may account for Euripides' use of this illogical phrase implying that the murder definitely has taken place. The notion intended is presumably that Argives might be alerted by cries from Helen in time to save her.

357-9 truly see the slain Helen ... or else hear word: i.e. either see the body displayed on the ekkyklema or hear a "messenger's speech". The second alternative foreshadows what is about to happen, without giving any hint that it will happen in a wholly unexpected way.

361-2 the gods' disapprobation: the common English use of "nemesis" does not correspond to the early Greek sense of the word, which is "disapproval", "indignation", "resentment", whether by men or by gods, at some form of behaviour. The gods' indignation issues in punishment, and in that sense it has "visited Helen", but this does not make *nemesis* mean "punishment".

364-5 because of ... Paris: Euripides liked tracing the woes of Troy back to their origin; see T.C.W. Stinton, *Euripides and the Judgement of Paris* (1965). Here it tends to detract from Helen's responsibility by reminding us that Aphrodite brought about her seduction for her own reasons.
Idaean: Paris was exposed on Ida as a baby and brought up there (Eur. *Alexandros; IA* 1284-90), and it was there that he judged the three goddesses (*Hel.* 24 ff., etc.).

366-8 But the bars – things inside: there is an apparent contradiction between these lines and 1371 f., where the Phrygian seems to be saying that he has escaped by way of the roof, not the front door. The ancient commentator shrewdly conjectured that later actors, afraid of hurting themselves by jumping off the roof, substituted entrance through the door and interpolated 1366-8. Other ancient scholars argued that 1371 f. were to be interpreted differently, for example, of roofs inside the palace which the audience could not see. Modern commentators are at variance. My view is that 1371 f. should indeed describe an unconventional way of arriving on stage: triglyphs (carved beam-ends) belong on the face of a building and should be visible to the audience (cf. *IT* 113, *Ba.* 1214). If the man was merely describing an internal route that brought him to the door, we might have expected these details, if anywhere, at 1499. The height of the stage building in the fifth century is not known, though it was too high to scale from below without a ladder (*IT* 96-8), and *Phoen.* 90 seems to refer to an upper room (cf. Ar. *Wasps* 379 ff.). There is no need to suppose that the Phrygian was expected to jump down; he may have let himself down by his arms and dropped the last few feet, or the façade may have offered some hand- and toe-holds by which he could clamber down. It is even conceivable that he used a rope. And it may be that he does not start on top of the roof but wriggles out through one of the spaces between the triglyphs; cf. *IT* 113 with commentators.

Yet we cannot simply excise 1366-8. Something is needed to mark off the Phrygian's song from the chorus', and to introduce him. Perhaps only 1366 is interpolated. "Is coming out" in 1367 is a surprisingly neutral way of adverting to a man appearing from the roof; but such announcements became very stylized, cf. Hourmouziades 142.

the bars ... are clanking: for this audible warning of an impending entry cf. *Ion* 515, *Hel.* 859. It becomes commonplace in New Comedy. Cf. Taplin (1977) 71 n.3.

Be quiet: 1311 n.

1369-1502 The Phrygian's aria. Our astonishment at the manner of his arrival is compounded when he bursts into song instead of following the conventional procedures of a tragic newsbringer (cf. on 844-956, 852 ff.). But Euripides has carefully prepared for this in 1110-2,

1126-8: Helen's attendants were not to be mere bystanders at the assassination, they were to be terrorized and routed, so it is no wonder that this fellow uses such an emotional medium of discourse. He does not come out with the aim of telling people the news; the chorus has to guide him into this role. This has the advantage that he need not, like a normal newsbringer, announce at the outset what has actually happened, viz. that Helen is not dead but vanished. This surprise is saved up for the end. On Euripides' liking for monodies see on 982-1012. The longer ones (and this is much the longest, if we disregard the chorus' interposed questions) mostly occur in his last plays, and show considerable metrical diversity, which implies elaborate multiformity of music. See West (1982) 135-7. This is the kind of thing Aristophanes was parodying in *Frogs* 1331-63.

Normally monodies are sung by important characters (especially women), not by anonymous slaves. But the Phrygian is a novel type of character altogether. Seven years earlier Euripides had given his chorus of Trojan women no special national characteristics. More recently he had developed a taste for exoticism (harking back to Phrynichus and Aeschylus); it is seen in his chorus of Phoenician women (gratuitously introduced in a play set in Thebes), and later in *Bacchae*. (Cf. H.H. Bacon, *Barbarians in Greek Tragedy* (1961) 115 ff.) Like the Phoenician chorus, the Phrygian sings and behaves in an explicitly oriental way (1370, 1374, 1385, 1396, 1426, 1507 n.). Unlike them, he is a semi-comic character, ludicrous in his unmanly fear and his native lack of dignity. In comedy he would have been made to talk pidgin Greek, and Timotheus ventures this in his *Persians* (*PMG* 791.150-61); but it is not the way of tragedy. The language of the song is articulate, high-flown, typical of late Euripidean lyric. Its incongruity in the mouth of such a character is part of the humour of this delectable scene.

370 moccasins: *eumāris* is a foreign loan-word denoting an Asiatic, unisex type of shoe made of deerskin. Darius' ghost wears yellow ones (Aesch. *Pers.* 660).

373 gone, gone: either agreeing with "timbers" or a vague nominative neuter plural meaning "everything's finished". The invasion of the house seems to be run together in his mind with the sack of Troy (1381 ff.).

1377-8 <u>by flying - or to the sea</u>: he feels that nowhere on
earth is safe. The extravagant cosmic alternatives are a
Euripidean cliché, see Barrett on *Hipp.* 1290-3. (Cf. also
above on 982.)
<u>the white heaven</u>: for the sense of *polios* see my n. on
Hes. *Op.* 477.
1379 <u>the bull-headed</u>: Ocean is the great river surrounding the
earth in the traditional poetic cosmology, and river-gods
were represented with bull's horns in art. Cf. *Ion* 1261
with Owen's n.
<u>winds in his arms</u>: infinite air "embraces the earth in its
pliant arms" in fr. 941.
1380 <u>footman of Helen, Idaean soul</u>: the high tragic phrases
have an effect of parody. Aristophanes could have written
the line.
1384 <u>with barbarian cry</u>: like the Phoenician chorus, *Phoen.*
1301.
<u>chariot melody</u>: *harmateios nomos* was the technical name
of a traditional melodic form used by Stesichorus and said
to have been invented by Olympus. It was in the
Phrygian mode and a high register, exciting in character,
and associated (but not exclusively) with aulos-playing.
See *CQ* 21 (1971) 309-11 (adding now a reference to Phot.
Lex. [ed. Theodoridis 1982] *a* 2835). For Euripides the
Phrygian association is the dominant one.
1385 <u>all because of the bird-born</u>: cf. *IA* 793 "all because of
you, the child of the long-necked swan" etc.
1386 <u>swan-plume</u>: oddly transferred to Helen from the
swan-mating of Zeus and Leda that produced her. A
deliberate absurdity?
1387 <u>lion-cub</u>: 1213 n.
<u>Ill-Helen</u>: modelled on "Ill-Paris" (*Il.* 3.39 = 13.769, Alcm.
PMG 77). Again in *IA* 1316.
1389 <u>Apolline</u>: Apollo and Poseidon built the walls of Troy; see
Stevens on *Andr.* 1009 ff. In the *Iliad* Apollo is the chief
pro-Trojan god.
<u>Vengeance incarnate</u>: after Aesch. *Ag.* 749. Medea is
called an Erinys in *Med.* 1260, as is Cassandra in *Tro.*
457.
1390 <u>the dirges</u>: those heard at the fall of Troy. Some take the
genitive not as exclamatory with *ottotoi* but as defining
tlāmōn, "unhappy in your dirges".
1392 <u>the riding</u>: this can hardly be in apposition to *Dardaniā*

or mean "the place where he rode". If the text is sound, it is presumably a separate exclamation, like Soph. *El.* 504 "O ancient toil-laden riding of Pelops". But no story of riding by Ganymede is known. His grandfather owned vast herds of fine horses (*Il.* 20.219-29), and Tros his father received a new breed from Zeus in compensation for Ganymede's abduction (5.265 f.). Heracles sacked Troy on account of Laomedon's horses (5.640-2, [Hes.] fr. 43a.64). In epic formula Trojans are *hippodamoi*, Ilios and Dardania are *eupōlos*.

1393 **Tell us plainly:** the increasingly incoherent and inconsequential threnody has to be diverted to a more informative path. The Phrygian adjusts gradually.

1394 **[For what you said - certainty]:** this line is omitted in Π 19 and was absent from many ancient copies; cf. 957-9 n. The chorus' other interpellations are all of a single line.

1395 **Ailinon:** see Bond on *HF* 348. In explaining why he has begun with a lengthy lament, the Phrygian maintains the impression that Helen is dead.

1396 **to inaugurate death:** an obscure expression, but *Andr.* 1197-9 may lend it some support. Kirchhoff's emendation "at the death of rulers" is attractive.

1399 **Hades-swords:** the genitive *Hāidā* is used as if an adjective. See Fraenkel on *Ag.* 1235.

1400-1 **There came - a matching pair:** modelled on Aesch. *Cho.* 937 f.

1402 **the son of the Commander:** the Phrygian of course knows all about Agamemnon, but Orestes is new to him. His wartime experiences provide his standards of comparison (1404, 1479-81).

1404 **like Odysseus:** Odysseus' cleverness is as a rule portrayed unfavourably in Euripides. For Pylades' inventiveness cf. 1158-60.

1409 **the bowman:** in the *Iliad* he wounds several Greek heroes with his arrows, and in the *Aethiopis* he killed Achilles.

1416 **Up at a run they leapt:** it may or may not be relevant that Phrygians are accustomed to prostration before royals (1507), not knee-clasping.

1424 **matricidal snake:** after 479. The mixture of metaphors is probably not intentional grotesquerie.

1426-8 **Phrygian, Phrygian ... a breeze, a breeze ... of Helen, of Helen:** the concentration of anadiploses is

279

accurately parodied in *Frogs* 1352-3. But it is really self-parody to start with.

1429 a roundel of firm-set plumes: an exotic touch. Egyptian, Assyrian and Persian kings had themselves fanned by slaves. The plumes (peacock or ostrich) were attached to a round or semicircular centrepiece at the end of a handle. On a 4th-century vase in the Hermitage a female slave holding just such a fan stands beside Helen, who is seated on a throne with a footstool (*Or.* 1440), with Paris on her other side in his Phrygian costume (*Compte-rendu de la Commission archéol. de St.-Pétersbourg*, Atlas 1861 pl. v 2.1). On a 5th-century vase in the British Museum (London E 447, *ARV²* 1035) the Phrygian Midas is similarly enthroned with a female slave fanning him. F. Chapouthier, *RÉA* 46 (1944) 209-16, adduces some comparable scenes in oriental art (ladies being fanned while spinning).

1431 ⟨golden⟩ distaff: the noun is too bare without an adjective, and the metre is unsatisfactory; my insertion gives an anapaestic dimeter. For Helen's golden distaff see *Od.* 4.131. That passage is Euripides' model for this spinning scene, and the word *klismos* in 1440 comes from there.

1433 making for the floor: as it grew in length, both twisted together and pulled down by the whirling spindle dangling from its lower end. The distaff in Helen's left hand had the unspun yarn wound round it.

1434 finery for the grave-mound: Euripides combines the Homeric picture of Helen spinning with the motif from earlier in the play of offerings for Clytaemestra. (For offerings of clothing at tombs cf. Thuc. 3.58.4.) The purple cloth adds to the splendour of the scene evoked (cf. 840 n.) and to our impression of Helen's luxury.

1439 set down your foot: from the footstool on which her feet rest (*Od.* 4.136, cf. 1429 n.; a common article in vase paintings).

1441-2 ancient hearth-seat: i.e. anciently established hearth. The central hearth is the holiest place in the house, the best place for a suppliant to sit (*Od.* 7.153, Thuc. 1.136.3), but also a place of sacrifice (Aesch. *Ag.* 1056 f.). They had to separate Helen from her servants.

1444 led her, led her: here the anadiplosis is expressive, as in *Ba.* 1065 *katēgen ēgen ēgen*. Note the vivid present tense (1005 n.); again in 1461, 1475 (?).

1447 Won't you clear off: the absence of a verb of speaking is extraordinary. Possibly something has fallen out, but there is no unclarity.

elsewhere: *allāi* (cf. *Ion* 162) is far superior to *all' aei*. Neither "but Phrygians are always cowards" nor "are Phrygians always cowards?" makes sense here.

1449 stables: as an improvised prison again in *Ba.* 509 f., 618. On the importance of the stable being a secure place cf. Xen. *Eq.* 4.1-2.

verandahs: lit. "sitting-out places"; cf. LSJ. We cannot tell just what Euripides had in mind, but they must be outlying rooms of some sort. One scholiast takes them as latrines.

1452 the next phase: the imperfect *egigneto* anticipates that the reply will not include the final climax.

1453 Idaean Mother: a Mother goddess, associated especially with mountains, was widely worshipped in Anatolia under various local names. (One form of the cult took root in Greece in the 5th century, cf. Dodds on *Ba.* 78-79.) The Phrygian cult round Mt. Ida was well known (Strabo 10.3.12 etc.). "Idaean Mother" was doubtless an established title among Greek-speakers in the area, though not found again till early Hellenistic times. This was the obvious deity for the Phrygian to cry out to. Cf. Tim. *Pers.* (*PMG* 791) 124 ff.

1457 purple-bordered: *amphiporphyros* is a poetic variation on the usual term *periporphyros*.

1465 She screamed aloud: this corresponds to the (more articulate) cries heard at 1296/1301.

1468 her golden sandal-sole: another touch of rich colour. The sole was what she presented to the view in her flight.

1469 flinging his fingers in her hair: for this unheroic but practical way of controlling a woman cf. Aesch. *Sept.* 328, Eur. *Andr.* 710, *Hec.* 1166, *Tro.* 882, *Hel.* 116, *IA* 790 f., 1366; extended to Persian captives by Tim. *Pers.* 144. The clash between trochaic and iambic rhythm in 1469 f. suggests that "Orestes" may be a gloss that has replaced a descriptive word or phrase, e.g. *ho tou stratēlatā* "the Commander's son".

1473 And where were you: the question sidetracks the Phrygian so that the main story is held at the peak of suspense. For *ēste* as the correct Attic form of "you were", see Fraenkel on *Ag.* 542.

1476 slings: the meaning of *ankylai* here is a guess. In Aesch. fr. 281a.35 Radt it may signify a cleaving weapon, but the line is incomplete and the word may be an adjective qualifying a lost noun. In both of the other tragic occurrences (Soph. *OT* 204, Eur. *IT* 1408) it is a twisted cord (bow-string) or cable. Javelins with a sling attachment are *mesankyla*, "with *ankylai* at the middle", and the slinging action of throwing the kottabos is expressed by *ankylēi* (Anacr. *PMG* 415) or *ap' ankylēs*.

1480 triple-helmèd: what this means is obscure; cf. Dodds on *Ba*. 123. Hector's helmet has three layers of material in *Il*. 11.353.

1481 at Priam's gates: this simply means those of Troy. Possibly the poet is thinking of the battle for Achilles' body at the Scaean Gates, in which Ajax distinguished himself (*Aethiopis*).

1483 showed up outstandingly: it sounds as if the Phrygians fought heroically, until the word "inferior" pricks the bubble with comic effect.

1491 just as the mother – to the ground: lit. "upon the ground-falling murder of the mother", a phrase cunningly contrived to convince us that Helen is dead.

1492 lacking only the thyrsus: cf. 319 n. The simile implies that they look as if they are about to tear her limb from limb. She was already a "cub" in 1213.

1496 O Zeus, O Earth, O Light and Dark: a call to the all-seeing and omnipresent cosmic powers to bear witness to the truth of his statement. Cf. *Med*. 148 "did you hear, O Zeus and Earth and Light"; Barrett on *Hipp*. 601; *Il*. 19.258 f. (Zeus, Earth, Sun, Erinyes). The formula reflects Zeus' original nature as the sky; see my n. on Hes. *Op*. 267 (with the addendum p. 383).

1497 either by magic drugs etc.: emphasizing that the disappearance is miraculous; Helen did not simply slip away while her attackers were distracted. In *Od*. 4.220 ff. Helen has marvellous drugs which she was given in Egypt on the way home from Troy, but Euripides does not seem to be thinking of this.
sorcerers': *magos* and derivatives had come to have this general sense; cf. *Supp*. 1110, *IT* 1338, Soph. *OT* 387, Hp. *Morb. Sacr*. 1.10, 26, 31, 18.6 Grensemann, Gorg. *Hel*. 10.
gods' deceits: or "theft". The true explanation is

mentioned as one possibility, but we must wait till 1633 for confirmation.

1498 **What followed, I know not:** note the common idiomatic use of *ouketi*, not "I no longer know" but "my knowledge does not extend to". There is nothing more for us to be told (it only remains for the Phrygian to get himself out), but we are left aware that the drama is still continuing indoors.

1502 **all to no avail:** similarly in *Hel.* 603 this is the newsbringer's immediate reaction to the disappearance of (the phantom) Helen – the whole war has been for nothing. The Phrygian has no real reason for supposing that she is gone for ever, but Euripides has confided in him.

1503–36 Dialogue of Orestes and the Phrygian. The Phrygian has to serve as informant not only to the chorus but also to Menelaus; and in any case he must be sent away soon so that the serious action can proceed. Euripides might simply have made him say at the end of his song "Well, I can't stay any longer, I'm off". But he has not shown any thought of seeking Menelaus, only of escaping as far away as possible. The problem is solved far more skilfully in the little scene that follows. It is both functional and hilarious. In dialogue the Phrygian emerges as a witty fool, akin to the typical slave in comedy, and with a similar talent for philosophical observations (1509, 1523). There is no funnier scene in Greek tragedy. For the trochaic metre cf. 729–806 n.

1503 **another novel situation:** cf. *Tro.* 1118. The words emphasize the eventfulness of the drama. For the rest, this entrance-announcement is hardly more than a versified stage-direction, and might have been omitted without disadvantage.

1506 **from my sword:** actually it was Pylades who was dealing with the Phrygians.

1507 **the barbarian procedure:** similarly the chorus in *Phoen.* 293 f. prostrate themselves (or, more strictly, bow to the ground· from a kneeling position) and explain that they are following their native custom. Aeschylus' Persians do it less self-consciously (152, cf. 588; Hdt. 1.134.1, 7.136.1).

283

1510 for people to aid Menelaus: the reply proves that this is
the meaning (not "shouting to Menelaus to give aid").
Though not present, Menelaus is the person really being
attacked.

1512 So it was right – perished: here and in 1534 and 1536
Orestes apparently speaks as if he had killed Helen. But
he knows he has not (1580 ff., 1614), and there is no
reason for him to pretend to the Phrygian that he has. If
one wrote *diōllyto* or *diollytai* here ("so it is right that
she was/is being killed"), it would be possible to suppose
that Orestes thinks Helen is hiding somewhere in the
house and will soon be caught. Otherwise it seems
necessary to convict Euripides of carelessness.

1513 to stab: the MSS "to die with" is less convincing. The
general idea is "if you could have killed her three times
over I would approve even more".

1515 Phrygians and all: for this idiom with the dative of *autos*
(especially in contexts of destruction) cf. Stevens 52 f.
There is a deliberate absurdity in treating the Phrygians
as an appendage of Greece.

1517 I swear: the aorist answers Orestes' *omoson*, marking the
oath as something conclusive. Cf. *Cycl.* 266, Soph. *Phil.*
1289; below, 1672.
which you can expect me to: he is *philopsychos*, so
concerned with saving his life that he runs away from
danger. For the assurance that the thing sworn by is
held in especial esteem by the swearer cf. *Il.* 15.40, Pl.
Alc.I 109d, Theoc. 6.22.

1520 Are you afraid – Gorgon: i.e. are you frightened of just
looking at it?

1524 You're saved by your intellect: the Phrygian's remark
suddenly makes a link between the two of them.

1526 I'm going to reconsider: the Phrygian thinks he may be
going to kill him after all, but Orestes is changing his
mind about letting Menelaus hear what has happened. It
is dramatically necessary that he should.

1528 you're neither – among men: cf. Aesch. *Sept.* 197 "man,
woman, and whatever is in between". One would expect
Helen's chamber-attendants to be eunuchs, but Euripides
makes no allusion to this: the present line is a comment
on the man's cowardice. He lacks manly qualities without
having the excuse of being a woman.

1530 when Argos – sharp: cf. *Hcld.* 339.

1532 **with his dandy blond shoulder-locks:** Menelaus is *xanthos* in Homer. Euripides has portrayed him on the model of the elegant type of general deprecated by Archilochus 114 (tall, striding, with dandy locks and trimmed beard).

1533 **lead them against this house:** this is the basis for my stage-direction before 1549. Cf. 1621 n.

1535 **together with - this business:** Paley's deletion of this line is unjustified. All three need to be saved, and Euripides does well to keep the issue before us in these terms.

1536 **as well as his wife:** see 1512 n.

1537-48 A notional interval is necessary before Menelaus can arrive. The brief song responds metrically with 1353-65. This device of delayed antistrophe occurs in *Hipp.*, *Phoen.*, *Rhes.* (twice), and often in comedy; see West (1982) 80. There are other parallel features between the two strophes: both begin *Iō iō*, and have anaphora in the next line, and both end with a return to an original sin ("because of that accursed Paris" - "because of the fall of Myrtilus").

1539 **What do we do?:** at moments of crisis choruses sometimes consider active intervention, but stop short of making it: Aesch. *Ag.* 1347 ff. (where raising the alarm in Argos is the first suggestion), Eur. *Med.* 1275, *Hipp.* 782, *HF* 747. Here the device is rather incongruous (arousing the city's attention is the opposite of the chorus' policy in 1354-6; in any case Menelaus is already being told, and is expected to bring an Argive posse with him), and it seems to be used merely to emphasize that the play's climax is imminent.

1540 **Safer so:** choruses generally play safe; cf. *Hipp.* 785, Aesch. *Ag.* 1347.

1541 **this smoke:** for unexpected phenomena during a choral performance cf. *HF* 904 ff. (house shaking), *Ba.* 585 ff. (earthquake, fire at Semele's tomb), Soph. *OC* 1456 ff. (thunder and lightning). It is not essential to suppose that the smoke is visible to the audience, any more than at *Hec.* 823.

1543 **ready to fire the house:** at 1149 this was planned as a second best if the attempt on Helen failed. Since 1203 the aim has been to pressurize Menelaus, and the threat to burn the house serves to increase his discomfiture. In theatrical terms it adds to the spectacle and excitement; cf. the (revised) ending of *Clouds*, and *Tro.* 1256 ff., *Ba.* 595.

1545-8 <u>God controls the outcome</u> etc: divine intervention may yet produce a surprise ending, but at the moment the story of the Pelopid house looks like one long vendetta which is about to destroy it finally. For *daimōn* (here translated "God") cf. 341-4 n. That the gods or Zeus control the outcome (*telos*) is a commonplace, see my n. on Hes. *Op.* 669; only the sharpest in the audience will have picked up the hint of a *deus ex machina* conclusion.

1546 <u>that of the vengeance-demon:</u> the MSS *di' alastorōn* satisfies neither sense nor metre (1363), and is evidently affected by *di' haimatōn* below. The scholiast apparently read *alastōr*, which is acceptable with a short syllable supplied in place of *di'*. On the word cf. 336-7 n.

1547 <u>These halls have fallen:</u> for this idea cf. Aesch. *Ag.* 1532, *Cho.* 263, *Eum.* 516, Eur. *Hipp.* 812.

1548 <u>Myrtilus:</u> 988 n.

1549-1693 Final confrontation and resolution. Menelaus arrives, having heard the Phrygian's report. He discounts the miraculous disappearance of Helen and assumes that she has been killed. He finds himself locked out of the palace and forced to deal with an Orestes who holds all the cards. The tone of the dialogue is very different from that of their previous encounter. Menelaus is pompous and indignant, and has shed his intellectualism. Orestes, who was at Menelaus' knees and is now above his head, is insolently self-confident.

Just as everything seems about to go over the precipice, with Menelaus admitting defeat and the palace on the point of being fired, Apollo appears in the sky with Helen beside him. A 41-line speech from the god suffices to compose the quarrel, explain about Helen, solve the problem of Orestes' guilt, assign him Agamemnon's throne, and settle two marriages - in short, to put everything right so that the play can stop. All that remains is for Orestes and Menelaus gratefully to accept Apollo's solutions and for everyone to withdraw.

Euripides likes *deus ex machina* endings, especially

in the melodramas where everything turns out well (*Ion*, *IT*, *Helen*, *Hypsipyle*, *Antiope*, and *IA* in the version of fr. 857). They do not occur in Aeschylus, and in Sophocles only in *Philoctetes*. Their structure is generally as in *Orestes*, a substantial address by the god followed by brief, admiring acceptances and an anapaestic exodus, with the chorus having the final word. The god's functions in these scenes are principally (*a*) to tell people things that they cannot otherwise know about what has been happening – especially about divine actions and motives; (*b*) to issue such instructions and predictions as will tie the plot of the play up with other traditions about what happened to these persons, subsequent reigns, marriages, descendants, cults, etc.; (*c*) to deal with loose ends in the drama as it stands. Occasionally, as in *Philoctetes* and *Orestes*, the poet has spellbound the audience by threatening an outcome incompatible with firmly established tradition, and here, under the (*b*) heading, the god has to put a stop to the irregular proceedings and prescribe what everyone knows really happened. The god chosen is always one relevant to the play. Here none is more appropriate than Apollo, Orestes' patron, who has been the object of so much criticism earlier. This criticism, like the impossible plot, has to be cancelled before we go home.

1549–53 Well, now I can also see: an abnormal entrance announcement (cf. 348 n.), perhaps for the sake of explicit reference to the barring of the doors. Euripides did not want to write another scene in trochaic tetrameters, but by putting the announcement in this metre he sets the tone. Cf. again 729–806 n.

1551–2 You can't – you Atridae: this is not necessarily shouted so that they can hear. But the doors do get bolted.
bolt the staples: lit. "penetrate them together" (join them by penetrating) with bolts.
A man enjoying success: a late reprise of the motif in 86, 354, 449.

1557 is – not dead, but vanished: he has come believing that she *is* dead; this is not what he has been told, but what he infers from what he has been told. He thinks that Orestes has somehow concealed the murder from the foolish Phrygian, but he himself is not to be taken in.

287

1561 <u>Someone open the house:</u> this is perhaps addressed to servants inside, cf. *Med*. 1314, *IT* 1304, *Phoen*. 1067 f. If so, there is then a pause during which nothing happens, and Menelaus finally orders his followers to force the doors. But one might expect the text to be more explicit about the first order having no effect.

1562 <u>press through:</u> this shows that house doors in drama opened inwards. Cf. A.M. Dale, *JHS* 77 (1957), 205 = *Collected Papers* (1969) 104; Hourmouziades 16 f.

1564-6 <u>[and take possession – my consort]:</u> these inept lines are particularly unsuitable after *alla* in 1562, which implies "it is too late to do anything for Helen, but let us *at least* try to save Hermione". The interpolator may have been influenced by 1585. He took the second half of 1566 from 1556. Willink oddly deletes 1563-4 ("so we may at least recover my daughter, with whom ..."). This makes Menelaus assume groundlessly that Hermione is dead, and the language remains clumsy.

1567 <u>You there:</u> a startlingly rude way for a young man to accost a senior relative. The situation resembles *Med*. 1314 ff., where Jason, having heard that Medea has killed their children, is trying to get into the house when she suddenly addresses him from above, telling him to leave the doors alone. On the tragedians' use of the roof see Hourmouziades 29-33, Taplin (1977) 440 f. It was rare enough to be a distinct surprise for the audience.

1574 <u>beleaguered:</u> as if defending a city wall. Cf. 762.

1580 <u>robbed by the gods:</u> cf. 1497. Orestes does not intend the phrase in the literal sense which presently turns out to be appropriate.

1583 <u>Done what? – to be afraid:</u> cf. 757. But why does Menelaus feel a *new* fear of what Orestes will say he *wishes he had* done? Perhaps, convinced that he has killed Helen, he thinks he is about to admit to some yet more frightful design (such as Achilles' in *Il*. 22.347, for instance).

1589-90 These lines must precede the transition from Helen to Hermione in 1586; they refer to the killing of Helen, not that of Hermione, who does not belong in the class of "bad women".

1587 <u>The mother-killer – another:</u> a variation on 1579 (again as a response to "I will kill your child") for the sake of a different riposte. 1589 has now brought the matricide to mind.

592 <u>He says yes in silence:</u> Pylades and Hermione are played by non-speaking extras in this scene. The actor who played both parts earlier is now needed to be Apollo.

595 <u>your father's:</u> or "our ancestral".

598 <u>Oh, oh, don't do it:</u> the closest parallel for this urgent protest is Soph. *Phil.* 1300 (just after *all' ou ti chairōn* = *Or.* 1593).

602 <u>touching lustral vessels:</u> before making sacrifices on behalf of the city. The *chernips* is for ritual hand-washing at the start of the ceremony, but will itself be polluted by a polluted person, cf. Aesch. *Eum.* 656, Soph. *OT* 240, Dem. 20.158.

603 <u>before battle:</u> as e.g. *Il.* 2.400 ff., Aesch. *Sept.* 43, 379, Eur. *Hcld.* 399, 673, 821, *Phoen.* 174, 1255, *Rhes.* 30; W.K. Pritchett, *The Greek State at War* iii (1979) 83-90; Burkert (1985) 60.

604 <u>my hands are pure. – But not your heart:</u> this untraditional antithesis also in *Hipp.* 317. The concept of purity of mind was of recent development, see Parker 323.

606 <u>Lucky man:</u> fortunate in having a mother worthy of respect. Cf. 541.

608 <u>You are false:</u> a somewhat unnatural answer, preparing for the inversion in the next line (cf. 1525-6). The insertion of *d'* ("But –") would ease it.

613 <u>O unhappy Helen:</u> Menelaus takes stock of his whole situation for a few moments before admitting "you've got me".

614-5 <u>only to be slaughtered ... after I'd toiled endlessly:</u> cf. 1500-2.

616 <u>I have been treated outrageously:</u> a standard phrase of formal protest (*Alc.* 816, *Ba.* 642, *IA* 847, Soph. *OC* 595, 892, Ar. *Wealth* 967).

617 <u>You've got me:</u> a wrestling metaphor, cf. Ar. *Ach.* 571 and above on 265.
<u>You caught yourself, by being a swine:</u> cf. the Clouds' reproach to Strepsiades, *Clouds* 1454 f. (just before the house-burning finale), but also Aesch. *Cho.* 923.

618 <u>Ahoy there, Electra:</u> he shouts down into the building; the unseen Electra is not to be left out of the action. Menelaus' admission of defeat ought to mean that he goes to address the Argives, not that the house-burning goes ahead. This development, though illogical, is dramatically

justified in that it brings the crisis to the highest possible pitch before Apollo's intervention, rather as in the *Iliad* the danger that the ships will go up in flames is all but realized before Achilles takes action.

1621 O land of the Danaans: the cry for help need not imply the presence of a body of Argives (cf. 1296 n.), but Menelaus had probably brought some with him (1533 n.), and excitement is maximized if there is now a rush at the palace. Without this, these four lines merely hold up the action. Cf. the first Hypothesis to the play ("set himself to storm the palace"), and *IT* 1422 ff.

knightly: lit. horsy. Cf. 1000 n.

1625 Menelaus, take the edge off your temper: as in *IT* 1435, *Hel.* 1642, *Antiope* fr. 48.67 K., the god calls a halt to action that is proceeding at a fast pace; there is no time for the entrance-announcement that introduces some other divine epiphanies. See Halleran 24 f. There can be no doubt that Apollo and Helen appear at a higher level than the people on the roof: she is in the sky (1631), and he is conducting her (1684). On the staging see Introduction V.

There is now a spectacular tableau on four levels, unique in ancient drama: the chorus in the orchestra; Menelaus and his followers in battle array before the house; the conspirators with their swords and torches on the roof, probably symmetrically stationed on either side of their captive; and the two beautiful deities above them all. Perhaps about forty persons in total.

1626 I am Phoebus: gods regularly introduce themselves, cf. *Hipp.* 1285, *Andr.* 1232, *Supp.* 1183, etc.

1629 As for Helen: the other visible figure has to be explained before anything else.

1631 at the gates of heaven: i.e. about to enter it; cf. the gates of Hades, 1019 n. Those of heaven are mentioned in *Il.* 5.749 = 8.393. Apart from this excellent marginal variant *pylais* in M, the MSS have *ptychais* by anticipation of 1636.

1633 I rescued her: such rescues were familiar from Homer. Apollo had no special concern for Helen; it is merely for dramatic economy that the poet has her rescued by him rather than by, for instance, the Dioscuri.

1634 at my father Zeus' bidding: Zeus himself never appears *ex machina* – he only deals with mortals through intermediaries - but it is often mentioned that what is being communicated is his will (*Andr.* 1269, *El.* 1248, etc.).

635 Zeus' daughter: the form *Zēnos* is used for the sake of the "etymologizing" connection with *zēn* "to live". This sense was already heard in Zeus' name in Aesch. *Supp.* 584 f. (see Friis Johansen & Whittle on 585), Eur. *Tro.* 770 f. As a historical etymology it is false; but the poets in such cases had no idea of inquiring into the evolution of their language, only of identifying an essential aspect of a god's or a person's nature which had somehow embodied itself in his or her name.

636 the vales of heaven: also *Hel.* 44, 605, *Phaethon* 174, *Phoen.* 84, a Euripidean development from Homer's "vales of Olympus" (*Il.* 11.77, 20.22). *Aithēr* in tragedy is "air", "sky", "heaven", in all their functions.

637 a saviour for sailors: a traditional function of her brothers the Dioscuri from Indo-European times (as of the Aśvins, the twin equestrian sons of Dyaus in the Rigveda); cf. *h.Hom.* 33.6 ff., Alc. 34.5 ff., Eur. *El.* 992, 1241, 1347 ff., *Hel.* 1495 ff., 1664 f. Helen as a goddess was associated with them (Pind. *O.* 3.1, Eur. *Hel.* 1666-9, below on 1688), but not in this role, and it may be an *ad hoc* innovation by Euripides; otherwise it is hard to explain why he did not mention it in *Hel.* l.c. However, there was a sailors' superstition, possibly ancient, that a double corposant = the Dioscuri (good sign), a single one = Helen (bad sign) (Plin. *HN* 2.101, Stat. *Theb.* 7.792 with schol., *Silv.* 3.2.8-12; cf. Sosibius *FGrH* 595 F 20), and a goddess who is destructive to sailors must also have the power to save them.

638 Take another wife: there is no tradition that he did so, and if Euripides had known one he would have named the lady. In other accounts Helen lives out her natural life on earth with Menelaus.
Menelaus: the vocative is strangely absent in the Greek. Willink suggests that 1638-42 belong after 1663, where no vocative is required. I suspect that Euripides originally wrote the lines in that context but moved them here when he expanded the speech; see 1643-52 n.

639 the gods' instrument: her purpose on earth being fulfilled, she is to stay no longer. Cf. Introduction II.

291

1641-2 Earth's oppressive ... complement of mortals: as in *Hel.* 36 ff. (cf. *El.* 1282), Euripides follows the story in the *Cypria* (fr. 1) that Zeus conceived the war to give the Earth-goddess relief from overpopulation.

1643-52 These details of Orestes' rehabilitation look like an expansion, as the rest of the speech implies a simpler conception of his destiny: he is to marry, with no mention of any delay; he is to rule in Argos forthwith (1660), and Apollo will put things right between him and the city. The vocative in 1653 points to a change of addressee in the original draft, which may have run 1625-37, 1660-3, 1638-42, 1664-5, 1653-9.

1645 live on Parrhasian ground: in southern Arcadia. There was a town Orestheion or Oresthasion, a few miles east of the later Megalopolis. The similarity of its name to Orestes' gave rise to the legend that he had fled to that region (cf. Pherecydes *FGrH* 3 F 135, Eur. *El.* 1273-5, and the location of his grave at Tegea in Hdt. 1.67-8).

for a year's full circle: in *El.* l.c. Orestes goes to Arcadia after his trial at Athens, and apparently remains there, being forbidden to dwell in Argos (1250). Here Arcadia and Athens are combined with assumption of the Argive throne, so the exile is limited to a year – a typical period in myth (Parker 376, 378, 386, 391; Nicolaus of Damascus *FGrH* 90 F 13), as perhaps in Attic law for involuntary homicide (*apeniautismos*; but see MacDowell 122).

1647 [for Azanes – Oresteion]: against the authenticity of this line are the inept repetition of "call", the inapposite mention of the Azanes, who belong to *north* Arcadia (Hdt. 6.127.3, Polyb. 4.70.3, etc.), and the parallel of *El.* 1275, where the town to be called after Orestes is referred to in similar terms without its name being spelt out. A sciolist's interpolation, like 933.

1650 the three Benign Ones: 408 n. This trial on the Areopagus was a familiar story at least since Aeschylus; cf. *El.* 1254-72, *IT* 943-67.

gods as judges: the Twelve Gods (Dem. 23.66). This detail is transferred from the myth of their trying Ares for the killing of Halirrothius (*El.* 1258, etc.). In Aeschylus Orestes is tried by Athenian nobles (*Eum.* 487).

1651 most righteously: the justness of the Areopagite vote is also stressed in *El.* 1262, after *Eum.* 483, 489, 704 f., 748 f.

654 Hermione you are destined to marry: in *Od.* 4.5-9 she is married to Neoptolemus. Fifth-century authors (Pherecydes *FGrH* 3 F 63-4, Soph. *Hermione*, Eur. *Andr.* 966 ff., Philocles *TrGF* 24 F 2, Theognis *TrGF* 28 F 2) variously combine this with a previous or subsequent marriage to Orestes. Here Euripides only wants the marriage to Orestes, and the Neoptolemus tradition is explicitly negated. In the Orestes tradition, he and Hermione are the parents of Tisamenus, who united the kingdoms of Argos and Sparta before falling to the Heraclidae.

656 to die by Delphian sword: Pind. *Pae.* 6.110-20, *N.* 7.40-3, Pherecydes and Soph. ll.cc., Eur. *Andr.*; the circumstances vary.

657 compensation for Achilles: whom Apollo helped Paris to kill. Sophocles gave this as the reason for Neoptolemus' visit to Delphi; cf. *Andr.* 53. But there he was represented as already married to Hermione.

658 Give your sister to Pylades: 1078 n.

659 awaits him: *nin* could mean "them", but for this Euripides prefers *sphe* when metre allows. For ignoring the wife cf. 1677.

662 enjoying the dowry: the Spartan throne itself is principally meant.

665 I who made him: as in Aesch. *Eum.* 83 f., Apollo accepts the responsibility for seeing Orestes out of the difficulties that his instructions placed him in. His succinct promise to "set things right" disposes of a major unresolved problem.

667 truthful: in telling him that everything would be all right if he killed his mother.

668-9 the fear – some vengeance-demon: this doubt already in *El.* 979. The chorus has interpreted events as the workings of an *alastōr* (337 n., 1546), and that is not exactly wrong. But what matters to Orestes is that he had genuine divine sanction for his deed. For the aorist optative referring to something past at the time of fearing cf. *IT* 1341; similarly the subjunctive in present sequence, *Il.* 1.555 and elsewhere.

670 I will do as you say: similarly *Supp.* 1227, Soph. *Phil.* 1447.

1671 <u>I release Hermione:</u> he has been motionless all this time.

1672 <u>and agree:</u> the aorist as in 1517.

1673 <u>O daughter of Zeus:</u> Orestes' salute to Apollo is balanced by Menelaus' to Helen. He must address his ex-wife in new terms.

1675 <u>I betroth my daughter:</u> a common element in the happy endings of New Comedy, where, however, the Attic ritual formula (553 n.) is regularly used.

1676 <u>from a noble house:</u> lit. from a noble father, cf. Thgn. 189 f., 1112, Eur. *Hcld.* 299, *Andr.* 975, fr. 59.

1678 <u>Proceed, then:</u> setting the exodus in motion. Cf. *Ion* 1616, *Ba.* 1371.

1679-80 <u>end your quarrel:</u> a recurring motif in *ex machina* endings, cf. *Hipp.* 1442, *Hel.* 1681, *Antiope* fr. 48.116 K. <u>One can only obey. – I feel so too:</u> cf. Soph. *Phil.* 1447 f.

1682 <u>Go on your ways, then:</u> Sophocles' and Euripides' plays nearly all end with a short passage of choral anapaests, and sometimes, as here, the anapaestic section begins earlier and is inaugurated by one of the characters. It would have been recited with musical accompaniment; see *DFA*[2] 160-2.

1683 <u>fairest of deities, Peace:</u> the ancient commentator sees this as a comment on the prolongation of the war (cf. 772 n.). However, Euripides had praised Peace in the same terms before 422 B.C. (*Cresphontes* fr. 71 Austin); cf. also *Supp.* 488 ff. On Peace as a goddess cf. Dodds on *Ba.* 419-20 and my n. on Hes. *Th.* 902.

1686 <u>Hera and ... Hebe:</u> as Zeus' daughter she is to be seated with other goddesses of his immediate family, his wife and his daughter by his wife. There is a trivial inconsistency with 1636 f. <u>Heracles' wife:</u> *Od.* 11.603, Hes. *Th.* 950, [Hes.] fr. 25.28, 229.8.

1688 <u>honoured in libations together with the Tyndarids:</u> cf. *Hel.* 1667-9. It is hard to believe that anyone at Athens poured libations to Helen; at Sparta perhaps. The Dioscuri were honoured at Athens in a minor festival, the Anakia; at which three animals were sacrificed, and one of these was (later) said to be for Helen (Paus. *Gr. a* 111 Erbse).

1689-90 <u>queen of the restless sea:</u> 1637 n. The marginal variant in M, *hygrās* ("fluid", not just "wet"), is correct as against *hyiois*, a form not used in Attic until *c.*350 (the dative in use being *hy(i)esi*).

691-3 <u>O Victory</u> etc.: the same tailpiece is found at the end of *IT, Phoen.*, and in one manuscript *Hipp*. In those places it is probably an addition by actors or scribes; on such additions see Barrett on *Hipp.* 1462-6. In *Orestes* the case is less clear. We expect the chorus to have the last word, but not something so wholly unconnected with what has gone before. The prayer for victory (for the poet) is conventional in Menander (*Dyscolus, Misumenus, Sicyonius*), and may have been so in 4th-century tragedy. The idea goes back to Bacchylides (*Epigr.* 1 Snell = 2 Page).

<u>crowning it with garlands:</u> the victorious poet was crowned with ivy in the theatre, see *DFA*² 98.

INDEX

Other Greek Texts in this series include:

ARISTOPHANES *Acharnians* (ed. A.H. Sommerstein)
　　　　　　　Knights (ed. A.H. Sommerstein)
　　　　　　　Clouds (ed. A.H. Sommerstein)
　　　　　　　Wasps (ed. A.H. Sommerstein)
　　　　　　　Peace (ed. A.H. Sommerstein)
　　　　　　　Birds (ed. A.H. Sommerstein) [1987]
EURIPIDES *Trojan Women* (ed. Shirley A. Barlow)
　　　　　　Alcestis (ed. D. Conacher) [1987]
GREEK ORATORS I Antiphon & Lysias (ed. Edwards & Usher)
MENANDER *Samia* (ed. D.M. Bain)
PLATO *Meno* (ed. R.W. Sharples)
　　　　Phaedrus (ed. C.J. Rowe)
　　　　Symposium (ed. R.G. Bury) - no translation
SOPHOCLES *Antigone* (ed. A.L. Brown)
THUCYDIDES *Pylos 425 B.C.* (ed. J.B. Wilson)